OXFORD EARLY CHRISTIAN STUDIES

General Editors

Gillian Clark   Andrew Louth

Communities of the Blessed

Social Environment and Religious Change in Northern Italy, AD 200–400

MARK HUMPHRIES

OXFORD
UNIVERSITY PRESS

OXFORD
UNIVERSITY PRESS

Great Clarendon Street, Oxford OX2 6DP
Oxford University Press is a department of the University of Oxford.
It furthers the University's objective of excellence in research, scholarship,
and education by publishing worldwide in

Oxford New York

Athens Auckland Bangkok Bogotá Buenos Aires Calcutta
Cape Town Chennai Dar es Salaam Delhi Florence Hong Kong Istanbul
Karachi Kuala Lumpur Madrid Melbourne Mexico City Mumbai
Nairobi Paris São Paulo Singapore Taipei Tokyo Toronto Warsaw

and associated companies in Berlin Ibadan

Oxford is a registered trade mark of Oxford University Press
in the UK and certain other countries

Published in the United States
by Oxford University Press Inc., New York

British Library Cataloguing in Publication Data

Data available

Library of Congress Cataloging-in-Publication Data
Humphries, Mark.
Communities of the blessed : social environment and religious
change in northern Italy, AD 200–400 / Mark Humphries.
p. cm.
Includes bibliographical references and index.
1. Italy, Northern—Church history. 2. Church history—Primitive
and early church, ca. 30–600. I. Title.
BR877.NC7H65 2000
274.5′01—dc21 99-25813
ISBN 0-19-826983-8

1 3 5 7 9 10 8 6 4 2

Typeset by Graphicraft Limited, Hong Kong
Printed in Great Britain on acid-free paper by
Bookcraft (Bath) Ltd., Midsomer Norton

To my parents, for everything

'uincuntur tenebrae noctis lumine deuotionis'
Chromatius of Aquileia, *Sermo* 16. 3

PREFACE

This book is a revised version of a St Andrews doctoral thesis written between 1993 and 1996; it is anticipated that a second volume will continue its analysis of north Italian Christianity through the fifth and sixth centuries. Although this is a social history of religion, I write neither as a devout Christian nor as a sceptical atheist, but as one sympathetic to all shades of religious belief. At the same time, however, I write as one whose formative years were spent in a country where Christian churches exercised considerable social leverage, and where religious hatred extended to murderous extremes. It seems incredible to me that this should not have influenced the present study, especially where matters of tolerance or intolerance are at issue.

During the preparation of the thesis and its subsequent transformation into a book I have incurred many debts of gratitude, although none of those mentioned below should be held responsible for the shortcomings of the finished product. I owe most to Jill Harries, who supervised my thesis with exemplary skill and sympathy, and who has continued to encourage me during the preparation of the book. In St Andrews I was also fortunate to enjoy the camaraderie and support of a lively group of ancient historians and classicists (many now dispersed to other universities): Colin Adams, Philip Burton, Jon Coulston, Mary Harlow, Tom Harrison, Peter Maxwell-Stuart, Helen Parkins, Roger Rees, John Serrati, Christopher Smith, Shaun Tougher, and especially Michael Whitby and Mary Whitby. My examiners, Julia Smith and David Hunt, made many useful corrections and suggestions, and encouraged me to publish. I was able to conduct some of my research and field-work in Italy and Slovenia, and I am grateful to all who facilitated my work there. The David Russell Trust in St Andrews supported my travel with a generous grant. For a month I was a guest at the Istituto di Filologia Classica at the University of Urbino. I should like to thank the Director, Roberto Pretagostini, for his hospitality; Adrian Gratwick (St Andrews) and Rosaria Falivene (Urbino) for helping to arrange my visit; and Maria Cesa, who kindly took time to discuss my work with me. At Udine, the staff of the university library provided a warm welcome even though I arrived unannounced, and they did much to find obscure Aquileian material for me. A productive period of study at the University of Bari was facilitated by the kindness of Aldo Corcella, Liana Lomiento, and Gennaro Lomiento (Director of the Istituto di Studi classici e cristiani at Bari). Graham Shipley, Thomas Wiedemann, and Wolf Liebeschuetz (who kindly allowed me to see the typescript of sections of his forthcoming book on late antique cities) all provided timely encouragement, while Bryan Ward-Perkins, as editor of my contribution to *The Cambridge Ancient History*, helped refine my ideas about late antique Italy. As editor for Oxford Early Christian Studies, Gillian Clark has provided endless inspiration, without which I could never have finished the book.

At Oxford University Press, Hilary O'Shea and Georga Godwin provided abundant assistance, encouragement, and reassurance, while David Sanders copy-edited the typescript most conscientiously, thus saving me from many errors and inconsistencies.

Other debts are more personal. Friends in Italy, the United Kingdom, and Ireland have provided encouragement and coffee in abundance. For support and tolerance during the completion of both thesis and book, I owe more to Catherine Parker than words can express. Finally, none of this would have been possible without the love, patience, and understanding of my parents. Neither has ever had leanings towards academe, but I have learned most from them.

M.D.H.

CONTENTS

ILLUSTRATIONS

ABBREVIATIONS

(a) Primary sources

Acta conc. Aquil.	Acts of the Council of Aquileia
Altercatio Heracliani	*Altercatio Heracliani laici cum Germinio episcopo Sirmiensi*
Ambr., *C. Aux.*	Ambrose of Milan, *Contra Auxentium*
Ambr., *De obitu Theod.*	Ambrose of Milan, *De obitu Theodosii*
Ambr., *De Sacr.*	Ambrose of Milan, *De Sacramentis*
Ambr., *Ep.*	Ambrose of Milan, *Epistolae*
Amm. Marc.	Ammianus Marcellinus
Arnulf, *Lib. gest.*	Arnulf of Milan, *Liber gestorum recientorum*
Athan., *Apol. Const.*	Athanasius of Alexandria, *Apologia ad Constantium*
Athan., *De Syn.*	Athanasius of Alexandria, *De Synodis*
Athan., *Ep. ad Afros*	Athanasius of Alexandria, *Epistola ad Afros*
Athan., *Hist. Ar.*	Athanasius of Alexandria, *Historia Arianorum*
Aug., *ad Don. post coll.*	Augustine of Hippo, *Ad Donatistas post collationem*
Aug., *Brev. Coll.*	Augustine of Hippo, *Breviarium Collationis cum Donatistis*
Aug., *c. Cresc.*	Augustine of Hippo, *Contra Cresconium*
Aug., *Conf.*	Augustine of Hippo, *Confessiones*
Aug., *Ep.*	Augustine of Hippo, *Epistolae*
Aur. Vict., *Caes.*	Aurelius Victor, *Liber de Caesaribus*
Basil, *Ep.*	Basil of Caesarea, *Epistolae*
Chrom., *Sermo*	Chromatius of Aquileia, *Sermons*
Chron. 354	*Codex Calendar of AD 354*
Conc. Chalc.	*Council of Chalcedon*
Conc. Nic.	*Council of Nicaea*
CTh	*Codex Theodosianus*
Damasus, *Ep.* *Confidimus quidem*	Damasus of Rome, *Epistola* 'Confidimus quidem'
Eus., *HE*	Eusebius of Caesarea, *Historia Ecclesiastica*
Euseb. Verc., *Ep.*	Eusebius of Vercelli, *Epistolae*
Filastrius, *Div. her. lib.*	Filastrius of Brescia, *Diversarum hereseon liber*

Gaud. Brix., *Tract.*	Gaudentius of Brescia, *Tractatus*
Greg. Mag., *Dial.*	Gregory the Great, *Dialogues*
Hier., *Chron.*	Jerome, *Chronicon*
Hier., *De vir. ill.*	Jerome, *De viris illustribus*
Hier., *Ep.*	Jerome, *Epistolae*
Hil. Pict., *C. Aux.*	Hilary of Poitiers, *Contra Auxentium*
Hil. Pict., *Coll. Ant. Par.*	Hilary of Poitiers, *Collectanea Antiariana Parisina*
Lact. *De mort. pers.*	Lactantius, *De mortibus persecutorum*
Lact., *Div. Inst.*	Lactantius, *Divinae Institutiones*
Landulf Senior, *Med. hist.*	Landulf Senior, *Mediolanenis historiae libri IV*
Liberius, *Ep. ad Euseb. Verc.*	Liberius of Rome, *Epistolae ad Eusebium Vercellensem*
Lucifer, *de Athan.*	Lucifer of Cagliari, *de Athanasio*
Mart. Hier.	*Martyrologium Hieronymianum*
Not. Dig.	*Notitia Dignitatum*
Not. Gall.	*Notitia Galliarum*
Pall., *Apol.*	Palladius of Ratiaria, *Apologia*
Pan. Lat.	*Panegyrici Latini*
Paul. Diac., *HL*	Paul the Deacon, *Historia Langobardorum*
Paul. Med., *V. Ambr.*	Paulinus of Milan, *Vita Sancti Ambrosii*
Ruf., *Apol. c. Hier.*	Turranius Rufinus, *Apologia contra Hieronymum*
Ruf., *HE*	Turranius Rufinus, *Historia Ecclesiastica*
Sid. Ap., *Ep.*	Sidonius Apollinaris, *Epistolae*
Sulp. Sev., *Chron.*	Sulpicius Severus, *Chronica*
Sulp. Sev., *V. Martini*	Sulpicius Severus, *Vita Sancti Martini*
Venant. Fort. *Carm.*	Venantius Fortunatus, *Carmina*
Venant. Fort. *V. Martini*	Venantius Fortunatus, *Vita Sancti Martini*
Vigilius, *Ep.*	Vigilius of Trento, *Epistolae*
Zeno, *Tract.*	Zeno of Verona, *Tractatus*

(b) Journals, collections, and modern sources

For journals, I have usually used the conventions of *L'Année Philologique*. Note also the use of the following.

AASS	*Acta Sanctorum*
AE	*L'Année Épigraphique*
ANRW	*Aufstieg und Niedergang der römischen Welt*
An. Tard.	*L'Antiquité Tardive*
AqN	*Aquileia Nostra*
Arh. Vest.	*Arheolski Vestnik*

BHL	*Bibliotheca Hagiographica Latina*
BS	*Bibliotheca Sanctorum*
CCL	*Corpus Christianorum, series latina*
Cessi, *Origo*	R. Cessi (ed.), *Origo Civitatum Italiae seu Venetiarum* (Rome, 1933)
CIL	*Corpus Inscriptionum Latinarum*
Comm. Mart. Hier.	H. Delchaye (ed. H. Quentin), *Commentarius perpetuus in Martyrologium Hieronymianum* (*AASS* Nov. 2/2: Brussels, 1931)
CSEL	*Corpus Scriptorum Ecclesiasticorum Latinorum*
DACL	*Dictionnaire d'archéologie chrétienne et de liturgie*
DHGE	*Dictionnaire d'histoire et de géographie ecclésiastiques*
EAC	*Entretiens sur l'antiquité classique, Fondation Hardt*
Giardina, *Società*	A. Giardina (ed.), *Società romana e Impero tardoantico* (Bari and Rome, 1986)
Gryson, *Scolies ariennes*	R. Gryson, *Scolies ariennes sur le concile d'Aquilée* (*SChr* 267: Paris, 1980)
IG	*Inscriptiones Graecae*
II	*Inscriptiones Italiae*
ILCV	*Inscriptiones Latinae Christianae Veteres*
ILS	*Inscriptiones Latinae Selectae*
IMU	*Italia medioevale e umanistica*
Inscr. Aquil.	G. B. Brusin, *Inscriptiones Aquileiae* (Udine, 1991–3)
Jäggi	C. Jäggi, 'Aspekte der städtebaulichen Entwicklung Aquileias in fruhchristlicher Zeit', *JbAC* 33 (1990), 158–96
Krautheimer, *Capitals*	R. Krautheimer, *Three Christian Capitals* (Berkeley, 1983)
Lowe, *CLA*	E. A. Lowe, *Codices Latini Antiquiores*
MGH, AA	*Monumenta Germaniae Historica, Auctores Antiquissimi*
MGH, SS	*Monumenta Germaniae Historica, Scriptores*
Milano Capitale	*Milano Capitale dell'impero romano 286–402 d. C.* (Milan, 1990)
Munier, *Conc. Gall.*	C. Munier (ed.), *Conciliae Galliae, A.314–A.506* (*CCL* 148: Turnhout, 1963)
Noy, *JIWE* i	D. Noy, *The Jewish Inscriptions of Western Europe*, i (Cambridge, 1993)
NSc	*Notizie degli Scavi*

PG	*Patrologia Graeca*
PL	*Patrologia Latina*
PLRE	*The Prosopography of the Later Roman Empire*
PLS	*Patrologia Latina Supplementum*
RIS	*Rerum Italicarum Scriptores*
Ruggiero, *Diz. Ep.*	E. de Ruggiero, *Dizionario epigrafico di antichità romana*
Savio, *Piemonte*	F. Savio, *Gli antichi vescovi d'Italia. Il Piemonte* (Turin, 1898)
SChr	*Sources Chrétiennes*
Sett.	*Settimane di studio del Centro italiano di studi sull'alto medioevo*
TLL	*Thesaurus Linguae Latinae*
Verona	*Verona e il suo territorio* (Verona, 1960)
Ward-Perkins, *CAMA*	B. Ward-Perkins, *From Classical Antiquity to the Middle Ages: Urban public building in northern and central Italy*, AD 300–850 (Oxford, 1984)
White, *God's House*	L. M. White, *Building God's House in the Roman World: Architectural Adaptation among Pagans, Jews and Christians* (Baltimore, 1990)

INTRODUCTION

Regional history and religious history

This is a study of religious change in northern Italy under the Roman empire, focusing on the origins and development of Christianity down to the end of the fourth century. It aims to liberate that history from the conventional models of ecclesiastical narrative, by demonstrating the unreliability of many of the traditional sources and by constructing a new methodology which locates the development of the Church in the context of what will be termed the north Italian human environment. In other words, it is an attempt to understand the growth of Christianity in the social and cultural context of a region of the Roman empire. Before beginning my investigation, it is necessary to offer some explanation and justification for the subjects discussed and the methodologies adopted.

Authority, history, and the study of early Christianity

On 2 February 1351, the faithful of the patriarchal see of Aquileia entered the cathedral in Udine at the end of their procession to celebrate the Feast of the Purification of the Blessed Virgin Mary. This procession concluded with a recitation of the names of all the previous patriarchs of the Aquileian see, beginning with St Mark the Evangelist and concluding with Bertrand de Saint-Geniés, who had been murdered seven months earlier.[1] Thus the history of the see was presented as a seamless succession, stretching back to the time

---

[1] The nature of the ceremony is evident from the rubric at the beginning of the patriarchal list: 'In die purificationis beate Marie virginis post processionum recitantur nomina patriarcharum' (*MGH, SS* 13. 367). The MS of the list is written in various hands, but the first hand concludes with Bertrand's name; the names of his successors have been added by different scribes (ibid., 368). For Bertrand, see Mollat, 'Bertrand de Saint-Geniés'. That the ceremonies took place at Udine rather than Aquileia or Cividale, the other major centres of the patriarchate, is impossible to prove, but it seems most likely bearing in mind the artistic embellishment of the city by Bertrand and his predecessors: Casadio, 'Vitale da Bologna a Udine', 49–60.

of the apostles. To the participants in this fourteenth-century ceremony, the need to research the early history of Christianity in northern Italy would be superfluous. That early history was self-evident
in the living traditions surrounding them.[2]

It may seem absurd to invoke medieval opinion as a justification
for this study, but views that we may term 'medieval' have had an
enduring influence on the conventional historiography of north
Italian Christianity. Traditions prevalent in the middle ages have been
collected and handed down to the modern era, albeit in a rather more
refined form. An important medium was the monumental *Italia Sacra*
by the Cistercian historian Ferdinando Ughelli (1596–1670), published in Rome between 1644 and 1662.[3] This seminal work has had
a defining influence on Italian ecclesiastical historiography: subsequent enterprises such as Fedele Savio's *Gli antichi vescovi d'Italia
dalle origini al 1300* (1899–1932) and Francesco Lanzoni's *Le origini delle diocesi antiche d'Italia* (1923) proceed along similar lines
taken by Ughelli's masterpiece, even though both ostensibly seek
to replace it.[4] The similarity is methodological: like Ughelli, both
Savio and Lanzoni sought to put the early ecclesiastical history of
Italy on a firm footing by rationalizing divergent traditions;[5] also
like him, they were obsessed by episcopal successions, defined within
the geographical parameters of modern—or in Ughelli's case, early
modern—diocesan boundaries.[6]

This reflects the constraints imposed on the shape of the *Italia
Sacra* by Ughelli's methods. Ensconced at Rome, where he had access
to fine archival resources, Ughelli nevertheless relied on contributions by assistants elsewhere in Italy for the history of other bishoprics.[7] This not only explains the uneven quality of the work, but also

---

[2] The Aquileians were not alone in this active commemoration of the past: cf.
Ch. 2 below.

[3] Despite its faults, I have, for reasons of accessibility, used the second edition
prepared by Niccolo Coleti (Venice, 1717–22). For a critique of the relationship
between the two editions, see Ditchfield, *Liturgy, Sanctity, and History*, 331–2.

[4] For their views of Ughelli's work, see Savio, *Piemonte*, pp. v–xiii; Lanzoni, *Diocesi*,
61–4.

[5] For Ughelli's aims, note especially his letter of 3 February 1625 to fellow
scholar Cesare Becelli, in which he bemoans the scale of his labours in trying to
distinguish the truth between imprecise and contradictory writings (quoted in
Ditchfield, *Liturgy, Sanctity, and History*, 338).

[6] Otranto, *Italia meridionale*, 3–21; cf. Ditchfield, *Liturgy, Sanctity, and History*, 341:
'It remained for Ughelli . . . to lay the foundations of Italian ecclesiastical geography.'

[7] The scale of this dependence is evident from the lengthy list of his correspondents: Morelli, 'Monumenta Ferdinandi Ughelli', 262–80.

highlights its polemical context. Such local ecclesiastical histories were, as Cardinal Carlo Borromeo of Milan (1538–84) noted, essential for the good governance of the Church, which depended on the maintenance of tradition.[8] Borromeo's interests were intensely political: a dedicated agent of Tridentine reform in his own archdiocese, he belonged to the same intellectual milieu as the effective founder of modern ecclesiastical historiography, Cesare Baronio (1538–1607), whose *Annales Ecclesiastici*, a chronological compendium of church history, began to appear in 1588. Baronio (usually known by the Latin form of his name, Baronius) was not just a scholar, but a dedicated defender of papal supremacy in the face of challenges issued by the rising tide of Protestantism. His *Annales* were designed to demonstrate the primacy of the Roman church by emphasizing Peter's preeminence among the apostles and the superior legitimacy of his successors as bishops of Rome.[9] Ughelli's interests were the same: his work began with 'Rome, that first of all churches, the mother of sane dogma, the pinnacle of Apostolic honour, the most noble seat of the Supreme Pontiff'.[10] Even so, Ughelli's appeal has proved to be wider: his reliance on local historians has meant that his work, or that of his correspondents, has underpinned much of the *campanilismo* (local patriotism) that has characterized Italian historiography, including that of an ecclesiastical variety.[11]

This traditional approach has been challenged by searching analysis of the source materials—mainly literary—upon which it depends, as well as the marshalling of other types of evidence—primarily archaeology and epigraphy—to add detail to our picture of early Christian life. That chronicles of episcopal successions were later concoctions has been obvious since Duchesne subjected the Gallic lists to criticism,[12] while his extension of his methodology to Italian material, in the form of his edition of the Roman *Liber Pontificalis* (1886–92), has shown that the manipulation of the ecclesiastical past was a broad phenomenon. In recent years, such critical analysis has been applied to north Italian episcopal lists and

[8] Ditchfield, *Liturgy, Sanctity, and History*, 285–91.
[9] Baronius, *Annales*, i. 65–7, 285–9, and esp. 293–7.
[10] *Italia sacra*, i (1717), 1 A.
[11] For Ughelli's appeal to those with local and Italian, rather than papal, interests uppermost in mind, cf. Ditchfield, *Liturgy, Sanctity, and History*, 352–6. Much local historiography is criticized by Otranto for its 'eccesivo amore municipalistico' (*Italia meridionale*, 11).
[12] Duchesne, *Fastes épiscopaux*.

cults by Jean-Charles Picard with dazzling results (see Chapter 2) which effectively undermine those sources used by Ughelli and his successors.

Scholarship has moved on too from the political or theological mentality which determined the shape of much analysis of early Christian writings. The development of social-scientific criticism of New Testament texts, for example, has opened up new vistas of historical discussion, by moving towards an interpretation of early Christian thought which locates it in an anthropological, social, and cultural context.[13] Instead of using patristic texts to write histories of doctrine or hierarchy, historians such as Lellia Cracco Ruggini and her followers, most importantly Rita Lizzi, have quarried them to write the social history of north Italian Christianity for the late-fourth, fifth, and sixth centuries.[14] What this new breed of Italian ecclesiastical historians is seeking to reject has been elegantly set out in Daniela Rando's recent study of the emergence of the Venetian church, where she characterizes the work of her predecessors 'by the schism between a secular historiography and a confessional ecclesiastical historiography'.[15] Yet even where modern ecclesiastical historiography is not to any major degree confessional, much of it still concentrates on church hierarchies and matters of dogma, despite the considerable advances made in recent decades on the social history of late antiquity.[16]

Religious and regional diversity

My own study aims to fit into the new trend which seeks to reconcile ecclesiastical and social history. By setting it firmly in its social context, I will offer an explanation, rather than just a description, of the origins and development of the Christian communities of northern Italy. It seems to me that, even where the causes of church development are not explicitly narrated, it is possible to reconstruct the

[13] For a sample of such studies, with a useful consolidated bibliography: Esler, *Modelling Early Christianity*.

[14] Note especially Ruggini, *Economia e società*, and Lizzi, *Vescovi*. Even so, a lively tradition of works espousing theological concerns continues to flourish: e.g. Padovese, *L'originalità cristiana*; Truzzi, *Zeno, Gaudenzio, e Cromazio*.

[15] Rando, *Una chiesa di frontiera*, 7–8.

[16] I have discussed this issue at some length in a review of Williams's *Ambrose*, forthcoming in *Hermathena*.

mechanisms that would have encouraged Christian expansion. In a recent, challenging, if not altogether satisfactory, analysis of the spatial dynamics of religion, Chris Park has identified the sorts of circumstances conducive to the diffusion of a proselytizing faith like Christianity.[17] His typology of diffusion practices explains that 'the number of people who adopt the innovation grows by direct contact [where] an idea is communicated by a person who knows about it to one who does not, so the total number of knowers increases through time'. This can happen either by 'contagious diffusion', where conversion occurs 'as a product of everyday contact between believers and non-believers'; or by 'hierarchical diffusion' where a deliberate missionary strategy is developed which targets major centres and social élites. Christianity will have spread in a variety of ways, mixing the various types of diffusion which Park distinguishes, but the paucity of explicit sources means that the exact nature of the process in various parts of the Mediterranean is often unknown.[18] Much of this is common sense. Religion, like any ideology, requires direct human interaction to ensure its diffusion.[19] Urban centres, places where such direct contact occurred most frequently, provided fertile ground for the propagation of religious ideas. This fertility increased concomitantly with the extent to which a town or city attracted diverse and changing populations, because they were centres of either trade or administration. Ports and markets were more than just centres for the exchange of material goods. They were environments where people like Demosthenes' defendant against Apaturius could mix with foreigners (*Or.* 33. 5). They were also places where new ideas and new cults would make their first mark, although the precise link between the presence of foreigners and the adoption of new gods by natives is often unclear.[20] Nevertheless, it is interesting to compare the similar distributions of Christianity, Judaism, and Isis worship in northern Italy, suggesting that similar

[17] Park, *Sacred Worlds*, 93–127.

[18] Park, *Sacred Worlds*, 99–101 (typology), 105–9 (application to Christianity). Park's interpretation of early Christian diffusion (pp. 105–6) is, however, flawed, since he derives his picture from sources, such as Acts and the Pauline Epistles, which emphasize the role of aggressively proselytizing missionaries: cf. Humphries, 'Trading Gods', 206 and n. 3.

[19] Cf. Matthews, 'Hostages, Philosophers, Pilgrims', emphasizing how diffusion frequently depends on unofficial channels of communication.

[20] Note the cautious remarks of von Reden, 'The Piraeus', 30–4; and Parker, *Athenian Religion*, 152–98, esp. 161: 'The point is that the role of non-Athenians and non-Greeks . . . needs to be treated as a problem, not taken for granted.'

social circumstances influenced the diffusion of each cult (see Chapters 1 and 3).

Of course, any such generalized picture requires qualification. Areas other than urban centres could provide conditions advantageous to the spread of new cults. In Chapter 6, for example, it will be shown how the Val di Non (ancient Anaunia), in the Alps north-west of Trento, enjoyed a diverse religious life which confounds simple models of a society divided between culturally rich urban centres and relatively poorer rural peripheries. Moreover, no two religions are identical in terms of their beliefs, organization, or the constituency to which they appeal. For instance, both Mithraism and Christianity are soteriological cults in that they offer initiates a picture of the afterlife of the soul. Yet Mithraism, open only to men and favoured by male organizations such as trade associations and the army, had a very different pattern of distribution to that of Christianity. Nor are religions static. Judaism, from which Christianity is traditionally assumed to have inherited its missionary ethos, seems not to have developed this expansionist impulse until the uncertain times after the destruction of the Jerusalem Temple by the Romans in AD 70.[21] Even traditional Roman religion, for all its alleged inertia, was open to change: cults and rituals could be added or jettisoned as required, sometimes quite suddenly.[22] More starkly, Roman religion was intensely local, and the regional varieties of ritual and cult across the empire—or even within a province—were myriad.[23] Diversity, then, is the key factor: diversity of religions, diversity of experiences, and, finally, diversity of regions.

Regional analysis and the ancient world

The ancient Mediterranean world presents a bewildering array of linguistic and cultural zones which defies any attempt to reduce its dynamics to a single formula.[24] To be sure, it is different from North America or the Far East, and there are some common features shared by the peoples who live around its shores; but equally the Mediterranean, both now and in antiquity, boasts a remarkable diversity of cultures. This raises a primary difficulty with beginning

[21] Goodman, *Mission and Conversion*, 38–48.
[22] North, 'Conservatism and Change'. For the *histoire du question* see Feeney, *Literature and Religion*, 2–6.
[23] Mellor, 'Local Character'; North, 'Religion and Rusticity'.
[24] See Meeks, 'Review of P. F. Esler, *The First Christians*', 317.

any form of regional analysis. As the anthropologist Carol Smith warns, '[t]here is no single regional level of analysis, but rather many different regional levels of analysis'.[25] Even Fernand Braudel, who more than anyone focused the historian's attention on the Mediterranean and highlighted those elements which lend it unity, warned that:

The Mediterranean is not a single sea but a succession of small seas that communicate by means of wider or narrower entrances. In the two great east and west basins [into which the Mediterranean is divided by Sicily]... there is a series of highly individual narrow seas between the land masses, each with its own character, types of boat, and its own laws of history... Even within these seas smaller areas can be distinguished, for there is hardly a bay in the Mediterranean that is not a miniature community, a complex world itself.[26]

Socrates famously thought of the entire Mediterranean as a large frog pond (Plato, *Phaedo* 109b), but instead of them all croaking the same language, the frogs would have given off an even more discordant noise than normal. Any institution aiming to interact with Mediterranean society had to develop a variety of responses to its disparate cultures. Witness how, as the Romans extended their rule over the Mediterranean in the middle and late Republic, they had to devise different strategies for dealing with the highly developed states of Carthage and the Hellenistic east, and the diffuse tribal societies of the Celtic west.[27] On a more local level, it is clear that particular regions of the Mediterranean basin, both now and in the past, have their own peculiar dynamics, defined by factors such as landscape, social networks, language, culture, religion, lifestyle, and the absence or presence of urbanization.[28]

Regional diversity in early Christianity

The Christian Church, like any institution in the ancient Mediterranean, was compelled to meet the challenges of this diverse environment. Recent studies of the early development of the Church have

[25] Smith, 'Analysing Regional Social Systems', 4.
[26] Braudel, *The Mediterranean*, i. 108–10.
[27] Dyson, *Creation of the Roman Frontier*, 4.
[28] The most obvious area where this has been realized is in archaeological survey, although several important historical studies exist. The French *Annales* school, particularly Braudel's *The Mediterranean*, has exercised a profound influence: Bintliff, 'Contribution of an *Annaliste*/Structural History Approach to Archaeology', 4–9; cf. Purcell's editorial remarks in Frederiksen, *Campania*, p. xiii.

emphasized the importance of regional, as well as social, contexts.[29] In the first place, the dissemination of the faith was dependent on local and inter-regional networks of interaction. The earliest traceable Christian missionary enterprise, that of Paul described in Acts, is indicative of such trends. Paul's background as a Hellenized Jew from the bustling centre of Tarsus underpinned his missionary strategies: his was a quintessentially urban world view, and it is no surprise that, in contrast to the rural origins of Christianity in the highlands of Galilee, he chose to take the gospel to the cities of the Mediterranean coast.[30]

At other times, when Paul's mission was less self-directed, the influence of Mediterranean networks continued to exert a profound influence. For example, it has been shown that Paul's curious inland detour in southern Asia Minor, away from the coastal cities of Pamphylia to the region of Pisidian Antioch, was due to his personal connection with the proconsul of Cyprus, Sergius Paullus, scion of one of the greatest Antiochene families.[31] This haphazard relationship between Paul's journeys and the Mediterranean environment is even more apparent in the route taken by him on his way to judgement at Rome. Paul's party passed through Myra in Lycia where, using a practice recorded by other ancient travellers, they hitched a ride on 'a ship sailing for Italy from Alexandria' (Acts 27: 5–6).[32] This was clearly a merchantman engaged in the grain trade between Egypt and Rome, because when it got caught in a storm, its cargo of wheat was jettisoned in an effort to lighten the ship's load (27: 18, 38). It was eventually wrecked off Malta, but Paul was able to pursue his journey on another Alexandrian ship that had wintered at the island (28: 11). From Malta he travelled through the straits of Messina to Puteoli (28: 12–13), precisely the route taken by the grain ships from Alexandria which supplied Rome. Apart from these maritime connections, Paul's use of travel networks is evident from his entirely typical behaviour when seeking accommodation: en route from Puteoli to Rome he called at the revealingly named

[29] Two excellent examples: Mitchell, *Anatolia*, ii. passim; Rives, *Religion and Authority*. For general principles: Beard, North, and Price, *Religions of Rome*, i. 245–312.
[30] Meeks, *Urban Christians*, 9. Status and world-view: Hengel, 'The Pre-Christian Paul', 29–33.
[31] Mitchell, *Anatolia*, ii. 5–8.
[32] Cf. Libanius asking around the port for ships when he hoped to travel from Constantinople to Athens (*Or.* 1. 31).

Tres Tabernae (28: 15); in Rome itself, having nowhere else to stay, he rented lodgings (28: 30).[33]

Christian expansion is not so well attested in the west as in the east, but it is clear that local social dynamics were important there too. One of the outstanding features of Paul's mission in Asia Minor and Greece had been its dependence on an existing network of Jewish communities and synagogues.[34] It is unlikely, however, that Judaism was a substantial vehicle for the dissemination of Christianity in the west. Apart from centres such as Rome and Puteoli, the spread of Judaism there was so retarded that it may have expanded not in advance of but concurrently with Christianity.[35] Others have sought to identify the earliest western Christians as traders from the Greek east.[36] Yet even when there is explicit evidence of links with the Greek east, explaining them is not easy. For example, the southern Gallic churches of Lyon and Vienne had contacts with Asia Minor (Eus. *HE* 5. 1. 2–3), prompting the interpretation that Greek traders were instrumental in their origins.[37] More critical analysis of the evidence suggests that the first Lyonnais Christians may have come from Rome. This of course does not rule out a mercantile factor, but it is startling that the church at Lyon seems older than those in other southern Gallic ports, such as Arles and Marseilles. A more elaborate explanation is required, and it is not difficult to find. Lyon was not just a commercial city but the effective capital of the Three Gauls, at the hub of an extensive communications network, and a centre of political, cultural, administrative, and cultic activity: there were many reasons, then, why Lyon should have attracted foreigners able to spread the gospel.[38]

[33] Humphries, 'Trading Gods', 207, discusses the significance of this route in full.
[34] Meeks, *Urban Christians*, 26–9. Cf. Georgi, 'Early Church', esp. 37–46, showing that Paul's polemical strategies, even those which appear most anti-Semitic, derive in no small measure from a Jewish tradition.
[35] Lane Fox, *Pagans and Christians*, 272–6 with references. Cf. Rives, *Religion and Authority*, 226 n. 116, on Jewish origins—or the lack thereof—for Christian communities in north Africa; Otranto, *Italia meridionale*, 26–7, for southern Italy.
[36] For summary and critique, see Humphries, 'Trading Gods', 203–4, 220–2.
[37] Frend, 'Influence of Greek Immigrants', 126–8.
[38] Humphries, 'Trading Gods', 220–1. Similar circumstances are described in Acts, when Paul and Barnabas are alleged to have preached to 'all the residents of Asia' at Ephesus (19: 10). As the seat of the governor of Asia, and as an important cult centre, Ephesus would have attracted traders, petitioners, litigants, and worshippers from all over the province: Lane Fox, *Pagans and Christians*, 490; Price, *Rituals and Power*, 135–6, 254–7.

Once established, these new Christian communities remained susceptible to the influences of local and regional social dynamics. The life of the early Church, like that of many other cults in the empire, was characterized by a certain tension between unity and diversity, in ritual, organization, and patterns of belief, that owed much to the Roman imperial environment.[39] For all its unity, the empire preserved a rich mosaic of regional diversities in terms of cultural, economic, and institutional development.[40] Such tensions are neatly illustrated by liturgical differences. Christians throughout the Mediterranean world would have shared notions as to what constituted normative liturgical practices, such as the eucharist, baptism, and so forth. But liturgical evolution was neither linear nor monolithic, and it proceeded at different rates and in different ways in the various Christian communities across the empire.[41] That different liturgical observances obtained contemporaneously in different parts of the Roman world is clear from, for example, Egeria's need to describe the Jerusalem liturgy to her fellow Christians in the west, or Jerome's assertion, for a southern Gaulish audience, that in eastern churches it was normal to light candles for the Gospel reading, regardless of the time of day.[42] While these examples may imply a simple division between east and west only, it is clear that liturgical variations could exist also on a much more local scale, like those between the baptismal rites of Rome and the north Italian cities.[43]

Similar variation is also apparent in the development of the episcopate. Bishops were present in most parts of the Roman world where there were Christians, but the nature of episcopal office varied from place to place. In Africa, for example, bishops seem to have resided even in very small towns;[44] but in Asia Minor there was a distinction between ἐπίσκοποι ('bishops') in cities and χώρεπισκοποι ('country-bishops') in more rural areas.[45] Finally, not even belief was immune to these tensions. It is clear that the concept of an 'orthodox' or 'normative' Christianity opposed to 'heresy' predates the fourth century:

[39] Beard, North, and Price, *Religions of Rome*, i. 301–11.

[40] Garnsey and Saller, *Roman Empire*, 178–95, 203.

[41] Bradshaw, *Christian Worship*, 111–30, 158–60, 161–84, 205.

[42] e.g. *Itin. Egeriae* 18. 2; cf. Hier., *C. Vigilantium* 8. For Jerome's audience, cf. Kelly, *Jerome*, 286–90.

[43] The key text is Ambr., *De Sacr.* 3. 5: 'Non ignoramus quod ecclesia romana hunc consuetudinem [i.e. the washing of feet] non habet.' See further Bradshaw, *Christian Worship*, 179–81.

[44] Lane Fox, *Pagans and Christians*, 272; cf. Lepelley, *Cités de l'Afrique romaine*, i. 371–6.

[45] Meyendorff, *Imperial Unity*, 41–3; Mitchell, *Anatolia*, ii. 69–71.

how else could Irenaeus have written his *Adversus haereses* in the late second century?[46] Nevertheless, as dramatic discoveries such as the Gnostic texts from Nag Hammadi remind us, the definition of what was normative could change from time to time or place to place. As Elaine Pagels has noted: 'during the first and second centuries, Christians scattered throughout the world, from Rome to Asia, Africa, Egypt, and Gaul, read and revered quite different traditions, and various groups of Christians perceived Jesus and his message very differently'.[47]

The comparative—though never total—isolation in which early Christian communities scattered across the empire developed came to an end with the conversion of Constantine to Christianity, and his proclamation of religious freedom. Bishops from distant territories could now meet freely to discuss ecclesiastical business; but far from fostering the harmony that Constantine craved, Christians became increasingly and uncomfortably aware of differences between their own practices, organization, and beliefs, and those of their brethren elsewhere. This produced a varied response. On the one hand, there was an effort to impose liturgical unity in certain areas. For example, the Council of Arles (314) sought a solution to the problem of the date of Easter, announcing that 'it should be observed by us on the one day at the same time throughout the whole world'.[48] Likewise, organizational patterns that had developed before the fourth century now began to cause problems. At the Council of Nicaea in 325 a serious attempt was made to formalize the provincial hierarchy of the Church, which had hitherto developed informally. The fourth canon laid down the supremacy of the bishop of the provincial capital over the other bishops within the secular administrative province. This arrangement could not apply in Palestine, however, where the provincial capital was Caesarea, but where the church of Jerusalem had traditionally possessed greater prestige. Hence the bishops at Nicaea attempted to provide also for the authority of Jerusalem (canon 7).[49] Similarly, the tension between doctrinal unity and diversity persisted into the fourth century and beyond. Far from

---

[46] See esp. Williams, 'Pre-Nicene Orthodoxy'. Bauer, *Orthodoxy and Heresy*, is the seminal work; Christie-Murray, *History of Heresy*, 1–12, discusses general problems of definition.

[47] *Adam, Eve, and the Serpent*, 152.   [48] Munier, *Conc. Gall.*, 9.

[49] Detailed analysis in Rubin, 'Church of the Holy Sepulchre'; also Hunt, 'Constantine and Jerusalem', for the self-conscious assertion of the Jerusalem church's prestige in the period leading up to Nicaea. Cf. Chadwick, 'Faith and Order', for similar problems in relation to the jurisdiction of Alexandria and Antioch.

facilliating unity, the advent of imperial involvement in ecclesiastical matters added a new dimension to the forces seeking to impose
their version of orthodoxy. With emperors taking up highly partisan positions in these doctrinal disputes, orthodoxy often meant
the side best able to coerce its opponents into submission.[50] Such
ample evidence for the diversity of early Christianity—both before
Constantine's conversion and after—begs more studies of early
Christian communities that set them against their particular social
and regional contexts.

Defining a region

This, then, is what a study of north Italian Christianity between about
200 and 400 aims to achieve: a demonstration of how, in a given area,
the development of the Church is influenced by the features of the
environment within which it evolves. For such an approach to be
useful, the definition of the region must itself be valid. This question
has particular relevance for the study of early Christianity in Italy,
much of which has been concerned with the origins of bishoprics
and diocesan administration. The very methodology used by Ughelli,
Savio, and Lanzoni has been justifiably interrogated by Giorgio
Otranto's studies of the early Church in southern Italy, especially
Apulia. He asks why studies of the genesis of ecclesiastical administration proceed from the assumption that the territorial definition
of a bishopric today should in any way reflect its definition—or an
aspiration to such—in late antiquity. Instead he advises that any search
for the origins of Italian bishoprics must begin by setting their development in the context of ancient social relations and administrative
structures.[51] Otranto highlights a problem which has been particularly taxing to archaeologists interested in developing regional analysis, and which should likewise present difficulties for historians:
'Very often . . . regional analysis starts from a definition formulated
by modern or early modern observers.'[52] This, as we have seen, is
precisely the problem with the approach taken by Ughelli. Furthermore, the definition must also go beyond merely physical geography. Braudel lamented 'the traditional geographical intoduction to

---

[50] Gottlieb, 'Les évêques et les empereurs'; Hanson, *Tradition in the Early
Church*, 177; id., 'Achievement of Orthodoxy', 146–7. This theme is explored in detail
in Ch. 4 below.

[51] Otranto, *Italia meridionale*, 16–21.   [52] Hodges, 'Spatial Models', 128.

history that often figures to little purpose at the beginning of so many books.'[53] Little wonder, for as Braudel's detailed analysis showed, 'human life responds to the commands of the [physical] environment, but also seeks to evade and overcome them'.[54]

Defining northern Italy, as Chapter 1 demonstrates, is no easy matter. Of course, the region has already been the subject of studies which overlap, to a minor extent, with this one. Two, in particular, have been influential on the formulation of my own ideas: Jean-Charles Picard's monumental study of the cult of bishops in northern Italy down to the tenth century; and Bryan Ward-Perkins's analysis of urban public building in northern and central Italy between tetrarchic times and the reign of Charlemagne. It is interesting to note why each author chose to study northern Italy. Picard chose the area because of the richness of its documentation which he believed, rightly, deserved to be studied independent of material from Rome and from that found in Germanic Europe north of the Alps.[55] Ward-Perkins is refreshingly blunt on the issue:

In geographical range I have tried to cover the whole of mainland Lombard Italy, from Salerno northwards, and the whole of the Byzantine North. I would feel happier if I had included the deep south and Sicily, at least until the Arab invasions. However time and lack of familiarity with these regions excluded any comprehensive treatment.[56]

In both cases, the choice of northern Italy is informed by the identity of the region in the early medieval period. Neither definition, therefore, is appropriate for a study which seeks to explain the emergence of an institution in late antiquity.

How, then, is it possible to define a region? At the outset it must be stated that a single definition is not really feasible, since it will shift depending on the criteria used, whether temporal or geographical, cultural or economic. Some indication of the potential for overlap between different regions, and different definitions thereof, is clear from the evidence of periods better-documented than late antiquity. In mid-sixteenth-century France, for example, a plethora of factors meant that several different regions—ecclesiastical, administrative, economic, linguistic—overlapped in the tiny village of

---

[53] Braudel, *The Mediterranean*, i. 20.   [54] Ibid., i. 267.
[55] Picard, *Souvenir*, 1–5: he does not adequately explain, however, why he ignores the *gesta episcoporum* from Naples (mentioned by him at p. 1).
[56] Ward-Perkins, *CAMA*, p. vi.

Artigat near Toulouse.[57] The experience of one of my friends, a
Scottish nationalist, sums up this potential for disparity between
definitions of regional identity drawn up according to different criteria. We recently made a train journey northwards from Peterbor-
ough to Edinburgh, and as we were crossing the bridge at Berwick
upon Tweed, my friend shifted in his seat and muttered with pleas-
ure, 'That's better.' For him, Scotland begins at the river Tweed,
even though in administrative terms, laid down by a government in
London, the English border is a few miles further north. Between
my friend's cultural geography and the government's administrative
geography there lies a considerable divide.[58]

My own definition of northern Italy is sensitive to the disparity
between such different 'geographies'. The social compass of Roman
Aquileia, for example, will be seen to stretch into the Balkans in
apparent defiance of the physical frontier constituted by the Julian
Alps.[59] This is because that physical frontier has never been an effective barrier to human movement. Anyone who lives near these
mountains is acutely aware of this. In the course of fieldwork
undertaken for this project, I found myself having breakfast on the
balcony of a friend's apartment overlooking Trieste. As I took in
the view leading up the valleys behind the city, into what is now
Slovenia, my friend's mother, with a dramatic sweeping gesture of
her arm, sighed nostalgically, 'In the past, all this was Italy.'

Less frivolously, these disparities reflect how difficult it is to come
up with a single comprehensive definition of a given region. They
are reminders, in Edward Said's words,

of how oddly hybrid historical and cultural experiences are, of how they
partake of many often contradictory experiences and domains, cross national
boundaries, defy the *police* action of simple dogma and loud patriotism.[60]

The northern Italy of this study is not constrained by the rigid strait-
jacket of its physical boundaries. Even as I have defined it in
Chapter 1, it is an amorphous thing, sometimes inward-looking, sometimes open to influences from the Balkans, Gaul, peninsular Italy,

[57] Davis, *Return of Martin Guerre*, 8–11, 19.
[58] Cf. Hobsbawm, *Nations and Nationalism*, e.g. 132–3 on the 'utter impractic-
ability of [Woodrow Wilson's] principle to make state frontiers coincide with the
frontiers of nationality and language'.
[59] This is in itself a highly terrestrial definition: Aquileia's population comprised
overseas groups too.
[60] Said, *Culture and Imperialism*, 15 (author's own emphasis).

and overseas from Africa and Egypt. Sometimes these influences are intertwined, at other times one or more may dominate. In short, the regional dynamics of northern Italy represent a tension between the internal social, cultural, and economic matrices of life, and the pressure exerted upon them by external influences. In real terms this means northern Italy was a region where the complex interrelationships (in themselves never static) between its various communities were periodically confronted with, and sometimes confounded by, factors such as imperial presence and mercantile exchange. In themselves, such factors, both internal and external, provoked the movement of people around, into, and out of the region.

Approaches

These phenomena, and their impact on the early development of Christianity in northern Italy, are the subject of the first part of this study. The social dynamics of the north Italian environment are explored in Chapter 1. Chapter 2 examines the conventional views of Christian expansion in the region as defined by medieval tradition. Although the story they tell obscures the regional dynamics actually responsible for shaping early Christianity in northern Italy, their own formulation was very much a product of the north Italian environment. These traditions arose in circumstances of inter-episcopal rivalry, which provided the impetus for developing the traditions, exacerbated by events such as the collapse of western Roman imperial rule in the fifth century, and the disastrous Justinianic reconquest followed by the Lombard invasions in the sixth. The medieval texts are by no means useless, but what they really narrate is an effort to articulate the early Christian past by persons active in an uncertain late antique and early medieval present. Chapter 3 provides a reconstruction of the early diffusion of Christianity in the region, liberated from the model provided by later traditions. Of course, some elements of those traditions remain useful: late antique and early medieval historians of the Church did not invent wholesale, but manipulated (to a cynical mind) or rationalized (to a more sympathetic one) the material they had before them. This was probably a haphazard process; hence there can be no all-inclusive theory which determines when a later tradition is or is not reliable. Each instance must be assessed on its own merits.

The second part of the study pursues the theme further, examining how the social context of northern Italy in the fourth century aids an understanding of how its Christian communities developed. Once again, this context was diverse, especially with the regular presence of outsiders, such as the emperors and their courts, or exiles such as Athanasius of Alexandria. In general terms, it strikes me that the western *adventus* of Constantius II in the 350s was an important determinant of ecclesiastical development in northern Italy. In grand terms, the Christological debate, hitherto confined largely to the eastern provinces, was physically brought to the west. Relations between church and emperor, already an important feature in the east, became a factor in the life of north Italian Christian communities as never before. Chapter 4 will show the pivotal role of Constantius' reign in the developing relationship between local churches and the imperial government in the decades between Constantine and Theodosius. It also transformed the intellectual outlook of the north Italian episcopate, involving them in the theological controversies of eastern Christianity and providing the ideological backdrop to Ambrose of Milan's pro-Nicene campaigns in the 380s.

At the same time, Constantius' intervention made clear the disparity between north Italian structures of ecclesiastical power and those with which the emperor was familiar in the east. Northern Italy did not have a highly developed metropolitan administration, but Constantius' imposition of Auxentius on the church of Milan assumes that he saw Milan as possessing the same sort of eminence as Alexandria had in Egypt or Antioch in Syria. Hitherto, north Italian ecclesiastical administration had lacked any formal centralization, being conducted, as far as it is possible to tell, on an *ad hoc* local basis. But the polarization of the region's episcopate into various Christological camps, and efforts by some bishops to displace others, provided conditions which favoured the emergence of leadership by a domineering individual prelate. Northern Italy found him in Ambrose of Milan. At the same time, transformations of a bishop's prestige in relation to his peers cannot be cut adrift from his relationship with his flock. Thus Chapter 5 deliberately examines side-by-side the emergence of episcopal hierarchies, albeit informal ones, and the reflection of this process at a local level in the manifestations of a bishop's authority within his community.

The last two chapters will return to the themes of the early part of the book: the expansion of Christianity in northern Italy.

Whereas Chapters 4 and 5 show that the Church had become a cru-
cial social institution in the region's interaction with the rest of the
empire, and that bishops had become important players in regional
and local politics, it still remains uncertain to what extent northern
Italy was a Christian territory by the end of the fourth century. In
Chapter 6, an effort will be made to establish to what extent the
Church had expanded in the years between Constantius II and
Theodosius. It will be shown that, as for the pre-Constantinian period,
Christian expansion continued to be a piecemeal process, following
established social networks, sometimes into surprising places such
as the Alto Adige. Chapter 7 continues this theme, by addressing
the question of what it was like to live as a Christian in northern
Italy in the late fourth century. Concentration on ecclesiastical
affairs to the exclusion of all others tends to lend support to glib
views of Christian triumph. Yet it is clear that by the time Ambrose
of Milan died in 397, northern Italy was far from being an entirely
Christian space. Other religions maintained their vitality nearly a
century after Constantine's conversion. Here, perhaps more obviously than in other areas of this investigation, the importance of social
context will be evident: Christian communities of the blessed there
certainly were, but the north Italian human environment they
inhabited was not yet their own.

The social history of early Christianity in northern Italy is a large
subject, and it is inevitable that some areas have been treated more
cursorily than others. There is little here on popular piety, which
could be studied in inscriptions from Christian gravestones. Any dis-
claimer is likely to be unsatisfactory, but I will offer one nonethe-
less. The absence of Christian funerary practices from these pages
has less to do with a cheerful determination to concentrate on the
affairs of the living than that the evidence for such an investigation
begins to occur in substantial (and datable) quantities only from the
early fifth century. This topic will, however, loom large in my sequel
to this book.

Finally, I ought to explain why the figure of Ambrose of Milan
is less prominent in this book than in some other studies of late antique
Christianity. Ambrose has practically defined the course of investigations into early north Italian Christianity, and with good reason.
His extensive writings, including a valuable collection of letters,
the biography of Paulinus, and his obvious significance for a figure
like Augustine, all make Ambrose an attractive, richly documented

subject. In no small measure, the fascination with Ambrose in the works of my predecessors reflects his own self-conscious image-making. He single-handedly created a network of bishops in northern Italy who looked to Milan for leadership, while his dealings with the emperors Gratian, Valentinian II, and Theodosius I have invested his episcopate with legendary status. As a result many studies of the north Italian church take his career as a starting point,[61] or at best see the previous history of the region's churches as a prologue for the Ambrosian achievement.[62]

Yet to allow Ambrose to dictate the narrative is to take too narrow a view of early north Italian Christianity. No doubt many, like Augustine, knew him and admired him; but others, like Palladius of Ratiaria, Ambrose's major adversary at the Council of Aquileia in 381, saw him as a self-serving and domineering bully.[63] So north Italian Christianity has an existence and logic independent of Ambrose. To concentrate on Ambrose is narrow in another sense, in that it privileges one variety of evidence—writings by or about Ambrose—above all others.[64] There exists, however, other evidence, much of it archaeological, demanding interpretation on its own terms and for what it can tell us about the regional development of Christianity in the Roman world. This, then, is the basic task of this study.

[61] Lizzi, 'Ambrose's Contemporaries'; ead., *Vescovi*; cf. Bradshaw, *Christian Worship*, 115–16, 179–81.

[62] Williams, *Ambrose*.   [63] See further Ch. 5 below.

[64] For the extent to which Ambrose has dictated the study of his own episcopate, and, indeed, events outside it, see the judicious comments of McLynn, *Ambrose*, pp. xiii–xix.

PART I

Religion and environment: Christian origins in northern Italy

Why do I tell you this instead of getting on with my story?
Because I want you to understand that, in the Little World
between the river and the mountains, many things can happen
that cannot happen anywhere else.

Giovanni Guareschi

1

The north Italian human environment

In later chapters, I will argue that the arrival, expansion, and development of Christianity in northern Italy were determined by the environmental dictates of the region. To understand these processes, then, it is crucial to have a picture of the region's dynamics, and in this chapter I aim to provide a sketch of the conditions that shaped north Italian Christianity. Since the first Christians arrived in a region already deeply influenced by a Roman presence, it is not enough to examine the north Italian environment in purely geographical terms. We must also consider the human structures which existed within the geographical context. These human structures were highly complex, ranging from visible, concrete features which added to the physical appearance of the region, such as roads and settlements, to more intangible ones, like the social, economic, and cultural networks through which the local populations of northern Italy interacted with each other and the outside world. Together with the enduring influence of the physical landscape, these factors constitute what I call the north Italian human environment. In what follows I will naturally concentrate on towns and cities, since Christianity was at first a primarily, if not exclusively, urban phenomenon. Towns, moreover, offered the ideal environment for the direct personal contact crucial to the dissemination of religious ideas. Yet physical geography is a good enough place to begin, since it provides the canvas upon which human activity is painted.

Landscapes

When Caesar and his army crossed the Rubicon, they performed a deed resonating with profound symbolism for Rome. Hence Suetonius made the crossing a watershed, a moment of high drama (Suet., *Div. Iul.* 31. 2). Five centuries later when Sidonius Apollinaris, en route from Gaul to Rome, encountered the river, he paused to

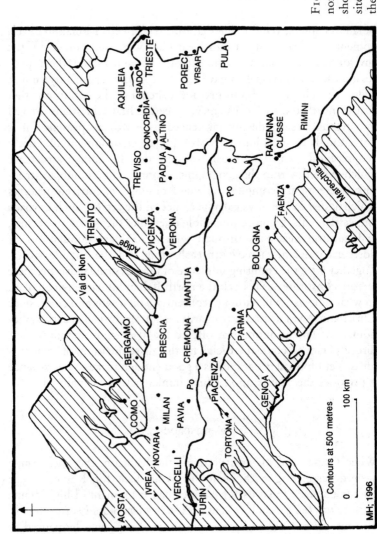

Fig. 1. Map of northern Italy showing important sites mentioned in the text

contemplate Caesar's action (*Ep.* 1. 5. 7). It is Sidonius who most explicitly expounds the symbolism: the Rubicon was once the boundary between Italy and Cisalpine Gaul (*olim Gallis cisalpinis Italisque veteribus terminus erat*). It was close to Rimini from where the road from the north led south to Fano and thence inland through the Apennines towards Rome. The Rubicon, then, was a neat conceptualization, an articulation in Roman terms of the frontier between two parts of Italy, one north and the other south of the Ligurian and Tosco-Emilian Apennines. The distinction went further: north of the Rubicon was not even properly part of Italy. Designated Cisalpine Gaul, it was where barbarian Europe encroached closest on the comfortable heartland of Roman Italy (cf. Strabo 5. 2. 10). By the time of Augustus, however, northern Italy had come to be seen as a geographical unit in its own right, a gulf of land bounded by mountains (Strabo 5. 1. 3; cf. Polybius 2. 16. 6–10). This view was the product of a gradual process of experience, perception, and definition, beginning with the first Roman forays into the region in the third century BC.[1]

Mountains

Mountains, as Strabo noted, defined northern Italy: the Alpine arc stretching from the Riviera in the west to Istria and the headwaters of the Adriatic in the east; and the diagonal sweep of the Apennines, running south-east from Liguria, where they are contiguous with the Maritime Alps, to Rimini, where they hem the Adriatic coast.[2] Of these the Apennines are far the greater obstacle to human movement. Even at their narrowest point, between Tortona and Genoa, they still separated societies with profoundly different social and economic bases.[3] For all its importance as a

---

[1] Purcell, 'Creation of Provincial Landscape', 9–12.

[2] Degrassi, *Il confine nord-orientale d'Italia romana*, 11–13.

[3] Garnsey, 'Economy and Society of Mediolanum', 16–17, 21, employs a Vercellese inscription (*CIL* 5. 7373) recording C. Marius Aelianus, a native of Tortona who was magistrate at both Genoa and Vercelli, to demonstrate active commercial links between Genoa and the Po valley. But the evidence he used was, by his own confession, too sparse to permit such conclusions. Moreover, I cannot agree with Garnsey (17 n. 17) that Strabo's description of Genoa as the emporium of Liguria (Strabo 5. 1. 3) means that its trade ordinarily stretched as far as the banks of the Po. This is to make Strabo's definition of Liguria conform to that of the Augustan *regio IX*, called Liguria, which extended this far (Thomsen, *Italic Regions*, 126–31). But Strabo's conception of Liguria is patently different. Towns such as Tortona, which

trading port (Strabo 5. 1. 3), Genoa seems to have enjoyed only limited commercial contacts with the regions north of the Apennines:
as in the middle ages, its trade seems to have focused primarily on
the sea.[4] In the early middle ages, the relative isolation of Genoa from
the rest of northern Italy across the Apennines was emphasized not
least by political differences:[5] in 569, for example, when the Lombards
took Milan, the bishops of that city fled to exile at Genoa, at that
time still in Byzantine hands.[6]

The easiest crossing of the range was further east, via the
Marecchia valley from Arezzo to Rimini (Strabo 5. 2. 9). This sector, the Umbrian Apennines, was the crucial channel of communication between the Tyrrhenian coast and northern Italy.[7] It was here
that the earliest contacts occurred between Italians from the north
and those of the centre and south. In the fifth century BC the
Umbrians seem to have occupied territory in the Romagna, including Ravenna, Rimini, and Sarsina (Strabo 5. 2. 10).[8] The first Roman
penetration of northern Italy also came by this route. Rimini was

---

were part of Augustan Liguria, are included in Strabo's description of the Po valley
(5. 1. 11), which he clearly distinguishes from Liguria (5. 2. 1), a region which he
apparently considered no more extensive than an insignificant coastal strip (cf. 5.
2. 1). Brunt, *Italian Manpower*, 180–1, offers, to my mind, a more sensible appraisal
of the economic realities of attempting to transport goods overland from Genoa across
the Apennines. This is a useful reminder that administrative and commercial geography do not always overlap.

[4] For example, analysis of the Italian amphorae retrieved during the excavations
between 1982 and 1985 in the S. Silvestro district of the castle hill revealed that most
of them came from Etruria, Latium, and Campania: Milanese, *Genova romana*, 82–91,
esp. 88–91. Perhaps in antiquity, as in the middle ages, Genoa's economic importance lay not in its role as an entrepôt between Liguria and the wider Mediterranean
world, but as a centre of exchange from where imported goods were re-exported:
Abulafia, *The Two Italies*, 217–54, noting instances of luxury goods from the east
being exported to Sicily, via which they had come to Genoa in the first place; cf.
Origone, *Bizanzio e Genova*, 51–60.

[5] Wickham, *Early Medieval Italy*, 11.

[6] Paul. Diac., *HL* 2. 25; cf. Origone, *Bizanzio e Genova*, 18–23, for the importance of Genoa at this period. Note, however, that this was not entirely the upshot
of geographical factors, since the passes of the Ligurian Apennines were heavily gar-
risoned at this time: Christie, 'Byzantine Liguria', 257–64; and in greater detail, id.,
'The Limes Bizantino Revisited'.

[7] It remained so in the early middle ages, when the duchy of Perugia formed
a vital link between Rome and the Byzantine Pentapolis round Ravenna: Diehl,
Études sur l'administration byzantine, 68–72. This route was, however, never secure,
and was regularly under attack from the neighbouring Lombard duchy of Spoleto:
Noble, *Republic of St Peter*, 5, 156–7. This emphasizes the continued strategic
importance of the Umbrian Apennines, which the Romans knew only too well: cf.
Tabacco, *Struggle for Power*, 75.

[8] Pallottino, *History of Earliest Italy*, 104.

founded at the estuary of the Marecchia in 268 BC and a road, the Via Flaminia, was constructed nearby along the route of the river Metaurus in 232 BC. This was the route taken by Caesar and Sidonius in later centuries. Even in the early modern period it remained the most convenient crossing from northern Italy to Rome.[9] Yet, as Sidonius' graphic account suggests, crossing the Apennines via this route, even with the *cursus publicus* at one's disposal, could be extremely gruelling (Sid. Ap., *Ep.* 1. 5. 2, 8–10).[10]

By contrast the Alps, punctuated by a greater profusion of easily negotiable passes, were a less serious barrier to communication. This was especially so in their central and eastern reaches. North of Verona, the valley of the river Adige cut a cleft through the mountains that allowed easy passage to the lands bordering the upper Danube. In the north-east, the gentle, low-lying Julian Alps have never offered any serious barrier to human movement to and fro between northern Italy and the middle-Danubian region. From prehistoric times, the peoples of northern Italy have had more in common with their neighbours north of the Alps than those south of the Apennines.[11] When the Romans first entered the plain, much of it was occupied by Celtic peoples, and this affinity with Gaul was accentuated by the similar climates enjoyed by both regions. Consequently the Po valley came to be known as *Gallia Cisalpina*: Gaul on the nearer side of the Alps. Apart from the connections with Gaul through the Maritime Alps, there were contacts through the central Alps with the Celts of Rhaetia, who established *oppida* at Trento and Verona.[12] In the east, the Venetic peoples had long-standing connections via the Julian Alps with the peoples of the Balkans and the Hungarian plain.[13] This tradition of contact between these areas has persisted into modern times, as the sway of political fortunes has

[9] Braudel, *The Mediterranean*, i. 281.

[10] I am informed by a friend, who works in Urbino, lives in Florence, and commutes weekly, that even with a car, the autostrada, and a comprehensive system of tunnels, trans-Apennine travel is still tortuous.

[11] The recent discovery (September 1991) of the quasi-mummified corpse of 'Ötzi the Iceman', dating perhaps as early as the fourth millennium BC, has shown human activity high in the Alto Adige at a very early period. Konrad Spindler, the prehistorian involved in the recovery of Ötzi's body, advanced amongst others the theory that he may have been involved in trade between one side of the Alps and the other. For other interpretations, and a full review of the issues: Barfield, 'The Iceman Reviewed'.

[12] Richmond and Holford, 'Roman Verona', 69.

[13] Dyson, *Creation of the Roman Frontier*, 45–8. See the various essays in *Aquileia e l'arco alpino nord-orientale* (*AAAd* 9: 1976), esp. those by Vonwiller and Cattacchio; also Buora and Plesnicar-Gec, *Aquileia-Emona*, esp. 6–21.

seen national borders creep back and forth across these miniature Alps. In our own century, the bloodshed on the Carso above Gorizia during the First World War and the march of d'Annunzio to Fiume in 1919 are violent testimony to Italy's lack of geographical definition at its north-eastern frontier.[14]

Rivers

Within the arena formed by the encircling mountains, the other great geographic feature of northern Italy was its network of rivers, above all the Po.[15] Snaking its way from the Alps to the Adriatic, drawing its waters from the mountains north and south, it is the Po that gives unity to the plain. To the Romans, with their penchant for conceptualizing the landscape, it could function as a barrier. Both Polybius (2. 16. 6–7) and Strabo (5. 1. 4) talk of the regions of northern Italy in terms of Transpadana (across the Po) and Cispadana (on the near side of the Po). This view informed the Augustan division of northern Italy into *regiones* in which the Po acted as a dividing line.[16] Occasionally, such as when it was in flood, the Po could indeed constitute a physical barrier.[17] More important, however, was its role as a major communications artery.[18] It was used for personal travel as well as for trade: when Sidonius went to Rome, his journey from Pavia to Ravenna was made by boat on the Po (Sid. Ap., *Ep.* 1. 5. 3–5; cf. Strabo 5. 1. 11). But the Po was just one of a number of rivers used for transport, especially in the areas closest to the Adriatic coast, and above all in the damp, flat plains of Venetia. It was possible to sail from lake Garda to the Adriatic, via the Mincio and then the Po.[19] Padua, some 250 *stades* from the sea, had its own port on the river Medoacus, while minor channels also connected Oderzo, Concordia, Adria, Vicenza, and others to the Adriatic. Indeed Aquileia, the major port of northern Italy, lay more than 60 *stades* inland on the river Natiso (Strabo 5. 1. 8).

---

[14] Cf. Tibiletti, *Storie locali*, 35–45, esp. 38.

[15] Brunt, *Italian Manpower*, 173–5, 179–81, esp. 179: 'The most striking difference between Cisalpina and the rest of Italy was its inland water-system.'

[16] On the Augustan *regiones* see Chilver, *Cisalpine Gaul*, 1; Thomsen, *Italic Regions*, pt. i, esp. 144.

[17] The Po in flood: Brunt, *Italian Manpower*, 173–5 with references; cf. Braudel, *The Mediterranean*, i. 247 (on Mantua in the sixteenth century).

[18] Brunt, *Italian Manpower*, 179–81; Chevallier, *Romanisation*, 23.

[19] Chevallier, *Romanisation*, 23.

The impact of Rome

By the time Christianity arrived in the region, human activity had added its own features to the environment, and these were to be profoundly influential on the growth of the new faith. In the first place there were physical structures, often built in response to environmental conditions. The construction of canals and drainage ditches in much of the Po valley and Venetia was necessary to bring once marshy ground into agricultural use.[20] Similarly, the development of Roman cities and road networks in northern Italy amply demonstrates the influence of the physical environment on human activity.[21] For the Romans, moreover, both were fundamental to asserting control over newly conquered territories north of the Apennines. Together with them came the chequerboard division of agricultural land by centuriation, which has been justly called 'a reduplication of Roman political structures in a conquered zone'.[22]

We have already seen that the easiest point of access to northern Italy, the Umbrian Apennines, had an impact on the historical development of the Roman conquest, with the foundation of Rimini and the laying of the Via Flaminia. Routes taken by other early roads were similarly dictated by environmental factors. The Po was most easily crossed at the point straddled by the twin Latin colonies of Piacenza and Cremona, both founded in 218 BC. As with Rimini and the Via Flaminia, roads followed the cities. In 187 BC[23] the Via Aemilia was built, hugging the northern fringe of the Apennines, running north-west from Rimini to Piacenza (Livy 39. 2) and flanked on either side by centuriated land.[24] The central position of Cremona and Piacenza (cf. Strabo 5. 1. 11) was emphasized again in 148/7 BC with the construction of the Via Postumia from Genoa to Aquileia, which crossed the Po at the twin colonies.[25]

[20] Brunt, *Italian Manpower*, 175–6; cf. Menant, *Campagnes lombardes*, 182–203. For examples of drainage ditches associated with land divisions, see the many valuable contributions to *Misurare la terra*, esp. the photographs at figs. 60–4, 103, 123–4, 133, 138, 166–7.

[21] Chevallier, *Romanisation*, 297–9.

[22] Centuriation: Purcell, 'Creation of Provincial Landscape', 12–20, quotation from 16; cf. *Misurare la terra*, 15–21, esp. 21; Whittaker, *Frontiers of the Roman Empire*, 10–30, esp. 18–26. Cities: Garnsey and Saller, *Roman Empire*, 189–95. Roads: Chevallier, *Roman Roads*, 202–6.

[23] Dyson, *Creation of the Roman Frontier*, 32–5.

[24] Chevallier, *Romanisation*, 7–8, pls. 5–14.

[25] Chevallier, *Romanisation*, 9; Purcell, 'Creation of Provincial Landscape', 13.

While Cremona and Piacenza were built in advance of the Roman road, most other foundations were later developments.[26] Along the Via Aemilia, for example, lay Bologna, Modena, and Parma, together with a host of minor settlements.[27] Similarly, once the Alps began to be brought under Roman control in the reign of Augustus, cities were established commanding the mountain passes, as at Turin, Aosta, Susa, Verona, and Trento.[28] In the subdued zone these cities, echoing the rhythms of urban life at Rome, became the major centres of a cultural conquest. If native customs were to persist, they would do so in the areas most remote from urban influence, particularly in the mountains. Even in the late sixteenth century, pre-Christian fertility cults endured in the mountain valleys near Cividale in Friuli, not far from Aquileia, one of the oldest centres of Christianity in the region.[29] But while this shows how in remote areas pre-existing traditions could persist, there can be no all-encompassing rule. In the Val di Non near Trento, an area both rural and mountainous and therefore surely a classic peripheral zone, there was a strong Roman presence. This warning reminds us that local factors are extremely important for understanding cultural change. In the Val di Non the presence of the brick industry and aristocratic estates in the early empire and its importance as a military zone after the fall of the Rhaetian *limes* in 383 meant that, for all its apparent remoteness, the area saw constant and intensive Roman activity.[30]

The material fabric of the cities constituted an important part of the north Italian environment by the beginning of the Christian period. Cities here were often based on a strict orthogonal plan which in many cases persisted throughout the middle ages into the modern period. Roman street grids survive at Bologna, Brescia, Como, Parma, Pavia, Piacenza, and Verona;[31] until 1585, when Carlo Emmanuele I, Duke of Savoy, initiated a century of total rebuilding, Turin too retained its Roman plan.[32] The persistence of these

[26] For the social dynamics of road building: Laurence, 'Land Transport in Roman Italy', 138–46.

[27] Dyson, *Creation of the Roman Frontier*, 40.

[28] Gabba, *Italia romana*, 278–9.

[29] Ginzburg, *I benandanti*, esp. 61–88 on parallels and origins.

[30] Lizzi, *Vescovi*, 70–80; id., 'Ambrose's Contemporaries', 170.

[31] Chevallier, *Romanisation*, pls. 15, 19–23; Fevrier, 'Permanence et heritages de l'antiquité', esp. 100–1; Ward-Perkins, *CAMA*, 178–96; La Rocca, 'Public Buildings and Urban Change'.

[32] Gutkind, *Urban Development in Southern Europe*, 248–56, esp. 252.

street grids—and the continuity of effective public control over the urban fabric it implies[33]—emphasizes the need of the Church, like any private organization, to develop within the strict confines of this 'built environment'.[34]

Human geography

Within the physical environment provided by landscapes, urban centres, and roads, there developed a complex set of interpersonal relationships. These networks were the vehicles of change in society, and early Christianity was heavily dependent on them for its expansion and development. Plotting such networks is a difficult task: a tension exists between the methodological tendency to view them as distinct categories, and the demonstrable circumstance that they were blurred and not differentiated in practice. Thus while I will now analyse these networks individually, it must be remembered that together they constitute a complex, multi-layered, and interwoven social fabric.[35]

Economic networks

Economic activity in the form of trade provided an ideal environment for the personal interface so important to religious change. I have already alluded to the economy with reference to the transportation of goods, but we should not confuse commercial networks with communications networks. The two were certainly linked, but as is known from elsewhere in Italy and the empire, a good location in respect of communications was not always enough to guarantee a settlement importance as a market centre.[36] The road network, however, was important in that it provided easy communications to such

[33] Ward-Perkins, *CAMA*, 180.
[34] The term is taken from Bagnall, *Egypt in Late Antiquity*, 45–54. For religious implications: White, *God's House*, ch. 3 (esp. 48–59) and ch. 4 (esp. 85–101) on Mithraism and Judaism respectively.
[35] For central and southern Italy: Dyson, *Community and Society*, 147–79.
[36] Roman Apulia provides some well-researched examples. Aecae (modern Troia) commanded the two ancient roads from Benevento to Lucera, but never became an important market. That it was overshadowed by Lucera itself highlights the equal importance of locally available commodities to the location of markets: Frayn, *Markets and Fairs*, 41–2, 79–84. Cf. the prosperity of Canusium (Canosa di Puglia) in the fourth century: Dyson, *Community and Society*, 233.

markets as existed: it is particularly noteworthy that, in the wake
of the construction of the Via Aemilia, a number of small market
towns, some bearing the giveaway name *Forum*, sprang up along its
length.[37] It must also be remembered that trade operated on a number of different levels: some goods would have been traded at the
most limited, local level, particularly perishable agricultural pro-
ducts of everyday use. But where goods could be classed as luxuries,
or where a market had access to specialized commodities, then the
likelihood of long-distance trade was greater.[38]

In northern Italy there were a number of such markets that
attracted traders from the Po basin and beyond. The textile industry was particularly important: Milan was an important centre for
distribution in the upper Po valley, while the linen industry bene-
fited Faenza. In the Venetic plains especially, ideal grazing conditions which rendered transhumance virtually redundant fostered a
flourishing woollen trade, with important markets at Brescia, Verona,
Padua, and Altino.[39] In many of these instances, towns were not
important commercial centres simply because they were markets for
raw goods; rather, as Strabo's description of Padua (5. 1. 7), references
to Altino in Diocletian's Price Edict (21. 2; 25. 4), and numerous
epitaphs from Aquileia remind us, a city's ability to process goods
added to its significance as a trading centre.[40]

With excellent communications added to locally available goods
and thriving industry, some towns and cities became important markets not just for northern Italy but for the wider world. Milan, for
example, commanded a number of trade-routes across the Alps to
Rhaetia and Gaul, and consequently became an important node
in both transalpine and cisalpine trade-networks.[41] The city's trade
may even have stretched southwards, if the inscription recording the
presence of an Apulian *negotiator sagarius* (*CIL* 5. 5925) represents

[37] Dyson, *Creation of the Roman Frontier*, 40.
[38] Duncan-Jones, *Structure and Scale in the Roman Economy*, 7–58, esp. 39–47,
58. Frayn, *Markets and Fairs*, 74–7, with fig. 7; Dyson, *Community and Society*, 125–6;
cf. Jones, 'Cloth Industry', esp. 186.
[39] Conditions: Frayn, *Sheep-Rearing and the Wool Trade*, 25. Brescia: Tozzi,
'Iscrizioni latine sull'arte lanaria bresciana'. Altinum: Diocletian's Price Edict (25. 4).
In general: Brunt, *Italian Manpower*, 182; Chilver, *Cisalpine Gaul*, 163–7.
[40] Brusin, *Aquileia e Grado*, 115–18; Calderini, *Aquileia romana*, 297–332;
Chevallier, *Aquilée*, 55–60, 90.
[41] *CIL* 5. 5911: a corporation of traders operating in these areas. For comm., Garnsey,
'Economy and Society of Mediolanum', 19–22.

anything more than an isolated contact.[42] Likewise Verona, at the opening of the Adige valley onto the plain, controlled an important route into the Alps to markets in Noricum.[43] The fast-flowing Adige seems to have become navigable from Verona, which would have increased the city's commercial potential.[44] Explicit evidence confirms that markets at Cremona in the centre of northern Italy flourished because of its situation on the Po (Tac., *Hist.* 3. 30, 34).

The greatest centres of trade would have been the sea-ports on the Adriatic. Padua, as we saw, was connected with the sea, which undoubtedly helped its cloth trade in the late-Republic and Augustan period (Strabo 5. 1. 7). Ravenna was situated in antiquity at the mouth of the Po (Sid. Ap., *Ep.* 5. 1. 11), while the elder Pliny records that the river allowed the penetration of foreign goods deep into the north Italian plain (*HN* 3. 123). This makes Ravenna a likely entrepôt for goods coming up the Adriatic.[45] Distributions of imports in Cispadana suggest that there must have been a commercial port somewhere along its coast,[46] but identifying this with Ravenna is not easy. The city's maritime importance was attributable mainly to the great naval base at nearby Classis, which would certainly have generated its own trade because of the need for supplies.[47] Yet the precise location of a commercial port is still debated, and its significance prior to 402, when the imperial court moved to Ravenna, is impossible to define.[48] Furthermore there was an important port nearby at Rimini (Strabo 5. 1. 11), which, unlike Ravenna, was also at the hub of an important road network.[49] This is not to deny that Ravenna itself was important, but to suggest that imports may have reached Cispadana through more than one port.

There is no such ambiguity for Venetia, where economic inter-action with the outside world was dominated by Aquileia. The city was ideally situated on the navigable river Natiso, which linked the city to the Adriatic, and near the passes through the Julian Alps to

[42] Jones, 'Cloth Industry', 192.
[43] Hyde, *Roman Alpine Routes*, 116–58; De Laet, *Portorium*, 157–8, 182–3; Sartori, 'Verona romana', 222–3.
[44] *CIL* 5. 4017 records Veronese *navicularii*.
[45] Thus Garnsey, 'Economy and Society at Mediolanum', 17–18.
[46] Gelichi, Malnati, and Ortalli, 'L'Emilia centro-occidentale', 557.
[47] Excavations in the Chiavichetta district of Classe have revealed *horrea* and ceramic manufacturing facilities by the quayside: Deichmann, *Ravenna. Kommentar*, iii. 33, 45, 48, 263–4, 266, and pls. 12–18.
[48] Chevallier, *Romanisation*, 24–7; Reddé, *Mare Nostrum*, 183–6.
[49] See above, pp. 24–5.

the Balkans and the Danube. Contacts with the regions across the mountains began very early indeed and persisted into the Roman period and beyond.[50] Strabo emphasized this trade, calling Aquileia an 'emporium for those Illyrians living near the Danube' (Strabo 5. 1. 8; cf. 4. 6. 10). This sentiment is echoed by Herodian some two centuries later, but he draws greater attention to the role of Aquileia as a centre of exchange between land and sea, as well as being a considerable agricultural and industrial centre in its own right (Herodian 8. 2. 3). Archaeological and epigraphic evidence confirms this picture. At Aquileia itself there are the impressive remains of the harbour and its *horrea*, as well as numerous finds associated with trade. The distribution of inscriptions, pottery, and amphorae attests the activity of Aquileian traders in the Julian Alps and the Danubian provinces in the early imperial period.[51] The extent to which the tentacles of this trade extended westwards into northern Italy is unclear, but it is possible to infer its existence from the social networks that linked Aquileia and other centres in Venetia.

Social and cultural networks: the matrix of interaction

The movement of goods meant the movement of people, and it is in connection with trade that we have the clearest evidence of the local populations of northern Italy interacting with each other and with the outside world. The epigraphic record throws up many instances of people moving around and beyond northern Italy for commercial purposes. Members of the Barbii *gens* from Aquileia, for example, are attested in trading contexts throughout the Danubian provinces, the north-eastern Alps, the ports of the Adriatic, and in cities in northern Italy.[52] Foreign traders too are mentioned in inscriptions found in and around the city, confirming Herodian's early third-century description of Aquileia as 'teeming with local citizens, aliens, and traders' (8. 2. 3). The Gavii, a prominent Veronese family, had freedmen at Aquileia, and it is possible that they too were engaged in trade.[53] It was not just merchants,

---

[50] The foundation of Aquileia in 183 BC was soon followed by early Roman military expeditions into Pannonia: Dyson, *Creation of the Roman Frontier*, 74.

[51] Cipriano, 'Aquileia', 139–43; Jäggi, 163–5, 169–70. Pavan 'La provincia romana della Pannonia Superior', 441–3, 466–7.

[52] Sasel, 'Barbii'.   [53] Chilver, *Cisalpine Gaul*, 90–1.

however, who moved around northern Italy because of trade. Commerce across provincial boundaries attracted the scrutiny of the imperial government, which established customs stations staffed with imperial officials and their slaves. Transalpine routes in north-eastern Italy came under the aegis of the *portorium* (customs network) of Illyricum, and the distribution of personnel associated with the *portorium* confirms the picture of close links between north-eastern Italy and the Danubian provinces. The activities of one Ti. Iulius Saturninus, a *praefectus vehiculorum* of the customs network in the reign of Antoninus Pius, are recorded on inscriptions along the road leading east through Moesia Inferior and Thrace;[54] his slaves and stewards (*vilici*) are attested on the routes from Venetia to Noricum, and on the Dalmatian coast.[55] Around the same time, two other officials of the *portorium*, C. Antonius Rufus and Q. Sabinius Veranus and their staff were active in precisely the same areas.[56] These networks cluster along a number of trade-routes, both overland and maritime, emanating from Aquileia, where, moreover, a bureau of the Illyrican *portorium* was based.[57]

State influence on the social dynamics of the region is visible in other matters. When Roman armies began to bring the Balkans under control, this expansion was buttressed by the foundation of colonies, some of whose settlers seem to have come from northern Italy: at Emona (Ljubljana) and Savaria (Szombathely), for instance, members of the Tiberii-Barbii *gens* which had died out at Aquileia by the early imperial period are found holding civic office in the first and second centuries AD.[58] Not only did state directives 'export' people from northern Italy: it drafted them in too, such as at Ravenna, where the marines associated with the imperial naval base came from diverse racial backgrounds.[59]

These last examples remind us that social networks were not always dependent on trade. Politics and religion provide further instances

[54] *AE* 1928, no. 153; 1934, no. 107.
[55] Venetia–Noricum networks: *CIL* 3. 4720; 5. 5079. Dalmatia: *AE* 101 (1940).
[56] Antonius Rufus etc.: *CIL* 3. 13283 (Dalmatian coast), 5117 (Atrans in Noricum); *ILS* 4244 (Poetovio in Pannonia). Sabinius Veranus etc.: *CIL* 3. 4875, 5184 (Noricum); *ILS* 4243 (Poetovio).
[57] Calderini, *Aquileia romana*, 245–8; De Laet, *Portorium*, 175–92, esp. 179–80, and 386 on the links between these three officials; cf. Selem, *Les religions orientales*, 36, 69–74.
[58] Sasel, 'Barbii', 137; cf. Mócsy, *Pannonia*, 76–8, for further examples.
[59] Chevallier, *Romanisation*, 204–6; Starr, *The Roman Imperial Navy*, 204–6.

of non-commercial interaction. Analyses of epigraphic material
reveals that certain individuals from one city held priesthoods and
magistracies at others. Although the evidence is far from comprehensive, it is possible to see a number of regional clusters. For example, there seem to have been particularly strong links between
the cities of Piedmont. An inscription from Tortona reveals that one
C. Marius Aelianus held office in Vercelli and Tortona, as well as
in Genoa (*CIL* 5. 7373). Tortona and Vercelli can also be shown
to have had political and religious connections with nearby Novara
and Ivrea.[60] Doubtless, all of these centres will have fallen within
the networks emanating from Milan as that city became increasingly
important as the focus of local administration,[61] just as numerous
Milanese came to fill administrative posts in neighbouring cities,
such as Como and Lodì.[62] Meanwhile, similar circumstances probably obtained in the cities of *Venetia et Histria*: we find Barbii,
probably related to the Aquileian *gens*, in priesthoods at Altino
and Vicenza.[63] Such connections might suggest commercial links,
especially when a trading family like the Barbii is involved, but it
would be rash to assume that every connection reflected economic
interests. Milan's links with Como could certainly be seen in a commercial context,[64] but those with Lodì more probably resulted from
the traffic between Rome and Milan.[65] Some of this would have
involved trade, but during the late republic and early principate
there would have been also much accruing from the political relationship between Milan, an important administrative centre, and the
imperial capital and court at Rome. Another example of this non-
commercial interaction is provided by the inscription of Marius
Aelianus from Tortona, which mentions that he had been *iudex inter
selectos ex V decuriis*, recording his jury service at Rome.[66]

---

[60] *CIL* 5. 6494 (a *flamen civitatis Vercellensis* recorded on an inscription from between
Vercelli and Novara), 6771 (an inscription from between Vercelli and Ivrea record-
ing 'T. Sextius Secun[...] | Eporediae'), 7373 (on magistracies held at both Vercelli
and Tortona).

[61] Tac., *Hist.* 1. 70, associates the cities of Novara, Ivrea, and Vercelli with Milan.

[62] Tibiletti, *Storie locali*, 279–82; cf. Mirabella Roberti, 'Milano e Como', 479–98,
arguing that Como was originally the more important city.

[63] Sasel, 'Barbii', nos. 62 and 94.

[64] A Milanese trader was *patronus* of a guild of sailors on lake Como: *CIL* 5. 5911.

[65] Tibiletti, *Storie locali*, 1–4.

[66] *CIL* 5. 7373; cf. 7375 for another Tortonese at Rome for jury service. On the
formula: F. Bozza, art. 'Iudex', in Ruggiero, *Diz. Ep.* 4. 1. 1 (1924–46), esp. 161–3.

To social networks deriving from the administrative actions and ambitions of family groups we must add those connections fostered by the urban culture of northern Italy. There is good evidence for the role of civic spectacles, such as shows at the theatre or games in the arena, in creating social networks.[67] Such public spectacles would probably have attracted large crowds of spectators, especially to a city like Verona, which boasted one of the largest amphitheatres in Italy. At Verona we have evidence that at least the gladiators came from other parts of the Po valley: epitaphs were set up in honour of fallen combatants from Modena (by his wife and fans!) and Tortona.[68] Verona also demonstrates how such entertainments could provide opportunities for local grandees to play the role of civic patrons. At the highest level of the *cavea* of the theatre, there were porticoes from where the Veronese could admire the view across their city: these arcades were built, as inscriptions record, at the expense of the great families of the city, the Gavii among them.[69] Indeed patronage, as the glue which cemented Roman society, both urban and rural, was to be of enduring importance in the development of Christianity, particularly in terms of organization within the community, as well as in relationships between communions. The personal role of the bishop echoed that of the civic *patronus* as benefactor and protector, administrator and politician.[70]

This pervasive role of patronage at so many levels in ancient society serves to remind us of the complexity of interpersonal networks which existed in northern Italy at the time Christianity first arrived. The matrix of social relations so important to Roman administration, based above all on the cities, was to have important ramifications for the growth of the Church in the region, providing the loosely defined framework within which Christians would operate. Trading centres, teeming with foreigners and natives, were ideal places for religions to spread, and, as we will see in Chapter 3, there is good reason to suppose that they were important in the process of

[67] Chevallier, *Romanisation*, 508.
[68] *CIL* 5. 3466 (to Glaucus, set up by Aurelia and his *amatores*), 3468; also 3471 recording a troupe of gladiators (*familia gladiatoria*); cf. Wiedemann, *Emperors and Gladiators*, 114–15.
[69] *CIL* 5. 3441; cf. Beschi, 'Verona romana. I monumenti', 422; Zanker, *Power of Images*, 329.
[70] Dyson, *Community and Society*, 206–8; cf. Garnsey and Woolf, 'Patronage of the Rural Poor in the Roman World', esp. 162–6.

evangelization. But trade did not take place in a vacuum: it was deeply
embedded in the social fabric, as is shown by the roles of various
Barbii and Gavii as patrons, priests, and magistrates, as well as traders.

Divine geography

The landscape into which Christianity was introduced was one
already saturated with gods. It is impossible to give here anything
other than the briefest survey of north Italian religious society
prior to the advent of Christianity: the story is a complex one, involving the imposition and interaction of successive layers of religious
activity, from the pre-Roman period, through the process of conquest and colonization, and down to the profusion of cults under
the empire.[71] Nevertheless, even a cursory analysis shows that there
was profound interpenetration between the dynamics of north
Italian society and the region's religious landscape. As will be seen
later, in Chapter 3, certain of these characteristics are to be found
also in the pattern of Christian expansion into the region.

The earliest comprehensible strata of north Italian religious history belong to the period just before the conquest. In certain
respects this pre-Roman substrate followed the tribal dispositions
of the population. Thus, for example, the religion of the peoples
in the west and centre of the Po plain was imbued with Celtic
deities.[72] Yet the different regions did not develop in isolation: that
Aquileia, in the old Venetic territories, could boast as its tutelary
deity a Celtic god of the central Alps, Belenus, is emblematic of this
phenomenon.[73] Also, some elements of the north Italian religious
milieu were altogether more exotic. A festival in honour of the Trojan
hero Antenor was held at Padua once every sixty years. The precise
origins of this remarkable cult are unknown, but by the Augustan
period the people of Padua—and indeed of Venetia generally—were
confident of their Trojan origins.[74]

---

[71] For comprehensive surveys and catalogues: Chevallier, *Romanisation*, 421–502;
cf. Pascal, *Cults of Cisalpine Gaul*.

[72] Chevallier, *Romanisation*, 429–32.

[73] Pascal, *Cults of Cisalpine Gaul*, 123–9; Calderini, *Aquileia romana*, 93–111,
assembles all the evidence for the cult.

[74] Festival: Dio 62. 26; Tac., *Ann.* 16. 21. 1. Trojan origins for Padua and the Veneti
are noted by Livy 1. 1, and Verg., *Aen.* 1. 242–9. A dedication to the *Antenoridai*
occurs at Aquileia: *Inscr. Aquil.* 211.

This pre-Roman religious geography proved resilient, albeit reshaped by *interpretatio Romana*. During his account of the siege of Aquileia during the civil war of AD 238, Herodian paused to re-mark on the vitality of the cult of Belenus, by now identified with Apollo, which served to inspire the city's defenders.[75] In the pan-theon of north Italian gods, Belenus was a remarkable success: dedi-cations to him are known from outside northern Italy at Rome, Tivoli, and in southern Gaul.[76] Yet local deities who did not enjoy this wide dispersal continued to be venerated: at Aquileia, for example, we find a dedication to Aesontius (associated with the local river Isonzo);[77] and in the Alps, local gods of the mountain passes found willing dedicants well into the imperial period.[78] The survival of these local deities often depended on syncretism with gods of the Roman pan-theon. The Alpine god Poeninus, under whose protection lay the Great St Bernard Pass, is known primarily through dedications which associate him with Jupiter.[79] In some areas, however, there seems to have been a more general retreat of the local cults in the face of Roman gods. The Val di Non, for example, seems to have taken Saturn as its tutelary deity: when the emperor Claudius granted the local inhabitants Roman citizenship in AD 46, the bronze plaque commemorating this gift was set up at the temple of Saturn in the local centre of Cles.[80] Once again we see that this par-ticular valley in the Alto Adige, far from being remote, enjoyed strong contacts with the outside world.

Saturn was prominent in the Val di Non precisely because that area came under the direct supervision of the Roman state and its administrative apparatus. An examination of what may be termed Roman state religion—that is, the worship of gods venerated at Rome, together with devotion to the imperial cult—suggests, however, that its impact on northern Italy was far from comprehensive. This is amply demonstrated by the case of the Capitoline triad—Jupiter, Juno, and Minerva—as worshipped in the immense temple domin-ating the Forum in Rome. Temples of the Capitoline gods, situated,

[75] Herod. 8. 3. 8–9, actually calling the god 'Beles'; but the identification with Belenus is certain, thanks to Herodian's assertion that the god was identified with Apollo. Epigraphic testimony of this identification survives: *CIL* 5. 737, 741, 748–9, etc.
[76] Calderini, *Aquileia romana*, 102–3.   [77] Calderini, *Aquileia romana*, 158.
[78] Pascal, *Cults of Cisalpine Gaul*, 128–31.
[79] Pascal, *Cults of Cisalpine Gaul*, 129–30.
[80] *CIL* 5. 5050; cf. *ILS* 206, with additions. On the religious topography of the Val di Non: Degrassi, 'Culti romani'.

as at Rome, in a position commanding the forum, are explicitly attested at Verona and Brescia,[81] and others may be identifiable with the remains of similar stuctures at Trieste, Iulium Carnicum (modern Zuglio), and Pula.[82] Yet dedications to the Capitoline triad as a group are remarkably rare. Jupiter with the Capitoline epithet *Optimus Maximus* is attested on his own; more usually, however, the Capitoline deities are found in association with local gods.[83] In general, the imperial cult, frequently associated with the goddess Roma, is more prominent in northern Italy than worship of the Capitoline gods. There were early cults of the emperor at Como and Pula, the latter boasting a magnificent temple, and priesthoods of the cult are found in every city in the region.[84] Veneration of the emperors retained its vitality throughout the period of the principate, and, as we will see, underwent a revival in the late third and early fourth centuries.[85]

In addition to such cults from the city of Rome, others of a less official nature began to make their appearence in the imperial period. Although devotion to such gods, among whom are numbered the deities of foreign cities and the mystery cults, was entirely compatible with the worship of other deities,[86] the dissemination of such cults depended on private initiative, not state sponsorship. As such, the means by which they spread through northern Italy can provide a framework within which some attempt can be made to understand the dissemination of Christianity. This question will concern us at length in Chapter 3; here, however, it will suffice to show how the distribution patterns of such cults were sporadic, and how their diffusion owed much to the dynamics of north Italian society.[87]

It is not at all surprising that cities should provide the context for much of this new cultic activity. The evidence is abundant for Aquileia, which boasts the most diverse religious profile of any city in northern Italy. It seems that in most cases, the city's migrant

---

[81] The *capitolium* at Verona is mentioned in an inscription: *CIL* 5. 3332. The impressive structure at Brescia still survives: Chevallier, *Romanisation*, 112–13.

[82] Chevallier, *Romanisation*, 116.

[83] Pascal, *Cults of Cisalpine Gaul*, 14–18.

[84] Pascal, *Cults of Cisalpine Gaul*, 18–25; Chevallier, *Romanisation*, 453–5, 456–7.

[85] See below pp. 208–9.

[86] Burkert, *Ancient Mystery Cults*, 10–11, 31–51; Beard, North, and Price, *Religions of Rome*, i. 307–9.

[87] Cf. Humphries, 'Trading Gods', 208–10, 214–16.

population was involved in the process of dissemination. Among the foreign gods who had shrines there was Artemis of Ephesus. An inscription of the mid-third century shows how the cult could provide a focus for links between Aquileia and the goddess's Asian homeland. In stately Greek, Ti. Claudius Magnus, 'an Ephesian and decurion of the city of Aquileia', records how he restored and decorated Artemis' portico (*stoa*).[88] The Egyptian goddess Isis was also the focus of a popular cult in northern Italy. The scatter of Isiac material in the region generally is instructive, with concentrations in and around the ports of Aquileia, Ravenna, Trieste, and Rimini.[89] From these centres, the cult was diffused through northern Italy, and also the bordering Alpine territories, along the region's commercial and communications networks. For example, the pattern of activities that we were able to trace for the *praefectus vehiculorum* Ti. Iulius Saturninus and his assistants (above p. 33) was reconstructed entirely from the dedications that they set up to Isis.[90] In the dissemination of the cult of Isis we have explicit evidence for the interpenetration of north Italian economic, social, and religious systems. This complex web of interrelationships would in turn influence the spread of Christianity in the region. Before addressing that question directly, however, one further factor needs to be considered: the changed status and dynamics of northern Italy in the late Roman period.

Late antique transformations

Although in the late republic and early principate northern Italy was still largely peripheral to Roman interests,[91] the bloody conflicts fought out there in the civil war of AD 69, particularly near the crossing of the Po at Cremona, demonstrated the political significance of the zone. From the late second century, and especially during the third, the strategic importance of northern Italy became incontrovertible as the need arose for emperors, from Marcus Aurelius onwards, to react promptly to breaches in Rome's defensive curtain along the Rhine and the Danube. Under Gallienus (253–68) this process

---

[88] *Inscr. Aquil.* 182 (dating to AD 256).
[89] Malaise, *Inventaire préliminaire*, 4–13, 23–32.
[90] Malaise, *Conditions de pénétration*, 321–32, 335–51. Cf. nn. 54–5 above.
[91] Brunt, *Italian Manpower*, 180.

was accelerated with the establishment of mobile squadrons of troops in the Po valley, the refortification of strategic centres like Verona, and the establishment of garrisons in the Alpine passes.[92] With the embellishment of Milan as an imperial capital in the 290s, the transformation neared completion. By the mid-fourth century, northern Italy, far from being peripheral, was on the central axis of communications between important imperial cities, from Trier in the north, and eastwards, via Aquileia, Emona, and Sirmium, to Constantinople and Antioch.[93] The presence in northern Italy of the emperor and his court for extended periods made new demands on the cities. At Milan, the primary seat of the court, and Aquileia, an important transit city and strategic centre, the presence of the emperor and his entourage heralded the erection of new buildings, such as palaces and enormous hippodromes, which reflected their new-found status.[94] This reflects a general prosperity in northern Italy during the fourth century, which is particularly evident in the cities, some of which, such as Pavia, even expanded.[95] Aquileia too grew in size, with new walled districts to the south and south-west. This seems particularly linked to the increased economic and strategic importance of the city as a supply base for the troops garrisoning the passes of the north-eastern Alps. Among the new buildings erected was a large *horreum* which in its plan and location, in the new part of the city, recalls the late-imperial military warehouse at Trier on the Moselle.[96] Similarly, imperial intervention added new vitality to the industrial life of the region, with the establishment of mints, operating at various times in Aquileia, Pavia, and Milan, as well as arms factories at Concordia, Verona, Mantua, Cremona, and Pavia.[97]

[92] Christie, 'The Alps as a Frontier', 413; Garnsey, 'Economy and Society at Mediolanum', 22; for Verona see *CIL* 5. 3329.

[93] Brown, *Power and Persuasion*, 6–7.

[94] Palace at Aquileia: *Pan. Lat.* 6 (7). 6. 2; Jäggi 171–2. Hippodromes: Humphrey, *Roman Circuses*, 613–20 (Milan), 621–5 (Aquileia). Maximian's transformation of Milan: Arslan, 'Urbanistica di Milano Romana', 196–203; Cagiano de Azevedo, 'Northern Italy', 477; Krautheimer, *Capitals*, 69–70. For general principles: Braudel, *The Mediterranean*, 312–52, esp. 344–52 on capitals.

[95] Bullough, 'Urban Change in Early Medieval Italy', 83, 89.

[96] In general: Whittaker, 'Late Roman Trade and Traders', 165–7; Cipriano, 'Aquileia', 140–3; Gentili, 'Politics and Christianity in Aquileia', 193; Panella, 'Le merci', 441; Chevallier, *Aquilée*, 17–19, 36. For the *horreum*: Bertacchi, 'Edilizia civile', 340–8 and fig. 3; cf. Rickman, *Roman Granaries*, 264–5, on Trier. Cf. Ceresa Mori, 'Gli horrea', on the *horrea* at Milan.

[97] Mints: Jones, *Later Roman Empire*, 435–7; factories: *Not. Dig. Occidentalis* 9. 23–9, also mentioning sword manufacture at Lucca in Tuscany.

This expansion of Aquileia and Pavia, together with the embellishment of Milan and Aquileia with imperial buildings, points to how the imperial presence led to a modification in the social, economic, and cultural dynamics of northern Italy. From the time of Augustus, the presence of foreign imperial marines at Ravenna had constituted an artificial distortion of the composition of the region's population. During the late third and fourth centuries, this situation was exacerbated. At Milan there developed an increasingly cosmopolitan population, attracted by the patronage of the imperial court, or the need to present petitions directly to the emperor.[98] The heterogeneity of the north Italian garrison troops buried at Concordia was a symptom of the same process.[99] Even the transformation of trading patterns resulting from the new strategic importance of northern Italy caused changes in the social dynamics of the region, as increased imports brought a new influx of foreign merchants, above all to Aquileia.[100]

Late antiquity brought considerable continuity too in the vitality of north Italian cities. Even with the increasing bureaucratization of the empire and the apparent 'decline' of urban centres in late antiquity (never a uniform process anyway), cities continued to fulfil their former role.[101] As 'the secret of government without bureaucracy',[102] their impact on the Church's organizational development, therefore, was likely to be substantial. Their urban institutions provided a template for the behaviour of bishops in cities, and their dominance over smaller settlements in their territories could serve as a model for the development of major episcopal sees with suffragans in their hinterland.

Above all, it was the penetrability of the Alpine passes which was confirmed by the changed circumstances of the late empire. Much imperial energy was devoted to their fortification, as Rome's grip on her Danubian frontier loosened. After the fall of the Rhaetian *limes* in 383 there was an increased military presence in the valleys

---

[98] Patronage at court: Matthews, *Western Aristocracies*, 41–3, 183–6; Van Dam, *Leadership and Community*, 9–16. Cf. Chadwick, *Priscillian of Avila*, 40–2, for Spanish petitioners in Milan.

[99] Lettich, 'Concordia e Aquileia', esp. 68–9; Matthews, *Western Aristocracies*, 183–4.

[100] Ruggini, 'Ebrei e orientali'; Cuscito, 'Africani in Aquileia'.

[101] Liebeschuetz, 'End of the Ancient City'; Matthews, *Roman Empire of Ammianus*, 383–403. For local variations see e.g.: Lepelley, *Les cités de l'Afrique romaine*, esp. i. 409–14.

[102] Garnsey and Saller, *Roman Empire*, 26.

around Trento so that, once again, the area of the Val di Non was brought under direct imperial supervision.[103] Not surprisingly, the most vulnerable area was Venetia, owing to the inadequacy of the Julian Alps as a barrier. From the mid-third century onwards there was considerable effort expended on the defence of this region. Walls were built in the mountain passes, forming a network known as the *Claustra Alpium Juliarum*. In the later years of his reign the emperor Gratian (375–83) identified the Julian Alps as a weak point, vulnerable to the Goths then at large in the Balkans. His judgement was repeatedly confirmed in the next two centuries when Theodosius I (twice), Alaric's Goths, Attila's Huns, Theoderic's Ostrogoths and Alboin's Lombards all invaded Italy by this route.[104]

These invasions draw attention to a shift in the way northern Italy was viewed within the empire's political geography. Its designation as Cisalpine Gaul was a perception shaped by prevailing conditions in the late republic. At this stage southern Gaul and its inhabitants were well-known, so comparison between two such neighbouring areas was natural. Conversely the Balkans were little known: the main thrust of Roman conquest here did not come until the age of Augustus.[105] The development of trading and social networks under the empire led to a stark change in the perception of northern Italy, which emphasized its links with regions along the upper and middle Danube, beyond the central and eastern Alps. By the fourth century these ties were formalized in the administrative structure of the empire, in that Italy formed part of the same praetorian prefecture as the western Balkans.[106] Significantly, northern Italy had now lost the remoteness that had characterized its political and economic development in the republic and early empire, and had far outstripped Rome and southern Italy in every way. The Eternal City and peninsular Italy were effectively political backwaters, and it was thanks only to a certain cultural nostalgia that they were at all important. Northern Italy had usurped the position once held by the centre and south, and it was Milan—and subsequently Ravenna—that sat

[103] Lizzi, *Vescovi*, 76.

[104] Duval, 'Aquilée sur la route des invasions'; Christie, 'The Alps as a Frontier', 417–18, 427.

[105] Sasel, 'Lineamenti dell'espansione romana'.

[106] Gaudemet, 'Mutations politiques et géographie administrative', 260–1, 264; Chastagnol, 'L'Administration du diocèse italien au Bas-Empire'.

at the centre of Italian political activity.[107] Nomenclature reflected the change. The arena bordered by the Alps, the Apennines, and the Adriatic was no longer known as Cisalpine Gaul: henceforth its official title was *Italia Annonaria*; often, it was simply known just as *Italia*.[108]

Conclusion

To sum up, northern Italy at first seems to be a geographically distinct region, defined by its natural boundaries, particularly the Alps, which also seem to serve as the frontier between peninsular Italy and Europe. Closer analysis, however, reveals that this convenient conceptualization is misleading. Human activity shows that from an early period, the peoples of the north Italian plains had closer links with the neighbouring territories beyond the Alps, with the Danube and the Balkans, and also with Gaul. Following the Roman conquest, this pattern persists, even though political domination from Rome brought close administrative and some economic connections with central and southern Italy. The advent of the Roman peace also saw the rise of inter-regional trade via the Adriatic to the wider Mediterranean world. In late antiquity this maritime trade continued, especially at Aquileia, where supplies were imported to provision the garrisons guarding the north-eastern Alpine passes.

In addition to these relationships with the outside world, we have seen within northern Italy a complex set of networks on both regional and local levels. Communications along the roads and the rivers did much to unify the region and encourage economic and social interaction. At the same time, however, it is clear that much would have happened on an extremely local scale. This includes not just commerce in perishable, everyday goods, but also networks of social and political interface. For example, we have seen connections between urban centres, viewed in the light of those persons holding civic offices, clustering in a number of local patterns: Milan, Como, and Lodì in Lombardy; Tortona and Vercelli in Piedmont; Aquileia, Altino, and Vicenza in the Veneto. The religious geography of pre-Christian northern Italy underlines the importance

---

[107] Krautheimer, *Capitals*, 93; cf. the case of Augustine (*Conf.* 5. 13. 23) moving from Rome to Milan for advancement: Brown, *Augustine*, 69–72.

[108] Cracco Ruggini and Cracco, 'L'eredità di Roma', 37.

of these matrices. Distinct patterns of the distribution of cults, particularly of privately sponsored ones, shows how the religious life of the region is inseparable from broader social, economic, and cultural networks. Finally, in late antiquity, the establishment of a quasi-permanent court at Milan superimposed a new set of political relationships on the region.

These personal networks were as important a determinant of human activity in northern Italy during the early Christian period as the landscape itself. Driving this activity were the towns and cities founded by the Romans in the wake of their conquest of the region. With their social, cultural, and economic networks, these urban centres provided the template for human behaviour, while their physical fabric was a crucial facet of north Italian environment as encountered by Christianity. The new religion entered a region, therefore, where the elaborate workings of the human environment were determined by a combination of natural landscapes, social networks, and urban centres. It is time now to observe the interaction between the region and its new religion.

2

*Subscribing bishops and invented apostles: the
search for the earliest north Italian churches*

It is impossible to be precise as to when and how the Christian faith
arrived in northern Italy, but this chapter and the one following will
attempt to reconstruct as much of this process as is feasible. A substantial difficulty arises from our sources. The *Ecclesiastical History*
of Eusebius of Caesarea says nothing about north Italian churches
in the pre-Constantinian period, in marked contrast to the rich detail
it provides on aspects of the early Christian history of Gaul, Africa,
and other parts of Italy. Nor do we have any writings produced
by north Italian Christians to compare with Cyprian, Tertullian,
Irenaeus, or Hippolytus. Rather, Christianity in northern Italy
only breaks its silence in the fourth century, after the joint proclamation of religious freedom by Constantine and Licinius at Milan
in 313. Our first glimpses of the north Italian churches come when
their bishops attended the synods called by Constantine in 313 and
314 in a vain effort to resolve the Donatist dispute in Africa.
Afterwards they slip back into the shadows, to re-emerge some three
decades later in the records of the Trinitarian conflicts of the mid-
fourth century.

Such bland snapshots of north Italian bishops are not, however,
the only materials at our disposal. In the medieval period, historians of early Christianity, unlike their modern counterparts, claimed
detailed knowledge of the first Christian arrivals in northern Italy.[1]
This is manifested in a wealth of literature recording bishops, martyrs, and confessors, sometimes listing their deeds too. Yet as accounts
of the early history of north Italian Christianity, these medieval
sources are at least equally as problematic as the conciliar documents
mentioned above. Taken together, however, they have constituted
the traditional body of evidence for the study of the origins of north

---

[1] On such traditions, see in general Pilsworth, *Sanctity in Early Medieval
Northern Italy*.

Italian Christianity (see Introduction). This chapter will examine the nature, problems, and limitations of these different sources; then Chapter 3 will interpret the data they yield in the context of the north Italian human environment.

Councils and conflicts in the fourth century

For the purpose of studying Christian origins in northern Italy, the records of five church councils provide useful data: Rome in 313, Arles in 314, Serdica in 343, Milan in 355, and Rimini in 359. The use of such documents must take into consideration the circumstances in which they were produced. When these councils concluded, their pronouncements were signed by the bishops who attended and who agreed with the decisions reached. It is immediately clear, then, that the lists of bishops found in such documents are likely to be both partial and partisan, since those who disagreed with the decisions of the council would not have signed. This situation is especially obvious at the Council of Serdica, where the assembly split into two diametrically opposed groups. Each promulgated a statement of their findings, together with a list of signatures, so that we have not one but two lists of subscriptions for this council. Moreover, the preservation of these lists is at best haphazard, with many of them surviving in only one version or manuscript. In some cases, the conciliar subscriptions have been incorporated into historical narratives, while others are preserved in semi-official dossiers of documents for use by churchmen. It will be easiest to analyse this material council-by-council, noting first if the survival of the document presents particular problems, and second the north Italian bishops who are mentioned.

Rome, 313

The list for the Roman synod of 313 survives not as subscriptions, but as part of the introductory narrative to the account of the council given a half-century later in Optatus of Milevus' anti-Donatist work (1. 23). It probably derived from the official documents of the council, which are referred to as *gesta* by Augustine, writing in the aftermath of the Conference of Carthage of 411 (*Brev. Coll.* 3. 17. 31; cf. 3. 12. 24). It is clear, however, that the version preserved in

Optatus has become corrupt. His dating has gone awry, since he states that the bishops 'met in the house of Fausta in the Lateran, when Constantine, for the fourth time, and Licinius, for the third time, were consuls, on the sixth day before the Nones of October, the sixth being a feast day'. This yields the date of 2 October 315: but this is impossible since the council was presided over by Pope Miltiades, who died on 11 January 314 (*Chron. 354*, pp. 70, 76). Augustine's version of the date provides a solution: addressing the Donatists after the Conference of Carthage he referred to the judgement made against them by Miltiades 'when Constantine for the third time and Licinius for the second were consuls, on the sixth day before the Nones of October (*ad Don. post coll.* 33. 56).[2] This yields the more credible date of 2 October 313. These textual problems do not diminish when we move to Optatus' list of bishops. Above all, many of the names of sees given by Optatus are corrupt.[3] Happily, however, there is no such ambiguity for the bishoprics of northern Italy: 'Merocles a Mediolano', 'Stennius ab Arimino', and 'Constantius a Faventia' make it clear that the sees represented were Milan, Rimini, and Faenza.

Arles, 314

The list for the Council of Arles survives in two forms. First there is a synodical letter addressed to Pope Sylvester at Rome, which may, or may not, be genuine.[4] In its preamble, the bishops are listed without the names of their sees (Munier, *Conc. Gall.* 4). Second, there is a list of subscriptions, this time naming both the bishops and their sees, preserved in a plethora of manuscripts, drawn up in southern Gaul in the sixth century, originally functioning as dossiers of canonical documents.[5] Presentation of the lists, as well as the spelling of names, varies considerably between the manuscripts. The most complete, in a manuscript from Corbie (now in Paris), puts the name of the bishop first, followed by the name of his see and province; all the others reverse this order (Munier, *Conc. Gall.* 14–22). This difference is inexplicable, but it is interesting to note

---

[2] Augustine is plainly referring to the Roman Council of 313: cf. *ad Don. post coll.* 15. 19, 'Romanum concilium Miltiadis'.

[3] Edwards, *Optatus*, 220; cf. Calderone, *Costantino*, i. 238–40.

[4] The debate is summarized by Gaudemet, *Conciles gaulois*, 38–9.

[5] Gaudemet, *Conciles gaulois*, 27–8; Munier, *Conc. Gall.* v–xi, 3, 7–8.

that the Corbie manuscript is not only the most complete, but also the earliest, dating to shortly after 523.[6] The subscriptions to Arles record the attendance of bishop Theodore and a deacon, probably Agathon, from Aquileia, and bishop Merocles and a deacon, probably Severus, from Milan.[7]

Serdica, 343

After a hiatus of nearly three decades, the north Italian churches re-appear at the Council of Serdica, when they became involved on the side of Athanasius in the Trinitarian conflicts during the 340s. There are two distinct lists of signatures, both preserved in the fragmentary and disordered *Opus historicum* of Hilary of Poitiers. The first follows the decrees sent to the African episcopate by that group of bishops at the council whom Hilary deemed heretical (*Coll. Ant. Par.* A. IV. 1–3; signatures at 3). The second (B. II. 4), in which the north Italian delegates are mentioned, is appended to letters and a list of heretics (B. II. 1–3) issued by bishops who supported Athanasius of Alexandria. At the end of the list it is written that the bishops who subscribed numbered sixty-one (*episcopi omnes numero sexaginta et unus*), but only sixty bishops are actually named, showing that some form of corruption of the text has occurred. Such anomalies are not uncommon in the extant form of the *Opus historicum*, which has been much altered at the hands of a late antique excerptor, and an early medieval scribe who copied out these selections.[8] It would be pointless to speculate as to whether or not the missing sixty-first bishop might have been from northern Italy.[9] As it is, five north Italian bishops are named: Lucius of Verona (*Coll. Ant. Par.* B. II. 4. 20), Fortunatianus of Aquileia (37), Severus of Ravenna (49), Ursacius of Brescia (50) and Protasius of Milan (51).

---

[6] i.e. the year of the death of Pope Hormisdas, the last Roman pontiff whose name is entered in the first hand in the dossier's papal list: Lowe, *CLA* v. 619.

[7] Munier, *Conc. Gall.* 14–22. The variants on the names are 'Theudorus' and 'Teudosus' for Theodore; 'Agustun' and 'Agaton' for Agathon; 'Meroclis', 'Horosius', 'Oresius' and 'Heresius' (!) for Merocles; and 'Servus', 'Nazareus' and 'Nazoreus' for Severus.

[8] Smulders, *Hilary of Poitiers' Preface*, 6–17, provides a convenient account of the work's complicated textual history.

[9] Cf. Colafemmina, *Apulia cristiana*, 36, suggesting that in addition to Stercorius of Canosa, who is mentioned in the subscriptions, 'è probabile che . . . partecipassero . . . altri vescovi pugliesi': the available evidence, however, does not permit such a conclusion.

To these should be added Crispinus of Padua, whom Athanasius mentions in his own account of the events leading up to the council (*Apol. Const.* 3. 42–3); he also refers to Fortunatianus and Protasius, as well as to the bishop of Verona, whom he calls Lucillus, rather than Lucius (3. 40–1, 43, 45–6).

Milan, 355

The Milanese council of 355 has always presented problems of interpretation, above all because the decision taken by Constantius II to exile three of the bishops who participated—Lucifer of Cagliari, Dionysius of Milan, Eusebius of Vercelli—made it an important event in the politics of the Trinitarian controversy. Most accounts of it, therefore, are primarily polemical, coloured by strong theological prejudices. In addition, there survive some documents issued at the time of the council, which were preserved in the church archives at Vercelli. Although these manuscripts are now lost, they were still extant in the sixteenth century, when they were edited by Baronius in his *Annales Ecclesiastici*. Among those archives, Baronius found a list of thirty bishops who had condemned Athanasius (*nomina episcoporum qui subscripserunt in Athanasium*), which, for some reason, he did not include in the first edition of the *Annales*. Even though they were printed in the second edition (1623), they were ignored by later scholars until comparatively recently.[10] The list does not mention the provenance of the bishops, but many are easily identifiable as either Constantius' supporters in the Balkans and the west (such as Ursacius of Singidunum, Valens of Mursa, and Saturninus of Arles) or easterners who accompanied the emperor on his journey to the West (Patrophilus of Scythopolis, Acacius of Caesarea, and Epictetus, who was set up as bishop of Centumcellae to watch over Pope Liberius at Rome). A Dionysius is listed: Baronius and later readers have identified him as the bishop of Milan.[11] This is surely correct, since bishop Lucifer of Cagliari, another participant at the council, recorded that a misinformed Dionysius of Milan had condemned Athanasius (*de Athan.* 2. 8). Apart from this, no other north Italian bishop is mentioned. But the list is not complete: it makes no mention, for instance, of the Eustomius who was one of

---

[10] Smulders, *Hilary of Poitiers' Preface*, 109–12.
[11] Baronius, *Annales*, iv. 537; cf. Smulders, *Hilary of Poitiers' Preface*, 111–12.

the delegates sent from the council to summon Eusebius of Vercelli.[12] Naturally, Eusebius himself does not appear in the list, because he refused to condemn Athanasius (Hil. Pict., *Coll. Ant. Par.* appendix II. 3). In sum, it seems that the only north Italian bishops we can identify at this council are Dionysius and Eusebius.

Rimini, 359

The sources for the twin councils held at Rimini in Italy and Seleucia in Isauria are so complex as to make those for Milan look like models of clarity.[13] Those sources which talk about the composition of the council are extremely vague, even on the total number of bishops attending.[14] Moreover, coverage of Rimini was affected by the controversial nature of the council. Sulpicius Severus, for example, makes much of how various bishops refused to accept state support for their travel expenses, believing this might compromise their independence of action at the council (*Chron.* 2. 41). The polemical purpose of most of our sources means that our detailed knowledge of participants is limited to those whom the vociferous, pro-Athanasian minority—who saw the whole enterprise as an attempt by Constantius II to impose his will on the western episcopates—identified as their enemies. Thus we learn that Ursacius of Singidunum, Valens of Mursa, and Germinius of Sirmium were there (Athan., *de Syn.* 8; *Ep. ad Afros* 3); the only north Italian bishop mentioned by name is, unsurprisingly, Constantius' appointee to the see of Milan: Auxentius (Athan., *Ep. ad Afros* 3). Yet considering the enormous importance of the twin councils of Rimini and Seleucia to Constantius' efforts to achieve doctrinal unity throughout the empire, it is unlikely that north Italian participation was limited to Auxentius. At the very least we might expect the bishop of an important city such as Aquileia to have attended—the limited evidence at our disposal, however, permits no firm conclusions. One other north Italian participant is possible. After the council, a delegation of its bishops brought the synodical letter to Constantius, and was

---

[12] *Epistola synodica*, ed. V. Bulhart, *CCL* 9, 119, 'carissimos *coepiscopos* nostros Eustomium et Germinium', leaves no room for doubt as to Eustomius' episcopal status.
[13] On the problem of sources for the council: Barnes, *Athanasius*, 284–5 nn. 8–9.
[14] e.g. Sulp. Sev., *Chron.* 2. 41: 'quadringenti et aliquanto amplius Occidentales episcopi'.

detained at Nike in Thrace. Among these bishops was a certain Urbanus, who may be the same as the bishop of that name who occupied the see of Parma.[15]

Summary

It will be convenient to present the findings of this survey in tabular form (see below).

It is immediately clear from the table that the material extracted from the attendance sheets of ecclesiastical councils is far from comprehensive. First, no list can be relied on to present a complete inventory of the bishoprics of northern Italy at a given date. This is most obvious when we compare the lists for the anti-Donatist councils of 313 and 314. No bishop of Aquileia attended the Roman synod, although one must have existed at this time (see Chapter 3). Similarly, Constantius of Faenza and Stennius of Rimini did not travel to Arles in 314, despite having taken part at Rome the previous year. The lists of the north Italian bishops attending the Councils of Serdica and Milan are equally anomalous. Crispinus of Padua did not go to Serdica, despite having joined Athanasius' entourage in seeking an

TABLE   Attested north Italian participation at church councils, 313–59

	Council				
Bishopric	Rome 313	Arles 314	Serdica 343	Milan 355	Rimini 359
Aquileia		*	*		?
Brescia			*		
Faenza	*				
Milan	*	*	*	*	*
Padua					
Parma					?
Ravenna			*		
Rimini	*				
Vercelli				*	
Verona			*		

[15] Hil. Pict., *Coll. Ant. Par.* A. V. 3. 1. Cf. Williams, *Ambrose*, 85; Mercati, 'Il più antico vescovo di Parma conosciuto', 3–6.

audience with Constans shortly before.[16] Similarly, Fortunatianus of
Aquileia, a formidable ecclesiastical politician (see Chapters 4 and
5), is a surprising absence from Milan in 355. Unfortunately details
on the participants of the Council of Rimini are too scanty for any
judgement to be made about who attended and who did not.

Further difficulties arise from the very mechanics of convening
a council. Imperial intervention could be crucial. Constantine personally wrote to bishops asking them to participate in the Rome
and Arles councils (Eus., *HE* 10. 5. 18–24). He provided imperial
resources to cater for the bishops' travel costs (ibid. 10. 5. 23), as
did Constantius II before the councils of Rimini and Seleucia.[17]
Furthermore, emperors took an interest in the bishops who attended
their synods. When summoning bishops to Arles, Constantine was
concerned to counter criticism that the previous year's Roman
council had been too narrowly based (ibid. 10. 5. 22). I will argue
in Chapter 4 that the haphazard north Italian presence at the
Councils of Rome and Arles had much to do with Constantine's
personal role in inviting the bishops to attend. Similarly, the list of
bishops whom Constantius assembled at Milan in 355 reads suspiciously like an anti-Athanasian quango. The survival of an imperial
letter shows that the attendance of Eusebius of Vercelli at the closing
session of the same council was also due to Constantius' personal
invitation.[18]

Another problem with this material is that it is useful in determining the extent of north Italian Christianity only in terms of episcopal sees. Yet it is abundantly clear from evidence throughout the
fourth century that there were many non-episcopal Christian communities in northern Italy, both in rural areas such as the Alto Adige,
and in sizeable towns such as Ivrea and Tortona.[19] In Eusebius' case,
there was a pre-existing Christian community at Vercelli which
appointed him bishop (Ambr. *Ep.* 63. 2). This is a helpful reminder
that the emergence of a bishopric often represents the culmination
of a process of evangelization, not its initiation.[20] This situation

---

[16] This should suffice to demonstrate the danger of conclusions, such as those of
Savio and Lanzoni, that the origins of the diocese of Pavia must come after the Council
of Serdica, since no bishop of that city appears in the subscriptions: see Lanzani,
'Ticinum', 366–7, with full references.

[17] Hefele and Leclerq, *Histoire des Conciles*, i. 935.

[18] *Epistola Constantii ad Eusebium*, ed. Bulhart, CCL 9, 120–1.

[19] See further the following footnote, and Chs. 6 and 9.

[20] Lanzani, 'Ticinum', 356. Cf. the cases of Tortona and Ivrea, the two communities dependent on Eusebius in the 350s, which eventually achieved episcopal status by 381 and 451 respectively: Lanzani, *Diocesi*, 476–81, 560–1.

matches conditions elsewhere in the Roman west, such as southern Gaul, where the bishop of Lyon seems for a long time to have had responsibility for non-episcopal congregations in nearby cities which acquired their first bishops only at a later date.[21] At best, then, the details of north Italian participation in ecclesiastical councils in the reigns of Constantine, Constans, and Constantius II provide only a partial guide to the extent of Christianity in northern Italy.

Traditions and innovations in the early middle ages

Our second body of sources dates from the early middle ages, and comprises collections of texts relating to the saints and early bishops of several north Italian sees. These texts divide into a number of categories: saints' lives, martyrologies cataloguing their feast days, and lists of bishops that enumerate those who had occupied the see since its foundation. We must be careful, however, not to drive deep distinctions between the categories. Even where they preserve apparent inconsistencies of attitude, taken together they represent a constantly evolving and metamorphosing map of the sacred past, crafted to meet the shifting needs of those who produced them.[22] Such texts, even when they appear most banal, are never jejune compilations of material: they enshrine particular views of the Christian past formulated with an eye to present needs. I will begin by analysing the general circumstances in which these genres arose, before considering in detail first the episcopal lists relating to a number of north Italian bishoprics, and then some examples of how the historical past was reshaped in hagiographical texts.

Sacred history and sacred power

From the very beginning of the relationship between church and state, the manipulation of the past to satisfy present needs has been a persistent feature of ecclesiastical politics. A good example is the Council of Nicaea, convened in 325 at the behest of the emperor Constantine himself. As the doctrinal statement formulated at that

---

[21] Griffe, *Gaule chrétienne*, i. 27–33.

[22] See esp. Geary, *Living with the Dead*, 9–29, with refs. Geary emphasizes well the importance of 'remaining sensitive to the context in which hagiographic production took place, which reflects not a[n abstract] "medieval mind" but a variety of minds, a spectrum of people reacting to the living tradition of the saints in their midst' (p. 28).

council achieved recognition as a definitive statement of orthodoxy, so the wider significance of the council changed. By the end of the fourth century, Nicaea had begun to achieve the status of an oecumenical synod, while the precise meaning of its rulings on the ecclesiastical jurisdiction of Alexandria, Antioch, Jerusalem, and Rome became the subject of heated debate.[23] The importance of those sees depended on their antiquity as foundations by Christ's apostles and this points to an important development in late antiquity which was to reverberate throughout the early medieval period. A city's status as an ecclesiastical centre depended in no small measure on its Christian past and in particular on the number and calibre of its saints.

The period between the fourth and sixth centuries saw an astonishing growth in the cult of saints throughout the western Mediterranean world.[24] In northern Italy, this phenomenon was already well developed by the opening years of the fifth century, as is clear from a list of saints' festivals known as the *Martyrologium Hieronymianum*.[25] Yet it is uncertain to what extent this text reflects traditions earlier than the later fourth century. Some spontaneous veneration of local saints probably developed in northern Italy as it did in the rest of Christendom, but the systematic cult reflected in the *Martyrologium* seems to be a later development.

In this process, the episcopate of Ambrose of Milan (374–97) has pivotal importance. Ambrose brought to his ecclesiastical career the organizational skills he had learned as a provincial governor prior to his election as bishop.[26] He also knew Pope Damasus I (366–84), under whom the cult of SS Peter and Paul was developed into a tool to help extend the influence of the Roman church.[27] Inspired by Damasus, Ambrose sought to develop the cult of saints in northern Italy in a similar fashion. At Milan he uncovered the relics of SS Gervasius, Protasius, Nazarius, and Celsus, and imported those of

[23] Chadwick, 'Faith and Order'.   [24] Brown, *Cult of the Saints*.
[25] For commentary, see especially the detailed *Comm. Mart. Hier.*; cf. also Picard, *Souvenir*, 654–6; Lucchesi, 'Ancora sull'antico calendario italico', 140–52. In general, see Dubois, *Martyrologues du moyen âge latin*.
[26] Lizzi, *Vescovi*, esp. 15–57.
[27] Pietri, *Roma Christiana*, 729–872. The clearest statement of Petrine supremacy comes from Innocent I, *Ep.* 25. 2: 'praesertim cum sit manifestum in omnem Italiam, Gallias, Hispanias, Africam atque Siciliam, et insulas interiacentes, *nullum instituisse ecclesias, nisi eos quos venerabilis apostolus Petrus aut eius successores constituerint sacerdotes*'. For discussion, cf. Otranto, *Italia meridionale*, 22 n. 45.

St Vitalis from Bologna.[28] Of these the discovery of SS Gervasius and Protasius is instructive: Ambrose's biographer Paulinus relates that these saints were unknown before their bodies were unearthed (Paul. Med.,*V. Ambr.* 14). Similarly Ambrose's excavation of the relics of SS Agricola and Vitalis at Bologna revealed hitherto unknown martyrs (Paul. Med.,*V. Ambr.* 29). The only secure evidence for veneration of saints at Milan prior to Ambrose's episcopate relates to SS Nabor and Felix, whose shrine in the cemetery west of the city walls is mentioned at the time of the discovery of Protasius and Gervasius (Paul. Med.,*V. Ambr.* 14).

Not only did the development of the cult of saints at Milan itself receive its great impetus under Ambrose: he also sent Milanese relics to other north Italian cities and appropriated their relics to Milan, and, by so doing, he sought to extend his influence from Milan just as Damasus had done from Rome.[29] In turn he was imitated by his fellow bishops in northern Italy, most notably Chromatius of Aquileia (388–407/8).[30] In northern Italy, as elsewhere in the Mediterranean world, late antique and early medieval bishops used the cult of saints to enhance the prestige of their sees.[31] Particularly where saints were associated with the veneration of relics, these cults made the cities that held them centres of pilgrimage. In turn, the prominence of a particular see in terms of its sacred heritage could serve to justify its leadership over a number of other ecclesiastical centres in its vicinity.[32] This could provoke deliberately stage-managed *inventiones*, as happened at Milan in the case of SS Gervasius and Protasius. Piacenza seems to provide a further example: here the *Martyrologium Hieronymianum* lists a certain St Antoninus (or Antonius in some manuscripts: *Mart. Hier.* 2 k. oct.). His antiquity

[28] Paul. Med., *V. Ambr.* 14 (Protasius and Gervasius), 29 (Vitalis), 32–3 (Nazarius and Celsus).

[29] Paul. Med., *V. Ambr.* 52 relates the story of a man who travelled to Milan from Dalmatia in order to receive a miraculous cure for blindness; en route he encountered the relics of the martyrs of Anaunia (the modern Val di Non) which were being brought from Trento to Milan. This happened after Ambrose's death, under the episcopate of his successor Simplicianus. It demonstrates, however, the influence that Ambrose exerted over his own city and Christian communities further afield: Simplicianus was imitating Ambrose's policy of acquiring relics, and the presence of the pilgrim from Dalmatia shows that Milan had a reputation as a centre where miraculous cures might be effected.

[30] Lizzi, *Vescovi*, 139–69, esp. 154–9.

[31] For example, Chromatius said that SS Felix and Fortunatus glorified Aquileia (*Sermo* 7).

[32] See esp. Picard, *Souvenir*. For relics: Hunt, 'The Traffic in Relics'.

is ambiguous, but later traditions, including an anonymous sixth-century pilgrimage, accord him the status of a martyr (*Antonini Placentini Itinerarium* 1). This is absent from the *Martyrologium*, however. The only other early source to mention him is Victricius of Rouen's *De laude sanctorum*, written in Gaul at the end of the fourth century.[33] Since Victricius, who was deeply influenced by Ambrose's use of the cults of saints,[34] mentions 'Antonius' (*sic*) in the same breath as Agricola of Bologna and Nazarius of Milan (*de laude sanctorum* 11. 7–10), all of whom were known only from the time of Ambrose, we cannot guarantee that Antoninus is any older.

North Italian episcopal lists

With so much at stake, it is not surprising that the sacred history of a city should have been subject to revision. As various episcopal sees competed for ecclesiastical authority, they sought to justify their pretensions by reinventing their past. This could take the form of rearranging historical material to make it seem older. Such tendencies are particularly evident in the redaction of episcopal lists for several north Italian sees, as indeed in the rest of the Christian world. Interest in the early history of bishoprics is as old as Christian historiography itself. Eusebius of Caesarea incorporated in his *Chronicle* and *Ecclesiastical History* lists of bishops from Alexandria, Antioch, Jerusalem, and Rome. It is also clear that such lists soon acquired a propagandist utility. When the unity of the Church was threatened by schism and heresy, episcopal lists were used by the squabbling groups to prove their continuity with the founders of their see, while their enemies were contrasted as interlopers who could claim no such heritage.[35] In such volatile circumstances, it was not unusual for competing groups within a church to produce different versions of a list to support their opposing claims to legitimacy. Thus, as we will see, the patriarchs of Aquileia and Grado both claimed to be the true successors of St Mark. Similarly, the lists would not mention bishops whose memories had been suppressed by succeeding

[33] I. Mulders and R. Demeulenaere, 'Préface', in *CCL* 64, 55–8; cf. Lanzoni, *Diocesi*, 448.

[34] I am grateful to Gillian Clark for showing me her forthcoming paper on Victricius.

[35] Eno, 'Lists of Roman Bishops', 158–69.

generations. At Rome the papal chronicle known as the *Liber Pontificalis* gives only a passing reference to the schism occasioned by the accession of Pope Symmachus in 498. It was influenced by another document, known as the 'Symmachan apocrypha', which recast certain episodes of earlier papal history to support Symmachus' claims.[36]

Similar revisions are obvious in the north Italian lists. The Milanese list, for example, makes no mention of bishop Auxentius (355–74).[37] This revision arose early in Milanese tradition, and once again Ambrose's episcopate was the catalyst. In a polemical passage recording his efforts to hold on to his sacred inheritance at Milan, Ambrose—who viewed Auxentius as a heretic and thus regarded his episcopate as invalid—omitted all mention of his immediate predecessor, presenting himself instead as successor to Dionysius, the Milanese bishop exiled at the council of 355.[38] Some revisions produced truly outlandish results: in the episcopal list from Trento, for example, some fifteen incumbents of the see are listed between Abundantius, who attended the Council of Aquileia in 381, and Vigilius, who was certainly bishop by 385![39] Not only material from the distant antiquity was subject to such manipulation: the recent past could be recast too. A neat example is provided by the list of patriarchs of Aquileia and Cividale, drawn up in the mid-fourteenth century. It excises an unhappy chapter from the history of the see by omitting any reference to Philip of Spanheim, who had been *de facto* patriarch from 1269 to 1273. Philip, brother of Duke Ulrich III of Carinthia, had been imposed on Aquileia when the previous patriarch, Gregory of Montelongo, had died in the course of the struggle between Aquileia and Ottokar II of Bohemia. Ulrich and Philip were Ottokar's cousins, and through them he sought to bring much of north-eastern Italy under his sway.[40] As we will see now, the evidence of several north Italian episcopal lists for the early Christian period is similarly vitiated by this tendency of later generations to reshape them.

[36] Davis, *The Book of Pontiffs*, xiv–xv, 29–30, 43–6.
[37] Picard, *Souvenir*, 18.
[38] Ambr., *Ep.* 21a. 18: 'Sed et hoc addidi: "Absit ut tradam hereditatem est Dionysii qui in exilio in causa fidei defunctus est, hereditatem Eustorgii confessoris, hereditatem Mirocletis atque omnium retro fidelium episcoporum."'
[39] Picard, *Souvenir*, 503.
[40] For events at Aquileia: Ughelli, *Italia Sacra*, v. 94; cf. Aubert, 'Gregoire de Montelongo'. For a Bohemian perspective: Dvornik, *The Slavs*, 27–31, 132.

At Brescia, the rearrangement of such material reflects the varying fortunes of the see. The earliest surviving list was written by the city's ninth-century bishop Rampert,[41] who lists only the successors of Filastrius (died 396). He refers, however, to a poem written by Peter, Rampert's immediate predecessor, in which Filastrius is designated Brescia's seventh bishop.[42] Of his alleged six predecessors, only one—Ursicinus, who attended the Council of Serdica in 343—is otherwise attested. For the names of the other early bishops, we must turn to a twelfth-century manuscript in the Bibliotheca Queriniana in Brescia, which records:

Primus episcopus brixensis fuit Anathalon, mediolanensis archiepiscopus. Secundus Clateus. Tertius Viator. Quartus Latinus. Quintus Apolonius. Sextus Ursicinus. Septimus Faustinus. Octauus Filastrius.[43]

An interesting change had been made to the list between the ninth and twelfth centuries. The proto-bishop of Milan, Anatelon, was placed at the head of the list, thus making Filastrius the eighth holder of the see.[44] It is impossible to know for certain how this alteration came about, but it may be related to the expansionist policies of certain Milanese archbishops in the tenth and early eleventh centuries. The last of these domineering bishops, Aribert II, is known to have attempted to impose Milanese candidates on other sees which, like Brescia, lay near Milan.[45] Indeed, we know that in the events leading to the coronation of Conrad II as emperor in 1027, Aribert invoked the legend of Anatelon to vindicate the right of the archbishop of Milan rather than the archbishop of Ravenna to present the imperial candidate to the pope.[46] So it is possible that the episcopal list of Brescia was revised at a time when the Church there was under Milanese influence. As for Clateus, Viator, Latinus, and Apolonius (*sic*), nothing at all is known.

A more interesting farrago is the list for Padua, which in its various forms dates from the 1260s and is extremely tendentious for any bishop before the ninth century.[47] The earliest Paduan bishop known from other sources, Crispinus, who held the see in the 340s,

---

[41] Edited in *AASS* (3rd edn.) July 4. 388–93. [42] Edited in ibid., 384–5.
[43] The only edition of this text is in Picard, *Souvenir*, 434. I have retained the idiosyncratic spellings of personal names found in the manuscript.
[44] Picard, *Souvenir*, 433–40. [45] Cowdrey, 'Aribert II', esp. 1–6.
[46] Ibid., 7. [47] Edited in *RIS* n.s. 8/1, 3–4.

does not feature in this list at all. Conversely, the first bishop listed, Prosdocimus, is unattested before the sixth century, when a sarcophagus for his relics was set up in a basilica dedicated to a local martyr, St Justina. On this sarcophagus, Prosdocimus is designated 'bishop and confessor', implying that his holiness derived not from the manner of his death, but from his exemplary life. We hear nothing else of him until the tenth century, by which stage his cult had spread to the hinterland of Verona. Then in the eleventh century, Prosdocimus was the subject of a trope-ridden *Vita*, in which he appears as a disciple of St Peter, but manages to survive until the persecution under the emperor Maximian (286–306)—a life span of nearly three centuries![48] Yet it seems that the cult of Justina was more important in the earlier period than that of Prosdocimus: after all, it was in her basilica that he was alleged to have been buried.

Both cults, however, may have had a common origin. Neither saint is attested in the *Martyrologium Hieronymianum*, and when the basilica was constructed in the sixth century, the dedicatory inscription stated that the church had been built 'from the foundations'.[49] Furthermore, the patron of the dedication, Venantius Opilio, was an important local aristocrat who had risen to high office in the Ostrogothic government at Ravenna.[50] This sort of aristocratic patronage of a cult has parallels elsewhere, most obviously in Merovingian Gaul.[51] It suggests that Justina's cult may have been primarily a local phenomenon. Indeed, one of the earliest references to it occurs in the *Life of St Martin* by Venantius Fortunatus, who came from Duplavis near Treviso, not far from Padua.[52] It is impossible to be certain why SS Justina and Prosdocimus appear so suddenly with Opilio's basilica. Yet the fact that the fifth and early sixth centuries, during which the cults may have been in gestation, saw the rise of Aquileia and Ravenna as the major metropolitan sees of north-eastern Italy perhaps offers a solution. Sandwiched between them, the Paduan church may have felt the need to produce some venerable saints of its own to increase its prestige.

[48] Picard, *Souvenir*, 466–70, 641–4.

[49] Picard, *Souvenir*, 641 n. 210; cf. Guillou, *Régionalisme et indépendance*, 278–82, with photograph.

[50] On his career: *PLRE* ii. 808–9. On his connections with the Italian aristocracy: Moorhead, *Theoderic in Italy*, 227.

[51] Van Dam, *Saints and their Miracles*, esp. 67–8.

[52] Guillou, *Régionalisme et indépendance*, 281–2; cf. George, *Venantius Fortunatus*, 18–20, on his connections with other cults in north-eastern Italy, including Aquileia.

The source for the early bishops of Ravenna is the *Pontificalis* of Agnellus of Ravenna written between 830/1 and the mid-840s.[53] The work clearly reflects the cultural ambience of Ravenna at this time, as well as the author's pride in his city's monuments.[54] It is also a vehicle for his political views. Agnellus is strongly anti-Byzantine and so he relishes the leadership by his forebear George of a revolt against Justinian II in 711 (Agnellus, *Pontificalis* 140);[55] he is less than favourable about the bishops of his own see.[56] But most important for our purposes is his distaste for papal jurisdiction over Ravenna, which he could accept in dogmatic matters, but nowhere else.[57] His ire is hardly surprising for a man displaying profound civic patriotism at a time when Ravenna's independence had been eroded by a sequence of Frankish–papal alliances since the 750s.[58]

This is significant because Agnellus makes Ravenna's first bishop, Apollinaris, a disciple of St Peter at Rome (Agnellus, *Pontificalis* 1), thus justifying Roman spiritual primacy over his own church. But Agnellus is reflecting rather than inventing a tradition: St Peter's instruction of Apollinaris appears in the writings of Paul the Deacon, more than fifty years earlier (*Liber de episcopis mettensibus*, p. 261). The origins remain obscure.[59] Peter Chrysologus, bishop of Ravenna in the mid-fifth century, makes the earliest extant allusion to Apollinaris, but says nothing of St Peter (*Sermo* 128). By 666, however, the emperor Constans II recognized that the Ravennate church possessed apostolic dignity.[60] Ravenna by now boasted two enormous churches dedicated to Apollinaris, one within the city, the other at Classe, its harbour suburb. They belong to the late fifth and mid-sixth centuries respectively, a time when the saint's legend was perhaps undergoing some sort of metamorphosis. At the same time the bishops of Ravenna increased their influence by exploiting their proximity to the successive courts of Roman emperors, Ostrogothic kings, and Byzantine exarchs.[61] The earliest bishop of Ravenna known from other sources is Severus, eleventh in Agnellus' list, a participant at the Council of Serdica. But

---

[53] Date: Brown, '*Romanitas* and *Campanilismo*', 108.
[54] Fasoli, 'Agnello Ravennate', 475–7.
[55] Brown, '*Romanitas* and *Campanilismo*', 111.
[56] Brown, '*Romanitas* and *Campanilismo*', 108.
[57] Fasoli, 'Agnello Ravennate', 487.
[58] Noble, *Republic of Saint Peter*, 71–95.
[59] For the period up to c. 600, see now Markus, *Gregory the Great*, 143–7.
[60] Brown, 'The Church of Ravenna', 15.   [61] Lanzoni, *Diocesi*, 464–8.

a church seeking to rival the prestige of Rome[62] would need a more ancient proto-bishop than a fourth-century incumbent, so the cult of Apollinaris may have been fostered in order to give the city an apostolic succession to rival that of St Peter.[63]

The earliest episcopal lists for Milan are preserved in eleventh-century manuscripts.[64] This date is crucial since, until 1075, the Milanese church was involved in a fierce struggle to preserve its independence in the face of an aggressive reform papacy.[65] Information in the lists may have been distorted, if not invented, to suit propagandist purposes, just as a papal polemicist such as Bonizo of Sutri spiced his works with wholesale untruths.[66] Of the bishops listed, the earliest otherwise known is Merocles, who attended the church councils of Rome in 313 and Arles in 314. Before him come five bishops: Anatelon, Gaius, Castricianus, Calimerus, and Monas. Ennodius (*Carmina* 2. 6) states that a *basilica sancti Calimeri* was repaired during the episcopate of Laurentius I (489–510/12). Although we cannot know exactly when this church was built, restoration in the late fifth or early sixth century suggests it may have been constructed before *c.* 450.[67] It was almost certainly on the same site as the present church of S. Calimero, not far from Ambrose's *Basilica Apostolorum*, now S. Nazaro, in a large ancient cemetery along the road to Rome.[68] The oldest references to Castricianus and Monas come from a flurry of *inventiones* between the mid-tenth century and the episcopate of Arnulf II (998–1018), while Gaius is first noted in the *Libellus de situ civitatis Mediolanensis* (p. 34), probably written in the eleventh century.[69]

It is perhaps significant that these 'discoveries' were made shortly before the lists were drawn up: together they attest to heightened interest at Milan in the years around 1000 in the early history of the see. This surge in activity may be linked to the new situation in which the Milanese archbishopric found itself in the tenth and early

[62] Markus, 'Ravenna and Rome', 556–78.
[63] Cf. Markus, *Gregory the Great*, 145 and n. 7, on a similar legend, reported by Agnellus, which alleged that Valentinian III granted Ravenna certain privileges so that it might exceed Rome in prestige.
[64] Picard, *Souvenir*, 442–3.
[65] Cowdrey, 'The Papacy, the Patarenes', 25–48.
[66] Robinson, *Authority and Resistance*, 36–7, 99–102.
[67] Picard, *Souvenir*, 26.
[68] *Depositio S. Calimeri*, in *AASS* (3rd edn.) 7. 184–5. A. Calderini, 'Milano archeologica', 558–63.
[69] Cf. Picard, *Souvenir*, 450–9.

eleventh centuries. Following the collapse of Carolingian authority
in Lombardy, the government of the region fell into the hands of
local power-brokers.[70] Among these, the archbishops of Milan maintained links with the Frankish kings north of the Alps who had retained
an interest in Italian affairs, even though they could impose their
will there only infrequently. The strength of the relationship was
most apparent when Otto I (936–73, emperor from 962) transferred
control of a number of his castles in Lombardy to archbishop
Walpert of Milan in 962.[71] Furthermore, this was also a period when
primacy in north Italian ecclesiastical affairs was hotly contested
between Milan and its rivals, Aquileia and Ravenna.[72] Perhaps the
Milanese church sought to boost its challenge for hegemony by promoting its ancient Christian heritage: the appearance of Anatelon as
proto-bishop at Brescia between the ninth and twelfth centuries could
reflect such a policy.

Ordinarily, of course, Milan's primary sainted bishop had been
Ambrose. The Milanese church was also the Ambrosian church,
with its own liturgical and administrative peculiarities.[73] Ambrose
himself behaved rather like a patron-deity from pagan antiquity,
actively protecting his city through supernatural appearances.[74] Yet
distinguished as he was, Ambrose was an inadequate ally when the
church of Milan came into ideological conflict with the reform
papacy in the third quarter of the eleventh century, not least
because popes such as Gregory VII (1073–85) included the great
Milanese bishop in their own armoury of Church Fathers who supported Petrine supremacy.[75] The proto-bishop of the Milanese lists,
Anatelon, provided an alternative solution to those desperately
seeking to counteract Roman propaganda.

When Anatelon first appeared in the eighth century, he was one
of a number of missionaries, including Apollinaris of Ravenna, sent
to northern Italy by St Peter.[76] By the mid-tenth century, however,

---

[70] Tabacco, *The Struggle for Power*, 151–76; Wickham, *Early Medieval Italy*, 168–81.
[71] Tabacco, *The Struggle for Power*, 173; and in more detail, Bognetti, 'Gli
arcivescovi', 850–4.
[72] Cowdrey, 'Aribert II', 2 n. 5.
[73] Cattaneo, 'La tradizione e il rito ambrosiano'; cf. Cowdrey, 'Aribert II', 3–4.
[74] e.g. Landulf Senior, *Med. hist.*, 2. 2; cf. Cowdrey, 'Aribert II', 11, for an
eleventh-century example described from the point of view of Milan's enemies.
[75] Robinson, *Authority and Resistance*, 23, on Gregory's use of arguments
attributed to Ambrose.
[76] Paul the Deacon, *Liber de episcopis mettensibus*, 261.

another form of the legend was current, this time making him the disciple of the apostle Barnabas, and so independent of Peter and Rome.[77] Even so, this account was not incorporated into the first of the episcopal lists of the eleventh century, which concluded with the death of Arnulf II in 1018, suggesting that the legend was not part of the official rhetoric of an autocephalous Milanese Church. Certainly, the historian Arnulf of Milan, writing *c.* 1070, made no reference to Barnabas, preferring to base Milan's prestige on the reputation of Ambrose (Arnulf, *Lib. gest.* 3. 13). The story was still not incorporated into the second eleventh-century recension of the episcopal list, which concluded with archbishop Tedald (1075–85), again suggesting that it may not have become part of official Milanese church propaganda. It was left to another late eleventh-century Milanese chronicler, Landulf Senior, to give a full account of the Barnabas story (Landulf-Senior, *Med. hist.* 2. 15). It is possible that Landulf reflects a revival of interest in the Barnabas legend by a distinct group of patriotic Milanese polemicists seeking to subvert the rhetoric of Gregory VII, who was invoking his apostolic succession to St Peter as the ideological basis for his authority.[78] If so, they had some limited success—the single pro-Gregorian response to the Barnabas legend is an angry denial:

Why do the Milanese stray from the truth?—they, who puffed up with scornful pride, say that their Church took its origins neither from Peter nor his successors, but from Barnabas.[79]

There, however, Milanese attempts to challenge the apostolic primacy of Rome ended, as the harsh north Italian policies of the emperor Henry IV (1056–1106) began to push Milan towards a reconciliation with the papacy.[80]

The problems posed by episcopal lists are more complicated at Aquileia than elsewhere. Two distinct traditions survive, both preserved in very late manuscripts: one set, from the thirteenth century, comes from Grado;[81] the other, of fourteenth-century date, from

---

[77] *Libellus de situ civitatis Mediolanensis*, 14–21, esp. 20; Hyde, 'Medieval Descriptions of Cities', 315–18.

[78] Paredi, ' "Barnabas, Apostel der Mailänder" '; Robinson, *Authority and Resistance*, 19–22.

[79] Bonizo of Sutri, *Decretum* (edited in A. Mai, *Nova Bibliotheca Patrum*, 7/3, Rome 1854), 4. 61, cf. 2. 6 and 4. 59.

[80] Cowdrey, 'The Papacy, the Patarenes', 39–48.

[81] Ed. in Cessi, *Origo*, 160–3.

Cividale.[82] This peculiar circumstance resulted from a split in the
Aquileian church, arising from the condemnation of certain writ-
ings known as the 'Three Chapters', a decision ratified by the Fifth
Oecumenical Council at Constantinople in May and June 553.[83]
Despite initial resistance, the papacy joined the chorus of condemnation. This move proved so unpopular in the west that in 556 only
two bishops could be found willing to consecrate the new pope.
Resistance was fiercest in northern Italy, where it crystallized under
Aquileian leadership. In 607, however, the bishop of Aquileia,
resident at Grado since the Lombard invasions of 568, re-entered
communion with Rome. But when the see next fell vacant, those
hostile to the rapprochement with Rome refused to accept Candi-
dianus, the new bishop at Grado, and elected their own candidate,
John. Thereafter there was a schism with two bishops claiming the
same see: one resident at Grado, the other at Aquileia and Cividale.[84]
The conflict was resolved in 723 when, under Lombard pressure,
Aquileia and Cividale returned to the Roman fold; but the see at
Grado continued to exist and its independence was guaranteed by
the new arrangement with the papacy.[85]

Consequently the two lists, recording the bishops of Cividale and
Grado, both claimed continuity with the ancient Aquileian church.
They diverge in various ways, not least in their versions of the schism
of 607.[86] There are also important differences for the early period:
the compilers of the Cividale list, not having access to the episcopal
archives at Grado, confused the order of the early bishops well
into the fourth century, as well as giving divergent lengths for each
episcopal reign.[87] Both lists agree, however, that the apostle Mark
was the founder of the see and that he left a certain Hermachora
as the first bishop. Legends associating the apostle, his relics and
northern Italy are heavily laden with apocryphal elements. Grado,
for example, claimed to have St Mark's episcopal throne, first mentioned at the synod of Mantua in 827.[88] The first datable association of apostle and region comes in Paul the Deacon's *Libellus de*

[82] Ed. in *MGH SS* 13. 367–8.
[83] For the impact of this controversy on the western churches: Markus, *Gregory the Great*, 125–42.
[84] Markus, *Gregory the Great*, 127–33.
[85] Noble, *Republic of St Peter*, 27–8.
[86] In general, see Picard, *Souvenir*, 411–31.
[87] For variants, see the notes to the edition in *MGH SS* 13. 367–8.
[88] Weitzmann, 'The Ivories of the So-called Grado Chair'; *contra* Picard, *Souvenir*, 584.

episcopis mettensibus (p. 261), written in the 780s,[89] where St Mark
is sent to northern Italy by St Peter. It has been argued that this
was designed to give Aquileia adequate prestige to rival that held
by Ravenna because of St Apollinaris.[90] We have seen, in connection with Ravenna, that when the initiative was given to St Peter it
meant that Rome had dogmatic primacy. Could it be the same at
Aquileia? Perhaps. But our earliest source, Paul, although a cleric
of the church of Aquileia at Cividale, wrote *after* the reconciliation
with Rome in 723, and displays a consistently favourable attitude
to the papacy.[91] So Paul's version, which gives the initiative to the
Roman apostle, reflects its author's favour towards Rome at a time
when, indeed, the bishops of Aquileia at Cividale were no longer
in schism with the papacy.

The legend, however, could predate Paul's account and even the
reconciliation of 723. During the Aquileian schism, Cividale had
renounced the dogmatic primacy of Rome by refusing to accept papal
rulings on the Three Chapters. It is possible that, in order to assert
their ideological independence, the bishops at Cividale invented a
legend of an apostolic mission to the Veneto, but without a Petrine
connection, rather as some Milanese may have invented a role for
Barnabas in the eleventh century. Only later, after the rapprochement with Rome had been achieved, could a role for St Peter be
inserted in the story. Indeed, such an invention could date back to
the sixth century: until 607, after all, the breach with Rome involved
the whole of the Aquileian see, including Grado, and later patriarchs
of Grado claimed that they too were successors of St Mark. All this,
however, is mere hypothesis: in the absence of more decisive evidence, the origins of the legend of St Mark's activities in northern
Italy must remain shrouded in mystery.[92]

Born-again saints: the coherence of inconsistency

Such manipulations of historical material to fit hagiographical
needs might seem shocking to some modern historiographical sensibilities. It seems to confirm a cynical view that when the Church

[89] Bullough, 'Ethnic History and the Carolingians', 87; Luiselli and Zanella, *Paolo Diacono*, 92–3.
[90] Picard, *Souvenir*, 585.
[91] e.g., he eulogized Gregory I, calling him 'beatus' and even 'beatissimus', quite an honour for a pope who, despite all his efforts, never held jurisdiction over Aquileia: Paul Diac., *HL* 1. 26; 3. 13, 23–4; 4. 5.
[92] Dale, '*Inventing* a Sacred Past', 56–7.

looks at its past it tends to revise it in order to 'get the distortions to match the mood of present times'.[93] Yet to take such a view is to impose modern constraints on late-antique and medieval perceptions of historical veracity that differed radically from our own. If such views appear inconsistent to us, that is because they represent a distinct manner of negotiating the past. Whereas we view personalities such as Ambrose of Milan, Eusebius of Vercelli, and Zeno of Verona as belonging to the remote past, they would have been far from distant to the minds of people in late antiquity and the middle ages. Instead they inhabited a crowded, supernatural cosmos where, as Gregory of Tours said of Eusebius of Vercelli, their miracles proved their continued vitality beyond burial ('post tumulos': *Gloria Confessorum* 3). As such then, it was the symbolic value of their lives which mattered most, not the fine detail of when, where, and among whom they had lived. Their lives provided maps of ideals to be emulated, or at least admired, and the traditions handed down about them amply demonstrate this symbolic function.[94] A number of traditions surrounding north Italian bishops evokes the nature of such constantly evolving views of the past. Eusebius of Vercelli, for example, was known to have withstood heresy and suffered exile for his determination. In contemporary writings, such as those of his friend and fellow pro-Nicene agitator Hilary of Poitiers, such resistance is portrayed as quasi-martyrdom.[95] Such behaviour earned him some form of veneration by the end of the fourth century,[96] which soon seems to have accorded him the status of martyr by associating him with the Maccabees.[97]

The case of Zeno of Verona provides an even more dazzling display of how a hagiographer negotiates the past. Like Eusebius of Vercelli, Zeno was commemorated locally soon after his death, and later he began to acquire the status of martyr, although this seems to have been an intermittent honour.[98] Zeno's spiritual power, like that of Eusebius, extended *post tumulos*: indeed, his most celebrated miracle, when he staunched the floodwaters of the river Adige

---

[93] Douglas, *How Institutions Think*, 69.
[94] Geary, *Living with the Dead*, 28.   [95] Humphries, '*In Nomine Patris*'.
[96] Ambr., *Ep.* 63. 2, 68–70; *Mart. Hier.* Kal. Aug.
[97] Dattrino, 'S. Eusebio di Vercelli', 175–84, on a sequence of eight late-antique and early-medieval sermons, five of which associate Eusebius with the Maccabean martyrs.
[98] Ambr., *Ep.* 5. 1; Greg. Mag., *Dial.* 3. 19. 2; *Versus de Verona* 45; cf. Dattrino, 'S. Eusebio di Vercelli', 170–1.

on 17 October 589,[99] occurred two centuries after his death! The crystallization of certain traditions regarding Zeno's life and career found form in the delightful *Vita Zenonis* written by Coronatus, a self-confessed *inutilis notarius*, probably in the late eighth century. The text seems to have had little propagandist use or intention, and was compiled primarily to provide a coherent narrative of Zeno's miracles.[100] The *Vita* begins with Zeno in his monastery, which he shortly leaves to go on a fishing trip, during which he prevents the Devil from drowning the driver of a cart in the swift waters of the Adige (Coronatus, *Vita Zenonis*, 2–3). Then Coronatus relates Zeno's miraculous cure of the emperor Gallienus' daughter, who is possessed by a demon (4–5), and having thus earned the emperor's gratitude—which includes a gift of his 'royal' crown which Zeno uses to provide for the poor—Zeno launches into an evangelical campaign which provokes the hostility of local pagans (6–7). This campaign of evangelization is treated as if Verona was a thoroughly pagan city, and it goes some way to explaining how Zeno came to be identified as its patron saint.[101]

Here we seem to reach a problem: Zeno was not the first incumbent of his see—we have already seen that Lucillus (or Lucius) was bishop at Verona in the 340s—but is nevertheless presented more or less as its founder. Yet the inconsistency may be more apparent than real. Witness the testimony of the anonymous *Versus de Verona*, written *c.* 800 (and so roughly contemporary with Coronatus' *Vita*), which lists seven previous bishops before turning to Zeno, who 'by his preaching brought Verona to baptism' (*Versus de Verona* 45–7). So Zeno as eighth bishop and Zeno as evangelizer of Verona are harmonized in the poem, as is Zeno's status as patron and the most important link in Verona's sacred panoply.[102]

It is in the narrative of Zeno's encounter with the emperor that Coronatus presents his most surprising detail: the emperor named is Gallienus, who lived a full century before Zeno's episcopate.[103] This link between Zeno and Gallienus may not have been Coronatus'

[99] Greg. Mag., *Dial.* 3. 19. 2; Coronatus, *Vita Zenonis* 9; Paul. Diac., *HL* 3. 23.
[100] On the *Vita*: Humphries, 'Zeno and Gallienus', 69–78; Vecchi, 'I luoghi comuni'.
[101] On his status as patron: Miller, *Formation of a Medieval Church*, 15–17.
[102] He is the only saint whose miracles are described at all (*Versus de Verona* 45–54), and the poem ends with a prayer to him (100).
[103] Humphries, 'Zeno and Gallienus'.

invention, so much as a reflection of local Veronese traditions.[104] More importantly, the choice of Gallienus is not as capricious as it first seems, but fits a context of active commemoration of the Roman past in early medieval Verona. The *Versus de Verona* makes explicit reference to the visible Roman remains, and an impression of the impact they had on the appearance of the city can be gleaned from the *Iconographia Ratheriana*, an eighteenth-century copy of a mid-tenth-century topographical drawing of the city showing various ancient monuments, including the amphitheatre, theatre, walls, marble bridge, and palace.[105] The period when such materials as the *Versus*, the *Vita*, and the *Iconographia* were produced—the eighth to tenth centuries—coincides with a renaissance of interest in the ancient heritage at Verona which found institutional form in the Capitular Library founded by the archdeacon Pacificius (776–844).[106] In this context, the choice of Gallienus makes perfect sense. The circuit of walls which defended Verona in the early middle ages depended on the work of refortification of the city by Gallienus in AD 265.[107] Above the arches of one of the principal gates of the ancient city, which retained its importance in the middle ages as the very portal leading to the basilica of S. Zeno, ran an inscription recording Gallienus' work of restoration which justified him, with egotistical panache, in renaming the city 'Colonia Augusta Verona Nova Gallieniana' (*CIL* 5. 3329).[108] For a local tradition seeking to have Zeno meet an emperor resident in Verona, Gallienus was the logical choice.

[104] Vecchi, 'I luoghi comuni', notes how Coronatus combines elements drawn from Zeno's own sermons with those culled from Veronese tradition. The story of the exorcism in particular is a familiar hagiographical *topos*.

[105] Ward-Perkins, *CAMA*, 224–8. On the attitude of the *Versus* towards the Roman past: Godman, *Poetry of the Carolingian Renaissance*, 29–30; but cf. Fumagalli, *Paesaggi della paura*, 183–4, dismissing the *Versus* as 'quasi solo un ricordo di tempi migliori e un'aspirazione', a part of 'il mito della città occidentale'.

[106] For Verona as a centre of learning: Turrini, *Millennium Scriptorii Veronensis*, 9–13. Bolgar, *Classical Heritage*, 119, admirably sets the scene: 'many Roman customs and institutions still survived in the Italian towns; and the prevalence of urban communities, the fact that Italian life had its cultural centre in the city rather than the monastery, made for a more secular outlook which was by that very token less distrustful of the pagan past'; cf. Ward-Perkins, *CAMA*, 226.

[107] On the medieval walls of Verona: Greenhalgh, *Survival of Roman Antiquities*, 69–70; cf. Ward-Perkins, *CAMA*, esp. 192–4, 219–20;

[108] Miller, *Formation of a Medieval Church*, 19, on the Porta San Zeno, or the Porta dei Borsari as it is better known today. Near the Roman amphitheatre there is a fragment of wall in a small square known as the Piazza Mura Gallieno, in which there is also the delightful Bar Gallieno, both testimony, of sorts, to the influence of the third-century emperor on Veronese toponomy.

The case of Coronatus' *Vita Zenonis* is instructive in terms of the apparent inconsistency of such hagiographical materials. In it we can see Coronatus, or the traditions he reflects, reacting to the vibrant past of medieval Verona, slotting the 'facts' of Zeno's life into the most visible Roman context presented by the city. This narrative of Zeno's life was popular and in the twelfth century it was immortalized in a series of sculptures above the main portal of S. Zeno Maggiore.[109] In this way the inconsistency was given monumental form. Observant citizens of Verona ascending the steps of the church could gaze up at the story set out before them. Yet next door stood the church of S. Proculo—dedicated to the fourth bishop in the city's episcopal list (*Versus de Verona* 42)—which by its very existence was a reminder that Zeno was not, as Coronatus' life presents him, the founder of the Veronese church. That the various traditions existed side-by-side demonstrates how the inconsistency may seem greater to us than to the medieval inhabitants of Verona. Coronatus' little *Vita* represented one negotiation of the past which granted apostolicity to Zeno; the list in the *Versus de Verona* gave voice to another; and at the neighbouring churches of S. Zeno Maggiore and S. Proculo, the two existed in apparent harmony.

Summary

Is it possible to view the cults of founder saints such as Zeno as a form of 'structural amnesia' which attempts a cynical manipulation of the past 'to get the distortions to match the mood of present times'?[110] This takes much too dim a view of the workings of medieval hagiographical production, since it argues for disingenuity at every juncture. Notwithstanding this, some patterns emerge. First, it is clear that traditions concerning founders, especially apostolic ones, developed in the early middle ages to enhance the prestige of certain sees in northern Italy. They reflect the competition between various bishoprics, especially in those cases—such as Milan, Ravenna, and Aquileia—where not just prestige, but also the justification of autonomy, authority, and jurisdiction was at issue. Second, the possession of apostolic relics itself became an important factor in establishing the eminence of a bishopric. Although

---

[109] Fasanari, *Il portale di San Zeno.*
[110] Douglas, *How Institutions Think*, 69–70.

Agnellus of Ravenna tacitly accepted Roman spiritual jurisdiction over Ravenna because of Petrine primacy, he could still speculate on how different things would have been had the city succeeded in acquiring the relics of the apostle Andrew from the emperor Justinian I (Agnellus, *Pontificalis* 76).[111] At the Council of Mantua in 827, part of the dispute between Aquileia and Grado had hinged upon whose collection of relics of St Mark was superior.[112] That same year, the citizens of Venice, unwilling to see their city overshadowed by its neighbours, pilfered the apostle's body from Alexandria, and established their city's prestige as the home *par excellence* of the relics of St Mark.[113]

Such actions are testimony to the radically different approach to the sacred past in the complexities of medieval minds.[114] Our needs are profoundly different, so that the information preserved in these medieval sources deserves to be treated with caution if not suspicion. In view of the propagandist nature of these documents, it must now seem incredible that, since Ughelli's day, they have been used as major sources for the history of earliest Christianity in northern Italy. Any new account of Christian origins in the region must look to other sources of information to reconstruct a narrative. Data from the episcopal lists can be retained—after all, it would be arrogant indeed to reject everything these medieval chroniclers wrote as nonsense—so long as it is viewed within a context constructed from other materials.

Conclusion

This chapter has shown the strict limitations of and the difficulties imposed by the traditional source material for early north Italian Christianity. The lists of bishops at councils have been shown to be unsatisfactory for a variety of reasons. First, they always represent a partisan group who agreed with the decrees of the council. Second, they cannot be assumed to offer a comprehensive list of bishoprics then extant since it is clear that attendance at councils was at best partial, so the absence of a bishopric from a list does not

[111] Brown, '*Romanitas* and *Campanilismo*', 109–11; Markus, *Gregory the Great*, 145–6.
[112] Above p. 64.   [113] Geary, *Furta Sacra*, 88–94.
[114] Geary, *Living with the Dead*, 28.

necessarily mean it did not exist. Third, the view they offer us of north Italian Christianity is, at best, severely restricted: they limit us to seeing only bishoprics when we know that there existed a few (and perhaps many) Christian communities without episcopal leaders. Similarly, to use medieval diocesan episcopal lists and local traditions as evidence is to ask them to bear a burden of proof they were never designed to take. Such texts were formulated in the middle ages for reasons wholly alien to our quest. They sought to articulate ideas of Christian origins, often in response to contemporary pressures, and, as the case of Coronatus' *Vita Zenonis* has shown most emphatically, their views of historical personalities negotiated a timelessness that confounds modern historical sensibilities.

This is not to say that such materials can tell us nothing, but we must acknowledge their limitations. Lists of conciliar subscriptions provide a secure if partial guide to the existence of episcopal sees. The names they list can be helpful, but again in a partial sense, in sketching the involvement of the north Italian episcopate in broader ecclesiastical affairs. But to reach a full understanding of these processes, it is necessary to use such documents in combination with other sources. This serves as a helpful reminder of the limitations of subscriptions. Likewise, medieval material can be used to a certain extent, if with caution. Episcopal lists and *vitae* often provide detailed information on the lengths of episcopates or the geographical origins of bishops themselves. It is impossible to be certain how much of this information is accurate. Tempting though it is to dismiss it all as fabrication, we must remember that the compilers of such texts could have had access to sources or traditions now lost to us.[115] Yet when embracing such material, we need to remain sensitive to the variety of forces which shaped its production. The next chapter will offer an explanation of Christian origins in northern Italy. It will use some of the material preserved in conciliar subscriptions and medieval traditions, but in order to make sense of this disparate and inconclusive body of evidence, it will be necessary to use the social matrix of the north Italian human environment as a template against which the process may be understood.

---

[115] As Vecchi, 'I luoghi comuni', 143, suggests is very likely to have been the case with Coronatus, who states that he was a *notarius*.

3

Portraits in a landscape:
Christian origins in northern Italy

The previous chapter outlined the traditional source material for earliest Christianity in northern Italy, highlighting its inadequacy on its own to provide a credible account of the arrival and growth of the new faith in the region. While certain of these early legends are demonstrably shameless fictions, it is possible that some of these medieval authors were reworking genuine material. Testing the reliability of such traditions is no easy matter, but this chapter will attempt just that by marshalling other types of evidence, and by viewing the picture that emerges within the context of the north Italian human environment outlined in Chapter 1. From this analysis we may be able to gain some idea of the mechanisms and the chronology of the evangelization of northern Italy.

The Christian communities

The first task of this chapter is to analyse all the evidence for early Christian communities in northern Italy, combining data from the traditions discussed in the last chapter with that offered by archaeology and epigraphy. Such evidence is frequently of a diffuse nature, and of itself is often difficult to interpret. In particular, we cannot always date archaeological remains with precision. Often the chronology is fixed by stylistic criteria which are, it must be admitted, extremely subjective: we will see that several divergent dates are sometimes assigned to the same items of evidence by different scholars. Nevertheless, when this material is taken as a whole, it will permit an attempt at interpreting how Christianity came to northern Italy.

Aquileia

The richest single site in northern Italy is Aquileia. Archaeological investigation over the last century has revealed much about the life of the Roman city, including substantial remains of early Christian edifices. These can be related to hagiographical traditions to render one of the most complete pictures possible for an early Christian centre in northern Italy. Even so, the evidence for early Aquileian bishops and saints is woefully poor: none of it securely predates the late fourth century when, particularly under bishop Chromatius (388–407/8), there was an explosion of activity at Aquileia promoting the city's saints. Imitating the Ambrosian model at Milan, Chromatius erected many new churches, founded several suffragan sees, and seems to have promulgated the cult of Aquileian saints.[1] Therefore it is impossible to know how many traditions date back to the earliest years of the church in Aquileia, or how many saints were, like Gervasius and Protasius at Milan, unknown before the late fourth century.

Of the various names listed in the medieval episcopal catalogues of Aquileia from Grado and Cividale, the *Martyrologium Hieronymianum* mentions at least two of the early entrants in those lists. On 30 and 31 May it mentions Chrysogonus (there are two bishops of this name in the episcopal lists) and on 16 and 17 March, Hilarus. The 'Armiger' listed on 12 July may be the same as the Hermachora whom we have encountered as St Mark's disciple, but this is uncertain.[2] Of these saints, a cult of Hilarus seems to have developed in the fourth and fifth centuries, with a small church dedicated to him inside the walls at Aquileia.[3] The burial of a 'Beatissimus martyrus Chrysogonus', probably one of the bishops, is attested by his sarcophagus, found near Aquileia at Aquae Gradatae, now S. Canzian d'Isonzo, where reputedly he was executed (*ILCV* 2018).[4] Here he seems to have been associated with a clutch of other Aquileian saints: Protus, noticed on 14 June in the *Martyrologium*, whose sarcophagus was also found here (*ILCV* 2017); and the trio of Cantius, Cantianus, and Cantianella (30–1 May, 15

---

[1] Lizzi, *Vescovi*, 154–9.   [2] Picard, *Souvenir*, 582; Lanzoni, *Diocesi*, 493–4.
[3] Chevallier, *Aquilée*, 108; Jäggi, 178–9.
[4] *AASS, Apr.* 1 (3rd edn.), 247–8; Picard, *Souvenir*, 253, 580.

and 17 June), who have given the town its modern name.[5] Their cult
is attested in the fifth century when Maximus of Turin delivered a
sermon in their honour (*Sermo* 15). Around this time it seems that
a church dedicated to them may have been built at S. Canzian d'Isonzo
itself. This was erected over a yet earlier Christian edifice, perhaps
dating from the mid-fourth century, but it is uncertain whether this
first building had any relation to a cult of the group of Aquileian
martyrs. Such a connection is possible. In antiquity, Aquae Gradatae
was the location of important Aquileian cemeteries: it is just the sort
of place where a martyr cult would be expected to develop.[6] Two
other early saints deserve attention: Felix and Fortunatus, recorded
on 14 August in the *Martyrologium*. Chromatius devoted an entire
sermon to them, although only a fragment remains (*Sermo* 7); there
was also a shrine to them outside the southern gate of the city.[7] This
position, near the river Natiso, was claimed to be the site of their
martyrdom in their fifth- or sixth-century *passio*.[8] Traditionally, however, these saints were shared with Vicenza, where there seems to
have been a church there dedicated to them by the end of the fourth
century.[9]

If the earliest Christian history of Aquileia is dimly lit, it emerges
spectacularly from the shadows in the episcopate of Theodore, who
attended the Council of Arles in 314 in the company of a deacon
Agathon. To have had deacons, the Church of Aquileia must have
had some formal hierarchy. The best evidence for the ability of the
city's Christian community to organize themselves comes from the
archaeological record. Beneath the eleventh-century cathedral of
Poppo lie extensive remains of a large church, consisting of two parallel halls (the northern one measuring 17.25 × 37.4 m, the southern 20.45 × 37.1 m) connected by a transverse hall (13.7 × 29 m),
off which lay anterooms and a baptistery (Figure 2).[10] The floors
are decorated with polychrome mosaics, which are particularly
elaborate in the southern hall. Most of this pavement is covered
with large panels, subdivided into emblemata (square, polygonal, and
circular) by intricate geometric networks, everywhere utilizing the

[5] Picard, *Souvenir*, 580.
[6] Cuscito, 'Testimonianze archeologico-monumentale', 641–2.
[7] *CIL* 5. 1678, 1698; cf. Chevallier, *Aquilée*, 108.
[8] *AASS, Iun.* 2 (3rd edn.), 457. For the date: Billanovich, 'Appunti di agiografia aquileiese', 5.
[9] *Mart. Hier.* 19 k. sept.; Venant. Fort., *Carm.* 8. 3. 165–6; id., *V. Martini* 4. 658–60.
[10] Chevallier, *Aquilée*, 106–7.

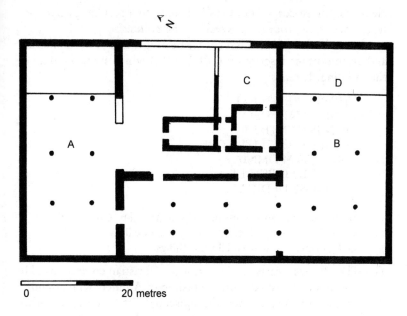

FIG. 2. Aquileia: the double church of bishop Theodore
(early fourth century)
KEY   A: northern hall   B: southern hall (?catachumeneum)
C: baptistery D: *transennae*

guilloche pattern that was to become so common in fourth-century
Christian mosaics in north-eastern Italy.[11] The emblemata are occupied by various devices: animals, birds, portraits, and, in the southern hall, some overtly Christian images. These include a Good
Shepherd, and a panel with a Victory flanked by a basket of loaves
and a chalice (presumably holding wine), almost certainly symbol-
izing 'Eucharistic Victory'. The most elaborate tableau, stretching
across the entire east end of the southern hall and occupying a quarter of its floor space, is an enormous seascape incorporating a narrative depiction of the story of Jonah. The prophet is shown, in a
sequence of images running from north to south, being cast into the
sea-monster's mouth, being belched up onto a beach, and resting
under a canopy of gourds. Apart from these overtly Christian

[11] On this motif: Glass, *Studies on Cosmatesque Pavements*, 29–30.

elements, the seascape could easily belong to a secular, pagan context, since it incorporates several fishing *erotes*.[12]

Also amid the seascape is a *clipeus* bearing a Chi-Rho monogram and an important inscription (*ILCV* 1863) which fixes the date of the building. It reads:

THEODORE FELI[X]
[A]DIVVANTE DEO
OMNIPOTENTE ET
POEMNIO CAELITVS TIBI
[TRA]DITVM OMNIA
[B]AEATE FECISTI ET
GLORIOSE DEDICAS
TI
(O happy Theodore, with the help of Almighty God and the
flock given you by Heaven[13] you have blessedly accomplished
and gloriously dedicated all these things.)

This Theodore is clearly the leader of the Christian community. He must surely be identified with the bishop of Aquileia who attended the Council of Arles, since the episcopal lists record no other bishop with this name occupying the see. Therefore this building can be dated quite closely. In the Aquileian episcopal lists from Grado, Theodore is allocated a reign of 11 years,[14] estimated to have been between 308 and 319.[15] As it is impossible that a church on this scale could have been built secretly,[16] it is perhaps most likely that it was erected late in Theodore's episcopate, after Constantine's proclamation of religious toleration in 313.[17]

---

[12] The bibliography on this pavement is immense. Among the most useful I have consulted are: Chevallier, *Aquilée*, 101–4; Dorigo, *Late Roman Painting*, 169–79; Menis, *I mosaici cristiani di Aquileia*; Tavano, 'La crisi formale tardoantica', 549–69.

[13] Opinions vary on the translation of 'poemnio caelitus tibi | [tra]ditum'. The reading adopted here is that of Chevallier, *Aquilée*, 101, and Menis, 'La cultura teologica', 465 and n. 6, 482–5. But A. Carlini (*AE* 243 (1986)) has suggested the reading 'for the flock given you by Heaven'. See further n. 30 below on the significance of *poemnio*.

[14] Cessi, *Origo*, 162. 19.

[15] Calculations are based on counting the lengths of episcopates, as recorded in the medieval lists, backwards from 388, when Ambrose of Milan installed bishop Chromatius: Truzzi, 'L'ordinazione episcopale di Cromazio', esp. 31.

[16] White, *God's House*, 129–31, 146–7.

[17] An earlier date cannot be ruled out. At Altava in western Mauretania a church may have been built in 309: Lane Fox, *Pagans and Christians*, 587. The inscription attesting the dedication is defective, however, and is especially worn in the part where the date is given: Ferrua, 'Due iscrizioni', 227.

The decorative scheme of the church provides valuable hints as to the socio-economic status and cultural profile of the city's Christian community at the beginning of the fourth century. The mosaics, particularly the seascape, show great affinity with contemporary north African work, where the device of fishing *erotes* is found in several pavements.[18] It is also found in mosaics laid by north African mosaicists working abroad, most famously in the late-third-century villa at Piazza Armerina in Sicily.[19] Furthermore an example also occurs at the late Roman villa at Desenzano, on the shores of lake Garda near Verona, where the mosaics may also be the work of African craftsmen.[20] If African mosaicists were active or influential elsewhere in Venetia, why not also in Theodorean Aquileia?[21] After all, strong contacts between Aquileia and Africa existed at this time.[22]

The scale and sumptuousness of these mosaics, together with the possibility of their African workmanship, raises questions about the size of the Christian community at Aquileia. To require such a large building the Christian community may have been quite numerous; to buy the property on which to build the edifice and to decorate it so lavishly implies the community had access to considerable wealth.[23] In a city which flourished on trade, it does not seem unreasonable to suppose that many Aquileian Christians were themselves merchants and businessmen. Such a hypothesis seems to be supported by other data. Theodore's church was built inside the walls, near the south-eastern perimeter. This part of Aquileia is close to the harbour area, and immediately to the south of the church there was, in the fourth century, a large warehouse and market-place.[24]

[18] e.g. the Triumph of Oceanus and Amphitrite from Constantine (Dorigo, *Late Roman Painting*, pl. 18), or the House of the Triumph of Dionysus at Sousse. See in general: Dunbabin, *Mosaics of Roman North Africa*, 125–30.

[19] Wilson, *Piazza Armerina*, 59 and pl. 33; cf. id. 'Roman Mosaics in Sicily', 413–18.

[20] Wilson, 'Roman Mosaics in Sicily', 426; id., *Piazza Armerina*, 80; Dunbabin, *Mosaics of Roman North Africa*, 214–16. For architectural affinities between Desenzano and Piazza Armerina: Scagliarini Corliata, 'La villa di Desenzano', 262.

[21] Cf. Wilson, 'Roman Mosaics in Sicily', 423. Duval, 'L'influence des écrivains africains', 196–7, paints a charming—though self-confessedly fanciful!—picture of Caecilian of Carthage, visiting Aquileia en route to Brescia and Milan, and suggesting the use of African mosaicists to Theodore.

[22] Cf. pp. 40–1 and nn. 96 and 100 above.

[23] This observation was made soon after the discovery of the mosaics in 1909: see the letter of V. Casarola *apud* Marucchi, 'Notizie', 165. Cf. Lizzi, *Vescovi*, 13.

[24] Bertacchi, 'Edilizia civile', 337–48 and figs. 1–3; Chevallier, *Aquilée*, 36–7, 39; Jäggi, 163–7.

Thus the church lay in a part of the city close to its mercantile quarter.

There may have been a tradition of Christian worship on this site which predates Theodore's church. Beneath it lie buildings of Augustan and mid-imperial date.[25] Elsewhere in the empire, such as at Dura-Europos and the *tituli* of Rome, church buildings often developed by a gradual process of architectural adaptation of a structure in which Christians met for worship. An analogous process may have occurred at Aquileia: Theodore's edifice, for example, reuses the foundation courses of some walls of earlier buildings, some of which seem to have been warehouses.[26] If the underlying buildings were used as a venue for Christian worship before the construction of the Theodorean church, it is possible that their owners then donated them for ecclesiastical use. While we cannot be sure who those owners were, it is possible that, in a commercial town like Aquileia, they came from the professional merchant classes.

This hypothesis seems to be supported by literary evidence which suggests that the clergy of the Aquileian church came from those areas with which the city had commercial contacts, especially the Balkans, Africa, and the eastern Mediterranean. Two of the bishops are designated as having Balkan origins: Hilarus 'fuit natione Pannonicus' and Chrysogonus II 'fuit natione Dalmatie'.[27] The African connections noted in the mosaics of the Theodorean church were also reflected in the origins of the clergy: in the mid-fourth century, the see was held by Fortunatianus, whom Jerome designates 'Afer' (*De vir. ill.* 97). Other names suggest links with the Greek world, not least those of Theodore himself and the deacon Agathon who accompanied him to Arles; moreover, in the episcopal list of Grado, Theodore is said to have been 'natione Tracie Grecie'.[28] By themselves, names are not always compelling evidence,[29] but epigraphic evidence seems to support the vestige of a Greek-speaking element in the Aquileian church in the early fourth century. In the mosaic inscription in Theodore's church, the term used to describe the Christian community is *poemnium*, deriving from

[25] George, *Roman Domestic Architecture*, 40 (Aquileia, no. 3).

[26] White, *God's House*, 115, 136, 198 n. 114. Warehouses: Chevallier, *Aquilée*, 106.

[27] Cessi, *Origo*, 162. 16, 18. Chrysogonus I is recorded as 'fuit natione Ursantinopoli' (162. 17): I have been unable to identify this place.

[28] Cessi, *Origo*, 162. 19.

[29] Mohrmann, *Études sur le latin des Chrétiens*, iii. 72–3.

the Greek ποίμνιον, meaning 'flock'.[30] So far as I know, there is no other example of this transliteration: the word is usually translated into Latin as *grex*.[31] That this ostentatiously Greek word should occur in an inscription recording the activities of a bishop from Thrace once again points to an immigrant element in the Aquileian church. Thus legendary, documentary, biographical, archaeological, and epigraphic data combine to present a portrait of a heterogeneous Christian community at Aquileia. Taken together with the evidence suggesting that Theodore's church may have been built with mercantile patronage, this evidence suggests that the origins of Christianity at Aquileia were closely bound up with the city's prominence as a centre of commerce, even if here (as elsewhere) individual traders cannot be indentified among the congregation.

Milan

Of the other cities in northern Italy, Milan can also boast extensive evidence for early Christianity. Here, however, we have seen clear examples of how already at the time of Ambrose, the Christian past was being manipulated, if not invented, for political ends. Unhappily, there is less of an opportunity at Milan to control the details recorded in tradition with archaeological data: the continuous importance of the city and occupation of its site throughout the middle ages mean that, unlike Aquileia, large tracts of ancient Milan are inaccessible to excavation. Worse, occasions such as Frederick Barbarossa's destruction of the city in 1162 mean that many early Christian remains may have perished forever.[32]

[30] Bauer, *Greek–English Lexicon*, 684; Lampe, *Patristic Greek Lexicon*, 1110. At first this interpretation of *poemnio* was controversial. Diehl, in his commentary on *ILCV* 1863 states 'Poemenio [sic] *martyris ignoti sive incerti nomen interpretor, non* poemnio, ποιμνίων', and offers a cross-reference to *ILCV* 1968B, a Roman inscription recording a 's(an)c(tu)s Pymenius'. But, Diehl's interpretation has never gained wide acceptance, and most scholars agree with the assertion made at the time of the mosaic's discovery that *poemnium* is a transliteration from Greek: Casarola, *apud* Marucchi, 'Notizie', 162–3 and n. 1; Zovatto, 'Il significato della basilica doppia', 362–4 esp. 364. Diehl's hypothesis is rejected in Ferrua's emendation of *ILCV* 1863 ('multo magis placet intellegere poemnio = grege'): *ILCV Suppl.* p. 15.

[31] Cf. Souter, *Glossary of Later Latin*, 166; *TLL* 6. 2. 2333–4. A possible derivation for the word is that it was a technical term used at Aquileia to refer to the Christian congregation: thus we would have a local equivalent of the more widespread phenomonen of retaining technical words such as *mysterium*: cf. Mohrmann, *Liturgical Latin*, 11–18, 29–32; ead., *Études sur le Latin des Chrétiens*, iii. 171–96.

[32] Geary, *Living with the Dead*, 243–56, on the removal of relics after Frederick's victory.

What, then, can we say about the early Milanese church before Merocles stepped out into the full light of history at the Roman synod of 313? Of his predecessors, we have seen that Calimerus had a church from about 450, probably in the cemetery outside the Porta Romana of Milan.[33] If so, a martyr shrine *may* have been on this site prior to construction of the church, although firm evidence for a formal cult (as opposed to informal veneration) of Calimerus is lacking before the eighth century.[34] Other martyrs—apart from Felix and Nabor, who seem, in any case, to have been imported from Lodì under Merocles' successor, Maternus[35]—are hard to trace before the intense activity of Ambrose. A complete portrait of earliest Christianity at Milan based on hagiographical material is not possible.

Archaeological evidence provides little extra help. Thanks to the ambiguity raised by Ambrose's vigorous promotion of Milan's sacred heritage, what little early-Christian material survives cannot be dated with certainty any earlier than the fourth century. The oldest church of which we have any record is that designated *basilica vetus* by Ambrose (*Ep.* 20. 10). Its precise location has been debated, but it seems likely to have lain to the east of the *basilica nova*, known in the middle ages as S. Tecla.[36] To be sure, this particular part of Milan, near the eastern walls, was on the periphery of the late-antique city: the palace complex and forum lay further to the west. Yet the building of a large church *within* the walls is, as we have seen at Aquileia, a significant indicator of the prominence of a Christian community.[37]

At any rate, when Merocles attended the council of Arles in 314, he was accompanied by a deacon, Severus.[38] That there were minor clergy at Milan suggests a formal ecclesiastical hierarchy in the city by 314; in turn this may imply that the Christian community there was well organized and probably numerous. This would not be surprising considering Milan's importance by this time as an imperial capital. Indeed, it is worth noting that Milan is the only north Italian

---

[33] Cf. p. 61.   [34] Picard, *Souvenir*, 251–6, 614–16, 623–4.
[35] Picard, *Souvenir*, 38–9.
[36] For the identification of the site: pp. 197–200 below.
[37] For a more detailed examination of the churches of Milan in their urban context see below Ch. 7.
[38] Munier, *Conc. Gall.* 14–24.

bishopric to have been represented at each of the Councils of Rome, Arles, Serdica, Milan, and Rimini.

Venetia

As in so much else, the situation at Milan and Aquileia cannot be used to draw generalizations for the whole of northern Italy, since these cities were privileged by virtue of their enormous importance as imperial centres. When we turn elsewhere, we find that information is rather less bountiful. For most other cities we must rely on meagre archaeological data supplemented occasionally by allusions in the literary sources. Yet a discernible pattern soon appears, and it is the cities of *Venetia et Histria* that provide the most abundant evidence for the existence of Christian communities by the mid-fourth century.

Verona, as we saw in the last chapter, has a rich and complex tradition relating to its Christian past. It too has an episcopal list, preserved in the *Versus de Verona*, which records five bishops before Lucilius, the first bishop for whom there is independent testimony. Of these, only Proculus was venerated in the medieval period: in the ninth century, there was a church dedicated to him west of the city.[39] It lay in the midst of an ancient necropolis, a location which sounds a convincing spot for a martyr shrine. Unfortunately we cannot assert with any confidence that there was a continuous veneration of Proculus in this area: the site seems to have been chosen in the ninth century for its proximity to that of San Zeno, which commemorated the most illustrious Veronese bishop of the later fourth century.[40] If this church of San Zeno, known from the late sixth century, marks the site of that bishop's actual fourth-century tomb, it could reflect a continuous tradition of Christians meeting in this cemetery dating back perhaps to the pre-Constantinian period. More convincing evidence for early Christian buildings is found in the north-west of the city, beneath the cloister of the medieval cathedral complex. Several different layers of ecclesiastical construction are superimposed on one another, of which a small, apsidal builing, measuring 31.70 × 18.30 m perhaps belongs to the mid-fourth century.[41]

[39] Picard, *Souvenir*, 259–60, 676.   [40] Picard, *Souvenir*, 260–2.
[41] Cuscito, *Primo cristianesimo*, 36–7, with full references.

Brescia, another important city on the road from Aquileia to Milan, presents little detailed evidence of Christian presence prior to the mention of its bishop Ursicinus at Serdica.[42] There is, however, one other literary allusion which suggests a Christian group at Brescia. In the mid-310s, bishop Caecilian of Carthage spent a brief sojourn in the city (Optatus 1. 26; cf. Aug., *c. Cresc.* 3. 71. 83). Despite the efforts of the Donatist party at the Conference of Carthage in 411 to depict this as a period of exile imposed by the emperor (*Brev. coll.* 3. 20. 38), it seems that Caecilian's residence at Brescia was part of Constantine's complex efforts to establish a peaceful settlement for the Carthaginian church, a process which reached its conclusion with the emperor's condemnation of Donatus at Milan in 316/17.[43] In this case, it is possible that Caecilian was hosted at Brescia by a Christian community there. Such an inference would place a Christian congregation at Brescia in the time of Constantine.

Archaeological data at Brescia is scarce, but it suggests that in the third century there may have been a martyr shrine in the cemetery south of the city on the site later occupied by the church of S. Afra.[44] This shrine is sometimes associated with a pair of Brescian saints, Faustinus and Iovitta, mentioned in the *Martyrologium Hieronymianum* on 16 February. But the cult of martyrs at Brescia is difficult to interpret. Strangely, Faustinus and Iovitta are never mentioned in the *Tractatus* of Gaudentius, bishop of Brescia in the last years of the fourth century, leading some to conclude that they were not venerated at Gaudentius' time.[45] The first mention of the cult outside the *Martyrologium* is in Pope Gregory the Great's *Dialogus*, in the late sixth century; but in this case only one of the pair, Faustinus, is mentioned (Greg. Mag., *Dial.* 4. 54. 2). The text makes clear, however, that there was a church at Brescia dedicated to him, since the patrician Valerian was buried there ('beatus Faustinus martyr, in cuius ecclesia corpus illius [*sc.* Valeriani] fuerat

---

[42] Cuscito ('Testimonianze archeologico-monumentale', 659) asserts that Brescia's Christian community was small enough to have escaped the attention of the imperial authorities during times of persecution. The evidence from which he deduces this situation, however, cannot bear such an interpretation: Ambrose's reference to a city 'sterile of martyrs' is clearly an allusion to Milan prior to the *inventio* of Gervasius and Protasius in 386 ('sterilem martyribus ecclesiam Mediolanensam' *Ep.* 22. 7).

[43] De Veer, 'Le séjour de Caecilianus à Brescia'.

[44] Picard, *Souvenir*, 219–23; Cuscito, *Primo cristianesimo*, 40–1.

[45] *BS* v. 483: 'fino al'inizio del sec. V erano assolutamente sconosciuto nella Chiesa bresciana'.

humatum'). No such church exists today, but local traditions associate the relics of the two martyrs with the church of S. Afra.[46]

We saw in the last chapter that the early medieval records of Padua's Christian past are extremely unreliable, and that we cannot be certain of the existence of any congregation there prior to the mid-340s, when Crispinus was bishop. Archaeological investigation of the church of S. Giustina confirms the relatively late development of this site associated with Opilio: none of the mosaics found there can be dated any earlier than the late fifth century. The area in which the church was built offers an explanation as to why a martyr cult developed here, since in the late-Roman period the zone was occupied by a necropolis.[47] As in the case of the extramural churches of SS. Zeno and Proculo at Verona, this cemetery may have been the scene of early Christian veneration.

Rather more secure evidence for an early Christian presence at Padua comes from a mosaic brought to light during excavations in 1931. In a pavement made up of geometric designs, there is a square panel framing a *clipeus* bearing an inscription which contains two acclamations, one mentioning a certain Eutherius and his family.[48] It is impossible to date this mosaic with certainty, but on stylistic grounds it most probably belongs to the fourth (or early fifth) century.[49] But the most significant aspect of the mosaic is its provenance. It was discovered during refurbishment of the Municipio at Padua, a building adjacent to the part of the modern city overlying the ancient forum. Thus we have a Christian cult building not only within the walls—as at Milan, Aquileia, and Verona—but in close proximity to the ancient political centre. Unfortunately not enough of the pavement survives to allow us to reconstruct the dimensions of the building it decorated. The excavators and subsequent scholars assume, however, that it belonged to a rather small structure, such as a private chapel.[50] It is known, however, that the Christian structure was built inside an insula block which at some earlier stage included a bath complex.[51] Furthermore, this property remained in church hands into the middle ages, and the church of S. Martino was

[46] Savio, 'La légende des SS. Faustin et Jovite'.
[47] Porta, 'Mosaici paleocristiani di Padova', 235–44.
[48] See below pp. 165–6 for full discussion of the inscription.
[49] Porta, 'Mosaici paleocristiani di Padova', 233–5 with figs. 2–3, examines the mosaic and concludes it belongs 'in un inoltrato IV secolo, se non agli inizi del V' (235).
[50] Cuscito, *Primo cristianesimo*, 9 n. 21; cf. Bellinati, 'Luoghi di culto', 4–6.
[51] Porta, 'Mosaici paleocristiani', 233, 235.

constructed on the site.[52] So Eutherius may have been the patron who donated the insula for ecclesiastical use. In any case, the real significance of the discovery of this mosaic is that it shows that the Christian community at Padua had the resources to build a chapel in the very heart of their city by the end of the fourth century.

Archaeological material allows us to postulate the existence of several other minor Christian centres in *Venetia* which have not left their mark in the documentary records of fourth-century councils. We have seen that Aquileia shared its cult of SS Felix and Fortunatus with Vicenza. Although no bishop is attested for this city until the sixth century,[53] archaeological testimony suggests a thriving Christian community existed there perhaps by the mid-fourth century. Outside the city's western gate, in a cemetery along the road to Verona, there rose a church which came to be dedicated to the two martyrs.[54] At first it was a plain rectangular hall with an attached baptistery, but later it was rebuilt as a three-aisled basilica.[55] It is impossible to be certain when the various phases of this church were built, and various solutions have been offered placing the earliest construction sometime in the early fourth century or perhaps as late as the fifth. The mosaics bear many similarities to those found elsewhere in northern Italy, with their use of guilloche patterns, geometric panels and *clipei* bearing inscriptions of donors who paid for the pavement.[56] There are important differences too: the elaborate four-pointed star commemorating the dedication by 'Splendonius et Iustina c(um) s(uis)' is quite unlike anything found

[52] Bellinati, 'Luoghi di culto', 6, 14.   [53] Lanzoni, *Diocesi*, 538.
[54] For the necropolis: Alfonsi, 'Vicenza', 337–40.
[55] For the earliest building, De Rossi, *Roma sotterranea*, iii. 436, suggested a date close to the time of the Diocletianic persecution. More recent ascriptions vary considerably: Cuscito, *Primo cristianesimo*, 38–40, favoured a late-fourth- or even early fifth-century date for the 'aula antica', with reconstruction as a basilica with three naves in the second half of the fifth; cf. however, his earlier assertion in id., 'Testimonianze archeologico-monumentale', 658, dating the first phase to the Constantinian period, the second to the late fourth century. This is the interpretation endorsed by the current custodians of the church of SS Felice e Fortunato, who have labelled the different phases of the mosaics as belonging to the Constantinian and Theodosian periods respectively (personal observation at Vicenza). Different still—and rather vague with it—is the dating offered by Billanovich, 'Appunti di agiografia aquileiese', 16 ('un'antica basilica . . . risalente . . . al IV secolo') and 18 ('[i]l grande rifacimento della chiesa, appunto alla fine del IV secolo o al principio del V secolo').
[56] Style: Glass, *Studies on Cosmatesque Pavements*, 29–30; Mirabella Roberti, 'Partizioni dei pavimenti musivi', 413–28. On the inscriptions: Cracco Ruggini, 'Storia totale di una piccola città', 296–7; Caillet, *L'évergétisme monumental*, 85–93.

in other early Christian pavements from the region, as indeed is the dramatic colour scheme of the pavement as a whole.[57] A crudely inscribed stele recording the 'Baeati mart | ures | Felix et | Fortun | atus' (*ILCV* 2002) is not much help in narrowing down the date, despite the efforts of various scholars to place it sometime between the early fourth century and the fifth.[58] Yet even if the church buildings cannot be dated more precisely than this, Cuscito's assertion that there was at Vicenza a well established Christian community by the end of the fourth century seems sensible.[59]

Moving eastwards again along the road to Aquileia, there is evidence of Christianity at Treviso, in the form of a fourth-century mosaic, from a circular building, probably a baptistery, measuring 10 m in diameter.[60] This material is the only testimony we have of a Christian community at Treviso prior to a mention of a bishop Felix who met with the invading Lombard king Alboin in the late 560s (Paul. Diac., *HL* 2. 12). But the Christian community at Treviso was clearly older. This same Felix it seems was a friend of the poet Venantius Fortunatus, who was born at Treviso, and the two made a pilgrimage to Ravenna sometime around 550,[61] which at least provides literary evidence for Christians in the city prior to Felix's episcopate. Further east, beyond Aquileia, there is no evidence for a bishop at Trieste prior to the Justinianic period, when a certain Fulgentius appears in our records.[62] Tradition and archaeology, however, place the origins of Triestine Christianity rather earlier. The *passio* of Justus, Trieste's patron saint, throws up a curious detail,

[57] Personal observation at Vicenza: the unique colours are the result of the materials used for the tesserae, and so could be determined by local geological factors.

[58] The inscription was erroneously ascribed a Roman location by De Rossi, *Roma sotterranea*, iii. 436, repeated by Diehl in *ILCV* 2002, but corrected by Marrou, *ILCV Suppl.* 2002. For illustrations see Billanovich, 'Appunti di agiografia aquileiese', Tav. 1, and *BS* v. 590. The stele has clearly been reused. Its original inscription was cut away to make room for the Christian one, which is in clumsy letters, badly arranged on the stone, and technically inferior to the carving of the architectural frame of the stele. For a thorough review of the difficulties posed by the inscription: Billanovich, ibid., 16–18.

[59] *Primo cristianesimo*, 38–9.

[60] Cuscito, *Primo cristianesimo*, 38 and fig. 5. My own efforts to find this mosaic were fruitless. Having followed the signs in Treviso which directed me to the mosaic, I found nothing but a gravelled pit. I made enquiries at the local archaeological museum, but the custodian on duty could not advise me as to the current whereabouts of the baptistery mosaic.

[61] Venant. Fort., *V. Martini* 4. 665–700; Lanzoni, *Diocesi*, 526.

[62] Lanzoni, *Diocesi*, 516, corrected by Degrassi in *II* 10/3. 74.

however, since nowhere does it mention a bishop of Trieste; instead, Christian leadership is identified with a priest called Sebastian.[63] We saw in the previous chapter that one of the limitations of episcopal lists and conciliar *acta* was that they obscured the existence of non-episcopal Christian communities. Could Justus' *passio* point to such a Christian communion? Unfortunately the text does not inspire much confidence,[64] so the question cannot be answered satisfactorily. The archaeological evidence for Christianity at Trieste does not appear until the fifth century; yet the two churches dating from this period were impressive structures. A suburban cemeterial church, now visible beneath Via Madonna del Mare, boasted magnificent mosaics; meanwhile a large cathedral rose on a site in the very heart of the city, adjacent to the forum.[65] Such impressive structures imply that the Christian community at Trieste had been in existence for some decades previously; even so, it is hard to demonstrate that a congregation in the city in the early fourth century was anything other than small.

Histria

The other north-eastern sites for which there appears to be good evidence for a Christian presence by the mid-fourth century are all in the Istrian peninsula. At Poreč (ancient Parentium) unequivocal literary evidence for a bishopric is—once again—late, referring to the energetic Euphrasius, who constructed the existing Byzantine basilica in the mid-sixth century.[66] Beneath this church, however, lie substantial remains which give unambiguous evidence for a much older Christian presence in the city. The earliest strata here belong to houses of the Roman imperial period, but above them in separate levels are remains of two distinct early Christian complexes. The first of these can be dated—by coins of Licinius, Constantine, and Valens found underneath its mosaic pavement—to the second half

---

[63] *AASS, Nov.* 1. 429.   [64] Cf. Appendix, under Trieste.

[65] Date of churches: Marusic, 'Krscanstvo i poganstvo', 569, 571 (French summary).

[66] Lanzoni, *Diocesi*, 512–15; cf. *II* 10/2. 80–1, 90, 92. It is possible that Rufinus' reference (*HE* 2. 28) to a certain Julian, who brought the relics of John the Baptist to Athanasius after they had been profaned by the emperor Julian, alludes to a bishop of Poreč in the second half of the fourth century, but this depends on preferring a reading in one of the three principal manuscripts of Rufinus' text at the expense of the others: cf. Thelamon, *Païens et chrétiens*, 290–4.

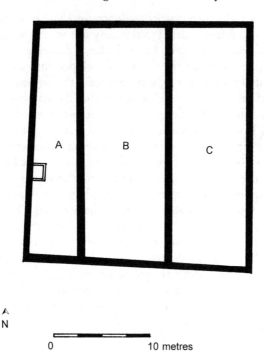

FIG. 3. Poreč: early Christian churches under the Euphrasian basilica
　　KEY　　A: catachumeneum/baptistery　B: assembly hall
　　　　　C: enlargement of early complex

of the fourth century.[67] When this building was destroyed by fire in the early or middle years of the fifth century, it was replaced with another church, known as the 'pre-Euphrasian basilica'.[68] Interpretation of these various remains is aided by a remarkable inscription found during excavations under the altar of the Euphrasian basilica in 1846.[69] The text records the dedication of the church as a memorial to the martyred bishop of Poreč, Maurus. Not only does this

---

[67] *II* 10/2. 26.
[68] Degrassi in *II* 10/2. 31; cf. Sonje, 'Krstionice', 321–2 (Italian summary).
[69] *II* 10/2. 64: 'Hoc cubile sanctum confessoris Maur[i] | nibeum contenet corpus | [h]aec primitiua eius oratibus | reparata est ecclesia | [h]ic condigne translatus est | ubi episcopus et confessor est factus | ideo in honore duplicatus est locus | [. . .]m s[uba]ctus | [. . .] s'. Analysis: Marucchi, 'Recente scoperti', 124–34. My transcription and description are based on the photograph of the stone in *II* 10/2. 30.

inscription yield such crucial evidence for the cult of the saints at Poreč; it also refers in detail to the early history of the site as a location for Christian worship. In particular, it describes three stages of construction by which the site was developed into a church.

The last of these stages to be mentioned is that to which the inscription itself belongs. It should be noted that the slab has been reused subsequent to its initial erection: the last two lines of the text (as it survives) have been chiselled away deliberately. Although the original location of the stone cannot be determined exactly, it certainly belongs to the earliest church on this site (that is, the building lying between the Roman houses and the pre-Euphrasian basilica). But the inscription tells us more, describing how this phase of the complex represented a doubling in size of the previous Christian edifice (*duplicatus est locus*). This concurs well with the archaeological record. The earliest church building consisted of two parallel halls, adjoined by a room indentified as a baptistery or catachumeneum; of these halls, the northern one seems to have been built first. By contrast, the southern hall was a later addition, contemporaneous with the development of the whole site as the earliest church. The addition of this second hall doubled the size of the Christian building (it now measured approx. 22.5 × 25 m), just as the inscription describes.[70]

The original complex consisting simply of the northern hall has its own chequered history. As this was the original church building, it is plainly the one referred to in the inscription as the place where bishop Maurus was martyred (*ubi episcopus et confessor est factus*). Yet the text makes it clear that this was not originally a Christian building; rather, there was a structure here that only became a church when it was used for prayer (*haec primitiva eius oratibus reparata est ecclesia*). Again, this detail can be correlated with the archaeological material from the site. Beneath both this southern hall and the later baptistery complex were found tesselated pavements belonging to the Roman house.[71] In the part of this Roman dwelling beneath the baptistery, moreover, there was uncovered a late third-century geometric mosaic with emblemata.[72] This room shows signs of being adapted to Christian use: at some stage pictures

---

[70] Zovatto, 'Basilica doppia', 380–1.
[71] Compare the illustrations in Sonje, 'Krstionice', 299, fig. 6, and *II* 10/2. 28–9.
[72] Marucchi 'Recente scoperti', 20–1; Marusic, 'Krscanstvo i poganstvo', 550.

of fish were inserted rather clumsily into the mosaic, partially destroying two of the original emblemata.[73]

What we are presented with here seems similar to the development of the Christian building at Aquileia. In the first place there was a Roman *domus*, and at some point one of its rooms was adapted for Christian use and its mosaics were altered accordingly. This may have occurred in the earliest years of the fourth century, prior to Constantine's victory, and perhaps before the persecutions since the inscription states that Maurus was killed in the building. Then during the course of the fourth century there were further adaptations of the building, culminating with the construction of the primitive church sometime after Valens came to the throne in 364.[74] At both Aquileia and Poreč, extant foundation courses were reused and this did much to determine the shape of their Christian edifices. The earliest stages of this process are obscure at Aquileia, but at Poreč they are clear in the insertion of the fish symbols into the geometric mosaic pavement of the Roman house. The analogy goes further: as at Aquileia, the early church at Poreč rose within the city walls. In both cases, the size of the early Christian edifice was substantial. Just as I have suggested in the case of Aquileia, these factors probably indicate that by the mid-fourth century, the Christian community at Poreč was numerous and had access to considerable wealth.

Apart from Poreč, however, there are few early-Christian remains in Istria which can be dated securely to the fourth century. Pula, the other great city in the region, may have had a community by the end of the third century: a *passio* dating from the central middle ages records the martyrdom of a certain Germanus, complete with local colour provided by the saint being tortured in the city's grand amphitheatre.[75] Archaeological evidence, however, does little to corroborate this picture,[76] and all the Christian inscriptions from the city are later.[77] Between Pula and Poreč, there seems to have been

---

[73] Marusic, 'Krscanstvo i poganstvo', 550–2 and fig. 1; cf. Snyder, *Ante Pacem*, 24–6, for the fish as a pre-Constantinian Christian symbol.
[74] White, *God's House*, 114–15, 128–9.   [75] Lanzoni, *Diocesi*, 511.
[76] Only one possible Christian edifice earlier than the fifth-century structures appears on the site of the cathedral. This is a mosaic (badly damaged) depicting a chalice with a swastika cross on it. This is not unequivocal evidence, and the case may be weakened by the inclusion of a splendid hippocampus in the plain, white border of the pavement: Marusic, 'Krscanstvo i poganstvo', 569–70 (French summary) and fig. 3.
[77] Lanzoni, *Diocesi*, 511 on *CIL* 5. 304–7.

another Christian building at Vrsar, also on the coast: the evidence here too is a mosaic pavement, measuring 9.30 × 15.20 m. It is only partially preserved, but enough survives to demonstrate that it was an elaborate piece of work. It consists of guilloche scrolls which enclose circular panels, occupied by abstract geometric motifs or by devices strikingly similar to those found in the Theodorean south hall at Aquileia: fish, birds, chalices, human portraits which are perhaps seasons. The date of the building is uncertain, but considering the stylistic similarities with Aquileia—and stylistic differences from other Istrian sites of the fifth century[78]—it does not seem unreasonable to suppose that the building belongs to the mid-fourth century.[79] Apart from this, however, Istria provides no further evidence for a Christian presence until the fifth century, during which the distribution of cult sites increases enormously.[80]

The Via Aemilia

Compared with *Venetia et Histria*, Christian remains dating from the mid-fourth century or earlier are extremely rare in the rest of northern Italy, with the exception of Milan. From the late fourth century and through the fifth, of course, the situation is profoundly different, but this seems to relate to a dramatic increase in Christian numbers throughout the region after about 350. We have seen that there are two securely attested Christian communities apart from Milan in the area of Lombardy at Rimini and Faenza, since their bishops attended the Roman synod of 313; apart from this, our information is sketchy.

While there is no archaeological evidence to add detail to our sparse knowledge of a Christian community at Rimini, the city does seem a likely candidate for an early see, considering its importance both as a port and as a hub of the road networks leading into and out from northern Italy.[81] There is, however, evidence for Christian communities in nearby cities. One of the most important early centres

[78] Such as the monastic complex of St Andrew at Betika, south of Vrsar: Marusic, 'Krscanstvo i poganstvo', 565; id. and Sasel, 'Complexe monastique de St. André à Betika', 307–42.

[79] Marusic, 'Krscanstvo i poganstvo', 569–70 (French summary) puts it in the mid-fourth century, and hypothesizes that it may have been a residence for the bishops of Poreč (unsubstantiated); cf. Mirabella Roberti, 'Partizioni dei pavimenti musivi', 419–20, advocating an early-fourth-century date.

[80] Marusic, 'Krscanstvo i poganstvo', *passim*.   [81] Cf. p. 27 above.

may have been Ravenna, although there is no documentary attestation of a Christian community until bishop Severus attended the Council of Serdica in 343. We saw in the last chapter that the city boasted a rich hagiographical tradition in the early middle ages concerning its apostolicity, but that the details of Apollinaris' mission were probably developed to suit the political needs of the Ravennate church. Yet this does not necessarily mean that there was no Christian presence in the city prior to the age of Constantine. It is significant that one of the great basilicas built in the saint's honour should have risen in the necropolis outside the southern walls of the harbour settlement of Classe where, according to his *passio*, Apollinaris was buried.[82] Excavations in the vicinity of the church of S. Apollinare in Classe have revealed many tombs, both pagan and Christian, dated to the third and fourth centuries.[83] Classe has provided other early remains, such as the basilicas of S. Probo and S. Eleucadio, both dedicated to early bishops of the see, and both in the cemeteries south of the town walls; there is also the intramural church of S. Severo, which like the others seems to date from the fifth century.[84] Such early churches are significantly more numerous at Classe than at Ravenna itself, where most basilicas seem to have been palatine foundations associated with the Roman, Ostrogothic, and Byzantine courts residing there in the fifth and later centuries.[85] In itself, however, the concentration of early Christian sites at Classe, and especially in the cemeteries, is not wholly surprising. This is precisely the sort of location where we would expect any early Christian group at Ravenna to congregate: Classe was Ravenna's port and saw some trading activity, thus providing the social conditions conducive to the spread of a new religion. Yet this is no more than an inference, and it would be wrong to forget that apart from the tombs around S. Apollinare in Classe, evidence for pre-Constantinian Christianity at Ravenna is sparse. The subsequent development of the city as the political centre of emperors, kings, and exarchs has probably done much to obliterate the earliest monuments of Ravenna's Christian community.

Also in the vicinity of Rimini, on the line of the Via Aemilia running inland from the coast, was the bishopric of Faenza, whose

[82] *AASS, Iul.* 5. 350.
[83] Deichmann, *Ravenna: Kommentar*, ii. 233–4, and fig. 109.
[84] Ibid., 323, 355–9, 361–9; Picard, *Souvenir*, 122–32.
[85] Deichmann, ibid., 49–53; von Simpson, *Sacred Fortress*.

bishop Constantius attended the Roman synod of 313. Apart from such documentary testimony, archaeological investigation in the city has yielded further evidence of the early Christian community of Faenza. Excavations in 1960 on the site of the former church of S. Terenzio, behind the cathedral, revealed a geometric mosaic pavement containing dedications similar to those found at Aquileia, Poreč, Trieste, and Verona.[86] These pavements seem to date sometime between the late fourth and early sixth centuries.[87] Yet even if the date is problematic, it is worth noting the location of the church to which the mosaic belonged relative to the topography of Roman Faenza. The Christian building is sited within the walls and is perfectly aligned with the urban street-grid; indeed, it seems to have been adapted from the Roman house on the site.[88]

Moving deeper into the Po valley along the Via Aemilia, the evidence for Christian communities becomes less prominent, and there is no documentary proof for many sees prior to the Ambrosian period (see Chapter 6), when bishoprics appear at Imola (Forum Cornelii), Quaderna (Claterna), Bologna, Modena, Parma, and Piacenza.[89] In the late fourth century, Jerome knew and corresponded with a papal secretary called Eusebius who came from Cremona (Hier., *Ep.* 53). If this Eusebius was born around the middle of the century, he could attest a Christian community at Cremona by that point: but this is to infer too much from our meagre sources. All we can say is that many of the cities along the Via Aemilia had developed bishoprics—and hence organized Christian communities—by the third quarter of the fourth century. Even though this probably represents the end of a process of evangelization,[90] it is impossible to say when the first Christian communities appeared in these cities.

The upper Po valley

Moving across the river into the central and north-western reaches of the Po valley, the area around Milan provides slightly better evidence for Christian communities by 350. There may have been a

[86] Monti, 'Faenza', 18–21.

[87] Susini, 'Pavimento musivo', 21–3. Cf. Maioli, 'Il complesso di via Dogana', 199–206, arguing a fifth- or even sixth-century date for the other early Christian pavements at Faenza.

[88] Monti, 'Faenza', 19–20; cf. George, *Roman Domestic Arhitecture*, 50 (Faenza, no. 1).

[89] Lanzoni, *Diocesi*, 431–42, 444–8.   [90] Lanzani, 'Ticinum', 356.

bishop at Bergamo, north-east of Milan, by this time. Our evidence is late and relates to a text which is no longer extant, but it has been universally accepted. In the ninth century, bishop Rampert of Brescia, writing in praise of his fourth-century predecessor Filastrius, quoted what he had read among writings—now lost—of Filastrius' successor, Gaudentius. He asserted that Gaudentius, himself writing in praise of Filastrius, had quoted examples of Filastrius' excellent reputation among neighbouring bishoprics. One of these snippets was an epitaph set up by the fourth bishop of Bergamo which stated that his predecessor had been consecrated bishop by Ambrose of Milan, and that sometime before he had been made a deacon by Filastrius.[91] Ambrose died in 397; Filastrius sometime shortly before.[92] If Bergamo had received its third bishop by the last decade of the fourth century, it is probable that a Christian community existed in the city by the middle of the century.

The last group of firmly attested Christian communities comes from the area around Vercelli. Bishop Eusebius of Vercelli was one of the most important north-Italian politicians of the pro-Nicene cast during the 350s and 360s, and was exiled at Constantius II's Milanese council of 355. From exile he wrote to his flock; but more importantly, he included in his greetings the clergy and faithful of the neighbouring towns of Novara, Ivrea, and Tortona (*Ep.* 2). None of these centres is known to have had a bishop before the Council of Aquileia in 381, which was attended by a bishop of Tortona, or the Milanese synod of 451, attended by bishops and clergy from Novara and Ivrea.[93] The existence of Christian communities in these centres prior to the appointment of bishops demonstrates how there were Christian communities in certain towns and cities *before* the appointment of a bishop. Furthermore, it seems that this was the situation in Vercelli itself. No bishop of Vercelli prior to Eusebius is recorded; nor was any commemorated in the middle ages.[94] But there is good reason to believe that the Christian community at Vercelli, like that of Ivrea, Novara, and Tortona, was older than its bishopric. Writing to the people of Vercelli sometime around 396, Ambrose of Milan stated that Eusebius had been made bishop

[91] *AASS, Iul.* 4. 393. Accepted by Cuscito, *Primo cristianesimo*, 46–8; Lanzoni, *Diocesi*, 573; Picard, *Souvenir*, 266–8.

[92] For Gaudentius' succession to Filastrius at Brescia, and his own dependence on investiture by Ambrose: Lizzi, *Vescovi*, 97–109.

[93] Lanzoni, *Diocesi*, 476–7, 560–1, 566–8.   [94] Picard, *Souvenir*, 667–73.

against his will by Christians of Vercelli who had seized him while he was travelling through their city (*Ep.* 63. 2, 68). Some of the details given by Ambrose need to be treated with caution: his account of Eusebius' involuntary election is suspiciously similar to the account, probably based on Ambrose's own propaganda, of his own episcopal election in 374 (Paul. Med. *V. Ambr.* 7–9).[95] But the detail of Eusebius coming to Vercelli from elsewhere may be trusted: Jerome tells us that Eusebius, a Sard, had been a lector of the Roman church prior to his election (*De vir. ill.* 96). During the period when Eusebius might have been elected—the mid to late 340s and the early 350s—several delegations from the bishop of Rome made their way north to visit the imperial court at Milan.[96] It is entirely feasible that Eusebius was a member of one such delegation and that he had been appointed bishop of Vercelli when it had passed through that city on its way to court.[97] Apart from that, however, we cannot be more certain of the events leading to his election; even the chronology remains unclear. Archaeology is of little help, since most early Christian remains from Vercelli are either of a later period, or impossible to date with precision.[98]

Summary

The evidence for early Christian communities in northern Italy is extremely scarce for the period up to 350, but it has been possible to make some advance on the number of congregations revealed by sources such as episcopal lists and conciliar *acta*, even to the extent of discovering non-episcopal groups such as those in Piedmont. Furthermore, analysis of the material remains of the early Christian communities reveals something of how each developed within its own particular social context. Most, it would appear, only had cult buildings outside the walls of their cities. Indeed, in some cities the invasion of the urban heart by Christian buildings would come only at a very late date indeed: at Pavia, for instance, there is no church recorded within its walls until the Ostrogothic period.[99] This serves

---

[95] McLynn, *Ambrose*, 44–52.   [96] See p. 154 below.

[97] Savio, *Piemonte*, 412–13.

[98] Panto and Mennella, 'Topografia ed epigrafia', provides a convenient summary of the archaeological data. The article should be used with caution, however, since the authors' dating criteria are often imprecise or over-confident: in particular, Mennella's section on inscriptions (pp. 384–98) seems too ready to see consular dates in the most fragmentary of inscriptions.

[99] Bullough, 'Urban Change in Early Medieval Italy', 99.

to emphasize that the picture of Christian expansion and its social consequences is extremely variable for the whole region. There were early concentrations in some areas, such as *Venetia et Histria*, but not in others, such as along the line of the Via Aemilia. Likewise, the individual profiles of each Christian community varied dramatically from city to city. Of all the cities in northern Italy, Aquileia provides the strongest evidence for a vigorous Christian community, the size and wealth of which must have been profoundly different from those in Ivrea, Novara, and Tortona. Explaining this variety and the dynamics that brought it about is not easy, but the rest of this chapter will attempt to account for some features of the dissemination of the gospel in northern Italy.

Patterns of dissemination

To understand more fully both the processes and chronology of Christian expansion in northern Italy, I propose to examine the diffusion of congregations against the wider background of religious change in the area during the middle and late imperial period, roughly between the second and fourth centuries. I will begin by examining the 'scatter' of the new faith, which has been acknowledged as a valuable tool for the study of the process of evangelization elsewhere in the Mediterranean.[100] It will be seen that there is a close correlation between the distribution of Christian communities in northern Italy and the important nodes of interaction in the north Italian human environment. This correlation is not, however, unique to Christianity, so next I will point to similarities—and divergences—between distribution patterns of fledgling churches and those of other religious groups, such as Judaism and the cult of Isis. This will point to some of the human mechanisms by which the Church spread its tentacles into the Po valley. At all times, the situation in northern Italy will be compared with what is known of the evangelization of neighbouring geographical areas.

Distribution and dissemination

As a result of the investigations undertaken in this and the preceding chapter, the number of probable early Christian communities

---

[100] Lane Fox, *Pagans and Christians*, 272.

in the first half of the fourth century presents a more substantial
picture than the meagre four bishoprics attested at the councils of
313 and 314. By about 350, it is possible to identify as many as twenty
Christian communities in northern Italy, with varying degrees of
certainty: at Aquileia, Bergamo, Brescia, Cremona, Faenza, Ivrea,
Milan, Novara, Padua, Poreč, Pula, Ravenna, Rimini, Tortona,
Treviso, Trieste, Vercelli, Verona, Vicenza, and Vrsar. It will be noted
that most of the sites occur close to the Adriatic coast, and that all
but Faenza, Ivrea, Milan, Novara, Ravenna, Rimini, Tortona, and
Vercelli are in *Venetia et Histria*. For northern Italy as a whole, this
suggests a gradual dissemination of the Christian message from east
to west, perhaps originating from maritime centres like Aquileia,
Ravenna, and Rimini. The cluster of Christian communities in the
Piedmontese centres of Vercelli, Novara, and Tortona may have arisen
from an independent pattern of religious dissemination.

There is a close correlation between the distribution of these
Christian centres and the communications networks discussed
in Chapter 1.[101] Several early communities were situated in cities
with good communications by sea: Aquileia, Padua, Poreč, Pula,
Ravenna, Rimini, Trieste, and Vicenza. Leading inward from the coast,
we see that the early Christian centres were scattered along the major
roads into northern Italy. Many lay along the main road from
Aquileia to Milan, at Treviso, Padua, Vicenza, Verona, and Brescia,
as well as at Bergamo. Turning eastwards from Aquileia, we note
that the Istrian churches also gather along the coastal road, at
Trieste, Poreč, Vrsar, and Pula. Moving inland from Rimini along
the Via Aemilia, it may seem disappointing to find only two early
Christian centres, at Faenza and Cremona. Yet this picture may be
misleading: by 400 this road was studded with Christian communities in all its major centres.[102] Moreover, it may be significant that
the first two churches on the Via Aemilia developed at centres which
intersected with other important transportation routes: Faenza was
the starting-point for an important road through the Apennines
to Etruria, while Cremona was a hub for communications on the
Po, as well as a crossroads for routes leading to Milan, Genoa, and
Aquileia. That Christian groups should appear at some centres
along a major communications artery but not at others reminds us

---

[101] In order to avoid unnecessary repetition, I will not cite evidence for these networks here. Full details will be found in Ch. 1 and its notes.
[102] For full discussion, see Ch. 6.

that specific local characteristics defined whether or not Christianity took root in a city. The primary prerequisite was that social conditions should favour the dissemination of the new religion: in short, there should be the opportunity for interpersonal contact through which ideas spread. A quick glance at the list of Christian centres suggests that this must have been an important factor in northern Italy, since many of the earliest communions developed in major market centres. In *Venetia et Histria*, for example, the church appeared in centres of the wool trade at Brescia, Padua, and Verona, as well as the important *emporium* of Aquileia; while Faenza on the Via Aemilia was important not just for communciations but also for the linen trade.

For some centres we can attempt a more detailed reconstruction of those social conditions, by locating north Italian Christian communities in their particular urban contexts. At Aquileia and Poreč, for example, we have seen that the earliest church buildings developed out of a process of gradual adaptation of existing edifices. In both cases these buildings lay within the walls, were of subtantial size, and came to be decorated with elaborate mosaics. Similarly, early Christian buildings at Faenza, Milan, Padua, and Verona rose within the city walls in the decades after Constantine's conversion. These factors suggest that by the time of Constantine, the Christian communities in certain cities included members with considerable personal wealth who acted as patrons, donating or paying for the plots on which such buildings were erected.

All these elements prompt the observation that the early Christian communities were deeply embedded in the social matrix of the north Italian towns and cities in which they developed. While trade patterns seem to have been important, they should not be emphasized to the exclusion of other networks. The early dependence of the Christian communities at Ivrea, Novara, and Tortona on the bishopric of Vercelli points to other ties. Under the Roman empire, there had existed between these centres a complex set of interrelationships involving magistracies and priesthoods, and it is perhaps as part of this web that we should see their early ecclesiastical contacts.[103] Similar circumstances may have helped foster early Christianity at Milan. The city had for long possessed administrative importance, but from the late third century onwards this was

---

[103] See pp. 33–4 above.

enhanced by its gradual metamorphosis into an imperial capital. There were thus many reasons, in addition to trade, why an outsider might come to Milan. The importance of the city might also explain why ecclesiastical administration was more elaborate at Milan than in the cities in its immediate vicinity. By 314, when it sent both its bishop and a deacon to Arles, the organization of the Milanese church was already more advanced than that in Bergamo or the towns of Piedmont, none of which had a bishop much before 350. That churches developed where they did in this early period seems to have been determined to a large degree by the social matrix within which Christianity operated. Towns and cities—where the face-to-face interaction crucial to the dissemination of ideas was to be found—provided perfect opportunities for evangelization. These same centres would have been those that attracted a wide range of people, both from their immeditiate vicinities and from further afield. In short, Christianity in northern Italy developed first in urban centres of economic and administrative importance which were advantageously sited on the communications network.

Similar factors had determined the spread of Christianity in other regions of the western Mediterranean where the evidence for early missions is rather more detailed than it is for northern Italy. In central and southern Italy, it has been seen that there were communities at Puteoli, near Naples, and Rome already in the apostolic period.[104] Their existence so early should occasion no surprise: Puteoli was one of the greatest emporia in Italy (Strabo 5. 4. 6),[105] while Rome, the imperial capital, was a magnet for peoples—and their religions—from across the entire empire.[106] From these instances it can be seen that the evidence for the earliest north Italian churches fits a pattern visible in other areas where Christian missions were embedded in social, cultural, and economic contexts. This should not obscure, however, the various peculiarities of Christian expansion in northern Italy. For example, Christianity seems to have come to north Africa via the great trading city of Carthage, a circumstance similar to the missions I have suggested for the ports at Aquileia, Ravenna, and Rimini. Yet in Africa it is clear that the new faith had spread not only to the cities, but also to many small towns and their rural hinterlands: indeed, one of the best known African

---

[104] See pp. 8–9 above.

[105] D'Arms, *Romans on the Bay of Naples*, 81–2, 138–9.

[106] It aroused the notorious disgruntlement of Juvenal: 'Syrus in Tiberim defluxit Orontes', and so forth (*Satires* 3. 62–5).

passiones, the *Acts of the Scillitan Martyrs*, describes a vigorous Christian community in a settlement so insignificant that it has never been properly identified.[107] In northern Italy, by contrast, Christian expansion seems to have been largely confined to the cities. The remains uncovered at S. Canzian d'Isonzo near Aquileia are the only testimony of a rural Christian presence before the events in the Val di Non in the 390s;[108] even in the fifth century, it is clear that the countryside around Turin remained largely untouched by the gospel.[109] There would have been differences too in terms of the specific networks used by the first Christians in northern Italy and in other regions. Whereas Paul's missionary journeys often relied on the network of Jewish communities in the cities of the eastern Mediterranean, no such circumstance will have obtained in northern Italy. There—as in much of the west—the dissemination of Judaism in general came late,[110] so that Jewish and Christian expansion occurred concurrently, rather than consecutively.[111]

Christians in a religious landscape

It is apparent that the early dissemination of Christianity was often subject to similar social constraints as those which influenced the spread of different religions. This section will compare the distribution of early Christian groups with that of some other religions, but the comparison cannot be indiscriminate, and it must involve cults that were subject to similar constraints to early Christianity. For example, a comparison with Mithraism would be inappropriate, since that cult appealed to a different constituency from Christianity: Mithraic initiates were exclusively male.[112] The cult of Isis, however, will suit rather better: although it was never subjected to the sort of sporadic repression suffered by Christians, it was a private cult under the Roman empire, and it appealed to both sexes.[113] Also worthy of consideration is Judaism, although

---

[107] Rives, *Religion and Authority at Roman Carthage*, 223.

[108] See in detail pp. 181–4 below.   [109] Lizzi, *Vescovi*, 193–202.

[110] An important exception is L. Aiacius Dama, a Jewish freedman and customs house worker (*portor*), who seems to have lived at Aquileia in the 1st cent. BC: Noy, *JIWE* i. 8 (pp. 11–13).

[111] Schürer, *History of the Jewish People*, ii. 1, 82–4.

[112] Martin, *Hellenistic Religions*, 118 with refs.

[113] Ibid., 72. For the spread of Isiac cult see esp. Malaise, 'La diffusion des cultes égyptiens', 1615–91. For northern Italy: id., *Inventaire préliminaire*; id., *Conditions de pénétration*; Budischovsky, 'La diffusion des cultes égyptiens', 207–27; ead., *La diffusion des cultes isiaques*.

allowance must be made for the methodological problem of relative chronology noted above.[114] Moreover, it is unclear as to whether individuals might actually convert to Judaism—which required drastic surgical procedures in addition to a change of faith—or whether there were individuals who became 'sympathizers' of the Jews or associates of synagogues, rather like the 'God-fearers' found elsewhere in the empire.[115] Through analysis of the correlation and difference between the patterns of distribution for Isis-worship, Judaism, and Christianity, we may be able to arrive at a more complete picture of the factors which influenced the evangelization of northern Italy.

Starting with the cult of Isis in northern Italy, we note that its distribution yields interesting parallels with Christianity. There is a similar regional variety in terms of the occurrence of material along the coasts of *Aemilia* and *Venetia et Histria*, with particular concentrations in port cities such as Rimini, Ravenna, Trieste, and especially Aquileia. Moving inland, most material is concentrated in the areas nearest the Adriatic, particularly in *Venetia et Histria*. As with Christianity, various communications networks seem to have been crucial to this pattern of distribution.[116] Yet the Isiac material differs from the evidence for early Christianity in one crucial respect. Because of the greater openness with which devotees of Isis could worship and raise commemorative inscriptions,[117] we know a great deal more about the ethnic and social profile of the cult, a luxury we are usually denied with Christians before Constantine. These inscriptions show us that often the propagators of the cult were foreigners, such as merchants and sailors, or Romans involved in such migratory activities, either as traders themselves or as customs officials, and their slaves.[118]

Similar correlations emerge when we examine the evidence for a Jewish presence in northern Italy.[119] Between the late third and early fifth centuries, Jews are found in many of the cities where

---

[114] Cf p. 99 above.

[115] Feldman, *Jew and Gentile*, 342–415, examines the problems and sources extensively. On circumcision, note esp. the judicious remarks of Goodman, *Mission and Conversion*, 67–8, 81–2. A possible north Italian 'God-fearer' may be recorded in an inscription, now sadly lost, from Pula: Noy, *JIWE* i. 9 (pp. 16–17).

[116] Budischovsky, 'La diffusion des cultes égyptiens', esp. 212–21; Malaise, *Conditions de pénétration*, 335–51.

[117] Beard, North, and Price, *Religions of Rome*, i. 264–6.

[118] Chevallier, *Romanisation*, 458–70; Malaise, *Conditions de pénétration*, 321–32.

[119] For full details: Noy, *JIWE* i. 1–10 (pp. 1–18); Ruggini, 'Ebrei e orientali', 187–241.

Christianity also developed. Their distribution is, however, rather more limited, perhaps because the fourth century brought increasing intolerance and pressure to convert to Christianity.[120] Nevertheless, the familiar patterns seen with Christianity and the cult of Isis reappear. Jewish records occur with greatest frequency in *Venetia et Histria*.[121] Once more, good communications seem to have fostered the spread of Judaism, with communities in cities such as Bologna and Brescia, lying on important roads, and in Ferrara on the Po.[122] Their concentration in such areas suggests that trade would have been an important activity for north Italian Jews. Again, however, it is clear that other factors will have played a part in bringing Jews to the region, as Honorius' law of 418 banning Jewish troops from service within the Prefecture of Italy demonstrates.[123] Despite certain differences between Christian diffusion and that of both Isis worship and Judaism, in terms of frequency, visibility, and chronology,[124] there are sufficient parallels between their patterns of diffusion to suggest that the evangelization of northern Italy fits into a context of exchange of religious ideas that was embedded in the region's social matrices. Christianity, Isis worship, and Judaism were all private cults, relying on direct personal contact for their dissemination. In the bustling cosmopolitan cities and towns of northern Italy all three religions found the ideal environment in which to attract new adherents.

Chronological questions

One question remains to be answered: if the urban societies of northern Italy were conducive to the spread of Christianity, why does the process seem so retarded by comparison with central and southern Italy? In part, the question itself ignores a significant problem. While it is incontrovertible that the development of Christianity in Rome between Paul and Constantine was rapid, we

---

[120] Ruggini, 'Ebrei e orientali', 192–213; Lizzi, *Vescovi*, 124–5, 158–9, 162–5, 193 with n. 116. Cf. for a broader picture: Millar, 'Jews of the Graeco-Roman Diaspora', 97–123.

[121] Detailed discussion in Noy, *JIWE* i, pp. xiii–xiv, 6–17.

[122] Ruggini, 'Ebrei e orientali', 224–8.

[123] *CTh* 16. 8. 24; cf. Ruggini, 'Ebrei e orientali', 231–41 with full refs.

[124] For example, the development of a Jewish community at Ravenna and Classe seems not to have occurred until as late as the Ostrogothic period: Ruggini, 'Ebrei e orientali', 228; cf. now also Noy, *JIWE* i. 10 (pp. 17–18).

must be vigilant to the likelihood that there existed in the imperial capital special social dynamics, and that what happened there is unlikely to have been representative of other parts of Italy, never mind the empire as a whole.[125] For example, although there is detailed evidence for 27 bishoprics in central and southern Italy, Sicily, and Sardinia by 314, it is equally clear that their distribution is variable. In particular there is a concentration of congregations along the western seaboard of the peninsula, especially around Rome. This factor points to a solution to the problem. The advanced rate of evangelization in the parts of central and southern Italy lying to the west of the Apennines is paralleled only in two other areas of the western Mediterranean: north Africa and southern Gaul (particularly in the Rhône valley).[126] All of these regions belong to one zone, hemming the Tyrhennian basin, making it likely that such parallels in the pattern and rate of Christian expansion reflect a particular regional dynamic.

Turning to other regions of the west bordering northern Italy, we find the progress of Christianity similarly retarded. In the Balkan and Danubian provinces, for example, pre-Constantinian Christian communities did not flourish, except in the cities of Greece.[127] For other parts of the region, the record is very poor indeed—and very late. Little can be said about Christianity in Dalmatia before the execution of Bishop Domnius of Salona in 304.[128] Salona seems to have been host to the earliest Christian community in the province, but there is no evidence which leads us to suppose that it was any older than the mid-third century.[129] A similar picture emerges along the Danube. During the Diocletianic persecution, several martyrdoms are recorded at Sirmium. This could mean either that the city was the most important centre of Christianity in the area, or simply that as the region's administrative capital it was the place where most trials took place.[130] It is certain, however, that the greatest

---

[125] Lane Fox, *Pagans and Christians*, 268–9, warns about the dangers of extrapolating from Roman figures.

[126] Lane Fox, *Pagans and Christians*, 271–6.

[127] Von Harnack, *Expansion of Christianity*, ii. 372–4.

[128] On early Christian contacts, see Zeiller, *Origines chrétiennes dans la province romaine de Dalmatie*, 1–5.

[129] Wilkes, *Dalmatia*, 427–30; Zeiller, *Origines chrétiennes dans la province romaine de Dalmatie*, 6–95.

[130] Mócsy, *Pannonia and Upper Moesia*, 325–9; Zeiller, *Origines chrétiennes dans les provinces danubiennes*, 79–88. Cf. Lane Fox, *Pagans and Christians*, 490, for the coincidence of martyrdoms and judicial processes at Ephesus in the 3rd cent.

concentrations of Christians in the middle Danube region were in the area around Sirmium (in towns such as Cibalae) and this seems to be connected with the growing strategic importance of the city from the mid-third century.[131]

The late growth of the Church in the Balkans seems to have been concentrated in areas of dynamic social interaction, such as the major cities. Salona was the most important port on the Dalmatian coast,[132] so it is possible that early Salonitan Christianity was fostered by the same conditions of cosmopolitan variety as have been postulated for northern Italy. Indeed, hagiographical material directly associates Salonitan Christians with the outside world: Domnius is said to have come from Nisibis in Mauretania; another martyr, Anastasius, is linked to Aquileia.[133] Otherwise, Christianity was rare in the Balkans before the fourth century. Its growth was limited to nodal points on the major communications networks that traversed this mountainous region.[134] Such factors continued to influence the post-Constantinian expansion of Balkan Christianity. In Noricum, for example, there were few communities in the mountains: most were concentrated in the valley of the river Drava, one of the most important communications arteries leading up from the Danube plain.[135] Such evidence implies that the advance of Christianity in the Balkans depended as much on environmental factors, both physical and human, as it did in northern Italy.

If the growth of north Italian Christianity bears most similarities to the situation along the Adriatic coast of Dalmatia and in the Danubian provinces, this may help us to appreciate something of the chronology of its evangelization. The churches scattered around the Adriatic and in the Balkans cannot be traced before the middle of the third century; nor can the congregations of northern Italy. It has been seen that in the archaeological record it is in most cases impossible to find any Christian community much earlier than c. 300. For once, the hagiographical record seems to be in accord with the testimony of other sources. The *passiones* of the various

---

[131] Mócsy, *Pannonia and Upper Moesia*, 259, 325–6.

[132] Rougé, 'Ports et escales', 121; Wilkes, *Dalmatia*, 220–3.

[133] Domnius: Wilkes, *Dalmatia*, 429. Anastasius: Zeiller, *Origines chrétiennes dans la province romaine de Dalmatie*, 60.

[134] On the influence of Balkan geography on its historical development in late antiquity and the Byzantine period: Obolensky, *Byzantine Commonwealth*, 5–24; Whitby, *Emperor Maurice*, 59–66.

[135] Alföldy, *Noricum*, 208–10, 279–81.

martyrs venerated in northern Italy do not—apart from some
patently fictional examples of first-century martyrdoms such as
the spurious *acta* of those Ambrosian discoveries Gervasius and
Protasius, or the eighth-century accounts of Hadrianic martyrs at
Brescia—put their narratives much earlier than the reigns of emperors from the mid-third century; most, indeed, are placed at the
time of the tetrarchs.[136] Taken by itself, it is impossible to know how
much hagiography is pure invention, and how much preserves half-
remembered realities; but in the case of northern Italy, all the evidence taken together seems to suggest that the Christians of that region
cannot have been very numerous prior to the middle of the third
century.[137]

Conclusion

This chapter has ranged widely in order to trace and interpret
Christian origins in northern Italy; it will be helpful, therefore,
to summarize its findings. At the outset it should be stated that
the archaeological record is fundamental for an appreciation of the
growth of north Italian Christianity. Not only does it increase our
knowledge of congregations beyond what can possibly be known
from medieval sources and conciliar *acta*; it also grants us tantalizing glimpses of the various Christian communities set in the context of their immediate surroundings. A warning, however, is also
necessary. For a statistical analysis, archaeological evidence is a
capricious ally, and what we know from it depends on accidents of
destruction and excavation.

By correlating all the evidence, it is clear that by the middle decades
of the fourth century there were some twenty identifiable—and probably an unknowable number of uinidentifiable—Christian communities scattered across the Po valley and in *Venetia et Histria*. This
'scatter' was not uniform: the density of Christian communities varied from region to region, with the highest concentrations closest
to the Adriatic coast, especially in *Venetia et Histria*, where they
cluster along the main communications routes emanating from

---

[136] See Appendix on the martyrs of northern Italy.

[137] Tramontin, 'Origini del cristianesimo nel Veneto', 105, concludes: 'Solo con le
ultime gravi persecuzioni, a cominciare da quella di Decio (250 d. C.), la *Venetia et
Histria* è bagnata dal sangue dei primi cristiani.'

Aquileia. It seems that Christianity took hold first in certain towns and cities which, for a variety of reasons ranging from trade to imperial and regional administration, had regular contacts with communities outside their immediate vicinities. That Christianity should exploit such pre-existing networks is not surprising: these matrices were the framework within which, to a greater or lesser extent, all private cults spread, as comparison with the expansion of Isis worship and Judaism has demonstrated. A similar analysis shows that while the chronology of the early evangelization of northern Italy is difficult to determine precisely, a number of factors point to late development. In the western Mediterranean, Christianity was distributed most widely first in those regions bordering the Tyrrhenian sea: Africa, southern Gaul, Rome, Latium, and Campania. Northern Italy, by contrast, seems to have shared in the slower development observable in the lands around the Adriatic coast and in the northern Balkans. These were the regions, after all, with which northern Italy had long and frequent cultural contacts. Neither archaeology nor literary and documentary evidence can demonstrate the existence of north Italian Christian communities earlier than the middle of the third century. Both in the manner and in the chronology of its dissemination, then, north Italian Christianity can be shown to have been deeply influenced by the human environment of the Po valley and *Venetia et Histria*. In the chapters that follow, we will trace how the north Italian churches continued to negotiate their social, political, and cultural milieu in the tumultuous years of the fourth century.

PART II

North Italian Christian communities in the fourth century

Some names count for more, and others that count for less are due to be struck out. The revisionary effort is not aimed at producing the perfect optic flat. The mirror, if that is what history is, distorts as much after revision as it did before.

Mary Douglas

4

Regional churches and imperial policy

If the origins and early development of north Italian Christianity were influenced by the region's human environment, so too was its further evolution in the fourth century. This was, of course, a period when successive emperors took a personal interest in the regulation of ecclesiastical matters, and throughout the century, north Italian social dynamics were transformed periodically by visits of the imperial court. This chapter will examine the impact of imperial intervention on north Italian Christianity between, roughly speaking, Constantine's involvement in the Donatist schism after his victory in 312 and the death of Theodosius I at Milan in January 395. Analysis of these events will proceed from the perspective of neither the Roman state nor the Church of the Mediterranean region as a whole,[1] but of the north Italian bishops themselves. This sequence of relations between bishops and emperors guided the transformation of many aspects of north Italian Christian life in terms of institutional, liturgical, and social development, some of which areas will be the particular concern of later chapters. Therefore this chapter will provide the framework within which those developments will be analysed. Its primary focus, however, will be the transformation of north Italian ecclesiastical relationships with other parts of the Mediterranean world, and how these contacts influenced the evolving theological outlook of the region's bishops. First it is necessary to examine how the north Italian episcopate came to be involved in these wider ecclesiastical debates.[2]

---

[1] I will not be using the term 'Imperial Church', which is probably an anachronistic concept: Barnes, *Athanasius*, 168–73; cf. the important analysis of Illyrican bishops such as Valens of Mursa in Hunt, 'Did Constantius II Have "Court Bishops"?'.

[2] My intention is not, however, to give an exhaustive survey of the *minutiae* of north Italian involvement in these doctrinal debates: that would repeat unnecessarily what has already been treated in several excellent recent studies: esp. McLynn, *Ambrose*, chs. 1–3, and Williams, *Ambrose*, chs. 1–6; cf. Barnes, *Athanasius*, and Hanson, *Search*, for an examination of ecclesiastical and doctrinal affairs from a wider perspective.

Emperors and bishops: patterns of interaction

Any study of north Italian church politics is fraught with difficulty because of the nature of our sources. Much of what we know about early Christianity in northern Italy depends on accounts of doctrinal or ecclesiological debates produced in confrontational contexts. Authors such as Hilary of Poitiers and Athanasius of Alexandria had particular aims which influenced their selection—even manipulation—of materials for inclusion in their writings.[3] They were often actual participants in the events they describe, with the result that such disputes could seem so all-encompassing to them that they might ignore developments elsewhere in the empire.[4] Also, the focus of the sources is rarely on northern Italy, so that for much of the fourth century we must depend on incidental mentions of Italian participants in events elsewhere. For example, we have seen how the very first appearance of bishops from the region in the historical record arises from Constantine's intervention in the Donatist schism in Africa. Only when the region hosted events important for doctrinal development do our sources focus on northern Italy: the holding of councils, such as that at Rimini in 359, was one such type of event; another was the imperial presence itself. Thus the history of the 'political' development of north Italian Christianity often consists of a sequence of snapshots, taken at times of imperial intervention, in the form of either passive presence or active involvement, in the region. There is, however, a qualitative and quantitative change in the evidence for the period after 374, when Ambrose was elected bishop of Milan. Thereafter, his own letters and works of exegesis and instruction, together with a rich seam of evidence from historical and biographical works, throw light as never before—and rarely after—on the minutiae of Christian life in late antique northern Italy. Even from this patchy testimony, however, it is clear that there was a development in the nature of this relationship between emperors and bishops, and that it did much to shape the character of north Italian Christianity, reinforcing existing foci of activity, and introducing new ones.

[3] Humphries, '*In Nomine Patris*'; id., 'Savage Humour'.
[4] Optatus of Milevus, for example, compiled an account of the Donatist schism which omits any reference to Athanasius or Constantius II, the great antagonists of the Christological dispute: Setton, *Christian Attitude*, 54 and n. 71.

Imperial guidance and ecclesiastical policy

The period under discussion is one in which the relationship between church and empire underwent radical change. With Constantine's conversion and proclamation of religious toleration, the Roman government ceased to be an agent of persecution (in theory) and its apparatus adopted a friendly attitude towards Christianity. Soon the north African clergy applied to Constantine for arbitration on the disputed episcopal succession at Carthage; but it was not long before they dispensed with their deferential timidity and happily pestered the emperor at court.[5] In northern Italy, however, the relationship seems to have retained its tentative character rather longer,[6] and until the death of Constantius II in 361, it was normally characterized by the region's episcopate responding to the demands of the emperor.

The tentative nature of these initial contacts is implicit in the selection of north Italian bishops who attended Constantine's councils at Rome in 313 and Arles in 314. At Rome we find bishops Merocles of Milan, Constantius of Faenza, and Stennius of Rimini, in addition to seven bishops from central and southern Italy, including Miltiades of Rome, as well as three from Gaul. While the presence of central and southern Italian clerics undoubtedly reflects the influence of Miltiades in summoning the tribunal,[7] the northerners probably attended because of personal invitations from Constantine himself. The emperor's role in assembling the bishops is sometimes underestimated,[8] yet it is clear that the presence of many participants at the synod was the direct result of Constantine's intervention. From Africa he had summoned bishops from both sides in the dispute (Eus. *HE* 10. 5. 19), and their dispatch was overseen by the proconsul Anullinus.[9]

---

[5] Frend, *Donatist Church*, 149–59.   [6] Cf. Turner, 'Adversaria Critica', 286.
[7] They are probably to be identified with the *septem eiusdem communionis* mentioned in Constantine's letter to Aelafius (*Corpus Optati* 3: Maier, *Dossier du donatisme*, i. 154, lines 16–25).
[8] Frend, *Donatist Church*, 148, writes: 'Constantine informed Miltiades of his intention [to hold a council] . . . Miltiades, however, appears to have used the opportunity to transform the small ecclesiastical tribunal which the Emperor convoked into a council under his presidency, dominated by Italian bishops.' But Frend seems to be imputing to Miltiades anachronistic pretensions to hegemony, of the type claimed by bishops of Rome only with the pontificate of Damasus (cf. pp. 156–8 below).
[9] Barnes, *New Empire*, 169–70. There is plenty of evidence of Anullinus' role in Carthaginian church politics, not least in the form of his own correspondence: apud Aug. *Ep.* 88. 2; cf. Eus. *HE* 10. 5. 15–17; 6. 4; 7. 1–2.

Miltiades' own participation was itself dependent on Constantine's wishes (ibid., 10. 5. 18–20). Constantine also wrote to the three Gallic bishops, Maternus of Cologne, Reticius of Autun, and Marinus of Arles, ordering them to make their way to Rome (ibid., 10. 5. 19). Their attendance provides a model for the participation of the northern Italians. That Constantine wrote to the Gallic bishops demanding their attendance at the forthcoming synod suggests that they had somehow come to the emperor's attention before, during the ten years when Constantine had resided in Gaul after assuming the purple,[10] and when, as Lactantius affirms, he had left Christianity unmolested (*De mort. pers.* 24. 9; *Div. Inst.* 1. 1. 3).[11] It would not be surprising to find Constantine in dialogue with bishops at this time: Ossius of Cordoba had already attached himself to the emperor's entourage, while Constantine's interpretation of his fateful vision before the Battle of the Milvian Bridge suggests that he had discussed religious matters with Christian teachers.[12]

Constantine's connections with the bishops of Milan, Faenza, and Rimini can be incorporated into this context. Prior to the Roman council, there were two periods during which the emperor was active in northern Italy and when he could have come into contact with the bishops who were to attend. First, there were his operations there in spring and summer 312, immediately before he marched on Rome. He had entered Italy via the Cottian Alps, through Susa and Turin,[13] whence he moved on Milan, Brescia, and Verona,[14] before turning south towards Modena, the Apennines, and Rome.[15] Our knowledge of Constantine's movements through the Apennines is defective: we hear nothing of him between his departure from Modena and his victory at the Milvian Bridge. Yet Aurelius Victor's

[10] Constantine in Gaul: Barnes, *New Empire*, 68–73. Maternus' see at Cologne was not far from Trier, where Constantine established his major residence. Reticius could have met the emperor when Constantine visited Autun during or just before his *Quinquennalia*. Marinus may have encountered Constantine during the war against Maximian in 310, in which the Rhône valley, Arles, and Marseille had been the major theatres of operations (*Pan. Lat.* 7(1). 14–20; Lact., *De mort. pers.* 29. 5–8). Pietri characterized these bishops as the emperor's spiritual confidants (*Roma Christiana* 160–1). Reticius could have fulfilled such a role: he was later famed as an exegete and polemicist against heresy (Hier., *De vir. ill.* 87).

[11] Creed (Lactantius, *De Mortibus Persecutorum*, 105–6) argues that this may simply mean that Constantine failed to implement anti-Christian legislation rather than make any formal legal statement himself; *contra* Barnes, 'Lactantius and Constantine', 43–6.

[12] Lane Fox, *Pagans and Christians*, 616–17; Barnes, *Constantine and Eusebius*, 43.

[13] *Pan. Lat.* 9 (12). 6; 10 (4). 17. 3; 21. 1; 22. 2.

[14] *Pan. Lat.* 9 (12). 7; 10 (4). 25–7.　　　　[15] *Pan. Lat.* 10 (4). 27.

remarks on Maxentius' defensive measures imply that Constantine journeyed along the Via Aemilia to Rimini and Fano, and then towards Rome along the Via Flaminia. Maxentius marched out of Rome to Saxa Rubra, nine Roman miles north of the capital (*Caes.* 40. 23).[16] Since Saxa Rubra lay on the Via Flaminia,[17] it is logical to assume that Constantine was advancing along the same road in the opposite direction. Thus Constantine's itinerary in northern Italy during 312, which had already included Milan, would have brought him through Faenza and then Rimini, affording him the opportunity to have contacted all three north Italian bishops who attended the Roman synod a year later. Certainly, these months had seen many cities abandon all allegiance towards Maxentius, while resistance offered to Constantine's progress had been offered only by detachments of troops sent out from Rome.[18]

It might be objected that the bishops might have been unwilling to side with Constantine while the war was as yet undecided, but this argument lacks force bearing in mind the wholesale defection of northern Italy to Constantine's cause and the probable presence of Ossius of Cordoba in the imperial entourage at this time. At any rate, in the aftermath of Constantine's Christian victory at the Milvian Bridge on 28 October 312, such reticence on the part of bishops will have disappeared. Constantine's northward progress in early 313—which probably retraced the route along the Flaminian and Aemilian roads[19]—would have afforded another opportunity for

---

[16] *Contra* Moreau, 'Pont Milvius ou Saxa Rubra?', 369–73 (followed by Barnes, *Constantine and Eusebius*, 305 n. 144), I see no reason for rejecting Aurelius Victor's version of events in favour of a reference from the *Historia Augusta*: even if Aurelius Victor has interpreted some events of Septimius Severus' battle for Rome in 193 in the light of what happened in 312, it does not follow automatically that he transferred details in the opposite direction from 193 to 312. Further, Moreau's faith in details provided by Lactantius' *De mort. pers.* 44 seems misplaced. Lactantius' account of the battle is couched in high-flown rhetoric—he quotes the *Aeneid* twice in the space of only a few lines (44. 6, 9)—and presents it as a cosmic struggle with Constantine's Christian dream (44. 5) opposed to Maxentius' consultation of oracles (44. 1, 8). It is also chronologically confused: in the middle of the battle, Lactantius suddenly returns to events in Rome immediately beforehand (44. 6–9). Similarly, Lactantius is ignorant of Maxentius' bridge of boats (see Barnes, *Constantine and Eusebius*, 305–6, now tacitly refuting Moreau!).

[17] Ashby, *Roman Campagna*, 247–9.

[18] Barnes, *Constantine and Eusebius*, 41–2.

[19] As with the previous year, we have no precise information on Constantine's route through the Apennines. Details of imperial journeys between Rome and Milan are scarce, but they seem to point to use of the viae Flaminia and Aemilia: e.g. *CTh* 9. 35. 5 (Theodosius at Forum Flaminii in 389). This was also the route taken by Sidonius, en route to Rome from Gaul (*Ep.* 1. 5).

the bishops to have greeted the new emperor. By March, Constantine was established in Milan (*CTh* 10. 8. 1), and succeeding events make it probable that bishop Merocles will have met him soon afterwards.

Constantine's visit to Milan would have been celebrated with customary civic ceremonial, and its significance would have been heightened by the arrival there also of the eastern emperor Licinius,[20] who married Constantia, Constantine's sister, in an ostentatious display of imperial unity (Lact., *De mort. pers.* 45. 1). The imperial ceremonies may have been given a Christian flavour: Easter fell on 29 March, and Constantine, rejoicing in his victorious new faith, perhaps joined the Christians of Milan for their celebrations of the feast, much as he did at other cities later in his reign.[21] The Christian hue of the western emperor's new interests was made explicit during this double imperial visit, when both Constantine and Licinius promulgated a directive on religious freedom for all their subjects, and especially the Christians. Copies were posted throughout the empire. We know of their existence at Caesarea in Palestine (Eus., *HE* 10. 5. 2–14) and at Nicomedia in Bithynia (Lact., *De mort. pers.* 48. 2–12), and the same must have been true at Milan. By this time, moreover, Constantine will have become involved in efforts to settle the Donatist dispute in Africa, thereby advertising his sympathy for Christian causes. Bearing in mind such aspects of the emperor's behaviour at Milan, it is hardly credible that bishop Merocles would have remained unknown to him or his officials.[22]

Direct imperial intervention is the most likely explanation for the north Italian presence in 314 at Arles too. Constantine was concerned that the Council of Arles should have a broader basis of authority to resolve the African schism: the Donatists had complained that the previous year's assembly had been drawn from too narrow a selection of bishops. In summoning bishops from a wider area, therefore, Constantine intended the pronouncements of Arles to be

[20] Coins minted at Pavia proclaimed the double imperial epiphany: Sutherland, *Roman Imperial Coinage*, vi. 277–8 and 296 (no. 111); cf. 297 (nos. 112–14).

[21] Most famously on the occasion when he delivered his *Oration to the Assembly of the Saints*, perhaps at Antioch in 325: Lane Fox, *Pagans and Christians*, 627–32.

[22] Eus., *HE* 10. 5. 18–20 preserves a letter from Constantine to Miltiades and a certain, unidentified Marcus. Some have claimed that the 'Marcus' of Eusebius 'is a misrendering or corruption of "Merocli", and that Merocles of Milan ... is meant': Turner, 'Adversaria critica', 285. But the emendation of 'Marcus' may be unnecessary: Pietri, *Roma Christiana*, 154; id., 'Appendice prosopographique', 386; Maier, *Dossier du donatisme*, i. 149 n. 4. He may have been a minor cleric who acted as legate from Miltiades to Constantine.

representative of a catholic Church (Eus., *HE* 10. 5. 23). The attendance of the bishops of Milan 'ex prouincia Italia' and Aquileia 'ex prouincia Dalmatia',[23] therefore, formed part of the emperor's plan. Constantine's links with Milan have been demonstrated; they can be shown also for Aquileia. It had been one of the cities which had defected to Constantine during his march on Rome (*Pan. Lat.* 9 (12). 11. 1). In the early years of uneasy peace between Constantine and Licinius the city lay on the sensitive frontier between their respective jurisdictions; and when war did eventually flare up, the spark was ignited at Emona, just across the Julian Alps.[24] Aquileia was, therefore, an important city in Constantine's strategic planning during his conquest of Italy and the consolidation of his power. In this context Theodore of Aquileia may have come to Constantine's attention, especially if, as will be argued in the next chapter, his episcopal influence extended across the mountains to Christians living under Licinius.[25]

Constantine's increasing concentration on eastern affairs after his war against Licinius in 316/17 marks the end of one phase in the relationship between emperor and church in northern Italy. The next glimpse of the region's bishops involved in the religious politics of the empire is during the Christological controversy. The next council after Arles attended by north Italian bishops was that at Serdica in 343. This had only met, so we are told, because Constans had threatened civil war on his brother Constantius II if no synod was called.[26] That Constans was so insistent on convening a council was in no small part due to the energetic representations at his court of the exiled Athanasius of Alexandria, in which he had been assisted by north Italian episcopal colleagues. This does not represent newfound bravado among the north Italian episcopate: any ecclesiastical manoeuvring would have been undertaken by Athanasius, by now an adept player in palace politics.[27]

The most decisive example of imperial summons being issued to north Italians, however, came after Constans' death, when Constantius II extended his mopping up operations after his victory over the

---

[23] The ramifications of this designation for Theodore's ecclesiastical jurisdiction are discussed in the next chapter (p. 143).

[24] Barnes, *Constantine and Eusebius*, 66.   [25] Cf. p. 143 below.

[26] For a sceptical discussion of the sources, cf. Hanson, *Search*, 307–8. Athanasius, however, was concerned to exonerate himself before Constantius of any charge that he had fomented Constans' hostility (*Apol. Const.* 2 and *passim*).

[27] Barnes, *Athanasius*, 47–93 *passim*.

western usurper Magnentius to the ecclesiastical sphere.[28] In 353, Constantius had called a second Council of Arles, where those who opposed his attempts to achieve theological conformity across the empire were summarily exiled and replaced with more malleable candidates.[29] Two years later it was Italy's turn to learn the full ferocity of direct imperial intervention in ecclesiastical affairs: the resulting council, at Milan in 355, was to prove a turning point in the political development of north Italian Christianity. Our sources for this council are lamentably poor, even to the extent that we do not know with full certainty beyond a few names who attended its debates.[30] Yet one aspect of the meeting is undeniable: whereas previously north Italian Christians had been used to the rather remote exercise of imperial power to summon bishops to meetings, the arrival of Constantius II heralded an altogether more interventionist policy, the aftershocks of which continued to rumble until the time of Ambrose.

At Milan, as at the Councils of Sirmium in 351 and Arles in 353, Constantius' wishes were communicated to the assembly by a group of bishops from Asia Minor and Illyricum, bound by their common subscription to the emperor's current favoured credal formula—*homoios*, that Christ was *like* the Father—and by their opposition to Athanasius.[31] Yet any semblance of ecclesiastical autonomy ended here, as it was the emperor himself who determined the composition and outcome of the synod.[32] The surviving records of the council show that Constantius' aim was once again to achieve ecclesiastical harmony throughout his domain,[33] with condemnation of Athanasius certainly part of the scheme.[34] Constantius' presence lurked in the background throughout the proceedings, and when it seemed that the meeting would not deliver the outcome desired by the emperor, the bishops were transferred to the imperial palace for the final sessions (Hil. Pict., *Coll. Ant. Par.* App. II. 3). This sort of imperial intervention in a council must have been shockingly new to the north Italians. Worse ensued. When Dionysius of Milan (after some vacillation) and Eusebius of Vercelli refused to submit to

[28] Even before his outright victory in 353 Constantius was crafting his ecclesiastical policy for the west: Barnes, *Athanasius*, 105–15.

[29] Barnes, *Athanasius*, 115–17; Hanson, *Search*, 329–32.

[30] Above pp. 49–50.   [31] Barnes, *Athanasius*, 109–20.

[32] Pietri, 'La politique de Constance II', esp. 146–65.

[33] This was clear to Eusebius of Vercelli, who, writing to Constantius, acknowledged the emperor's desire to secure 'per orbem terrarum firma pax ecclesiastica' (*Ep.* 1. 1).

[34] Barnes, *Athanasius*, 117.

Constantius' wishes, they were exiled to the eastern Mediterranean. At Milan, moreover, a new bishop was installed to replace Dionysius: the non-Latin-speaking Cappadocian Auxentius (Athan., *Hist. Ar.* 75). The remainder of Constantius' reign saw the bishops of northern Italy content to follow the emperor's demands. In 359, in a further effort to achieve unity throughout his realm, Constantius called a universal council, split into two assemblies. The easterners met at Seleucia in Isauria, while the westerners converged on northern Italy, at Rimini. No complete list of the participants survives, but we can be sure that Auxentius of Milan was there; we can hypothesize that bishops who were not stridently pro-Nicene or pro-Athanasian— such as Fortunatianus of Aquileia and Urbanus of Parma—may also have attended. At precisely this time, Fortunatianus was active on Constantius' behalf in another way, bringing the once defiant Liberius of Rome into the homoian camp.[35]

The next example of imperial intervention in the affairs of the north Italian church comes early in the reign of Valentinian I (364–75). By the early 360s, the exiles of Constantius' councils had returned to the west, where they sought to undo the achievement of the previous decade; in northern Italy, Auxentius of Milan found himself a target of their activities.[36] During Valentinian's residence at Milan in 365, Hilary of Poitiers, and perhaps also Eusebius of Vercelli, sought to topple Auxentius, by stirring up trouble against him.[37] The plot soon came to the attention of Valentinian. Despite his famed reluctance to become embroiled in religious disputes (Amm. Marc. 30. 9. 5), Valentinian chose to act in a manner reminiscent of the newly converted Constantine: unwilling to impose his own decision on the Church, he nevertheless sought to expedite their decision-making process. He summoned ten bishops—of unknown origin but possibly north Italians—to Milan where they met under secular scrutiny (*in foro*) to consider Auxentius' case. The bishop of Milan answered charges of heresy with a clever Latin phrase, the ambiguity of which satisfied the ten bishops that he was orthodox.[38] This

---

[35] Below, pp. 154–6.   [36] Williams, *Ambrose*, 76–83.

[37] The source for this is Hilary's own *Contra Auxentium*, a very imprecise text: cf. Williams, 'Anti-Arian Campaigns of Hilary of Poitiers', 7–22, arguing—against the standard interpretation—that Eusebius did not participate in the 365 campaign.

[38] Auxentius' creed is given in Hil. Pict., *C. Aux.* 14. The crucial passage is where Auxentius affirms 'credo ... in filium eius unigenitum Dominum nostrum Iesum Christum, ante omnia saecula et ante omne principum natum ex Patre *Deum verum filium* ex vero Deo patre'. Hilary noted at the time that it was unclear whether Auxentius' formula 'Deum verum filium' ascribed *veritas* to God (i.e. 'Deum

was sufficient to convince Valentinian, but when Hilary persisted in trying to undermine Auxentius' position, the bishop of Poitiers found himself expelled from the city by the imperial authorities (Hil. Pict., *C. Aux.* 9). Valentinian's intervention over Auxentius was the last time a fourth-century emperor imposed a decision on the north Italian church. The issues at stake, moreover, had been primarily ones of ecclesiastical and social order, rather than doctrine. When Valentinian expelled Hilary, he was probably more worried about the threat posed by the bishop of Poitiers to peaceful civic life in Milan.[39] This was markedly different from the domineering attitude of Constantius II, and it marks a stage in the transformation of relations between the Church and the Roman state in northern Italy. When next an emperor becomes involved with north Italian bishops, it is Gratian tacitly submitting to the persuasion of the new bishop of Milan, Ambrose.

Episcopal action from Eusebius to Ambrose

While much of the north Italian involvement in wider ecclesiastical disputes was determined by the emperor himself, the period after Constantine also saw mounting self-confidence on the part of bishops who were determined to negotiate religious issues rather than submit to imperial dictate. In the dynamic characters of Eusebius of Vercelli and Ambrose of Milan, north Italian Christianity found leaders willing to champion the autonomy of the Church from imperial control. The first attempt was unsuccessful. When Eusebius of Vercelli arrived at the Council of Milan in 355, he sought to take control of the proceedings by insisting on an affirmation of the creed of Nicaea. To this end, he produced a copy of the creed and gave it to Dionysius of Milan for his signature, thus provoking the Illyrican bishop Valens of Mursa's notorious outburst in which he snatched the pen from Dionysius' hand before he could sign (Hil. Pict., *Coll. Ant. Par.* App. II. 3). The significance of Eusebius' intervention is clear from the list of signatures which records Dionysius of Milan among those who subscribed to the council's

verum') or to the Son (i.e. 'verum filium'), and that in this way he obscured his heresy (*C. Aux.* 8). Cf. McLynn, *Ambrose*, 26, for discussion.

[39] The substance of Auxentius' complaint to Valentinian was that Hilary and Eusebius had stirred up the Milanese plebs against him: apud *C. Aux.* 13; 'aliqui ex plebe . . . nunc amplius excitati ab Hilario et Eusebio, perturbantes quosdam . . .'.

condemnation of Athanasius.[40] Eusebius' aim in submitting the creed of Nicaea for ratification had been to overturn the previous achievements of the council. Moreover, Eusebius had been concerned to come to the council on his own terms. It was already in session for some days by the time he arrived:[41] he had received letters from Constantius, the papal legates (among them Lucifer of Cagliari), and the assembly as a whole entreating him to come.[42] When at last he agreed to attend, he determined to set at nought the decisions the assembly had already made. It was to this end he produced his copy of the creed of Nicaea. A daring gesture, to be sure, but also one that ended in failure: Eusebius' actions came up against the resistance of an emperor determined to achieve a preordained outcome to the synod. As a result, Eusebius earned a sentence of exile for himself, and for Dionysius whom he had persuaded to change sides.

It was to be twenty years before another north Italian bishop stood up to an emperor as Eusebius had done. Elected to succeed Auxentius in 374, Ambrose of Milan set about expunging the last traces of Constantius' homoian achievement from northern Italy and Illyricum. That he was able to do so depended on his gaining the compliance of the emperor Gratian, who from 379 was to be a regular visitor to Milan.[43] It was to be no easy triumph, for at first he had to answer charges of heresy levelled against him by the homoian bishops of Illyricum.[44] Their capacity to undermine the new bishop of Milan's position was shown by their success—albeit fleeting—in persuading Gratian to hand over a Milanese basilica for the use of homoian Christians.[45] It was in response to such challenges that Ambrose penned the first two books of his *De Fide*, in which he sought to justify his theological position to the emperor and win imperial support for his anti-homoian campaigns.[46] Thus the work included a heavy dose of well-judged flattery directed at

[40] The list begins: 'nomina episcoporum qui subscripserunt in Athanasium', and Dionysius occurs twenty-first: Smulders, *Hilary of Poitiers' Preface*, 109–12. Cf. pp. 49–50 above.

[41] McLynn, *Ambrose*, 13–22, gives a better reading of these events than Williams, *Ambrose*, 52–8. Williams' extremely revisionist account is vitiated by his failure to acknowledge that Dionysius had initially condemned Athanasius.

[42] Ed. in *CCL* 9 (1957), 119–21.

[43] For the importance of Gratian's presence, due to the Gothic war beyond the Julian Alps, see McLynn, *Ambrose*, 88–106.

[44] McLynn, *Ambrose*, 92–8.

[45] For this obscure episode: Williams, 'Ambrose, Emperors and Homoians'.

[46] Full discussion in Williams, *Ambrose*, 128–53.

the emperor: facing the greatest crisis of his reign, a Gothic war
in the Balkans with effectively himself alone as emperor, Gratian
seems to have found Ambrose's confident predictions of victory
attractive. The predictions were couched, moreover, in language that
made victory inseparable from acceptance of Ambrose's brand of
Christology.[47]

In the years that followed, Ambrose exploited Gratian's frequent presence in the region to bring the emperor under his religious influence. Gratian was, it seems, now interested in resolving
the Christological controversy; embarrassingly, Theodosius I, his
eastern appointee as emperor—and hence of junior rank in the
imperial college—got there first with the Council of Constantinople in May 381.[48] Ambrose offered Gratian a solution: a western council convened immediately to investigate the orthodoxy of
two Illyrican bishops, the redoubtable Palladius of Ratiaria and his
fellow homoian, Secundianus of Singidunum.[49] The council met at
Aquileia in September, and Ambrose dominated proceedings from
the first, even though Aquileia's own bishop, Valerian, would have
had nominal presidency. It soon became apparent that Ambrose would
accept nothing less than the condemnation of the Illyricans for heresy.
Protest as he may that Ambrose was perverting the instructions given
for the council by Gratian (*Acta conc. Aquil.* 6–8), Palladius was
unable to stop the bishop of Milan savouring his triumph. With the
conclusion of the council, Ambrose wrote to Gratian to inform him
of its outcome (*Ep.* 10). To be sure, the letter observed all the conventions of respect due to an Augustus, but in Ambrose's relationship with Gratian, the wishes of the bishop had become the wishes
of the emperor.

Where Eusebius had found failure, Ambrose discovered success.
The infuriatingly intangible contribution of character is a crucial factor in understanding why. To be sure, Eusebius was a determined
advocate of Nicene orthodoxy, even to the point of defying the
emperor, but in Constantius II he had an adversary determined
to use the full weight of imperial force to achieve his own conception

[47] Particularly *De Fide* 1. 1 (where Ambrose flatters Gratian and assures him
of victory) and 2. 136–42 (where the victory over the Goths is made a reward for
orthodoxy).
[48] McLynn, *Ambrose*, 124–5.
[49] For the council, the best account remains Gryson, *Scolies ariennes*; cf. Williams,
Ambrose, 169–84, for a review of recent scholarship.

of ecclesiastical and doctrinal unity. In Ambrose too we have a dynamic bishop, but Gratian was no Constantius II. A serious young man of academic bent, Ambrose's emperor was malleable by theological persuasion. At the outset of his reign, he had found himself beset by protestations of orthodoxy from both Palladius and Ambrose; in the end Ambrose proved the more persuasive, and domination of the Council of Aquileia was his reward.

Ambrose was not to enjoy unqualified imperial support for much longer: in August 383, Gratian fell victim to the usurpation of Magnus Maximus, who now took control of Britain, Gaul, and Spain, while Italy, western Illyricum, and Africa passed under the supervision of the boy Valentinian II. At first Ambrose was willing to cooperate with Valentinian, and travelled on his behalf to Gaul to negotiate a truce with the usurper Maximus.[50] The relationship soon began to deteriorate, however, as Ambrose found it impossible to acquiesce in the actions of the real power at court, the emperor's mother, Justina. The kernel of the problem lay in Justina's own credal preferences, for she subscribed to the same homoian beliefs as those bishops condemned at the Council of Aquileia; indeed, among Justina's minions was another heterodox bishop, the fugitive Auxentius of Durostorum.[51] Robbed of imperial support, Ambrose's position now looked altogether more unstable: it would demand all the resources of his forceful personality, together with not a little ruthless opportunism, to win the day.

The conflict that followed focused on disputes over the use of Milanese basilicas for Easter services in 385 and 386.[52] By demanding a basilica for use by homoians, Justina and Valentinian presented a very real challenge to Ambrose's authority as bishop in his own city;[53] indeed, much of Ambrose's response was underpinned by his need to consolidate his position. Yet this was not merely a competition for political supremacy in Milanese affairs: in a very real sense, Ambrose's actions were directed to maintaining the integrity of the Milanese church, in terms both of its buildings, and, equally

---

[50] McLynn, *Ambrose*, 160–2.   [51] Williams, *Ambrose*, 202–10.
[52] It would be superfluous here to present another detailed account of these events, as two excellent recent studies have treated the subject exhaustively. McLynn, *Ambrose*, 158–219, is sensitive to the volatile nature of the politics of Milan, especially the tensions at the imperial court; Williams, *Ambrose*, 185–217, is less nuanced on the imperial context, but provides the most thorough analysis of the often overlooked theological dimension to the conflict.
[53] Cf. below pp. 168–9 for the context.

important, of the souls of its congregations. His characterization of Justina as Jezebel, while it is certainly extreme, eloquently evokes the intense danger she posed to the Church, both spiritually as a heretic, and physically in her willingness to mobilize Goths from the palatine guard against Ambrose and his supporters.[54] The bishop's responses, particularly during the events of 386, are well known. Augustine, who resided at Milan at this time and was witness to the whole crisis, testifies to the bishop's powerful and persuasive preaching in these years (*Conf.* 5. 13. 23; 6. 2. 2). By such virtuoso performances, Ambrose was able to galvanize his flock into a public display of resistance, as they occupied the basilica before Justina's troops could. The Milanese congregation famously sang praises to Heaven (Aug., *Conf.* 9. 7. 15; Paul. Med., *V. Ambr.* 13), and together with their bishop they soon received an astonishing sign of the divine favour they enjoyed. In the cemeteries to the west of the city, Ambrose and his flock unearthed relics of the martyrs Gervasius and Protasius. After some miraculous demonstrations of their power, the bodies were brought in triumphal procession to the newly completed Ambrosian basilica and interred there.[55] For Ambrose, these relics were heavenly trophies (*Ep.* 22. 4: 'animi sublimis tropaea'), and, together with the public acclamation that attended their translation, they provided Ambrose with a powerful endorsement of his resistance of Valentinian and Justina. Looking back on these events, Augustine believed that it was the discovery of the martyrs that secured Ambrose's victory over his would-be persecutors (*Conf.* 9. 7. 16). In any case, Valentinian and Justina soon had other worries, as the long anticipated invasion of Italy by Magnus Maximus grew ever more likely. With Ambrose once more in the ascendant, it was to him that Justina and Valentinian looked for a saviour to fend off the inevitable. Ambrose now made a second diplomatic mission to Maximus' court, but even he could not prevent the usurper's armies from pouring across the Alps in the summer of 387; bereft of all hope at home, the emperor and his mother fled to the eastern provinces.[56]

Maximus' conquest of Italy proved short-lived: a year later he was ousted by Theodosius I, who came to restore Valentinian. This turn

[54] Ambr., *Ep.* 20. 18: 'Quid dicam quod etiam Heliam Iezabel cruente persecuta est?'; the image is also evoked at *C. Aux.* 17–18.
[55] Main sources: Ambr., *Ep.* 22; Paul. Med., *V. Ambr.* 14; Aug., *Conf.* 9. 7. 16.
[56] Cf. McLynn, *Ambrose*, 218–19; Williams, *Ambrose*, 223–9.

of events presented Ambrose with an entirely new set of challenges. By now his old adversary, Justina, was dead, while Valentinian was soon dispatched to set up court in southern Gaul.[57] Milan became instead the principal residence of Theodosius, an emperor of unimpeachable orthodoxy, who had convened the Constantinopolitan council in 381 that had paved the way for a Nicene restoration throughout the empire.[58] Yet such theological sympathies were not enough to prevent a conflict between the emperor and the bishop. To an extent, some friction was inevitable: the entourage of easterners that followed Theodosius from Constantinople to Milan was a powerful group, bound by its own ties of friendship and patronage.[59] It was a group, moreover, over which Ambrose had no claims of influence.[60] For a bishop who had so recently trumped Valentinian and Justina, this situation looked uncertain. Yet the ensuing clash between emperor and bishop, although it certainly had much to do with conflicting political systems, was also deeply imbued with pastoral issues that were of the utmost importance to Ambrose. Early in his reign, during his campaigns against the Goths, Theodosius had fallen seriously ill, and, as it was anticipated that he should die, he had been baptized by Acholius, the Nicene bishop of Thessalonica.[61] Theodosius recovered, but the fact of his baptism was to add a distinctive texture to his relationship with Ambrose, permitting the bishop to act as arbiter for the emperor's soul. These were the years when Ambrose's reflections on baptism were to take shape in his *De Sacramentis*.[62] To a bishop who claimed that baptism had been devised 'lest the Devil's tricks and deceptions should prevail in this world' (*De Sacr.* 2. 6. 18), Theodosius' misdeeds simply could not be ignored.

The first breach came when Ambrose learned of events at Callinicum on the eastern frontier, where a Christian mob had destroyed a synagogue. In response, the imperial authorities in Syria had demanded that the bishop of Callinicum compensate the local Jewish community for their loss; when Theodosius heard of the dispute, he ratified this decision, but transferred the responsibility for making reparation to the local Roman military count.[63]

---

[57] Justina: Ruf., *HE* 12. 17. Valentinian: McLynn, *Ambrose*, 309.
[58] Hansen, *Search*, 804–23.   [59] Matthews, *Western Aristocracies*, 127–45.
[60] McLynn, *Ambrose*, 297–8, is most judicious.
[61] For these events, Ehrhardt, 'First Two Years', remains fundamental.
[62] Cf. Yarnold, *Awe-Inspiring Rites*, 98–9.
[63] Full and perceptive discussion of the episode in McLynn, *Ambrose*, 298–309.

Ambrose was incensed when he found out, and in a letter to Theodosius he complained at the injustice that made Christians, God's chosen people, pay compensation to the Jews, who denied the truth of the Incarnation (Ambr., *Ep.* 40. 9–20). Ambrose reserved his most devastating critique of Theodosius for the next church service attended by the emperor. Following a sermon in which he dwelt on the iniquity of the Jews in comparison to the gentleness of the Church (*Ep.* 41. 2–25), Ambrose challenged Theodosius to show gratitude for God's help in his recent victory over Maximus by rescinding the order to Callinicum (ibid., 26). A dramatic stand-off ensued, with the bishop refusing to perform the liturgy of the eucharist until Theodosius complied; in the end a begrudging emperor gave in to the bishop, and Ambrose resumed his service, in which, moreover, he claimed to feel the divine presence more strongly (ibid., 27–8). The Callinicum affair thus established the parameters for Ambrose's relationship with Theodosius. It was to be conducted on the basis of the emperor's membership of the Church, and the bishop's duty to see to it that Theodosius behaved as a baptized Christian. The next great rupture between them hinged upon precisely this issue.

In 390, and with Theodosius' consent, troops in Thessalonica massacred a crowd in the city's hippodrome in revenge for the linching of an imperial official. The ferocity of the action struck horror into the hearts of Theodosius' subjects, and in the aftermath, Theodosius did his best to restore confidence, issuing a law that, by granting a stay of thirty days between the issuing of a sentence and its implementation, sought to prevent any future lapse of imperial clemency.[64] So far as Theodosius' relationship with Ambrose was concerned, the massacre at Thessalonica precipitated one of their most memorable encounters, as the emperor submitted to the penitential rite at the Milanese cathedral. Whether or not this was merely an expedient demonstration of Theodosius' regret,[65] for Ambrose it offered another opportunity to act as spiritual impresario to the emperor. In his work on baptism, Ambrose remarked that the rite made the catechumen a participant in Christ's crucifixion: 'you are held with the nails of Our Lord Jesus Christ, lest the Devil drag

[64] *CTh* 9. 40. 13: cf. McLynn, *Ambrose*, 322–3 and n. 108 for discussion.
[65] Such is the complexion put on these events in McLynn's account (*Ambrose*, 315–30, esp. 323).

you away; the nail of Christ holds you firm, when human frailty calls you away'.[66] When Theodosius had condoned the massacre, such baptismal safeguards had deserted him, and he had fallen prey to the Devil and human weakness. Now Ambrose called upon him to cast sin from his kingdom (*Ep.* 51. 11) by seeking absolution.

The symbolism of Theodosius' willingness to join the penitents at Milan ought not to be underestimated, for it represented a significant reversal of the relationship between emperor and bishop since the time of Theodosius' arrival in the west. According to the historian Sozomen, the very first encounter between Ambrose and Theodosius had epitomized the awkward clash between their views of the relationship between church and emperor. During mass on his first Sunday in Milan, Theodosius, following his accustomed practice from Constantinople, had tried to enter the altar sanctuary, an area reserved for the clergy,[67] to receive the eucharist, whereupon he found himself summarily dismissed by an outraged Ambrose (Soz., *HE* 7. 25. 9). From equal of the clergy to selfless penitent was a remarkable journey for Theodosius to make, but it confirmed him as the most Christian of emperors, not just for Ambrose, but for generations to come. The transformation was manifest in the funeral oration Ambrose delivered over Theodosius' body after the emperor died at Milan on 17 January 395. In stark contrast to the rather disingenuous praise that Ambrose had delivered in a similar oration for Valentinian II less than three years before,[68] the impression given by the *De obitu Theodosii* is that the bishop had come to respect his emperor. Theodosius emerges as the most pious, merciful, and faithful of emperors (*De obitu Theod.* 12), and in tones of affecting sincerity Ambrose speaks of how the emperor truly deserves his place in heaven: 'I shall not desert him until, by tears and prayers, I will lead this man where he is called by his merits, "to the holy mountain of the Lord"' (*De obitu Theod.* 37). The funeral was emblematic of the change that had come over the relationship between emperor and episcopate in northern Italy. In 313 and 314, it was the emperor, Constantine, who had dictated the course of

---

[66] *De Sacr.* 2. 7. 23: 'clauis domini nostri Iesu Christi adheres, ne te diabolus inde possit abstrahere. Teneat te clauus Christi, quem reuocat humanae condicionis infirmitas.'

[67] For this, see p. 163 below.

[68] The *De Obitu Valentiniani*, on which see McLynn, *Ambrose*, 337–41.

events, summoning four north Italian bishops to attend the synods of Rome and Arles. By 395, however, amid the awesome splendour of his own cathedral, it was a bishop, Ambrose, who supervised the ceremonial dispatch of his emperor's soul to the realms of eternity.

Summary

The decades between 313 and 395 saw considerable development in imperial relations with the Church in northern Italy. For much of the period, the north Italian episcopate is no more than a shadowy presence, obediently following the summons of emperors to attend councils. Only later in the century, with Eusebius of Vercelli and, more particularly, Ambrose of Milan, is greater self-confidence apparent. When Ambrose sought Gratian's assistance in convening the Council of Aquileia, the resulting synod was organized along terms dictated by the bishop, not the emperor. Composed as it was of Ambrose's theological allies, the Aquileian synod was markedly different from Constantine's councils at Rome and Arles. The reasons for this change are bound up with the increasing involvement of north Italian ecclesiastics in the theological politics of the wider Mediterranean world, particularly the Christological controversy. With the advent of Constantius II, the character of north Italian ecclesiastical politics changed startlingly. For the first time, bishops from the region were confronted by an emperor whose ecclesiastical policy demanded adherence to a prescribed set of views. To some this proved intolerable, and their recalcitrance was rewarded by sentences of exile. In the resistance of Eusebius of Vercelli and, at his instigation, Dionysius of Milan, appears a germ of the strong-minded defence of ecclesiastical independence that becomes most visible in Ambrose. Yet, for all that, the development was by no means simple and without setbacks. As is clear from Valentinian I's role in the process initiated against Auxentius by Hilary, the emperor— even a relatively inactive one in the field of religious dispute—could still determine the course of ecclesiastical politics in northern Italy. Indeed, even Ambrose's preparations for the Council of Aquileia fit this pattern: the initial impetus for a council had been accusations of heresy filed against Ambrose by the homoian episcopate of Illyricum. That the council turned out to be a success for Ambrose owes much to his beguiling personality, a factor that was to be crucial in his ultimate domination of north Italian ecclesiastical affairs,[69] as well as in his defiance of emperors from Valentinian II to Theodosius I.

Defining deviance in northern Italy

These contacts with the state, intermittent though they were, brought the north Italian churches into more regular interaction with Christian communities throughout the Mediterranean. This served to change north Italian ecclesiological and theological perceptions, a phenomenon particularly evident in the Christological controversy. The manner in which the region's episcopate came to be involved in these disputes and the nature of the loyalties they adopted are instructive, for they reveal that while north Italian bishops were now participants in wider affairs, the character of their involvement was shaped by strong regional characteristics. This is evident not only in the nature of their Christological opinions, but in the geographical horizons of their activities. Like many in the west, the bishops of northern Italy were at first cut off from the theological and philosophical mainstream of the Christological debate, and their knowledge of and reaction to it depended on sporadic communications with the major centres of the dispute. Thus for the 340s and early 350s their actions were defined largely by their personal contact with the exiled Athanasius of Alexandria; between the councils of Milan and Aquileia, however, their attention was focused mainly on the activities of bishops in the Balkans, and to a lesser extent in Gaul.

Personal factors: Athanasius and Eusebius

There was no north Italian involvement in the councils of the Christological controversy prior to the gathering at Serdica in 343, and this was the first time that north Italians would have encountered at first hand the exponents of the rival Christologies. Their reaction was one of distaste: Lucius (or Lucillus) of Verona, Fortunatianus of Aquileia, Severus of Ravenna, Ursacius of Brescia, and Protasius of Milan joined with the majority of western bishops in condemning as heretics Ursacius of Singidunum, Valens of Mursa, Narcissus of Irenopolis, Stephen of Antioch, Acacius of Caesarea,

---

[69] Cf. below pp. 149–53.

Menofantus of Ephesus, and George of Laodicea (Hil. Pict., *Coll. Ant. Par.* B. II. 2. 5; 3–4). It is intriguing to observe how the Italian bishops and their allies arrived at their conclusion. There is little theology in the letters sent by this 'western' synod of Serdica to Julius of Rome and other western bishops. Condemnations of heresy merely rehearse standard pejorative formulae, such as that Ursacius, Valens, and the others had 'ventured against the servants of God who defend the true and Catholic faith' (ibid., B. II. 1. 1) and that 'their minds are tainted with the pestiferous Arian heresy' (ibid., B. II. 2. 2). Much more weight is given to accusations that these 'heretics' fomented violence within communities or constructed false accusations against their enemies (e.g., ibid., B. II. 2. 4). In particular, the bishops are concerned to defend the activities of Athanasius of Alexandria and his allies, such as Marcellus of Ancyra.[70]

This defence of the Alexandrian is couched in terms of close friendship: Athanasius is 'our dearest brother and fellow bishop' (ibid., B. II. 1. 1, 8), whereas his enemies are accused of lying, malice, and insidious assaults on a true son of the Church (ibid., B. II. 1 *passim*). The westerners' position is revealing, for it demonstrates that their quarrels with those whom they designated heretics were conducted primarily on grounds of personal allegiance. Thus, when Marcellus of Ancyra was accused of unorthodoxy it was enough for him, as an associate of Athanasius, to produce evidence of his own innocence to convince the westerners at Serdica that he had been wronged (ibid., B. II. 1. 6). How the north Italian bishops reacted to such arguments is easy enough to imagine. Of the five bishops from the region who signed the defence of Athanasius and the condemnation of his enemies, four—the bishops of Verona, Brescia, Milan, and Aquileia—had met him during his western exile (Athan., *Apol. Const.* 3); moreover, one of them—Fortunatianus of Aquileia—was at this early point a regular host of the exile on his western travels. Otherwise cut off from the Christological dispute, these north Italians would have learned about it first from Athanasius during his periods in the west.[71] For them, attachment to the hard-pressed bishop of Alexandria was inseparable from

---

[70] e.g. Hil. Pict., *Coll. Ant. Par.* B. II. 2. 5. For Athanasius and Marcellus: Leinhard, 'Did Athanasius Reject Marcellus?'.

[71] Barnes, *Athanasius*, 50–62.

their allegiances in wider church affairs. It is unsurprising, therefore, that a condemnation of Athanasius seems to have been one of the first aims of Constantius' Council of Milan in 355.

In this respect, the experience of north Italian bishops is similar to that of other western episcopates. Liberius of Rome made an outright rejection of Athanasius a central part of his accommodation with Constantius II, while loyalty to Athanasius proved dangerous for the likes of Paulinus of Trier and Ossius of Cordoba.[72] Not only does the centrality of Athanasius' personality make sense from an ecclesiastical perspective: in imperial terms too the bishop of Alexandria was an important concern for Constantius II, who saw him as a threat not only to Christian unity, but to the political stability of the empire.[73] But with Constantius' imposition of his wishes at Milan in 355, Athanasius ceased to be as important for the dispute as he had been hitherto. With the exile of Dionysius of Milan and Eusebius of Vercelli to the east, northern Italy, like the rest of the west, gained a new view of the Christological dispute, born of direct involvement in its debates in the eastern empire.

In this process, Eusebius of Vercelli occupies a place of central importance for northern Italy. He wrote to his congregations about affairs in the east (*Ep.* 2), and after Constantius' death he participated in a series of eastern councils by which Athanasius' partisans sought to reassert the orthodoxy of Nicaea. At the Alexandrian synod of 362, Eusebius was given the role of spreading the message of this Nicene restoration to the west (*Tomus ad Antiochenos* 2). By this stage Eusebius had travelled widely in the east, from his original exile at Scythopolis in Palestine to the Thebaid in upper Egypt and to Alexandria itself. He had become a different man in the years since the Council of Milan. In 355 he had been little more than a particularly single-minded Italian bishop, with few connections outside northern Italy apart from Rome and his native Sardinia.[74] By the time he returned to the west, however, he was a more mature, sober ecclesiastical politician. The stubbornness that had characterized his

---

[72] For Liberius, see below pp. 154–6; the danger to Paulinus and Ossius was acknowledged by Athanasius himself (*Apol. Const.* 27).

[73] Hence Athan., *Apol. Const.* 2–13.

[74] This much is implied by Liberius' letter to Eusebius, in which he commends to the bishop of Vercelli his delegation to the Milanese council, including Lucifer of Cagliari: Liberius, *Epp. ad Euseb. Verc.* 2. 1; 3. 1.

behaviour at Milan was replaced by greater circumspection, and he recognized, as his erstwhile associate Lucifer of Cagliari would never do, that accommodation was better than confrontation.[75]

This reflects his experiences in the east during his exile. Not only was he better placed to observe the theoretical underpinning of the Christological debate, but he was able to engage in discussion with many of the major participants. This much is clear from the *Tomus ad Antiochenos*, which records the proceedings of the Alexandrian synod of 362. Apart from Eusebius, it was attended by a large number of bishops from the near east, among them Athanasius himself (*Tomus*, 1, 10). The character of the debates there was, moreover, more elaborate than anything in which a north Italian bishop had been involved before. The central sections of the document deal with the complex question of the *hypostases* (substances) making up the Trinity (*Tomus* 5–6) and the nature of Christ's humanity (*Tomus* 7), and at the end of the document (*Tomus* 10), Eusebius expressly subscribes to the findings of the synod. If Eusebius was indeed the author of the *De Trinitate* ascribed to him by modern patristics scholars, then the complexity of its arguments would seem to confirm that he had learned much Christology during his eastern residence; regrettably, however, any attribution of that work to him must remain tentative.[76]

Little is known of Eusebius' return to the west and his activity there during the reign of Valentinian I. He travelled through the Balkans (*Altercatio Heracliani* p. 136) and Italy (Ruf., *HE* 10. 31) seeking to restore these areas to Nicene sympathies, and although his methods were usually viewed as conciliatory, it is clear that he was willing to confront any opposition. Thus Auxentius of Milan complained bitterly of Eusebius' interference in church affairs at Milan (apud Hil. Pict., *C. Aux.* 13). Not only did Eusebius exploit the knowledge and methods he had learned in the east; he also used contacts that he may have gained there. Somewhat earlier than Eusebius' homecoming, bishop Hilary of Poitiers had returned to Gaul to start a Nicene restoration. At some stage he seems to have joined forces with Eusebius, although the precise nature of their co-operation is unclear.[77]

---

[75] Gottlieb, 'Les évêques et les empereurs', 41–3; Hanson, *Search*, 347, 374–5, 529, 592–7; Speller, 'A Note on Eusebius'.

[76] For discussion of this difficulty, see p. 161, n. 90.

[77] See above pp. 117–18.

Geographical factors: Gaul, Italy, and Illyricum

The concerted efforts of Hilary and Eusebius point to another, geographical dimension in which the outlook of the north Italian church changed in response to theological debate, particularly after the intervention of Constantius II. It opened up new avenues of communication and reinforced existing ones. Those connections forged with the east depended largely on interpersonal contacts such as those of the emperor or of Athanasius and Eusebius. It is clear, however, that they persisted after Constantius' death. Eastern bishops were now actively interested in the affairs of their north Italian brethren, as Basil of Caesarea's correspondence with Valerian of Aquileia shows (Basil, *Ep.* 91). Opponents of Auxentius within the Milanese church looked to the east too for support, as the journeys made by the Milanese deacon, Sabinus, to Basil and Athanasius demonstrate.[78] Meanwhile, north Italian Christians of an ascetic bent, such as Turranius Rufinus of Concordia or the future bishop Gaudentius of Brescia, began to look towards the eastern Mediterranean as a venue for their endeavours.[79]

Another area where contact increased was with the churches in Gaul.[80] No connection is known prior to the joint participation of Gallic and north Italian bishops at Constantine's councils in 313 and 314. The most important period for increased contact between Gaul and northern Italy came with efforts to remove Auxentius from Milan. The first instance of this Gallic interest in northern Italy comes in the synod influenced by Hilary of Poitiers at Paris in 360. Here the assembled bishops of Gaul, writing to their eastern brethren, announced a general condemnation of homoian bishops in the west, among them Auxentius of Milan (Hil. Pict., *Coll. Ant. Par.* A. I. 4). Concrete action against Auxentius was taken by Hilary and Eusebius, but it is interesting to note that the one attempt to gain Auxentius' deposition by imperial intervention was perhaps the work of Hilary alone.[81] In the later 360s, a further condemnation of Auxentius was reported to Rome by a council composed of

---

[78] Basil, *Ep.* 91, mentions the mission of Sabinus to the east; cf. Damasus, *Ep. Confidimus quidem* 349C: 'Ego Sabinus diaconus Mediolanensis legatus de authentico dedi.'

[79] Rufinus: Spinelli, 'Ascetismo, monachesimo e cenobitismo', 285–8. Gaudentius: Lizzi, *Vescovi*, 97–109.

[80] In general: Duval, 'Les rapports de la Gaule'.   [81] Cf. above pp. 117–18.

bishops from Gaul and Venetia (Damasus, *Ep. Confidimus quidem* 348B). Ultimately, Auxentius retained his see until his death in 374, but the Gallic–north Italian axis of anti-homoian activity remained strong, and in 381 there were six bishops from Gaul at Ambrose's Council of Aquileia.[82]

The Aquileian council was, of course, directed against the Illyrican bishops Palladius of Ratiaria and Secundianus of Singidunum. There had long been social, economic, and cultural connections between northern Italy and the Balkans, and by the time of Theodore of Aquileia's participation in the Council of Arles in 314 it seems that these contacts also involved Christianity.[83] North Italian involvement in the Christological controversy did much to entrench these connections.[84] Constantius' intervention in the west was spearheaded by that posse of Illyrican bishops comprising Valens of Mursa, Ursacius of Singidunum, and Germinius of Sirmium, all three of whom were present at Milan in 355. During his episcopate, we most usually hear of Auxentius of Milan in connection with these Balkan homoians.[85] In this context, it is easy to see why, after the death of Constantius II, the restoration of a pro-Nicene consensus in northern Italy should have been inextricably bound up with the same process in the Balkans. This was reflected in Basil of Caesarea's view of Valerian of Aquileia as the bishop most likely to bring about the collapse of the homoian party in Illyricum (Basil, *Ep.* 91), and it had already found concrete expression in Eusebius of Vercelli's pro-Nicene agitation at Sirmium (*Altercatio Heracliani* p. 136).

The interpenetration between Illyrican and north Italian ecclesiastical politics persisted for much of the rest of the fourth century. It was an area in which Ambrose took an early interest, intervening to secure the appointment of Anemius as successor to Germinius of Sirmium in 378.[86] The Gothic revolt of 376–82 gave added urgency to north Italian interests in the ecclesiastical politics of the Balkans, particularly as homoian sympathizers fleeing the war, including clerics like Julianus Valens who came to Milan, posed a potential threat to pro-Nicene interests in northern Italy.[87] It was with such dangers in mind that Ambrose sought to convene the

---

[82] Williams, *Ambrose*, 174.   [83] Cf. pp. 140–5.
[84] Duval, 'Aquilée et Sirmium'.
[85] e.g. in the condemnation issued at the Council of Paris in 360 (Hil. Pict., *Coll. Ant. Par.* A. I. 4); cf. Athan., *De Syn.* 8, on Rimini.
[86] Paul. Med., *V. Ambr.* 11.   [87] Cf. pp. 168–9 below.

Council of Aquileia; among its members, moreover, were non-homoian bishops from the Balkans such as Maximus of Emona, Anemius of Sirmium, Diadertinus of Zadar, and Constantius of Siscia.[88]

Broadened horizons: the world view of Filastrius of Brescia

An index of the broadened cultural and theological horizons of the north Italian churches towards the end of our period can be gleaned from Filastrius of Brescia's *Diversarum hereseon liber*. Composed in the 380s, the work belongs to a tradition of anti-heretical polemic stretching back to Irenaeus of Lyon and Hippolytus of Rome. Its closest affinity, however, is to manuals produced in the Christological controversy, notably Epiphanius of Salamis' *Panarion*.[89] Yet Filastrius' book is not a diluted Latin version of its Greek predecessors; rather, it is a catalogue of heresies produced in an undeniably western context. The entry on Manichaeism, for example, refers to the presence of Manichaeans in Filastrius' own time in Spain and southern Gaul: a clear allusion to Priscillianism.[90] Particular elements reveal north Italian prejudices, notably the repeated references to Photinus of Sirmium (*Div. her. lib.* 65; 91. 2; 93. 5). Apart from their general interest in Balkan matters, north Italian bishops seem to have been deeply involved in the affair of Photinus,[91] and probably made up a large part of the council convened against him at Milan in 349 (Hil. Pict., *Coll. Ant. Par.* II. A. 5. 4).

Filastrius' description of the 'Arriani' (*sic*) conforms to this north Italian world view. He writes:

There are Arians following Arius, a priest of Alexandria who lived under bishop Alexander [of Alexandria] of happy memory and the holy emperor Constantine of happy memory, saying that the Son of God is 'like' (*similis*) God; however, in saying 'like', according to the meaning of the word, and not believing the son to be of the same substance (*substantia*) as the Father, Arius fell into perilous heresy. (*Div. her. lib.* 66. 1–2)

[88] *Acta conc. Aquil.* 55, 59, 61–2.
[89] McClure, 'Handbooks Against Heresy'; Williams, *Ambrose*, 89–90. For the date: F. Heylen, 'Praefatio', in *CCL* 9 (1957), 209–10.
[90] *Div. her. lib.* 61. 5: 'qui in Hispania et quinque prouinciis latere dicuntur, multosque hac cottidie fallacia captiuare'; cf. 84. Cf. Chadwick, *Priscillian of Avila*, 119–20.
[91] On which, see Hanson, *Search*, 235–8.

As a description of Arius' beliefs this is woefully inaccurate, but it is incredibly revealing of Filastrius' perspective on the whole Christological conflict. Its insistence on the heresy of a doctrine of 'likeness' which leaves out any consideration of 'substance' makes it clear what Filastrius has in mind: homoianism. While this might seem like sloppiness, it makes sense for a work composed in northern Italy, where the experience of Christological heterodoxy had been through the homoian ascendancy imposed by Constantius II. Filastrius' discussion of the heresy of these 'Arriani', which makes repeated appeals to the importance of *substantia* (cf. ibid., 66. 3, 4), is thus very much a product of its author's place and time. Likewise, Filastrius' references to the nature of the Holy Spirit (ibid., esp. 93. 3), show that the work belongs to the later stages of the Christological controversy, which by the 380s had moved on from disagreements about the relationship of Father and Son to consider all three persons in the Trinity.[92] Indeed, Filastrius demonstrates awareness of the various shades of Christological opinion at this time, including, for example, the followers of Eunomius (ibid. 68). To be sure, his descriptions often slip into 'glib caricature', but the needs of polemic required this strategy.[93]

Filastrius' work is an instructive point at which to conclude this survey of north Italian participation in the Christological controversy. His views are by no means unique: Zeno of Verona, for example, had much to say on the issue of *substantia*,[94] while it was left to Ambrose to produce the most extensive expositions of the pertinent theological issues in works such as his *De Fide*, *De Spiritu Sancto* and *De Incarnatione*. Yet Filastrius' book provides a snapshot view of how the intellectual horizons of north Italian bishops changed in the second half of the fourth century. At the Councils of Serdica and, to a lesser extent, Milan, north Italian participants had defined their activity in terms of personal allegiance to Athanasius. In the *Diversarum hereseon liber*, Filastrius presented an immeasurably more sophisticated picture of the conflict. In Filastrius we see a bishop more at home with the theological

---

[92] Hanson, *Search*, 738–90.   [93] *Pace* Williams, *Ambrose*, 90.

[94] Cf. the instances collected in Löfstedt and Packard, *Concordance*, 361–2. For Zeno's pronouncements on Christological matters, cf. Boccardi, '*Quantum spiritualiter intellegi datur*'; and esp. Truzzi, *Zeno, Gaudenzio e Cromazio*, 128–32, on the imprecision of Zeno's credal formulae.

debates of the universal Church, one whose world was very different from that of Merocles of Milan or Theodore of Aquileia.

Conclusion

The period between Constantine and Theodosius saw a radical change in the relationship between north Italian ecclesiastics and their emperors. Under Constantine and his sons, the relationship can be characterized by the north Italian episcopate reacting to, and usually acquiescing in, imperial decisions on ecclesiastical policy. In 355, however, north Italian bishops were expected to accept a more belligerently interventionist approach from Constantius II. The emperor desired ecclesiastical unity throughout his empire, and all who obstructed the achievement of this aim were exiled. Constantius' Milanese council proved to be a defining moment for north Italian Christianity, with Eusebius of Vercelli leading defiance of the emperor's wishes. To be sure, he and his fellows were disastrously unsuccessful, but their actions provided a template for future north Italian participation in the ecclesiastical politics of the empire: resistance, and not just acquiesence, was an option. The success of this stance depended on the relative strengths of character of emperor and episcopate. With Ambrose's accession to the bishopric of Milan in 374 and Gratian's succession to the western imperial throne a year later, the conditions were right for the achievement of episcopal autonomy in north Italian ecclesiastical politics. With the Council of Aquileia, Ambrose demonstrated how he sought to dictate the course of church politics and bring the emperor into accord with his decisions. Meanwhile, his defiance of a series of emperors showed how, through sheer force of personality, a north Italian bishop could presume to dictate terms to, and brook no compromise with, the imperial court itself.

As the north Italian episcopate's political outlook changed, so too did their cultural and theological horizons. The fourth century saw the region's bishops sucked into a wider Mediterranean arena of ecclesiastical politics and theological debate. This development is clearest in the Christological controversy. Until 355, the allegiances of north Italian bishops were dictated by personal ties, fostered during Athanasius' western exile in the 340s. From the 360s, however, it is clear that the bishops of northern Italy were much more capable of dealing with complex doctrinal issues. In Filastrius of Brescia's manual on heresies we gain a glimpse of this new theological sophistication of north Italian churchmen.

Such interaction of church and empire in northern Italy was played out in a manner influenced by distinctly regional dynamics. In particular, the Balkan focus of much north Italian involvement in the Christological controversy reflected long-standing connections between the two regions. It was a group of Balkan bishops who were instrumental in imposing Constantius II's homoian settlement on northern Italy; and it was the Balkan episcopate that bore the full brunt of the backlash after Constantius' death, culminating in the Council of Aquileia. Little wonder, then, that when Filastrius came to define 'Arianism' he described it as the homoian doctrine espoused by Balkan bishops such as Valens of Mursa, Palladius of Ratiaria, and Ursacius and Secundianus of Singidunum.

The fourth century transformed the way north Italian Christianity interacted with the outside world, but the events and processes described in this chapter had ramifications closer to home, and not just in terms of definitions of belief. The behaviour of particular bishops in the Christological controversy brought to the fore issues of ecclesiastical organization, both within individual communities and across the region as a whole. Once Eusebius of Vercelli took action against Auxentius of Milan, or Ambrose seized the initiative of a council under the nominal presidency of Valerian of Aquileia, they raised questions of when and where a particular bishop's authority had effect. Episcopal jurisdiction and the challenges to which it was subject, therefore, form the subjects of the next chapter.

5

The ordering of society

The last chapter showed how the interplay of imperial power and local society in northern Italy increasingly involved the Church and its hierarchy, especially from the time of Constantius II. This reflects a broader phenomenon, visible throughout the Roman world of the fourth century, whereby the Church was incorporated into a wider set of social power relations, with bishops beginning to act as leaders of their communities.[1] In northern Italy, this process was accelerated in the early fifth century,[2] but its genesis can be seen already in the fourth. The often bitter interaction between church and empire had ramifications not only for the theological outlook of north Italian bishops, but also for how they acted with or against each other. The purpose of this chapter in examining these developments is two-fold: it will examine first the emergence of ecclesiastical hierarchies in northern Italy; then it will analyse how those developing claims of regional authority were reflected at a local level, and how the Church competed with other interests in the region's cities.

The development of episcopal hierarchies

Our picture of developing administrative interrelationships between north Italian bishops in antiquity is often shaped by rigid and anachronistic hierarchical models.[3] Such an image is hard to sustain on

---

[1] The classic studies are: Bowersock, 'From Emperor to Bishop'; Brown, *Power and Persuasion*, esp. chs. 3–4; Cameron, *Christianity and the Rhetoric of Empire*, 123–41.

[2] See below, Epilogue; this theme will receive full exposition in the sequel to this book.

[3] For a recent example, see Williams, *Ambrose*, 76, describing Milan as 'the metropolitan seat of northern Italy' and how 'its bishop had episcopal jurisdiction effective over the whole of the political diocese of Italian Annonaria, which included Aemilia, Liguria, Venetia, the two Rhaetias, the Cottian Alps, Flaminia

the basis of fourth-century evidence from the region. It derives in
part from a tendency to generalize about adminstrative conditions
in the Church of the Roman empire, assuming that as the fourth
century progressed there developed a close correlation between
secular and ecclesiastical *metropoleis*, as laid down in the fourth canon
of the Council of Nicaea, in all areas of the empire.[4] Yet even in the
eastern provinces, which had a highly developed ecclesiastical hierarchy already at the beginning of the fourth century, there was ample
scope for dispute and variation.[5] The tendency to view the north
Italian church as having fixed hierarchies from the first is also
influenced by the picture of Christian origins presented in medieval
sources, which projected the political ideology of planned missions
and metropolitan bishoprics back into Christian antiquity. This
section will argue that the broader provincial organization of the
Church in northern Italy was more fluid, and that the ability of certain bishoprics to take on the characteristics of leadership depended
on constantly shifting circumstances. Only with the episcopate of
Ambrose at Milan was some measure of administrative rigidity
achieved, and even then it was reliant on Ambrose's force of character as much as the prestige of Milan as a provincial and imperial
metropolis.[6]

Conciliar sources and their limitations

Part of the difficulty in elucidating the origins of episcopal hierarchies in northern Italy is the lack of surviving information. As has
been noted before, there is no continuous narrative of north Italian
ecclesiastical history prior to the elevation of Ambrose. Any picture must rely on the minimal information given in conciliar subscriptions, on the occasional glimpses of north Italian bishops at work
given by Athanasius, Hilary, and others, and on the few statements
made by north Italian ecclesiastics themselves, such as Eusebius of
Vercelli.

and Picenum, and part of Tuscia'. Nowhere, however, does Williams offer any
justification for this claim, although his image clearly derives from the extension
of Ambrose's sphere of influence. This is a very old-fashioned view indeed: Menis,
'Le giurisdizioni metropolitiche', 275–80. Cf. pp. 17–18 above on the origins and problems of this approach.

[4] Above p. 11.   [5] Cf. above pp. 10–12 for such tensions.
[6] I will develop the ideas advanced, but not fully exploited, by Cattaneo, 'Il governo ecclesiastico', 175–87.

Even then the sources leave much to be desired. A good example
is the provenance of bishops as given in conciliar documents. At Arles
in 314, for example, Merocles of Milan is designated 'ex prouincia
Italia'. Superficially, this seems to present no problems, but the same
document lists Theodore of Aquileia as 'ex prouincia Dalmatia'. This
is curious indeed, since a tetrarchic inscription found at Miramare
near Trieste (that is, further east than Aquileia) shows that Aquileia
lay within the jurisdiction of the *corrector Italiae* (*CIL* 5. 8205). The
description of Theodore in the Arelate lists shows that such designations do not correlate closely with secular administrative districts,
as is sometimes assumed.[7] The situation is clearer by the time of the
Council of Serdica, where all the north Italian bishops are listed
simply as 'ab Italia', whereas those from central and southern Italy
are more precisely located, 'ab Apulia' and so forth (Hil. Pict., *Coll.
Ant. Par.* B. II. 4). Yet by the mid-fourth century, northern Italy
had been divided up into a number of provinces, such as *Aemilia et
Liguria* or *Venetia et Histria*.[8] Therefore the description of bishops
at Serdica as coming 'ab Italia' ignores the boundaries of secular
administration, and most probably reflects a growing tendency to
use 'Italia' on its own to describe northern Italy.[9] A further layer of
complexity is added because successive compilers of conciliar acts were
not themselves consistent in the criteria they used when appending
geographical designations to the sees represented at each council. The
case of Aquileia illustrates this point succinctly: at Arles, Theodore
came 'ex prouincia Dalmatia', whereas at Serdica, Fortunatianus
was numbered among the bishops 'ab Italia'. Determining what each
designation means, therefore, will assist evaluating the use of such
sources for the reconstruction of early north Italian ecclesiastical
administration. By themselves, moreover, these designations reveal
very little. For example, it would be too adventurous to assert that
the shift of Aquileia from 'ex provincia Dalmatia' to 'ab Italia' meant
that it, and presumably all the bishoprics of northern Italy, had come
under the thrall of the bishops of Milan. It is only when read in
connection with other texts that conciliar documents begin to make
any sense.

[7] e.g. Chastagnol, *La Préfecture urbaine à Rome*, 26–35, using evidence from the
subscriptions of Arles and Serdica to demonstrate administrative innovations.
[8] Chastagnol, 'L'Administration du diocèse italien', 355–8.
[9] Cracco Ruggini and Cracco, 'L'eredità di Roma', 37.

Aquileia and the genesis of episcopal jurisdiction

The first narrative depiction of north Italian bishops working together comes in Athanasius' report to Constantius II of his efforts at gaining an audience with Constans in the 340s (*Apol. Const.* 3). He recounts how he 'was always introduced [to Constans] in company with the bishop of the city where [he] happened to be, and others who happened to be there', among whom he mentions Fortunatianus of Aquileia (with whom Athanasius stayed for much of this time), Lucillus (or Lucius) of Verona, Crispinus of Padua, and Protasius of Milan. They, together with Vincentius of Capua, Ossius of Cordoba, Maximinus of Trier, and Dionysius of Elis, were Athanasius' sponsors before Constans (*Apol. Const.* 3).

Athanasius' audiences with Constans are difficult to distinguish. His account of them to Constantius was written for an emperor who already knew their basic chronology, but from the allusive account in the *Apologia ad Constantium* it is clear that there were four separate meetings: at Milan in 342 (*Apol. Const.* 3); at Trier in mid-343 and again in late 345 (ibid. 4); and at Aquileia during 345 (ibid. 14–15).[10] Athanasius' sponsors can be divided up between these audiences. He states explicitly that Ossius of Cordoba was with him at Trier (ibid. 4), as must have been that city's bishop Maximinus. Vincentius of Capua served for much of this period as papal legate,[11] and could have joined Athanasius at any of the audiences he mentions, as could Dionysius of Elis, who seems to have had dealings with the imperial court over the disputed tenure of his see in the mid-340s.[12] By fitting the north Italian bishops into this framework it is possible to reveal something of how they organized themselves when dealing with each other. For the audience at Milan we can assume that Protasius was present, as was the *magister officiorum* Eugenius (ibid. 3). None of the other north Italian bishops can be connected to this audience, which was convened at the orders of Constans himself.[13] The other north Italian bishops are more probably associated therefore with Athanasius' audience at

[10] See Barnes, *Athanasius*, 63–70, for analysis of the audiences which Athanasius describes.

[11] Pietri, *Roma Christiana*, 175, 239–42, 262–4.

[12] For Dionysius, see Barnes, *Athanasius*, 258 n. 9.

[13] Athanasius is clear on the order of events. While he was staying at Aquileia, Constans, then resident at Milan, wrote to Athanasius, summoning him to court (*Apol. Const.* 4).

Aquileia in 345. That the bishops of Padua and Verona should chance to be in the company of Fortunatianus at Aquileia is intriguing, because taken with other evidence it suggests that there was some form of provincial organization among the bishops of north-eastern Italy. This much seems to be implied by notice of a report from the bishops of Gaul and Venetia to Pope Damasus, sometime around 370, of attempts by Auxentius of Milan to disturb the peace of the Church.[14] Here there seems to be explicit confirmation of the bishops of Venetia working as a group.

Whether this means that the bishopric of Aquileia held any sort of hierarchical authority over the bishops of other cities in the region is harder to determine for the 340s. Certainly, once Fortunatianus disowned Athanasius, subscribed to the homoian creed promulgated at Sirmium in 351, and persuaded Pope Liberius to do likewise,[15] he may have found it hard to exercise any authority or influence over pro-Nicene or pro-Athanasian bishops. In 362/3, Liberius wrote to the Italian episcopate asking that any bishops who had lapsed into heresy—and he specifically mentions the Council of Rimini—should be received back into the orthodox communion.[16] Someone like Fortunatianus must have been intended in the pope's plea, and a letter of pro-Nicene Italian bishops to their Illyrican brethren suggests that anyone who now rejected Rimini would be readmitted to their company (Hil. Pict., *Coll. Ant. Par.* B. IV. 2). Whether Fortunatianus followed such a course of action, as Germinius of Sirmium seems to have done (ibid. B. V), cannot be known; nor can anything about his relationship with his fellow bishops in Venetia and Illyricum. By the later 360s, however, when Aquileia reemerges in the sources, there is a more cogent picture of its regional influence, if not leadership. It is worth examining this development in some detail as it provides a useful model for the development of ecclesiastical hierarchy in the region as a whole.

Among the major sources for this development are the writings of Jerome and Rufinus, which show that Aquileia exercised a form of influence over the Christian communities in the north-western

---

[14] Damasus, *Ep. Confidimus quidem* 348B: 'Sed Galliorum atque Venetensium fratrum relatione comperimus.' Cf. Williams, *Ambrose*, 81–2.

[15] For Fortunatianus' actions in the 350s, cf. pp. 154–6 below.

[16] Hil. Pict., *Coll. Ant. Par.* B. IV. 1. For the importance of *communio* in the Christological controversy: Monachino, 'Communio e primato nella controversia ariana', 339–47.

Balkans and north-eastern Italy. Links between Venetia and Jerome's home town of Stridon are confirmed by his account of how his sister, a wayward lass in her youth, ultimately succumbed to the spiritual life under the influence of Julian, a deacon from Aquileia (Hier., *Ep.* 6; 7. 4). The nature of this connection was probably informal, since Stridon had its own bishop, albeit a dissolute, inadequate one (*Ep.* 7. 5). Also within this sphere of influence may have been the Christians of Emona with whom Jerome corresponded in the 370s (*Ep.* 11–12), and whose bishop attended the Council of Aquileia in 381.[17] The city's social magnetism was powerful indeed: even after his self-imposed eastern exile, Jerome remained in close contact with his friends at Aquileia.[18]

A major reason for Aquileia's prominence was its reputation as a centre of spiritual excellence.[19] Writing his *Chronicle* at Constantinople in 380, Jerome looked back with fondness on the days he had spent at Aquileia and commented that the clergy there were considered a *chorus beatorum*, a community of the blessed (*Chron.* s. a. 374). This was a gathering of ascetics, whose activities reveal much about the prestige and influence of the see of Aquileia over neighbouring Christian congregations. Apart from the activities of the deacon Julian at Stridon, there was Turranius Rufinus from Concordia, who met and befriended Jerome at Aquileia, long before the days of their acrimonious debate over Origenist theology, and who shared happy memories of life in the *chorus beatorum*.[20] Others included Heliodorus, who became bishop of the neighbouring town of Altino before 381; Bonosus, Jerome's childhood friend; and the future bishop of Aquileia, Chromatius, and his brother, Eusebius. The lifestyle advocated by the *chorus beatorum* influenced neighbouring Christian communities: at Altino, Heliodorus was joined by his nephew, Nepotianus, who gave up a military career for the Church, and whose death was later to cause his uncle and Jerome great distress.[21]

Presiding over the whole community in the 370s, bishop Valerian had achieved a position of great prestige: he was 'papa Valerianus' to Jerome, 'Valerian of blessed memory' to a distraught Rufinus.[22]

---

[17] See below, p. 174.   [18] Kelly, *Jerome*, 30–5, 48–9.

[19] Full discussion in Spinelli, 'Ascetismo', 273–300; cf. Kelly, *Jerome*, 32–3.

[20] Spinelli, 'Ascetismo', 285–8.

[21] Hier., *Ep.* 52. 4–15; 60. 10. On Heliodorus, see esp. Scourfield, *Consoling Heliodorus*.

[22] Hier., *Ep.* 7. 4; Ruf., *Apol. c. Hier.* 1. 4.

This prestige was matched by a loose form of authority. In Asia Minor, Basil of Caesarea rejoiced at Valerian's piety, and wrote to him as 'bishop of the Illyrians' (Οὐαλεριανῷ ἐπισκόπῳ 'Ιλλυριῶν: *Ep.* 91), seeing in him an important agent who could lead Christians in the Balkans back to the creed of Nicaea.[23] Basil had received a letter from Valerian, carried to Asia by a Milanese deacon Sabinus,[24] making his designation of Valerian particularly interesting, for it is the first formal confirmation that the bishop of Aquileia envisaged for himself a role among the Christian communities beyond the Julian Alps. It helps to explain the designation of Theodore of Aquileia in 314 as 'ex prouincia Dalmatia'. Since its very foundation, the city of Aquileia had strong connections with north-western Illyricum in terms of trade, social interaction, pagan cults; now those links extended to Christianity.

The nature of the bishop of Aquileia's jurisdiction over western Illyricum is uncertain, but it is unlikely to have been at all formal in the fourth century. Certainly it did not go unchallenged. In the early 360s, Eusebius of Vercelli seems to have engaged in a mission at Sirmium,[25] while in 378, Ambrose of Milan was already extending his influence into the area when he took an active part in the appointment of Sirmium's new bishop, Anemius. Neither case, however, represents a permanent erosion of Aquileian interests in the Balkans. Eusebius' intervention coincided with the episcopate of Fortunatianus who, by his rejection of Athanasius, might have been seen by pro-Nicenes to have abdicated his responsibilities for the region.[26] Ambrose's activities at Sirmium, in the course of a mission to Gratian's court, are significant primarily as an example of his heavy-handed tactics wherever he went; his hijacking of the council of 381 might be seen as a similar infringement of Valerian's rights, but one in which the bishop of Aquileia acquiesced.[27] Certainly,

---

[23] Cf. Basil, *Ep.* 92. 2 (to the bishops of Gaul and Italy) announcing a programme designed to stamp out 'the evil of heresy which spreads from the frontiers of Illyricum to the Thebaid'. For discussion: Rousseau, *Basil of Caesarea*, 299–305.

[24] Rousseau, *Basil of Caesarea*, 296–7.

[25] *Altercatio Heracliani*, 136; for commentary, cf. Williams, *Ambrose*, 66–7.

[26] Cf. pp. 154–6 below.

[27] Ambrose and Anemius: Paul. Med., *V. Ambr.* 11. 1. Williams, *Ambrose*, 122–7, dismisses the entire story on the basis, first, that Paulinus is our only source for the episcopal election, and second, that the other evidence used to support Ambrose's presence there—Theodoret's account of a 'council of Illyricum' (*HE* 4. 8–9)—is fictional. That Theodoret's testimony is wholly untrustworthy is not in doubt, but this does not necessarily undermine the credibility of Paulinus' testimony: see McLynn, *Ambrose*, 88–106, esp. 90–8, for a more convincing reading of these events,

subsequent bishops of Milan could never claim jurisdiction over the Balkans; instead the area was gradually absorbed into the early medieval patriarchate of Aquileia.[28]

A similar degree of influence is evident in Aquileia's role in north-eastern Italy. Heliodorus, a monk of the *chorus beatorum*, was already bishop of Altino by 381, although the degree to which he was in any way a suffragan of Aquileia cannot be determined. That Turranius Rufinus should have joined the *chorus beatorum* suggests that the Christian community in his home town of Concordia was also under the influence of Aquileia, especially bearing in mind that Concordia had an ascetic attraction of its own in the learned, super-annuated monk Paul.[29] Such links were put on a more institutional footing when Valerian's successor, Chromatius, dedicated a *basilica apostolorum* at Concordia, sometime around 400.[30] No bishop of Concordia is known prior to the late sixth century, so its Christian community may have been dependent on Aquileia until then. Indeed, even when a bishop of Concordia does make an appearance, it is as a suffragan of bishop Helias of the see of Aquileia at Grado.[31] By that time, various other bishops along the Venetian coast and in the lagoons were also under Helias' jurisdiction, during whose episcopate the patriarchate of Aquileia was beginning to emerge.[32]

Moving within the urban hinterland of Aquileia, it seems that its relationship with neighbouring Christian communities was organized along lines suggesting a parochial structure. At S. Canzian d'Isonzo, ancient *Aquae Gradatae*, there was a small church by the

---

which acknowledges that Ambrose's motives were not entirely theological (this aspect is overestimated by Williams). Further, Williams's claim that Manlio Simonetti's analysis that 'l'azione di Ambrogio fu diretta sopratutto a debellare gli ariani nelle loro ultime roccaforti dell'Illirico' (*La crisi ariana*, 438) 'has little to undergird it' (Williams, *Ambrose*, 126) is curious indeed. From the time of writing the first books of *de Fide* in 378 down to the Council of Aquileia, it is clear that the opposition of characters such as Palladius of Ratiaria and Secundianus of Singidunum was a major consideration in Ambrose's manoeuvres in ecclesiastical politics.

[28] Menis, 'Rapporti ecclesiastici tra Aquileia e la Slovenia', 368–76.
[29] Hier., *Ep.* 5. 2; 10; id., *De vir. ill.* 53. In *Ep.* 10. 2, Jerome implies that Paul was an instructive character: 'futurae resurrectionis uirorem in te nobis Dominus ostendit'. For a discussion of Paul's career: Zovatto, 'Paolo da Concordia'.
[30] Chromatius gives an account of the dedication in *Sermo* 26. For commentary: Lemarié, *Chromace d'Aquilée. Sermons*, i. 103–7; cf. Lizzi, *Vescovi*, 151–4 setting the dedication in the context of Chromatius' activities to extend Aquileia's ecclesiastical jurisdiction.
[31] Cessi, *Origo*, 44.   [32] Rando, *Una chiesa di frontiera*, 21.

second half of the fourth century built in honour of the Aquileian martyrs buried there, staffed by deacon, lector, and *notarius*.[33] A similar situation seems to have obtained at Grado, Aquileia's port on the lagoon. The basilica in the Piazza della Vittoria there was built in the fourth century, but because no bishop ever resided in the city until the transfer of the Aquileian bishopric to the island in the sixth century, it seems that the church at Grado came under the aegis of Aquileia.[34]

By 381, then, the church of Aquileia lay at the centre of a network of ecclesiastical contacts straddling north-eastern Italy, the Julian Alps, and the north-western Balkans. It is necessary, however, to distinguish between two types of leadership exercised by the bishops of Aquileia. One was of a formal—or quasi-formal—nature, reflected in the existence of churches at Grado and S. Canzian d'Isonzo, both within the ancient territory of Aquileia, and perhaps also at Concordia and Altino. The other was more informal, based on the spiritual prestige of the bishops of Aquileia. This seems to have been the basis for the earliest contacts between Aquileia and north-western Illyricum, where it can only be seen to have been replaced by formal authority in the late sixth and seventh centuries. In every case, it is noticeable that spread of Aquileian influence followed the patterns of existing social networks. Venetia, Histria, and the north-western Balkans were areas with which Aquileia had long had contacts: they provided a template, therefore, for the emergence of its diocese and, later, its patriarchate.

Administration and influence at Vercelli, Trento, and Brescia

Moving westwards into the Po valley, a similar variety of administrative structures, and their development towards diocesan structures, can be seen at Vercelli, Brescia, and Trento. That Vercelli was the episcopal centre of a number of Christian communities in eastern Piedmont is clear from a letter written to the faithful of Novara, Ivrea, and Tortona by Eusebius of Vercelli during his eastern exile (Euseb. Verc., *Ep.* 2). In the opening address, and at several junctures throughout the letter, Eusebius refers to subordinate clergy who must have been among the personnel who governed the churches

---

[33] Lizzi, *Vescovi*, 155–6.   [34] Ibid., 151–9.

of these cities under Eusebius' overall direction.[35] By 381, however, Tortona had its own bishop, and Novara and Ivrea had theirs by 451, but, far from this representing the consolidation of Vercelli as a metropolitan see, these changes meant the erosion of Vercelli's pre-eminence in eastern Piedmont under pressure from Milan.[36]

In eastern Venetia, the church of Brescia seems to have exerted some influence over neighbouring congregations. If a ninth-century text can be believed, then it would seem that bishop Filastrius of Brescia was responsible for ordaining a deacon at Bergamo.[37] Such an action is impossible to verify, but it is in accord with what else is known of Filastrius' activities. Apart from his pungent writings against heresy, Filastrius, even before he became bishop, was active beyond his city when he attempted (and failed) to foment internal opposition against Auxentius of Milan.[38] Yet these activities illustrate nothing more than informal connections between the Brescian church and other Christian communities in its vicinity, and by the time of Ambrose's episcopate, they were turned in favour of Milanese interests.[39]

A surer picture emerges from the activities of the church of Trento in the Alto Adige at the end of the fourth century. Sometime around 397, three clerics sent out by bishop Vigilius of Trento died when violence erupted between pagans and Christians in the Val di Non, north-west of the city.[40] It is most probable that these clerics were sent out to minister to a pre-existing Christian community, and their activities represent a formalization of interrelationships between the bishopric of Trento and Christian congregations in surrounding valleys. It is interesting to note that the clerical structure of Vigilius' agents in the Val di Non—one was a deacon, another

[35] The letter is adressed 'Dilectissimis fratribus et satis desideratissimis presbyteris sed et sanctis in fide consistentibus plebibus Vercellensibus, Nouariensibus, Eporediensibus nec non etiam Dertonensibus'; in the course of it, Eusebius refers to Syrus a deacon and Victorinus an exorcist (at § 1. 2), and a priest called Tegrinus (at § 6. 2). He concludes by forwarding the salutations of 'nostri qui mecum sunt presbyteri et diacones' (§ 11. 2).

[36] McLynn, *Ambrose*, 285–6.

[37] Lanzoni, *Diocesi*, 573; also p. 96 above.

[38] Cf. below p. 167.

[39] McLynn, *Ambrose*, 221, on the Brescian Benivolus active among Ambrose's supporters at Milan. Cf. Lizzi, *Vescovi*, 97–109, on the installation of Gaudentius at Brescia, in which Ambrose played an important role.

[40] For full discussion of these events and the relevant source materials, see below pp. 181–3.

a lector, the third a porter—finds an almost exact analogy at S. Canzian d'Isonzo, and in the subordinate clergy whom Eusebius of Vercelli mentions at Ivrea, Novara, and Tortona. Such a similarity, taken together with the clear interest of Vigilius in the mission to the Val di Non, suggests the existence of a programme which sought to bind the Christian communities of the Alto Adige together under Tridentine leadership. At the same time, however, the activities of Ambrose were bringing Trento under Milanese sway: on his election, Vigilius had received a detailed exposition of his duties from the bishop of Milan (Ambr., *Ep.* 19).[41]

Milanese ascendancy

The extent to which Milan had developed any form of regional supremacy in the early to mid-fourth century is difficult to judge because of the distortion caused by Ambrose's energetic efforts at building up the authority of the Milanese church from the moment he was elected. There are, however, a few indicators that, already by 374, Milan was perceived to have some sort of important role in the region's ecclesiastical politics, by the imperial power at least. Merocles of Milan attended both of Constantine's councils seeking to resolve the Donatist dispute, and on both occasions he seems to have been summoned at the initiative of the emperor himself. It is probable, if unprovable, that Merocles and Constantine met at Milan when the new Christian emperor of the west and his eastern colleague, Licinius, promulgated their directive on religious toleration in the city in 313.

The first direct evidence for a meeting between an emperor and a bishop of Milan comes with Athanasius' audience with Constans in 342, which was attended by the city's bishop, Protasius. Thirteen years later, Constantius II chose to convene a council at Milan as part of his programme to engender unity in the Church throughout the empire. When bishop Dionysius, albeit under the influence of Eusebius of Vercelli, proved obstinate, he was not only ousted, but replaced by the more pliable Auxentius. Constantius' ecclesiastical policy in the west had been marked by a concern to ensure that compliant bishops were installed in, and their opponents removed from, important sees: thus Maximinus of Trier was exiled and his

[41] Lizzi, '*Codicilli* imperiali', 3–13.

role devolved on the shoulders of Saturninus of Arles; similarly, Liberius of Rome was forced from his throne and replaced with the deacon Felix and a watchful guard was installed nearby with Epictetus at Civitavecchia.[42]

The interest shown by both Constantine and Constantius II in the church of Milan surely attests to their perceptions of its importance. Protasius' presence at Athanasius' meeting with Constans helps to explain why this was so: the bishop of Milan, living at a city regularly occupied by the court, proved to be a useful intermediary between the emperor and other ecclesiastics, thus giving him a certain prestige outside his city. Yet there were limitations to this sort of influence. It was only of interest to those actually seeking an imperial audience, many of whom would have come, as Athanasius did, from beyond northern Italy. Therefore it might not reflect actual prestige or importance within northern Italy itself—certainly, Eusebius of Vercelli's ripping of the pen from Dionysius' hand at the council of 355 does not suggest that the bishop of Milan engendered any special respect. Within the city, moreover, the presence of the emperor could be as disruptive as it was advantageous to a bishop's authority.

Details about Milan's relationship with other north Italian sees before Ambrose's election are almost entirely concerned with efforts to remove Auxentius by those who saw him as a heretical interloper. Only one throwaway line in Ambrose indicates that Milan had any sort of hierarchical position before 374. Discussing the *inventio* of Gervasius and Protasius in the summer of 386, Ambrose describes Milan as sterile of martyrs of its own, having hitherto imported relics from other centres. These sacred imports included apostolic relics from Rome, but also the bones of Nabor and Felix, in whose shrine the bodies of Gervasius and Protasius were unearthed.[43] By the end of the fifth century, Milanese tradition held that Nabor and Felix had been brought from nearby Lodì by Maternus, bishop of Milan after Merocles. It is impossible to test the reliability of this account. The use of other cities' relics as a way of extending Milanese ecclesiastical influence is known from the end of the century, as when Ambrose used the relics of Agricola and Vitalis, which he had discovered at

---

[42] Constantius' attitude towards bishops was dominated by a concern to have like-minded bishops occupying the churches of provincial *metropoleis*: Pietri, 'La politique de Constance II', 134–7, 153–65.

[43] For full discussion of these events and their sources, see Appendix, s.v. Milan.

Bologna, to extend his influence.[44] For something similar to have
happened under Maternus would be a precocious development
indeed, since Ambrose's manipulation of the cult of martyrs to
bolster his own supremacy seems to have been in conscious imitation of the policies of Pope Damasus of Rome (366–84).[45] Certainly, Lodì was under Milanese jurisdiction later in the century: its
first known bishop, Bassianus, was one of Ambrose's henchmen at
Aquileia in 381, and he proved to be a devoted disciple of the Milanese
bishop to the end (Paul. Med., *V. Ambr.* 47). That the tradition of
the *inventio* of Nabor and Felix was embroidered later to justify
Milanese jurisdiction over its neighbour cannot be ruled out, but this
does not necessarily mean that they were not unearthed at Lodì.
Indeed, a close connection between the churches of Milan and Lodì
prior to Bassianus' election cannot be disqualified: Lodì lay on the
main road south from Milan towards Rome, and links between them
are evident in the social networks of the early and middle empire.
Bearing in mind how such networks have been shown to have
influenced interrelationships between the churches of Aquileia and
Vercelli and their neighbours, it provides a likely circumstance, if
not proof, for a similar interaction between the congregations of Milan
and Lodì in the early and mid-fourth century.

The crucial period in the aggrandisement of Milan was the episcopate of Ambrose. Any achievements of his predecessor Auxentius
have been largely consigned to oblivion, although his cooperation
in doctrinal affairs with bishops in the Balkans, such as Ursacius of
Singidunum and Valens of Mursa, provided Ambrose with a target
for his pro-Nicene policies in the early years of his episcopate. Twice
in that period—the investiture of Anemius of Sirmium in 378 and
the Council of Aquileia in 381—Ambrose actively intervened in the
affairs of Illyrican churches. Of course, Ambrose's connection with
Illyricum predated his episcopal election; for some years he had served
on the staff of the praetorian prefect at Sirmium (Paul. Med., *V. Ambr.*
5). His deftness as an administrator was enhanced by his holding of
the governorship of Aemilia and Liguria in the years leading up to
his election (ibid.). This is significant, because it indicates one source
of the skills Ambrose used to create a community of bishops in northern Italy. Ambrose's preeminence among the region's bishops was
in part achieved by negotiation, just as his consular jurisdiction over

[44] McLynn, *Ambrose*, 347–50.   [45] Brown, *Cult of the Saints*, 36–7.

his province had depended on dealings with local communities and their civic leaders. His skills as an administrator were intimately connected with his cultural outlook. Brought up on the fringes of the Roman élite, Ambrose used the genteel arts of aristocratic *amicitia* to cultivate friendship and loyalty among his fellow bishops in northern Italy.[46] Added to these abilities was that quality at once intangible and central to his success: his dazzling personality.[47]

Brought to the position of bishop, this combination of skills and talents proved a potent weapon in building Ambrose's influence. It allowed him to construct a friendship network throughout the region, upon which he called for support at moments of crisis, such as Aquileia in 381. In some cases, he was able to assert his preeminence in the most ostentatious manner, by presiding at, or endorsing, the elections and consecrations of his fellow bishops.[48] This was a tactic he adopted early on in his struggle against the heterodox bishops of Illyricum, when he officiated at the election of Anemius of Sirmium.[49] The strategy was applied with considerable success to northern Italy, where its workings and implications can be observed more closely. At times, Ambrose's role may not have been particularly proactive, such as in 388, when he seems only to have been a presence at the consecration of Chromatius of Aquileia.[50] At other times, however, Ambrose's actions were more aggressive and interventionist: at Brescia, he secured the accession of Gaudentius as bishop, despite the candidate's initial reluctance.[51] Even more belligerently, Ambrose intervened in the protracted episcopal elections at Vercelli, so ensuring the success of his own preferred candidate, Honoratus.[52]

At other times, Ambrose's influence was extended through the workings of patronage. Like his contemporary, fellow aristocrat, and friend, Q. Aurelius Symmachus, Ambrose was an energetic correspondent: he wrote to bishops all over northern Italy—and frequently

[46] Lizzi, *Vescovi*, 28–36.
[47] The classic description is Aug., *Conf.* 5. 13. 23–14. 24; cf. McLynn, *Ambrose*, 239–40.
[48] In general: Lizzi, 'Ambrose's Contemporaries', 158–9; McLynn, *Ambrose*, 284–5.
[49] See pp. 132–3 above.
[50] Truzzi, 'L'ordinazione episcopale di Cromazio'.
[51] Lizzi, *Vescovi*, 97–109.
[52] Ambrose gives a vigorous defence of his intervention in *Ep.* 63. Cf. Lizzi, *Vescovi*, 46–50.

further afield—advising them on matters practical and spiritual.[53] Through exercises such as the passing on of greetings from one bishop to another, Ambrose made himself the pivot upon which the north Italian episcopate hinged.[54] His most ostentatious display of patronage, however, was in his use of the cult of saints to enhance the prestige of Milan, just as Pope Damasus had done at Rome.[55] Moreover, by both importing important apostolic remains and sending gifts of relics of Milanese saints, he established himself and Milan as a power to be reckoned with not just in Italy, but also in Gaul.[56] By the time Ambrose died, Milan's place as a north Italian centre for the cult of saints had been firmly established. Shortly after their deaths, relics of the Val di Non martyrs made their way to Milan, where they were interred by Ambrose's successor, Simplicianus (Paul. Med. *V. Ambr.* 52).[57]

By investing his fellow bishops, giving them advice, and presenting them with gifts, Ambrose constructed a friendship network that welded the disparate Christian communities of northern Italy into a cohesive unit. This group made its first impressive appearance at the Council of Aquileia in 381, where bishops from various sees in Venetia and the Po valley reiterated Ambrose's condemnation of Palladius of Ratiaria and Secundianus of Singidunum. Ambrose's expansion of Milanese influence often entailed the erosion of other bishops' spheres of influence. Thus the Christian community of Tortona, which had been under the episcopal jurisdiction of Eusebius of Vercelli in the 350s, not only appears as a bishopric for the first time in 381, but its bishop remained a loyal ally of Ambrose, and supported him at the synod of Milan in 392/3. By this stage, however, Ambrose seems to have had few qualms

[53] The significance of Ambrose's correspondence is elucidated in full by Lizzi, *Vescovi*, 15–28; cf. McLynn, *Ambrose*, 281–4. They are apt, however, to give the impression that Ambrose's letter writing was more innovative than it actually was: cf. Lane Fox, 'Literacy and Power', 135–7.

[54] In *Ep.* 4. 1 Ambrose passed on the salutations of Bassianus of Lodì to Felix of Como. Cf. *Ep.* 63. 1: Ambrose communicates to the Christians of Vercelli that they are uniquely disadvantaged among the Christians of all of northern Italy.

[55] Cf. pp. 54–5.

[56] Importing relics: see esp. McLynn, *Ambrose*, 230–5. For Milanese 'exports', see Victricius of Rouen's *De laude sanctorum*, acknowledging a gift of relics: Clark, 'Victricius of Rouen'; cf. Brown, *Cult of the Saints*, 95–6; McLynn, *Ambrose*, 284.

[57] Nevertheless, bishop Vigilius of Trento sought to maintain a certain degree of Tridentine initiative, as is clear from the letters on the subject he wrote to Simplicianus and John Chrysostom: Lizzi, *Vescovi*, 81–6.

in asserting his authority at the expense of Vercelli: only a few years later we find him bullying the city's Christians into accepting Honoratus as their bishop.[58] Even where a bishop was firmly established, Ambrose showed no reluctance about subverting his authority. Thus poor bishop Syagrius of Verona found one of his judgements on the internal affairs of his community undercut by an intervention by Ambrose.[59]

Yet Ambrose could never assume that his leadership would remain unchallenged. Outspoken criticism of Ambrose's methods is rarely heard from northern Italy, but Palladius of Ratiaria was in no doubt as to the illegality of many of the bishop of Milan's actions. In a notorious outburst, he challenged Ambrose's authority at the Council of Aquileia. In tones of mounting desperation, he accused Ambrose of traducing the orders given by Gratian when convening the council:

Palladius said: 'Your bias (*studio*) has made it so that this is not a general and full council; in the absence of our colleagues, we [i.e. Palladius and Secundianus] cannot make a statement of our faith.'

Bishop Ambrose said: 'Who are your colleagues?'

Palladius said: 'The eastern bishops. . . . Our emperor Gratian ordered the easterners to come. Do you deny that he ordered this? The emperor himself told us that he had ordered the easterners to come'. (*Acta conc. Aquil.* 6, 8)

Writing an *Apologia* some time later to justify himself and his co-defendant, Palladius called the assembled bishops a *conspiratio* (Pall., *Apol.* 122), and expressly condemned Eusebius of Bologna as Ambrose's stooge (ibid. 117).[60] As Palladius was keen to point out, Ambrose's control over the the council was *de facto*, and not *de iure* (ibid. 89).

What *is* clear from northern Italy is that Ambrose's influence was by no means consistent. A comparison of the compositions of the Councils of Aquileia in 381 and Milan in 392/3 is instructive: at Aquileia there had been a strong contingent from Venetia; but some ten years later, the bulk of the bishops at the Milanese synod came from centres in Aemilia and Liguria. This suggests that Ambrose's influence was strongest over bishoprics in the hinterland of Milan. Even here, as the case of the disputed election at Vercelli shows, Ambrose's position depended less on any formal conception of Milanese jurisdiction than on the acceptance of his judgements by

---

[58] Above p. 150.   [59] Ambr., *Ep.* 5–6.   [60] McLynn, *Ambrose*, 134–6.

those captivated by the allure of his episcopal demeanour. From the very beginning of his episcopate, Ambrose had achieved his prominence in northern Italy by blending the skills he had acquired as a member of the Roman élite, as an official in the imperial administration, and as someone well placed to observe the activities of that most dynamic of fourth-century popes, Damasus I.

The shadow of St Peter

The Roman church has been glimpsed several times in our narrative, convening councils which north Italian bishops attended and providing templates for the activities of men like Ambrose. Yet because there is no evidence that the bishops of northern Italy submitted themselves to Roman ecclesiastical jurisdiction, it will be worth pausing to consider the nature of their relationship with the successors of St Peter. Contacts between them were largely limited to the participation of north Italians in councils convened at Rome, but it is also clear that some of the personnel of north Italian churches had close links with Rome, and after Constantius II's intervention in western ecclesiastical affairs, the religious politics of Rome and northern Italy became increasingly intertwined.

Assemblies of bishops at Rome had, since the mid-third century, demonstrated the influence, though not necessarily the authority, of the papacy over bishoprics in central and southern Italy, Sardinia, Sicily, and north Africa (cf. Eus., *HE* 6. 43. 3). Such gatherings reflected common interests and the ability of popes to summon other bishops; and in the fourth century, Rome proved to be a magnet for Christians from around the Tyrrhenian sea.[61] Together these factors must have influenced Constantine's decision that the first of his councils aimed at resolving the schism in the African church should be convened under Miltiades of Rome. The presence there of the bishops of Rimini, Faenza, and Milan does not indicate that their sees lay within the bishop of Rome's jurisdiction, since their attendance probably depended on the initiative of Constantine himself.[62] Once established, however, this connection proved to be a lasting

[61] Africa and Italy: Pietri, *Roma Christiana*, 729–48, 773–6, 888–909. Note also the composition of the Roman clergy: both Lucifer of Cagliari and Eusebius of Vercelli, who began their careers at Rome, were originally from Sardinia: Pietri, 'Appendice prosopographique', 393.
[62] As argued above pp. 111–14.

one, and thereafter the bishops of northern Italy were regular players in papal dramas, occasionally taking centre stage.

In large measure, the continuation of the connections established under Constantine was fostered by the regular presence of the imperial court in northern Italy, especially in the 340s and 350s. Not only for easterners like Athanasius did this prove an attraction, but also for the papacy, which dispatched a regular stream of legates to the region in these years, particularly at times of tension over doctrinal affairs, in which the bishops of Rome saw themselves —frequently despite all evidence to the contrary—as key players.[63] Hence, for example, a certain legate called Eusebius came north, at some indeterminate time in the 340s: he never returned to Rome, ending up instead as the celebrated bishop of Vercelli.[64] Vincentius of Capua, one of the most active papal agents in these years, seems also to have been a frequent visitor to northern Italy.[65]

As in so much else, the western expedition of Constantius II, and particularly his alliance with Valens of Mursa and Ursacius of Singidunum, transformed the relationship. As part of his effort to get the important western regional sees to adhere to his doctrinal definition, he came into conflict with Pope Liberius. Having attempted unsuccessfully a number of times to get Liberius to sign the decrees of the Council of Sirmium of 351, Constantius resorted to force, arrested the Pope, and interviewed him at Milan in late 355. When Liberius' obstinacy persisted, Constantius exiled him to Thrace and replaced him with a Roman deacon, Felix. After nearly two years' exile, Liberius capitulated; that he did so was entirely due to Fortunatianus of Aquileia.

Fortunatianus' dealings with or on behalf of Liberius are of particular interest for the developing relationship between Rome and the bishops of northern Italy. By 355, Fortunatianus had been bishop of Aquileia for more than a decade, and in that time had proved to be a key player in the Christological controversy insofar as it impinged on northern Italy, primarily in his role as host to the fugitive Athanasius. At Aquileia, the cross-currents of Christological politics converged in part because of the city's geographical position. That Constantius found support for his policies among bishops from the Balkans can only have increased Fortunatianus' interest in the

[63] Hanson, *Search*, 270–3, 854.
[64] Pietri, 'Appendice prosopographique', 393.   [65] Ibid., 373–4.

dispute, bearing in mind Aquileian ecclesiastical connections with the regions beyond the Julian Alps. In 347, for example, Ursacius and Valens, returning home after a council at Rome, encountered Athanasius' envoy Moses at Aquileia, while he was en route between Trier and Alexandria (Hil. Pict., *Coll. Ant. Par.* B. II. 8). During the usurpation of Magnentius, it seems that Valens and Ursacius were responsible for fomenting violent dissension in Fortunatianus' congregation (ibid. B. II. 2. 4). After the Council of Sirmium in 351, Liberius and the Italian episcopate had requested a council to be held at Aquileia (ibid. B. VII. 2. 6). At the same time, Liberius was in close contact with Fortunatianus, of whom he plainly held a high opinion (Liberius, *Ep. ad. Euseb. Verc.* 3. 2).

For reasons that can never be known, but which equally were not without parallel,[66] Fortunatianus gave up his allegiance to Athanasius around the time of the Council of Milan in 355, and, unlike Eusebius of Vercelli and Dionysius of Milan, retained his see. Little is known of his doctrinal beliefs, although it is most probable that Fortunatianus submitted to the Christology defined at Sirmium in 351.[67] It was at this time that he proved to be of greatest use to Liberius. With his exile to Thrace, Liberius was in special need of a trustworthy intermediary with the emperor. Before 355, he had used Eusebius of Vercelli and Lucifer of Cagliari, but after the Council of Milan, when they were exiled Liberius fell back on Fortunatianus. It was Fortunatianus who brought a letter to the eastern bishops in which Liberius repudiated Athanasius from communion with Rome (Hil. Pict., *Coll. Ant. Par.* B. III. 1–2), and according to Jerome, it was through the influence of the bishop of Aquileia that the pope succumbed to Constantius' demands (Hier., *De vir. ill.* 97).[68]

Fortunatianus never appears as anything more than a shadowy figure in the sources concerning Liberius' capitulation, but his

---

[66] Cf. the complaints, charged with pangs of regret, in Athan., *Apol. Const.* 27.

[67] This much is implied in Fortunatianus' willingness to carry to Constantius a letter in which Liberius asserted his acceptance of the creed of Sirmium (Hil. Pict. *Coll. Ant. Par.* B. VII. 8). Cf. Hier., *Ep.* 7. 6, claiming that, under Valerian, and through the efforts of clergy like Chromatius, Jovinus, and Eusebius, 'ab urbe vestra Arriani quondam dogmatis virus exclusum est'. This implies that Fortunatianus had accepted the Sirmian creed. For Jerome's equivocal attitude to Fortunatianus, see De Clerq, 'Fortunatien d'Aquilée', 1184. Athanasius, *Apol. Const.* 27, asserts, however, that Fortunatianus was forced into this position.

[68] For these events, see above all: Duchesne, 'Libère et Fortunatien'.

role can be compared with that of Vincentius of Capua and with Ursacius and Valens in the Balkans, to whom Liberius wrote, petitioning them to intercede personally on his behalf with Constantius (Hil. Pict., *Coll. Ant. Par.* B. VII. 10–11). Vincentius, Ursacius, and Valens were, like Fortunatianus, prominent western bishops who had rejected Athanasius and accepted the decisions of the Council of Sirmium. Much more than the bishops of Capua, Singidunum, and Mursa, however, Fortunatianus appears to have been Liberius' trusted friend. In 357, it was he who brought Liberius' letter to the eastern bishops and, when that failed to convince, brought a more strident one to Constantius. In the intervening period, the two bishops surely discussed what Liberius must do to regain favour with the emperor. This interpretation fits well with Jerome's later condemnation of Fortunatianus as the man responsible for Liberius' surrender to heresy.[69] The decision to which Fortunatianus directed Liberius was to have long-lasting consequences. It yielded a schism at Rome, where another pope, Felix, had been installed by Constantius and accepted by many of the clergy. In 366, when Liberius died, the election of a successor provoked bloody violence in Rome itself (Amm. Marc. 27. 3. 12–13). From a north Italian point of view, it seems that Fortunatianus' actions pushed him to the sidelines of ecclesiastical affairs. We hear nothing further about him, or his see, and it is not until the episcopate of his successor Valerian that Aquileia once more appears as an important regional bishopric.

The events of 355–7, however, meant that the affairs of the papacy and the churches of northern Italy had become intertwined, and they were not to be unravelled during the episcopate of Liberius' successor Damasus. In particular, Damasus was so distressed by Auxentius' continued tenure of the see of Milan that, in collusion with a number of north Italian bishops, he convened a council at Rome sometime between 369 and 372, at which Auxentius was condemned.[70] Yet his removal now, as when Hilary of Poitiers and Eusebius had tried some years earlier, would have required the intervention of Valentinian I, an emperor not given to an active role in theological politics. So Auxentius remained in place until his death

[69] Hier., *De vir. ill.* 97: 'Fortunatianus ... in hoc habetur detestabilis, quod Liberium, Romanae urbis episcopum, pro fide ad exilium pergentem primus sollicitavit et fregit et ad subscriptionem haereseos conpulit.'
[70] For this council see: Pietri, *Roma Christiana*, 733–6; Williams, *Ambrose*, 80–3.

in 374. Damasus' failure to secure Auxentius' deposition epitomized the bishop of Rome's lack of authority in north Italian affairs. There never seems to have been any recognition that the pope occupied a position of seniority over the region's episcopate: during the 350s, for example, there was never any hint that Pope Liberius conceived of the northern bishops as anything but equals.[71] Even after the accession of the emperor Gratian (375–83), who was more amenable than his father Valentinian I to listening to the requests of bishops, the capacity of the bishop of Rome to impose a decision on northern Italy remained restricted. A Roman synod of 378 sought to depose the wayward bishop of Parma, Urbanus, but he still seems to have been causing problems in 381.[72] For the rest of the century, all efforts by the bishops of Rome to impose their authority on northern Italy would have to be mediated through Ambrose, a bishop created in Damasus' own image.[73]

Ambrose seems never to have been anything but a willing servant of Damasus' ambitions for the papacy. In the early years of his episcopate, Ambrose built an enormous cruciform church, inspired by the Apostoleion at Constantinople, outside the Porta Romana of Milan, in which he interred the relics of the apostles, including SS Peter and Paul.[74] Damasus had fostered their cult as part of his expansionist plans,[75] so their installation in a Milanese church, especially one on the road to Rome, symbolized the connections between the two cities and their bishoprics.[76] But if Ambrose could be seen from a Roman perspective as 'our Ambrose' (Hier., *Ep.* 22. 22), the image proved largely irrelevant to his fellow bishops in northern Italy. With his consolidation of Milanese preeminence in northern Italy, Ambrose had created a communion of bishops which looked to him, not Rome, for leadership. Indeed, when it came to suppressing as heretical the teachings of the Roman ascetic Jovinian, the decision for northern Italy was not taken under direct papal leadership. Unsurprisingly, the offensive was led by Ambrose at the Milanese

---

[71] Even before the Council of Milan, Liberius addressed Eusebius on terms of equality, calling him 'frater' and 'coepiscopus noster' (*Ep. ad Euseb. Verc.* 3. 2. 1).

[72] McLynn, *Ambrose*, 287, giving a less positive appraisal than Pietri, *Roma Christiana*, 741–5.

[73] Pietri, *Roma Christiana*, 748–54, 782–6, 897–901.

[74] On the significance of the church's design: Lewis, 'Function and Symbolic Form'. For the relics of Peter and Paul: McLynn, *Ambrose*, 231–2.

[75] Huskinson, *Concordia Apostolorum*, 77–98.

[76] McLynn, *Ambrose*, 276–81.

synod of 392/3.[77] Even after Ambrose's death, the bishops of Rome
remained on the periphery of the world view of the north Italian
episcopate. When Vigilius of Trento sought to promote the cult of
the martyrs of the Val di Non, he wrote to Simplicianus of Milan
and John Chrysostom at Constantinople, but not to the bishop of
Rome.[78]

The shape of authority

The fourth century had seen a gradual transformation of the overall administrative structures in the north Italian church. At the
beginning of the period, it is impossible to see anything more elaborate than a loose regional affiliation between various congregations,
with or without bishops, because of geographical proximity. By the
third quarter of the century, a more formal kind of authority was
being exerted by bishops over Christian communities in their cities'
hinterlands, as is clearest at Vercelli and Aquileia. Neither these local
spheres of authority nor the broader areas of influence were inviol-
able. By the end of the century, the jurisdiction of Vercelli over neighbouring churches had eroded, while Aquileian influence over the
Balkans had been challenged by the activities there of Eusebius and
Ambrose.

The means by which such spheres of control were achieved and
maintained depended on a balance of administrative practice and
personal acumen. At various points in this discussion, an emerging
bureaucratic apparatus has been glimpsed. The sending of letters—
of which those by Ambrose and Eusebius represent perhaps only a
small sample—was crucial to the exercise of control. Such communication suggests that the bishops of northern Italy were beginning
to assemble administrative archives, even if only at a very unsophis-
ticated level.[79] Certainly, there is evidence that, like the imperial palaces
at Milan and Aquileia, the church buildings of northern Italy were
not just grand ceremonial spaces but also provided a focus for

[77] Ambr., *Ep.* 42; cf. McLynn, *Ambrose*, 280. For the issues: Kelly, *Jerome*, 179–
94.
[78] Lizzi, *Vescovi*, 93–4.
[79] Lane Fox, 'Literacy and Power', 136, on the implications of letter writing for
administration; cf. Noble, 'Literacy and Papal Government', for an excellent survey of how one special Italian church developed a highly bureaucratic administrative structure.

diocesan administration.[80] While such evidence has to be assumed for most north Italian churches for the fourth century, some precise indications of its workings can be seen in evidence from Aquileia. The detailed records of the council of 381—both its official *acta* and the defensive *Apologia* written afterwards by Palladius of Ratiaria —reveal much about the minutiae of ecclesiastical administration. In the *acta* of the council's proceedings, several references are made to stenographers (*exceptores*) employed by both Ambrose and his allies, and by Palladius and his fellow defendant Ursacius.[81] Following his condemnation at the council, Palladius wrote a pungent polemic challenging the authority of the council. Central to his case was the allegation that the council had been a secretive affair, and that its meetings had not taken place in public; on the contrary, the whole farce had been conducted behind closed doors in a place Palladius designates the *secretarium*.[82] Although the precise meaning of the term is unclear, it may indicate a room connected with the administrative apparatus of the church at Aquileia; certainly, there are several small rooms flanking the main halls of the Aquileian cathedral that could have served such a function. That such a quasi-bureaucracy existed in the emerging diocese of Aquileia seems to be implied by the personel of the church at S. Canzian d'Isonzo (*Aquae Gradatae*): one of the clergy recorded there was a *notarius*, a secretary.[83] By the episcopate of Chromatius, a substantial ecclesiastical archive at Aquileia must have existed, containing not only items of scripture,[84] but also volumes such as Rufinus' translations of Origen's homilies and Eusebius' *Ecclesiastical History*.[85] Indeed, it is possible that Rufinus exploited the skills of the Aquileian

---

[80] I owe this corrective to Kelly, 'Later Roman Bureaucracy', 163.

[81] *Acta conc. Aquil.* 34 (Palladius, addressing Ambrose and Eusebius of Bologna, refers to *tui exceptores*), 43 (Palladius challenges Ambrose: *Si uultis, exceptores nostri ueniant et sic totum excipiatur*), 46 (Palladius calls for *exceptor uester et noster*), and 51 (in the interests of a fair judgement, Palladius demands *Date auditores, ueniant et ex utraque parte exceptores*). On *exceptores*: Teitler, *Notarii and Exceptores*, 73–85, esp. 81–2 on their presence at the conference of Carthage in 411; cf. Gamble, *Books and Readers*, 120, 139–40.

[82] Pall., *Apol.* 89: '. . . ut licet concilium non esset, sicuti et angustiae secretarii in quo conuentum est . . .'. For comm., see esp. Tavano, 'Una pagina', 151–7.

[83] Cf. n. 33 above. For ecclesiastical *notarii*: Teitler, *Notarii and Exceptores*, 86–94.

[84] Jerome dedicated his translation of the Old Testament Chronicles to Chromatius: *PL* 28. 1389–90.

[85] Both of these works were dedicated to Chromatius: *CCL* 22 (1961), 267–8 (*HE*), 271–2 (homilies).

secretariat during his war of letters with Jerome over the orthodoxy of Origen.[86]

Beyond such administrative structures, a bishop's force of character was fundamentally important to the exercise of his authority over his peers. Eusebius and Ambrose had this aplenty, and exploited it as a way of extending their influence, or, in Ambrose's case, their episcopal authority. The importance of a bishop's background is particularly apparent in the case of Ambrose. Without the expertise gained as an imperial administrator or the dazzling model of Damasus to follow, it is hard to imagine the new bishop of Milan acquiring the leadership he had so obviously attained by 381. Determination and imagination were also important, as is clear from Ambrose's fearlessness even when dealing with the imperial court.[87] Perhaps the greatest testimony to the role of Ambrose's character in achieving ecclesiastical preeminence for Milan is the way in which the city's ecclesiastical jurisdiction waned after the great bishop's death in 397. Ambrose's influence had stretched as far as Florence and Sirmium; that of his successors went little further than the central plains of the Po valley (see Epilogue).

If the background of the bishops was important, so too were the long-standing social networks of the cities in which they preached. It is undeniable that the growth of regional spheres of influence followed the template laid down by centuries of Roman administrative, economic, and social networks. Thus Aquileia emerged as the leading centre of Christian communities in eastern Venetia and the north-western Balkans, while Vercelli's church had early links with other congregations in the cities of eastern Piedmont. This is a timely reminder of the importance of local contexts for the development of the north Italian church as a whole in this period. Each local conglomeration of Christianity emerged with its own distinct traditions, which would often defy the efforts of those interested in harmonizing them. Thus some of the most fundamental aspects of Christian life differed from city to city. To take one example, the baptismal liturgies of Aquileia and Milan were as different from each other, in terms of the order of rituals, as they were from the ceremonies of the Roman church.[88] The picture that emerges, therefore, is one which withstands any attempt at simplistic categorization. Administrative

---

[86] Cf. Hammond, 'Product of a Fifth Century Scriptorium', 372–5.
[87] Cf. pp. 119–26.
[88] Yarnold, 'Ceremonies of Initiation', 460–1; Jeanes, *The Day*, 206–12.

jurisdictions in northern Italy were still fluid and would remain so well into the fifth and later centuries.

The Church and local power

The mutability of regional episcopal hierarchies was mirrored at a more local level in terms of how bishops functioned as leaders in their own communities. Again this was a development which was tranformed utterly in the uncertain times of the fifth century, but the fourth century shows bishops negotiating their status with the other power brokers in the cities of northern Italy. That Christian congregations formed a distinct community within north Italian urban society is clear,[89] but this did not simplify the definition of a bishop's power. Rather, they found themselves engaged in competition with other claimants, both secular and clerical, for authority over their congregations.

Notions and expressions of episcopal power

The most obvious manifestation of episcopal power is evident in the literary corpus—albeit meagre—of the bishops of northern Italy. Zeno of Verona's *Tractatus*; Fortunatianus of Aquileia's *Gospel Commentaries*; Filastrius of Brescia's book on heresy; Eusebius of Vercelli's *de Trinitate* (if indeed it is by him);[90] the various letters they penned: all of them, whether aimed primarily at their congregations or not, were directed to the explanation of Christian truth. Until the beginning of Jerome's and Rufinus' literary and exegetical activities, it was the bishops of northern Italy who were the arbiters of orthodox doctrine. Sermons, such as those by Zeno, and like the ones upon which Fortunatianus' *Gospel Commentaries*

---

[89] Note, for example, Zeno of Verona's designation of his flock as the *aetheriae gentes* (*Tract.* 1. 38. 1); this suggests he is distinguishing them from less salubrious *gentes*. For discussion of who they were, see below pp. 209–13.

[90] It was long assumed that of its twelve books, only the first seven were actually by Eusebius. Doubt was cast on his authorship of even these by Manlio Simonetti in 'Qualche osservazione sul *De Trinitate*' (which includes, at pp. 386–7, a summary of the complex textual transmission of the work). Recently, however, Williams, *Ambrose*, 239–42, has put the case anew for Eusebian authorship. It is of little importance for my argument here whether or not it is a genuinely Eusebian work: the surviving letters of Eusebius, and the accounts of his action, are enough to show that he saw himself as an arbiter of doctrine.

probably drew,[91] were delivered by the bishops in their crucial role as interpreters of Holy Scripture.[92]

Such activity is mentioned by Zeno, whose spare references to the bishop's role in the Church are the most complete articulation of how the north Italian episcopate envisaged its role before Ambrose's voluminous writings on the topic.[93] In Zeno's concept of episcopal office it is exegetical and liturgical functions which demonstrate the position of the bishop among the congregation. His writings make frequent reference to explanations of the biblical readings which the congregation has just heard;[94] the bishop is the *predicator*, the *doctor legis* who interprets the two Testaments (*Tract.* I. 37. 9–10).[95] For Zeno, this exegetical activity was a regular duty, as part of daily services during which the eucharist was received and sermons preached.[96] At certain points in the year, the position of the bishop was particularly prominent, such as when he led the catechumens through the rites of baptism. The bishop was the intercessor between the human and the divine, as ordained by God:

by His own will He planted . . . the Mother Church, and tending it with the priestly office, and making it fruitful with holy waterings (*pia potatione*),

[91] The first discussion of the texts, which offer commentaries on Mt. 21: 1–11 and 23: 34–9, was by Wilmart, 'Deux expositons', 160–74. De Clerq, 'Fortunatien d'Aquilée', 1184–5, notes the place of their Gospel texts in the Aquileian liturgical year. As they survive, they quote a line of biblical text, followed by a short explanation. Thus they seem like notes, either derived from, or preparatory to, the delivery of exegesis while preaching. That Matthew was a popular text in the Aquileian liturgy is confirmed by the survival of seventeen *Tractatus in Evangelium Matthaei* by Fortunatianus' second successor, Chromatius (*CCL* 9 (1957), 389–442) which follow an identical structure, although they do not discuss the same passages.

[92] Gamble, *Books and Readers*, 211–31, on the use of Scripture in the liturgy.

[93] Zeno's views on the role of the bishop are explored in detail by Padovese, *Originalità cristiana*; and Truzzi, *Zeno, Gaudenzio e Cromazio*, ch. 1. For Ambrose: Gryson, *Le prêtre selon saint Ambroise*.

[94] e.g. *Tract.* 2. 26. 1: 'sicut lectio diuina testatur'; cf. the entries in Löfstedt and Packard, *Concordance*, 348–9, for similar phraseology.

[95] Zeno's ideas are expressed as profoundly allegorical readings of the Gospel. Commenting on the Parables of the Kingdom, he equated the role of the *praedicator* with that of 'the scribe who has been taught for the Kingdom of Heaven [who] is like the head of the household [*pater familias*] offering what is new and old from his treasure' (*Tract.* I. 37. 9 on Mt. 13: 52). Then, moving on to the Parable of the Good Samaritan, the bishop is like the innkeeper who accepts two denarii to care for the injured man, for the coins are the two Testaments which guarantee good health and salvation (1. 37. 10 on Lk. 10: 29–37).

[96] Cf. *Tract.* I. 37. 10: 'in ecclesia, quo pecora diuina succedunt, uenerabili sacramento susceptum cotidianis praedicationum medicaminibus curat'; cf. 2. 6. 11: 'Haec sunt, dilectissimi fratres, charisimata uestra, hae uirtutes, quibus Hierusalem spiritalis instruitur, quibus sacrae orationis iste locus nouus et populus cotidie Christi dei et domini nostri prouidentia comparatur.'

He trained it to bear an abundant harvest hanging from the fertile branches. (*Tract.* I. 10B. 2)

It was these liturgical functions that made the bishop's role most obvious.[97] In everything specifically Christian which Zeno's congregation did, their bishop was there to preside over them, and to explain how the events of the biblical drama were mirrored in the courses of their lives, especially at moments of crisis and resolution, such as baptism, death, or exorcism.[98]

This exegetical and liturgical prominence accorded the bishop was reflected in ritual. That this was an early development is clear from the parallel halls of Theodore's double church at Aquileia. Here, the spatial articulation of the building's interior did much to emphasize the prominence of the clergy in the church, and the supremacy of Theodore among them. The area where Theodore and his clergy would have presided over the liturgy, at the eastern end of both halls, was separated by marble *transennae* (cf. Figure 2).[99] As is clear from the mosaic pavement, which was designed to take these marble screens and their supporting jambs, this delineation of the floor space was part of the original plan of the church, showing how already by the time of Constantine, the bishops of Aquileia were emphasizing their preeminence within their communities. Here too there may have been an altar on which Theodore would have prepared and blessed the offerings for the eucharist.[100] With Fortunatianus' rebuilding of the complex, the ceremonial significance of the bishop was given increased emphasis: in the middle of the nave, a division of the mosaic pavement set aside a central, longitudinal strip of floor leading from the door of the church to the raised dais of the altar and sanctuary (see Figure 4). Further renovation of the building enhanced this architectural feature. In the early fifth century, some two-thirds of this central strip was raised as a *solea*: now the preeminence of the bishop was emphasized on his entry by his elevated physical position in the procession.[101]

---

[97] Padovese, *Originalità cristiana*, 24–5. Cf. Jeanes, *The Day*, 123–7, for the significance of the viticultural imagery.

[98] Padovese, *Originalità cristiana*, 18–26; Truzzi, *Zeno, Gaudenzio e Cromazio*, 111–17.

[99] Tavano, 'Il recinto presbiteriale', 105–21.

[100] Mirabelli Roberti, 'La posizione dell'altare', 181–94.

[101] Bertacchi, 'La basilica postteodoriana', 62–6; for the ceremonial use of this feature: Mathews, 'An Early Roman Chancel Arrangement', 73–95; cf. Bonnet and Perinetti, 'Les premiers édifices chrétiens', esp. 482–5, for a north Italian example.

Theodore's identity and prominence within the Aquileian communion was indelibly stamped on the building by this articulation
of its internal space, and the visual message of its mosaics served to
emphasize his position. Within the partitioned area of the southern hall, the mosaic decoration proclaimed the central role of the
bishop in salvation: an enormous seascape, depicting the story of
Jonah, symbolized the resurrection and its earthly counterpart,
redemption through baptism.[102] It was Theodore, moreover, who was
identified above all as the builder of the church. There were two
mosaic acclamations of his activity.[103] That in the northern hall
announced that his reconstruction of the building represented an
extension of the complex as a whole.[104] More impressively, the
clipeus in the Jonah seascape in the southern hall not only acclaims
Theodore in a standard formula (*Theodore felix*),[105] but accords him
alone the honour of having constructed the church.[106] Theodore knew
well how to appropriate the visual language of power to emphasize
his position in society. In the *clipeus*, his name was crowned by
the Chi-Rho symbol, an association which can be paralleled in a
number of fourth- and fifth-century contexts.[107] These dedicatory
acclamations set Theodore in the tradition of secular patronage
and munificence, where the position of a patron's name on a
building served to identify him (or her) as a prominent citizen.[108]

---

[102] Bagatti, 'Note sul contenuto dottrinale', 119–22; cf. Menis, 'Il pensiero teologico',
503–7. For the symbolism in a north Italian context: Zeno, *Tract.* 1. 38; cf. Y.-M.
Duval, 'Les sources greques de l'exégèse de Jonas', 98–115.

[103] For acclamations: Roueché, 'Acclamations', esp. 181–8.

[104] See in detail pp. 191–3 below.

[105] Both in the south hall (*ILCV* 1863) and in the nave of the north hall (Kähler,
Die spätantiken Bauten, 34). Cf. Roueché, 'Acclamations', 182–3; Ruggiero, *Diz. Ep.*
3. 44–9 on 'felix'.

[106] Although the assistance of God and the flock are mentioned, both verbs are
singular and emphasize the bishop's preeminent role in building the church:
'Theodore felix adiuuante Deo omnipotente et poemnio caelitus tibi traditum omnia
baeate *fecisti* et glorise *dedicasti*.'

[107] See esp. Brown, *Authority and the Sacred*, 13–14, for its use on the Hunting
Plate of the Seuso Treasure. It is also used on imperial monuments and artefacts: the
column of Arcadius in Constantinople; the diptych of Probus showing Honorius;
the Geneva missorium depicting Valentinian I or II where, significantly, the Chi-
Rho fills the nimbus around the emperor's head (compare the Hinton St Mary mosaic
from Dorset, now in the British Museum). On these, cf. MacCormack, *Art and
Ceremony*, 57–9, 204–5, 221.

[108] Ward-Perkins, *CAMA*, 51–84, also 242–3 on episcopal patronage at Ravenna.
For 'naming' as a strategy of episcopal patrons: Wharton, *Refiguring the Post
Classical City*, 113 and 187–8 nn. 31–3.

Together with the Chi-Rho, a symbol of Christian power, they identified Theodore as the leader of his congregation. A similar phenomenon can be seen at Milan, early in Ambrose's episcopate. The basilica outside the western walls in which he interred the relics of Gervasius and Protasius had become known as the *basilica Ambrosiana* already by the early 380s. This name was not imposed by the bishop, but was a popular designation attesting the pre-eminence of Ambrose among Milanese Christians.[109]

Popular acclaim and local competition

Yet neither Theodore nor Ambrose will have been without their local rivals, whether clerical or secular. As the position of bishop became invested with ever more power and prestige, so it was absorbed into the traditional rivalries and contingencies of local society. Theodore's acclamations and statements of his role as patron were themselves embedded in the etiquette of civic politics, and it would not be unsurprising to find others making similar claims. Other inscriptions in the mosaics of his church show that there were already other powers within the Aquileian church. Towards the eastern end of the north hall there is another acclamation: 'Cyriace vibas'.[110] This form of acclamation can be paralleled elsewhere in northern Italy, at Padua. The floor of the Christian building excavated near the ancient civic centre was covered by a mosaic, containing two acclamations, which are distinguished by the different sizes of the letters and the colour of the *tesserae* in which they are laid. The main body of the inscription, comprising its middle four lines, are in black *tesserae*, reading 'Euther | i Deus te c | um tuis | seruet'. The first and last lines of the inscription are in smaller letters of red *tesserae*, reading 'in hac uiuas'.[111] In both its appearance and form, the inscription is comparable to those in the Theodorean halls at Aquileia. Indeed, the formulae 'uiuas' or 'uiuas in Deo' were common throughout the Latin west on items such as Christian sarcophagi and metalwork.[112] Thus the examples from Aquileia and Padua

[109] Ambr., *Ep.* 22. 2: 'in basilicam quam appellant Ambrosiana.'
[110] Kähler, *Die spätantiken Bauten*, pl. 24.
[111] This description of the mosaic based on personal inspection in the Museo agli Eremitani in Padua. For further analysis of this mosaic, with full bibliography, see Porta, 'Mosaici paleocristiani', 233–5, with figs. 2–3 illustrating the mosaic (in black and white); and J.-P. Caillet, *L'évergétisme monumental*, 101.
[112] e.g. *ILCV* 2193–225.

show Theodore, Cyriacus, and Eutherius using the language of power to establish their prominence in their communities. What Cyriacus' inscription—and probably also that of Eutherius[113]—shows is that members of the community other than its bishops were willing to use these forms to put themselves in positions of prominence.

Close to the acclamation of Cyriacus in the Theodorean north hall there is another inscription, this time proclaiming the donation of money to pay for part of the mosaic pavement: 'Ianuari[us . . .] | de dei dono u[ouit] | p(edes) DCCCLXXX[. . .]'.[114] Ianuarius' identity cannot be established with certainty, other than that he was a private individual in the Aquileian congregation.[115] This donation was extremely generous, one of the largest known.[116] The style of Ianuarius' donation was not unique to northern Italy, but became particularly widespread there. During the fourth and fifth centuries, clerical and secular patrons of north Italian churches were using such payments for mosaic floors as a means of displaying their position in Christian society in buildings at Concordia, Emona (the baptistery and portico), Grado (Piazza della Vittoria), Trieste (Via Madonna del Mare), Verona (beneath the Duomo), and Vicenza (SS Felice e Fortunato).[117] At Aquileia itself it was used not only in the Theodorean church, but also at the Basilica di Monastero, while it has been suggested that the various portrait panels incorporated in the pavement of the southern Theodorean hall represent patrons of the local community.[118]

Inscriptions recording such donations point to one way in which the Church was being absorbed into north Italian local society.

---

[113] It is impossible to know who Eutherius was, but the formula adapted in the mosaic (*te cum tuis*) is similar to those used in other north Italian churches, where patrons use the formula *cum suis* to indicate that their donation is made on behalf of their family also. This might imply that Eutherius was a private individual rather than a member of the Paduan clergy.

[114] Cf. Kähler, *Die spätantiken Bauten*, 31–4.

[115] Stucchi, 'Le basiliche paleocristiane', 182 n. 1, proposed that this Ianuarius was the same as the fifth-century Aquileian bishop of that name. This is impossible, since the post-Theodorean north hall was constructed under Fortunatianus in the mid-fourth century; cf. Caillet, *L'évergetisme monumental*, 131–2.

[116] Caillet, *L'évergetisme monumental*, 131.

[117] The standard work is now Caillet, *L'évergetisme monumental*. For other examples in *Venetia*, cf. Pietri, 'Une aristocratie provinciale', esp. 132–7. Old but still useful is Leclerq, 'Pavement'.

[118] For a review of the various arguments: Brusin, 'Il mosaico pavimentale', 174–93.

Another was the rising importance of urban crowds in the region's ecclesiastical affairs.[119] Again, there are only tantalizing glimpses of this activity prior to Ambrose's episcopate, and what little there is focuses on Milan under Auxentius. The first instance comes at the Council of Milan in 355, where word of the rough treatment of bishop Dionysius provoked such popular indignation that the conclusion of the synod had to take place in the security of the imperial palace.[120] The next incident shows that in time Auxentius too won the loyalty of the Milanese. When Filastrius, the future bishop of Brescia, tried to stir up resistance against Auxentius, he found himself being whipped out of town by a crowd incensed at his treatment of their bishop (Gaud. Brix., *Tract.* 21. 6–7).[121] Similarly, Ambrose's intervention in the affairs of Verona was in response to requests from the laity within Verona who were dissatisfied with a judgement already made by their own bishop Syagrius.[122]

Yet the Milanese congregation was by no means so united a body as its angry reaction to Filastrius of Brescia might suggest. After Auxentius' death in 374, the election of Ambrose was preceded by a period when Milanese Christianity was wracked 'by grave dissension and perilous sedition' (Ruf., *HE* 11. 11). Paulinus' account of Ambrose's election (Paul. Med., *V. Ambr.* 6–9) makes much of the supposed unanimity of the group that selected him, but his insistence on a semi-mystical element in achieving this concord suggests that he is concealing real divisions among Milanese Christians.[123] As will soon be seen, Ambrose's rivals continued to find support in Milan, suggesting that a small anti-Nicene faction endured. Whether the pro-Nicene group during Auxentius' episcopate was any larger cannot be ascertained, but the most likely situation was that at Milan—as elsewhere—most Christians remained neutral, with only minorities taking up extreme theological positions. In their allegiance to three successive bishops—Dionysius, Auxentius, and Ambrose—holding different Christological views, it is most probable that the loyalty

---

[119] For the phenomenon in a Mediterranean context: Brown, *Power and Persuasion*, 84–9.

[120] Hil. Pict., *Coll. Ant. Par.* App. II. 3: 'res [*sc.* the treatment of Dionysius by Valens of Mursa] post clamorem multum deducta in conscientiam plebis est, grauis omnium dolor ortus est, inpugnata est a sacerdotibus fides. uerentes igitur illi populi iudicium e dominico ad palatium transeunt.'

[121] Williams, *Ambrose*, 77–8.

[122] Ambrose, *Ep.* 5–6; cf. McLynn, *Ambrose*, 286–7.

[123] Cf. McLynn, *Ambrose*, 1–7, for commentary.

of ordinary Christians at Milan was to their bishop as pastor, rather than as theologian. Some of Ambrose's rivals accused him of bribing crowds to secure their loyalty (Ambr., *C. Aux.* 33): this surely reflects the cynical manipulation by Ambrose's enemies of the bishop's almsgiving. Other north Italian bishops also distributed money to the poor, a helpful reminder that, in the eyes of the faithful, pastoral duties were as important as doctrinal ones.[124] Even those deemed by later tradition as heretics were active in this area. When Auxentius was appointed bishop of Milan in 355, he did not know any Latin (Athan., *Hist. Ar.* 75). By the time he died, however, he not only had picked up the language, but had acquired sufficient skill in it to use a grammatical ambiguity to trump no less a theologian than Hilary of Poitiers (Hil. Pict., *C. Aux.* 8, 13). It would be absurd to assume that Auxentius learned his Latin with a view to such theological tight spots; most probably he learned it, in part, to fulfil his pastoral role in the Milanese church.

This does not mean that bishops were never challenged by doctrinal opponents within their cities. Again, Milan provides the clearest evidence of clerical dissidence within a city. Whatever the nature of his successes as a pastor, Auxentius did not have complete control over his city's clergy: the deacon Sabinus who brought Valerian of Aquileia's letter to Basil of Caesarea and Damasus' letter *Confidimus quidem* to the pro-Nicene bishops of the east was from Milan. His activity on behalf of the pro-Nicene cause during Auxentius' episcopate shows that he must have been a renegade, refusing to associate with the bishop of his city. Nor was Ambrose unrivalled at Milan. From the late 370s it is clear that there was some sort of opposition movement within the city. Sometime after the Roman defeat at Hadrianople had left the Balkans at the mercy of the Goths, Julianus Valens, the bishop of Poetovio (modern Ptuj in Slovenia), had fled his city for the relative safety of northern Italy. He ended up at Milan, where he made common cause with another ecclesiastical renegade, Ursinus, a claimant to the bishopric of Rome, and hence a rival to Ambrose's friend Damasus.[125] More seriously, Valens had set himself up as a homoian rival to Ambrose,

[124] Cf. Lizzi, *Vescovi*, 36–57.
[125] Ambr., *Ep.* 11. 3. For commentary see McLynn, *Ambrose*, 58–9, a more sensitive appraisal of the situation than Williams, *Ambrose*, 137–8, who takes Ambrose at his word by surmising that Ursinus and Valens made a common anti-Nicene cause. McLynn rightly recognizes this as 'a smear'.

ordaining his own clergy (Ambr., *Ep.* 10. 9–10). While Ambrose
accused Valens of sowing the seeds of a homoian community,[126] it
is more likely that he appealed first to a kernel of homoian opinion
lingering in the city since Auxentius' episcopate.[127] At any rate,
Ambrose seemed curiously unable to deal with him: even after his
apparent triumph at the Council of Aquileia, he wrote to the
emperor Gratian requesting that Valens be sent back to the Balkans
(id., *Ep.* 10. 10–11).

The case of Julianus Valens was not unique. His presence in
Milan was mirrored in the presence there of the imperial court of
Valentinian II and Justina which, like Valens, had left the Balkans
for the security of Italy. In some respects, imperial presences could
be beneficial for a bishop's prestige: by giving him access to the
emperor, it could enhance the bishop's ability to act as an ecclesiastical politician of considerable importance, rather like those
bishops in whose cities Athanasius met Constans in the 340s.
As Ambrose would discover in late 388 when Theodosius arrived
in Milan, however, the imperial court could also be disruptive to a
bishop's position in his city, providing an alternative focus of
patronage and authority.[128] Under Justina's influence, Valentinian II
proved to be a rival to Ambrose within Milan, notably during the
conflict over the basilicas in 385–6.[129] Yet this threat to Ambrose's
preeminence in his own city had first manifested its potential in 378–9,
as soon as Valentinian and Justina arrived from the Balkans, when
the senior Augustus, Gratian, had sequestered a basilica for the
use of the newly established court (*de Spiritu Sancto* 1. 1. 21). It
was only when Ambrose interceded with Gratian directly that the
church was restored to the bishop's control.[130] Another instance of
the court acting as a rival attraction to the bishop seems to have
occurred in 345, when Athanasius spent Easter with Fortunatianus
at Aquileia, at the same time as the city played host to Constans
and his entourage. This was when Fortunatianus' new cathedral was

[126] *Ep.* 10. 10: 'nunc . . . et seminarium quaerit suae impietatis atquae perfidiae per
quosque perditos derelinquere'.
[127] McLynn, *Ambrose*, 185, talks of 'the homoean seedbed left at Milan by
Iulianus Valens', but it strikes me that Valens' initial success probably depended on
finding homoians in the city already. Paulinus' account of Ambrose's election
admits a Christological division among the population (*V. Ambr.* 6: 'et Ariani sibi
et Catholici sibi episcopum cupiebant').
[128] McLynn, *Ambrose*, 297–8.   [129] See pp. 121–3.
[130] For this confrontation: Williams, 'Ambrose, Emperors and Homoians'.

still under construction, and even though it was still unconsecrated, it had to be used for the Easter liturgy because of the unexpected size of the congregation (Athan., *Apol. Const.* 15).

Conclusion

In sum, the fourth century saw considerable fluidity both in the administrative interrelationships of north Italian bishops, and in their capacity to wield authority over their congregations. Both forms of episcopal administration relied upon a variety of circumstances ranging from the proximity or absence of the imperial court, to the particular character of an individual bishop. For all that, certain trends can be observed. Regional spheres of interest, and later metropolitan hierarchies, often evolved within a set of pre-existing social matrices which bound certain centres together. Thus the early influence of the church of Vercelli followed closely the pattern of administrative connections observable in secular Roman administration before the fourth century. Meanwhile the Aquileian bishops' sphere of influence was practically coextensive with the commercial networks which had long emanated from the city into north-eastern Italy and the western Balkans. Nevertheless, bishops were far from content to submit their authority to these constraints, and several sought actively to extend their jurisdiction beyond them. The example *par excellence* is of course Ambrose, but his example was soon followed by contemporaries, such as in Vigilius of Trento's direction of missions into the Alto Adige. Wedded to these pre-existing structures, bishops also extended their influence by exploiting very Christian principles and methods. Spiritual excellence is the most obvious example, and the rise of Aquileia in the days of bishop Valerian and his *chorus beatorum* shows how such prestige could benefit a church's local importance. At the same time, the appearance of members of the *chorus beatorum* as bishops of neighbouring sees—such as Heliodorus at Altino—shows how specifically Christian institutions could be used to build up a regional sphere of influence.

If regional hierarchies were in a state of flux, so too were the means by which a bishop exerted his power at the level of civic society. Apart from the acknowledgement that bishops had certain functions which established their leadership within their congregations—such as preaching—it is clear that they had to borrow methods from the secular sphere to buttress their authority. The careful articulation of space within church buildings and the use by bishops of visual symbols of power reflect this trend. But by setting themselves up in positions of authority, bishops also placed themselves within a wider network of power relations that permeated the life of the cities of northern Italy. Receiving the acclamations of the plebs was also something that civic grandees would expect. So just as Theodore was acclaimed by his flock at Aquileia, so too the Christians of Padua hailed their benefactor Eutherius and his family.

By the end of the fourth century, the north Italian episcopate was fully enmeshed in the politics of the region's cities. They can be seen manipulating crowds to get rid of rivals, and the erection of large church buildings gave them an opportunity to present themselves as patrons. Nevertheless, north Italian bishops could find themselves being opposed within their communities, for example, when certain groups refused to acknowledge their orthodoxy. The arrival of powerful outsiders, notably the emperor and his court, could also pose a threat by introducing a system of power relations over which the bishop had no control. Of course, these were experiences shared by bishops throughout the empire, but the way they were experienced in northern Italy was unique. The strategic importance of the region meant that its episcopate had to deal with the challenges offered by the imperial presence with alarming frequency. Similarly, the disruption of a bishop's doctrinal authority by local opposition seems to have been a problem for the north Italian episcopate only from the 350s onwards, as a direct consequence of the region's involvement in the Christological controversy. This same controversy also provided the environment within which various north Italian bishops sought to formalize their regional jurisdictions. Ambrose's efforts at achieving regional hegemony were directed towards the eradication of homoianism throughout northern Italy and its neighbouring territories. In other words, his actions aimed to undo the achievements of Constantius II at Milan in 355.

From the cities to the mountains:
Christian expansion, 350–400

By the time Ambrose had presided over the funeral of Theodosius I, north Italian Christianity had developed considerably from the small, secretive movement it had been at the outset of the fourth century. Its organization had become more elaborate, with bishops in certain cities—notably Aquileia, Milan, and Vercelli—wielding a loose form of authority over Christian congregations in other centres. Church buildings were rising in many of the cities of northern Italy, attesting the wealth and self-confidence of the Christians who built them. In social terms, the Church encompassed a broad constituency: from the archaeological remains of churches and hints in written sources, it can be seen that many wealthy inhabitants of the cities had joined their Christian communities. Local notables like Ianuarius at Aquileia saw Christianity as an outlet for their patronage, while some bishops, such as Auxentius and Ambrose at Milan, were able to mobilize large throngs of the urban population. But to what extent had the Church expanded since the early decades of the century? More importantly, did this expansion lead to the transformation of the religious geography of northern Italy, creating there a Christian landscape?

This chapter will be devoted to elucidating the evidence for Christian growth. In common with the analysis of the earlier phase of expansion in the late third and early fourth centuries, it will be shown that generalizations are impossible, and that instead variation from locality to locality within northern Italy is the key factor determining Christian diffusion. Similarly, it is impossible to know with certainty who precisely brought the faith to new areas within the region. Nevertheless, by looking again at the scatter of new Christian communities against the backdrop of the north Italian human environment, it is possible to identify the social dynamics conducive to the dissemination of the gospel. The scope of the chapter will be territorial, in that it will determine which new areas of northern Italy were brought within the evangelical horizons of the Church. Its source material will be primarily literary: letters and the proceedings of two church councils. Once again, however, archaeological data will be marshalled to add substance to the picture, providing detail about Christian communities listed in written sources and, occasionally, demonstrating the existence of congregations which have somehow failed to leave their mark on the documentary evidence. Having achieved a framework of Christian diffusion by these means, the following chapter will set these religious changes in the social context of the region's cities.

The growth of the episcopate

By the end of the period covered by this study, two further church councils had met in northern Italy, at Aquileia on 3 September 381,[1] and at Milan sometime in late 392 or early 393. These were not the only synods to have met in northern Italy since the dissolution of the Council of Rimini in 359: sometime in the late 360s or early 370s, for example, bishops from Gaul and Venetia met to condemn Auxentius of Milan.[2] But it is only from Aquileia and Milan that we have detailed lists of participants that can compare with the attendance records of councils convened by Constantine the Great, Constans, and Constantius II.

By 359, as has been seen, Christian communities with bishops were in place at Aquileia, Brescia, Faenza, Milan, Padua, Parma, Ravenna, Vercelli, and Verona, and it is likely that non-episcopal groups existed at several other centres.[3] At Aquileia in 381, however, the number of bishoprics had increased markedly. From within the confines of the Alps, the Apennines, and the Adriatic coast came bishops from several newly attested sees: Heliodorus of Altino (*Acta conc. Aquil.* 61),[4] Eusebius of Bologna (57), Bassianus of Lodì (60), Eventius of Pavia (56), Sabinus of Piacenza (58), and Abundantius of Trento (57). Tortona, which was under the jurisdiction of Eusebius of Vercelli in the late 350s, now had its own

---

[1] On the composition of the council, see M. Zelzer, *CSEL* 82/3 (1982), clii–clv; Gryson, *Scolies ariennes*, 130–2. But cf. also n. 19 below.
[2] See pp. 131–2 above.   [3] See Chs. 2–3 above.
[4] Numbers in parentheses hereafter refer to section numbers of these *acta*.

bishop, Exsuperantius (60).[5] In addition, there were three bishops from the Alpine fringes of northern Italy: Diogenes of Geneva (63), Theodore of Octodurum (62), and Maximus of Emona (59). The possibility that other north Italian churches were represented cannot be ruled out, since several participants at the council are given no provenance in the manuscripts of the *acta*; but to attempt any identification of these mysterious bishops with Italian sees would be purely speculative. Turning to the Milanese council a decade later we find three new sees listed, at Claterna (near modern Imola), Como, and Modena.[6]

As with any council, these lists of participants cannot be taken as a definitive picture of the extent of the north Italian church in 381 or 392/3. At the Council of Aquileia, for example, there were some notable absences, such as the bishops of Verona and Padua, two of the sees which had supported Athanasius in his efforts to gain an audience with Constans. More pointedly, the delegates assembled at Aquileia were a partisan bunch, a factor not lost on Palladius of Ratiaria, who questioned the very legality of the assembly.[7] Any picture of the expansion of north Italian Christianity based on the list of 381, then, must acknowledge the limitations of the text. Likewise, the Milanese list of 392/3 is far from comprehensive: indeed, it has already been suggested that this council amounts to little more than a local gathering of bishops directly dependent on Milan. Even so, it is possible to make some positive remarks about the picture these lists yield.

In the first place, it is noticeable that many of the new bishoprics arose along important roads: Bologna, Claterna, Modena, and Piacenza lay on the Via Aemilia, the latter on the important crossing of the Po, while Trento and Emona were on major transalpine routes. In addition, it is clear that Christianity did not spread evenly through the region. Just as for the period before 359, the growth of Christianity in the second half of the fourth century was patchy, with the new bishoprics arising in regional clusters. Pavia, Piacenza, Lodì, and Tortona, for example, fall in the area around the established Christian centres of Vercelli and Milan,

---

[5] This is a further reminder that the appearance of a bishopric in most cases represents the end of a process of Christian growth: Lanzani, 'Ticinum', 356.

[6] Subscriptions at the end of Ambr. *Ep.* 42. 14. For identification of the sees: Zelzer, *CSEL* 82/3 (1982), cxxviii, 311.

[7] See p. 152 above.

while Altino is close to Aquileia. Such local concentrations may reflect the influence of episcopal initiative in these established sees on the further development of those new sees, as is particularly clear in the cases of Milan and Aquileia in the later fourth century.[8] In the 350s, after all, Tortona had been dependent on Vercelli, while Heliodorus of Altino was a product of the *chorus beatorum* of the Aquileian church, where he had lived for several years as an ascetic.[9] At the same time, there is an important difference between the distribution patterns of new bishoprics in the periods before and after 359. In the earlier period, the expansion of the Church had shown greatest success in the regions nearest the Adriatic coast, particularly *Venetia et Histria*.[10] By the second half of the century, the diffusion of the faith was proving successful also in the central areas of the Po valley. Thus local variability and the importance of communications networks which had been so important to the spread of Christianity in the region in the third and early fourth centuries continued to play an important role in its further expansion in the decades after the Council of Rimini. In addition, episcopal initiative was becoming an important factor in directing Christian missionary activity.

The frontiers of evangelization

Perhaps the most remarkable aspect of Christian expansion in the second half of the fourth century was its move into areas which seem remote from the traditional—predominantly urban—centres of evangelization, to the countryside and the mountains.[11] This raises some important methodological questions in terms of interpreting literary sources for such expansion. The modern opposition

[8] See pp. 140–53 above. [9] Cf. p. 142 above. [10] Discussed in Ch. 3.
[11] For emphasis on the urban character of early north Italian Christianity: Lizzi, *Vescovi*, 59–81, 193–202. For cities as centres of civilization: Mumford, *The City in History*, 70, is the classic statement. The urban–rural division, with its ramifications for civilization, is neatly expressed in the various works of Fernand Braudel, esp. *The Mediterranean*, ii. 34–8 (on mountains), *Civilization and Capitalism*, i. 479 (dynamism of urban centres: 'towns are . . . electric transformers. They increase tension, accelerate the rhythm of exchange and constantly recharge human life'). Such views have been adopted wholesale by some ancient historians: e.g. Van Dam, *Leadership and Community*, 48–9.

between an urban 'centre' and a rural or mountainous 'periphery' is derived from a division common also in ancient perceptions.[12] In terms of evangelization, the concept is neatly encapsulated in Sulpicius Severus' assertion that Christianity came late to the Alps (*Chron.* 2. 32). His view was echoed in the bleak picture of Christian expansion in Piedmont painted by bishop Maximus of Turin early in the fifth century. Maximus' descriptions of pagan rites locate them in rural areas ('ad campum': *Sermo* 63. 2) beyond the city ('extra ciuitatem': *Sermo* 98. 3). Such sweeping generalizations ought not to be accepted at face value: as will be shown, Christianity was already seeping into rural and mountainous areas before the end of the fourth century. Another point at issue here is the distance between what a bishop like Maximus thought an acceptable level of piety and that shared by ordinary Christians in his congregation. Maximus' tirades against rural paganism occur, after all, in a sequence of sermons aimed at persuading Piedmontese landowners to crush pagan worship on their rural estates.[13] These local notables plainly did not see how their own devotion to Christ might be compromised by the pagan worship of their tenants, despite Maximus' protestations that they risked spiritual contamination (*Sermones* 106–8). In this they were not alone. At around the same time that Maximus was haranguing them about their duties as Christians, both Augustine of Hippo and Peter Chrysologus were seething at the presence of pagan elements in civic festivals at Carthage and Ravenna.[14] Others among the laity were more in tune with their bishops' expectations: Augustine's parishioner Publicola wrote a letter asking advice on the risks accruing from coming into contact with—or even just the presence of—pagan cult objects.[15] This represents nothing short of a gap between what bishops and the laity —even to the level of the emperor—perceived of as an acceptable

---

[12] See e.g. van Andel and Runnels, *Beyond the Acropolis*, 3–4; but cf. Aristotle's conundrum of the rural and urban parts of the *polis* (*Politics* 3. 1276a 19–25). Views of the natural world in antiquity—and indeed for much of the medieval and modern periods—were hopelessly anthropocentric: Clark, 'Cosmic Sympathies', 310–29; cf. Fumagalli, *Paesaggi della paura*, 15–90.

[13] Lizzi, *Vescovi*, 193–202.

[14] Aug., *Sermo* 62. 6. 10 (the *genius* of Carthage, and images of Mars and Mercury); Peter Chrysologus, *Sermo* 155 bis. 1 (the procession included effigies of Saturn, Jupiter, Hercules, Diana, and Vulcan).

[15] Publicola's letter is Aug., *Ep.* 46; cf. *Ep.* 47 for Augustine's reply.

demonstration of Christian devotion.[16] This touches on the issue
of what precisely is meant by a term such as 'Christianization': undoubtedly no single definition is possible, since views of what was
or was not acceptable varied from time to time, place to place, and
person to person.[17] Maximus was a hard-liner; so too was Sulpicius
Severus, as is clear from his approval of Martin of Tours' destruction
of pagan shrines.[18] Plainly their views of the limits of Christianization must be subjected to careful scrutiny, not least because at the
Council of Aquileia, four bishops came from mountain sees.

The western Alps

Of the bishops from Alpine sees at Aquileia in 381, Diogenes of
Geneva and Theodore of Octodurum (modern Martigny) more
probably belong to the Gallic, rather than the north Italian contingent (*Acta conc. Aquil.* 62–3).[19] The very existence of sees in
these centres is instructive, since they show the extent to which
Christianity was able to penetrate apparently peripheral areas. The
strength of these Christian communities is often hard to judge, but
rich archaeological evidence paints a picture of considerable vitality for Geneva. Excavations there in the cathedral of Saint Pierre have

---

[16] The emperor Arcadius was reluctant to grant the request of bishop Porphyry
of Gaza that the temples in that city should be destroyed as he did not want to aggrav-
ate the people of a loyal city: Mark the Deacon, *Vita Porphyrii* 41; on this episode
cf. Trombley, *Hellenistic Religions*, i. 237–9.

[17] To the uncritical analysis of (e.g.) MacMullen, *Christianizing*, see the critique
of Markus, *End of Ancient Christianity*. Cf. now also: Brown, *Authority and the Sacred*,
3–54.

[18] Stancliffe, *St Martin*, 328–40, collects the evidence.

[19] Many commentators have chosen to identify Diogenes as a bishop of Genoa
(e.g. Zelzer, *CSEL* 82/3 (1982), 326; Gryson, *Scolies ariennes*, 377). But his identification as bishop of Geneva is more secure, since the text of the oldest MS has
episcopus Genauensis, rather than *episcopus Genuensis*, that would be necessary for
Genoa to be meant: Zelzer, op. cit., clvi–clxii (on the codices), 363 with app. crit.
(for the forms in the MSS). To be sure, the form *Genauensis* may seem unusual, where
the genitive form *Genauensium* might be expected (cf. *Not. Gall.* 11. 4: 'Ciuitas
Genauensium'). But *Genauensis* is known from other contexts, such as the subscriptions to the Council of Orange, 441 (Munier, *Conc. Gall.* 87: 'Ex prouincia Vienninsi
ciuit. Genauensis Salunius Episcopus, Marius diaconus'). Cf. Holder, *Al-celtischer
Sprachschatz*, i. 1998–2000, s.v. *Genava*. Moreover, a Diogenes occurs in the episcopal list of Geneva: Duchesne, *Fastes épiscopaux*, i. 226: it is not at all certain that
his presence in the list reflects simply a corruption of the Geneva list by that of Grenoble
(*sic* Duchesne, loc. cit, with no discussion whatsoever).

revealed extensive remains of a Christian complex developed out of
a domestic building, which, by the mid-fourth century, had been
enlarged to include at least one church, residential quarters for the
clergy, and, possibly, a free-standing baptistery.[20] The presence of
large, vigorous congregations in the Alps might seem surprising,
but neither Geneva nor Martigny was really very remote. Both lay
along the important road from Italy through the Great St Bernard
pass, and from there to Gallia Narbonensis and the Rhône valley.
In late antiquity, this was a crucial strategic route which saw considerable renovation under the tetrarchy and Constantine.[21] So once
again, good communications seem to have been an important determinant in the distribution of Christian communities. Nothing, however, can be known with certainty about the Christians who first
preached the gospel in these valleys.[22] The bishops of Geneva and
Martigny had Greek names, Diogenes and Theodore, but by the end
of the fourth century these cannot be taken—however tempting it
might be—to indicate an immigrant element in the Christian populations of these cities.[23]

Crossing the Alps into northern Italy proper, we find a similar
correspondence between communications networks and the appearance of Christian communities in mountainous regions. Just over
the Alpine ridge from Martigny and Geneva there was a fledgling
community in Aosta. This city was not represented at the Council
of Aquileia and there is no documentary record of a bishopric there
until the appearance of a certain Gratus, a priest representing his
bishop Eustasius, at the Council of Milan in 451.[24] By that stage,
however, there were already several churches and shrines at Aosta,
including a substantial church building on the west side of the

[20] Bonnet, 'Origines du groupe épiscopal', 414–33; id., 'Developpement urbain',
323–38. There are numerous articles, with excellent illustrations, in *Archäologie der
Schweiz* 14/2 (1991) on early Christian remains from Geneva and its hinterland showing that by the early fifth century Christianity was flourishing in several centres in
this part of the Alps.

[21] Hyde, *Roman Alpine Routes*, 57–74; cf. Rivet, *Gallia Narbonensis*, 103, for the
renovations of 286–337.

[22] For what it is worth, the episcopal list of Geneva bears the heading 'Geneuensis
ecclesia a discipulis apostolorum Paracodo et Dionisio fundata, Viennensibus episcopis' (Duchesne, *Fastes épiscopaux*, i. 226).

[23] After all, Jerome and his father Eusebius had Greek names, but theirs was a thoroughly Dalmatian family by the early fourth century. Indeed, Rufinus alleges that
Jerome's acquisition of Greek came rather late (Ruf., *Apol. c. Hier.* 2. 9: 'mecum pariter
litteras Graecas et linguam penitus ignorabat').

[24] Lanzoni, *Diocesi*, 560; Savio, *Il Piemonte*, 70–2.

forum close to the ancient *capitolium*: thanks to a coin hoard found
in a channel leading to the baptistery, its construction can be dated
with confidence to shortly before 400.[25] Moreover, this early church
arose on the site of a large *domus* constructed in the late third century, and reused many of its walls as foundation courses,[26] so that
the construction of this church in the late fourth century could represent a renovation of a building already used for liturgical purposes.
In any case, the erection of a large church building within the town
walls, and so close to the traditional centre of civic and religious power,
suggests a growing Christian presence in the city during the second
half of the fourth century. The origins of the community are uncertain. A foundation at the initiative of Ambrose of Milan or even
Eusebius of Vercelli has been suggested,[27] but no surviving evidence
makes this connection.[28] Perhaps, then, the origins of Christianity
at Aosta are to be sought, not in any formal mission, but in the position of the city as an important staging point on the road over the
Alps to Gaul, just as may have been the case across the mountains
at Geneva and Martigny. Certainly, when we first hear of the local
activities of a bishop of Aosta it is in a collaborative venture with
his colleagues at Geneva and Martigny.[29]

The Julian Alps

At the opposite end of the region, Emona was represented for the
first time at a church council by bishop Maximus in 381. Emona
was a prosperous city by virtue of its position as an important node
on the road linking Italy to the Balkans.[30] It seems reasonable that
this was an important factor which contributed to the appearance

[25] Bonnet and Perinetti, 'Les premiers édifices chrétiens', esp. 477–88 on the intramural site.
[26] Ibid., 480–2, 487–8.   [27] Lanzoni, *Diocesi*, 560.
[28] There is no conclusive evidence for a strong connection with Milan. For example,
the church of Aosta did not boast any chapels dedicated to Milanese saints: the only
saint they share, the apostle Laurence, was popularly associated with episcopal necro-
poleis throughout northern Italy: Picard, *Souvenir*, 300–1. The fifth-century funerary church of S. Lorenzo at Aosta, which was used for the inhumation of the city's
bishops, is of cruciform plan, which has led some to hypothesize an influence from
Ambrose's *basilica Apostolorum* at Milan (Bonnet and Perinetti, 'Les premiers
édifices chrétiens', 493), but no such link can be proved.
[29] Together with bishops Domitian of Geneva and Protasius of Martigny, Gratus
of Aosta imported the relics of the martyr Maurice and his associates: *AASS, Sept.*
3. 74.
[30] Plesnicar-Gec, 'Aquileia ed Emona'; ead., 'Emona in età romana'.

of Christianity in the city, as indeed also for the presence of other foreign, private cults.[31] The nature of bishop Maximus' community is hard to assess, not least because the destruction of the city by Attila's Huns in 452 seems to have caused very real disruption in terms of settlement on the site.[32] What partial evidence survives, however, suggests a vibrant Christian community there already in the third quarter of the fourth century. Prior to his departure for the east sometime around 372, Jerome had written to Christians at Emona who had fallen out with him. These members of the faithful were predominantly of ascetic bent: a monk called Antony (*Ep.* 12) and a community of female virgins (*Ep.* 11).[33] In the late fourth or early fifth century, a liturgical complex was constructed in an insula within the city walls.[34] It comprised a portico, with an elaborate baptistery, where the font was covered by a baldachino supported by eight columns, and the floors were covered in sumptuous polychrome mosaics. These include various dedications including that of an archdeacon Antiocus (*sic*) who paid for the renovation of the building for liturgical use. Any precise relationship between this edifice and a larger church building is impossible to ascertain in the absence of further excavation, so it cannot be known if the church of Emona could boast a fine cathedral like those at other Alpine centres, such as Aosta and Geneva. Nevertheless the presence of the various dedications in the baptistery mosaics and the reference to an archdeacon, taken together with Jerome's evidence for the presence of an ascetic community in the city, suggests that the flock over which bishop Maximus presided in 381 was a flourishing one.

Another Christian community in the Julian Alps, but one not attested in any official document, was that at Jerome's home town of Stridon.[35] This community existed already in the first half of the fourth century, since Jerome's family was Christian.[36] The nature of the community is hard to judge, however. Jerome himself, by the

---

[31] Selem, *Religions orientales*, 2–5 (Egyptian deities), 72–8 (Mithras), 197–200, and 213–14 (Cybele and Attis).

[32] Gregory the Great (*Ep.* 9. 155 (*MGH, Epistolae* 2 (1909), 155)) records the movement of the people of Emona to a new settlement, in Istria, at the end of the sixth century: cf. *RE* 11A (1968), 576–8. For an archaeological appraisal see: Sivec, 'Il periodo delle migrazioni', 58–64.

[33] On Jerome's relationship with his sometime friends at Emona, see Kelly, *Jerome*, 30–5.

[34] Description in Plesnicar-Gec, 'La città di Emona', 367–75.

[35] For the location of Stridon: Kelly, *Jerome*, 2–5.   [36] Ibid., 7.

time he returned there from Trier in the early 370s, was deeply unim-
pressed by it. It was a conglomeration of boorish rustics where piety
was judged on wealth, and its leader, Lupicinus, who may have had
episcopal rank,[37] was a depressingly inadequate figure: 'a crippled
steersman . . . the blind leading the blind,' moaned Jerome (*Ep.* 7. 5).

Trento and the Alto Adige

Probably the most interesting and instructive example of Christian
expansion into the Alps is that in the Alto Adige, in the city of Trento
and in the Val di Non. Communications feature once more as an
important factor in explaining the dissemination of the gospel message in this region, and again it is striking how less remote these
high mountain valleys were than might be assumed. Since prehistoric times, the Adige valley was the most important transalpine route
from Italy to Rhaetia and the upper Danube,[38] and as a consequence
the region enjoyed considerable social and cultural diversity.[39] In the
Antonine period, officers associated with the customs bureaux of
Illyricum had brought the cult of Isis into these high mountain
valleys,[40] and Mithraism too had made its mark on the region.[41]
Among the other religions that came this way was Christianity.
The bishop of Trento who attended the Council of Aquileia,
Abundantius, is the first known to have occupied that see.[42] Even
if he had no episcopal predecessor, it is possible that Christianity
was established at Trento for some time prior to his election, just
as Tortona had a Christian community before Exsuperantius became
its bishop.

There is evidence from the end of the century that Christianity
in the Alto Adige was spreading to the countryside too. Sometime
around 397, three Christians—Sisinnius, Alexander, and Martyrius
—were killed in a violent confrontation with pagans in the Val di
Non (ancient Anaunia), north-west of Trento (Vigilius, *Ep.* 1. 3;

[37] Jerome describes him as 'Lupicinus sacerdos' which ought to mean he was no
more than a priest; but the Budé editor believes that *sacerdos* could be used inter-
changeably with *episcopus*: Labourt, *Saint Jérôme. Lettres*, i. 24 n. 2; endorsed by
Kelly, *Jerome*, 31.
[38] See p. 25 and n. 11 above.   [39] Lizzi, *Vescovi*, 70–6.
[40] Malaise, *Les conditions de pénétration*, 343–4.
[41] Lizzi, *Vescovi*, 75–6 and nn. 67–8.
[42] Picard, *Souvenir*, 502–4, on the extreme unreliability of the episcopal catalogue
for Trento which lists Abundantius second after an otherwise unknown Iovinus.

2. 2).[43] In the accounts of their deaths which he sent to Simplicianus of Milan and John Chrysostom at Constantinople, bishop Vigilius of Trento sought to portray them as martyrs who gave up their lives in missionary endeavour. The Val di Non is described as a thoroughly wild and uncivilized place,[44] an area which in terms of ethos as well as distance is 'a place cut off from the city' (*Ep.* 2. 2: 'locus . . . a ciuitate diuisus'). But this sits at odds with the tangible evidence for the social and cultural profile of these valleys, which demonstrates that for centuries they had been in regular contact with the lower reaches of the Adige and the north Italian plain. In the late fourth century, moreover, these contacts will have increased as the area witnessed an increased military presence after the collapse of the Rhaetian *limes* in 383.[45] In effect, Vigilius' description of the Val di Non is a literary construct: a dismissive statement of the barbarity of areas outside the cities in the same vein as Sulpicius Severus' claim that the Alps in his day had hardly been touched by the spread of Christianity.[46] In reality, it seems more likely that there was already a Christian presence in the Val di Non before its martyrs arrived. After all, the three Christians were clerics—Sisinnius was a deacon (*Ep.* 2. 5), Martyrius a lector (*Ep.* 1. 2), and Alexander a porter (*ostiarius*: *Ep.* 1. 3); moreover, Vigilius also recounts that they set about building a church (*Ep.* 2. 3). Such elaborate organization seems excessive if, as Vigilius would have us believe, the area was utterly pagan. Sending out clergy with designated roles suggests, rather, that there was already a Christian presence in the valley and that the three men were dispatched as part of a programme to bring the rural territory around Trento under episcopal control.[47]

If this is the case, then it has profound ramifications for the traditional picture of Christian expansion in peripheral zones such as

[43] For detailed accounts see Chaffin, 'Martyrs of the Val di Non', 184–203; and esp. Lizzi, *Vescovi*, 59–80.

[44] For example, in the letter to Simplicianus, Vigilius describes how Sisinnius 'nouam Christiani nominis pacem intulit barbarae nationi' (*Ep.* 1. 1); cf. 1. 2: 'Nam fumosa gentilitas contra uaporem fidei, zelo diaboli flamma furoris incaluit'; 2. 2: 'truculenta gentilitas'. Lizzi, *Vescovi*, 63 n. 9, assembles the various derogatory adjectives used by Vigilius.

[45] It is worth noting how Vigilius' description of the region includes the clause 'castellis undique positis in coronam' (*Ep.* 2. 2).

[46] Cf. Lizzi, *Vescovi*, 76–8, on Vigilius, *Ep.* 2, as a disingenuous literary *ekphrasis*. I suspect that the description in *Ep.* 2. 2 of the Val di Non as being remote from the *ciuitas* probably carries the implication that it is also distant from *ciuilitas*.

[47] Lizzi, *Vescovi*, 79–80.

the Alps and the countryside. Although the activities of Sisinnius and his colleagues date no earlier than the mid-390s, they were probably preceded by an informal process of evangelization which occurred as a natural consequence of the traffic passing through the valleys of the Alto Adige. By the mid-fifth century, at any rate, there had been a veritable explosion of church building in the region, with basilicas erected at Dos Trento, Bolzano, Altenburg, and even higher at Säben.[48] Indeed, the fifth century is the period of greatest consolidation by the Church throughout the north-eastern Alps, with concentrations of new communities along the major communications routes in the valleys of the Adige, Tagliamento, and Drava.[49]

Descending into the plain of Venetia we find further evidence of the diffusion of Christianity beyond the confines of urban centres. Two suburban settlements of Aquileia had Christian communities by the end of the fourth century. At Grado, the city's port on the coastal lagoons, there was a small rectangular church hall decorated with mosaic pavements incorporating dedications by the local faithful.[50] Inland, on the road to Trieste, there was a church built at Aquae Gradatae (modern S. Canzian d'Isonzo), where it was associated with the cults of SS Chrysogonus, Protus, Cantius, Cantianus, and Cantianella.[51] It is impossible to know how extensive was any Christian community actually residing at Aquae Gradatae. The site was a necropolis associated with Aquileia, and the building of the church was linked to the execution and burial there of the various martyrs.[52] Mosaic inscriptions from the church record a clerical hierarchy, with a deacon, a lector, and a notary,[53] but they could have been serving a flourishing martyr shrine rather than a significant rural Christian community.[54] In any case, the presence of the church is instructive. Together with the appearance of an episcopal see at Altino in the subscriptions to the council of 381 and the construction of churches at Concordia and Trieste by the early fifth century, it

[48] Menis, 'Basilica paleocristiana', 380, 385–6.

[49] See esp. Cuscito, 'Diffusione del cristianesimo'. The 4th cent. dates given for church buildings, such as that at Zuglio, by Menis, 'Basilica paleocristiana', 377–92, are probably too early: cf. Mirabella Roberti, 'Iulium Carnicum', 100.

[50] Lizzi, *Vescovi*, 157.

[51] Cuscito, 'Testimonianze archeologico-monumentale', 641–2.

[52] Necropolis: Cuscito, 'Testimonianze archeologico-monumentale', 642; execution and entombment of Aquileian martyrs: Calderini, *Aquileia romana*, lxxxvi–lxxxvii.

[53] Lizzi, *Vescovi*, 156.

[54] Maximus of Turin attests to the popularity of the cult in the fifth century (*Sermo* 15).

suggests that the coastal area around Aquileia also saw increasing diffusion of Christianity in the closing decades of the fourth century. In all cases it seems that the guiding hand in the consolidation, if not the expansion, of the Church may have been the bishop of Aquileia: Heliodorus had been a member of the *chorus beatorum* at Aquileia before becoming bishop of Altino; Concordia had its new church dedicated by Chromatius of Aquileia; a *defensor sanctae ecclesiae Aquileiensis* was to be among the patrons of the basilica in the Via Madonna del Mare at Trieste;[55] S. Canzian d'Isonzo was a *vicus* dependent on Aquileia as well as the resting place of some of the city's martyrs; and various churches across the Julian Alps in northern Dalmatia were clearly within the sphere of influence of the church of Aquileia already in the second half of the fourth century.[56]

Conclusion

Once again it has been shown that traditional forms of evidence—in this case the conciliar documents of 381 and 392/3—provide only a partial picture of the growth of Christianity in northern Italy during the third quarter of the fourth century. Not only is it demonstrable that some Christian communities are missing from such documents, but there is no hint in them of the processes by which Christianity spread through the region. Taking this evidence in conjunction with archaeological material, however, a more extensive —if still incomplete—picture emerges. It is clear that many of the characteristics of the process by which Christianity spread through northern Italy in the third and early fourth centuries are repeated in this later period. Once more, the diffusion of Christianity is uneven, varying from region to region. Most of the new congregations lie along the road leading from Rimini via Milan and northwards into the Alps: Claterna, Bologna, Modena, Piaenza, Lodì, and Como; Pavia, as Milan's nearest port on the river Po, belongs to the same group. There is also evidence of Christian penetration of the countryside and the mountains, although again there is considerable regional variety with communities in the Alto Adige, along the route from Italy

---

[55] *AE* 1973: 251: 'Eufemia | cum filio | suo Crysogono def(ensore) | s(an)c(t)ae eccl(esiae) | Aquil(eiensis) f(e)c(it) | p(e)d(es) C.'
[56] See pp. 141–2 above.

to Gaul through the Great St Bernard pass, and at Emona in the Julian Alps.

The means by which the faith spread to these areas has much in common with the earlier period, particularly the tendency of the new communities to cluster along important communications routes, whether those emanating from significant urban centres such as Aquileia and Milan, or those leading out of northern Italy towards neighbouring provinces across the Alps. Again, the constant movement of people along these avenues of communication will have provided the ideal social conditions for the propagation of the faith. Even if we can never know the identities of those Christians who first brought their religion to these new areas of northern Italy, we can identify the social context within which they operated. By the early 380s, however, the whole process was becoming less haphazard and informal, as bishops took an interest in the distribution of new Christian communities. Ambrose's effort, made obvious at the Council of Aquileia, to construct a community of like-minded bishops is one manifestation of this phenomenon. Throughout his career, the bishop of Milan took an active role in the investiture of bishops in other sees, some of them in neighbouring cities such as Piacenza, Como, and Vercelli, others as far afield as Aquileia and Sirmium.[57] Ambrose's activities were soon mimicked by his contemporaries, notably Chromatius of Aquileia.[58] Similarly, the confrontation between pagans and Christians in the Val di Non seems to have arisen because of efforts by Vigilius of Trento, another practitioner of Ambrose's methods, to bring areas of the Alto Adige under his episcopal jurisdiction.[59] Yet to see this more deliberate programme of evangelization entirely as a consequence of Ambrose's innovations is an over-simplification.[60] A self-conscious effort to increase the influence of a particular north Italian church is clear at Aquileia already in the third quarter of the fourth century.[61]

[57] For neighbouring bishoprics: Lizzi, 'Ambrose's Contemporaries', 158–61; cf. McLynn, *Ambrose*, 284–6. For Aquileia: Truzzi, 'L'ordinazione episcopale di Cromazio', 31–3. Sirmium: Paul. Med., *V. Ambr.* 11. 1. On the veracity of this account see pp. 143–4 n. 27 above.

[58] Lizzi, *Vescovi*, 139–69; ead. 'Ambrose's contemporaries', 158–9, 164–6.

[59] For Ambrose's influence on Vigilius, particularly in his manipulation of the violent deaths of Sisinnius, Alexander, and Martyrius to foster a martyr cult, see Lizzi, *Vescovi*, 86–96.

[60] It is implicit, if not explicit, in Rita Lizzi's analysis (in *Vescovi* and 'Ambrose's Contemporaries'), which takes Ambrose's episcopate as a starting point.

[61] See pp. 142–4, 175 above.

In sum, the later years of the fourth century were ones in which Christianity, on the face of it, extended its reach deeper into northern Italy. To be sure, the real explosion of self-conscious missionary effort seems to have come only in the wake of Ambrose's episcopate,[62] but the achievements of this half-century ought not to be underestimated. Christian communities, whether episcopal sees or not, were now more numerous, and the presence of the Church was beginning to be felt outside the cities in rural and mountainous areas. In addition, many of these congregations could boast fine church buildings with lavish decoration. Yet it is unclear from the evidence presented so far if northern Italy was to any extent a Christian space, as opposed to a pagan one. The scatter of Christian communities across the region does not of itself indicate a triumph over religious rivals. Christianity had, after all, been widespread in Asia Minor and north Africa by the second half of the third century, but that did not mean it was the dominant religion there: the violence with which it was suppressed during the tetrarchic persecutions demonstrates that well enough. So how can the rise of the Church be judged to have had any impact on the religious life of the region? To what extent was northern Italy really a 'Christian space' by Ambrose's time? Part of the essential transformation from a pagan to a Christian society will have been the redefinition of sacred space in, around, and between cities:[63] a mere catalogue of new congregations tells us little about the success of the Church in making these cities its own. Moreover, did the expansion of the Church always meet with unmitigated success? It seems unlikely that local non-Christians, whether pagan or Jewish, gave up their old beliefs without a struggle: the pagans of the Val di Non, as has been seen, did not. Again, merely cataloguing Christian communities largely fails to give any indication of *how* the Church did, or did not, win over the people of northern Italy. To answer these questions it is necessary to examine the life of the Christian communities within the framework of society, particularly urban society, in late antique northern Italy. This complex issue will be the theme of the next, and final, chapter.

[62] Lizzi, 'Ambrose's Contemporaries', *passim*.
[63] Markus, *End of Ancient Christianity*, 139–55.

Negotiosus cursus: *Christianity in the cities*

Views of Christian expansion in northern Italy during the fourth century risk being overtaken by a certain expectation of inevitability. The evidence presented in the last chapter for the greater number of bishoprics might lull us into seeing the period as one in which the new religion inexorably spread its influence over the entire region. Looking back from a vantage point in the episcopate of Ambrose of Milan, when vast crowds of Christians could be mobilized by their bishop,[1] it is easy to view such expansion as a *fait accompli*. Yet when Ambrose died, as his biographer Paulinus freely admits, there were Jews and pagans among the crowds at his funeral (Paul. Med., *V. Ambr.* 48). This requires us to qualify any picture we may have of a Christian triumph in northern Italy following on inevitably from Constantine's conversion. Religious diversity persisted in the region throughout the fourth century and beyond.[2] In this chapter it will be shown that for much of this period the Christians may have represented nothing more than a vociferous religious minority, competing for prominence in their communities with pagans and Jews. As bishop Zeno of Verona wrote, the Christian way of life was a *negotiosus cursus*, a 'troublesome path' weaving between ever present temptations, including other religions (Zeno, *Tract.* 1. 6). It will be shown that Christianity was engaged in competition and conflict with devotion to other gods, and just as bishops hoped for converts from Judaism and paganism, so lapses in the opposite direction were seen as a real danger. Before looking in detail at these consequences of religious pluralism, however, it is worth considering the most tangible evidence for a positive picture of Christian growth in the cities of northern Italy: the archaeological remains of church buildings. A close examination of these buildings can reveal much about the interaction between

[1] McLynn, *Ambrose*, 187–208; cf. Brown, *Power and Persuasion*, 103–15.
[2] Lizzi, *Vescovi*, 193–202, for continued paganism in rural Piedmont in the fifth century; cf. Ginzburg, *I benandanti*, 61–88, for the early modern period in Friuli.

Christian congregations and the communities within which they
developed. Such material, therefore, provides an essential backdrop
to the literary evidence for religious pluralism in fourth-century northern Italy.

Churches and urban space

The appearance of church buildings at various north Italian
centres raises difficulties of interpretation. How precisely are their
remains supposed to yield any information about the social status
of Christians? Most studies of religious change in late antiquity tend
to cluster around areas of enquiry where physical remains can be
interpreted in 'controlled' circumstances thanks to the survival of
detailed literary sources. For northern Italy, the case study *par
excellence* is Milan during the episcopate of Ambrose, where a
wealth of literary and archaeological material can be read side by
side to yield a coherent picture of the city's transformation from a
pagan, imperial capital to a Christian, episcopal metropolis.[3] While
the value of such literary evidence ought not to be denied, remaining too reliant on it limits the field of enquiry to certain traditional
topics. It fails, moreover, to explain a wealth of archaeological evidence attesting the erection of Christian buildings in cities other than
Milan.[4] Consequently, it is necessary to develop a methodology for
interpreting those remains. The first part of this section will outline
the strategy which I will use to understand the material evidence;
then it will look at the Christian presence in various centres, beginning with the rich seam of archaeological data at Aquileia.

Reading the architectural script

An appropriate methodological framework within which to understand the archaeological remains has been provided by a recent study

---

[3] Krautheimer, *Capitals*, 69–92; McLynn, *Ambrose*, 28–9, 175–9, 226–37.
Another important case study is the dedication of the new basilica at Concordia
by Chromatius of Aquileia: cf. Lizzi, *Vescovi*, 151–69.

[4] A most curious recent example is the study of late-antique Ravenna in Wharton,
Refiguring the Post Classical City, 105–47, where, despite the survival of an extensive corpus of sermons by the city's fifth-century bishop Peter Chrysologus, the analysis is guided primarily by a comparison of surviving monuments with Ambrose's
catechetical texts. This makes no allowance for the incidence of regional variations
in liturgical practice: cf. Ch. 6 above.

that has traced Christianity's 'progress from marginal cult to world religion' from the perspective 'that societies have characteristic discourses or "plots" [and] that the development and control of a discourse may provide a key to social power'.[5] Although the process is usually discussed in terms of oral or written modes of discourse, it clearly 'may pertain to the visual or any other means of communication'.[6] Architecture as much as art, is part of the visual discourse, by which one individual or group in society might communicate a power relationship with another, such as in the elaboration of a temple or commemorative monument.[7] Meanwhile, work on specific urban environments has demonstrated that the opening up of some architectural spaces to scrutiny along visual axes reflects a conscious division of houses and other buildings into public and private zones for the purposes of social and political rituals.[8] Thus the alignment and visibility of public and private architecture in an urban environment was manipulated in such a way as to convey social and political messages.[9] In religious terms, the spatial discourse of the early empire was controlled by the needs of a pagan society, where temples were often the most monumental buildings in a town, and were erected typically in prominent places, such as by the forum.[10]

This fits well with recent trends in the interpretation of early Christianity, which have emphasized the original embeddedness of Christian discourse in its Jewish and Graeco-Roman environments:[11] only later did Christian modes of expression develop their own distinct flavour.[12] Such modes of expression included architecture. The earliest patterns of Christian building are similar to those of comparable religious groups, such as Jews and Mithraists, where the development of cult buildings operates within a private context,

---

[5] Cameron, *Christianity and the Rhetoric of Empire*, 1.   [6] Ibid., 13.

[7] As Zanker has shown for the Augustan period: *Power of Images*. For late antiquity, see now Wharton, *Refiguring the Post Classical City*.

[8] For Pompeii and Herculaneum: Laurence, *Roman Pompeii*, 20–37, 100–3, 113–21; Wallace-Hadrill, *Houses and Society*, 38–61. Cf. Clarke, *Houses of Roman Italy*, 1–29; Elsner, *Art and the Roman Viewer*, 49–87.

[9] MacDonald, *Architecture of the Roman Empire*, ii. 74–142; cf. Carver, *Arguments in Stone*, 19–40. Any new building, however, was often constrained by pre-existing structures on a site. Even the imperial palace in Rome had no opening onto the forum until the destruction of aristocratic houses on the north-eastern slope of the Palatine hill during the fire of 64 allowed Nero the opportunity to develop one: Wiseman, 'Conspicui postes tectaque digna deo', 409–10.

[10] In detail, see Beard, North, and Price, *Religions of Rome*, i. 260–78.

[11] Cf. pp. 7–12 above.

[12] Cameron, *Christianity and the Rhetoric of Empire*, 15–46 and *passim*.

depending on private donations, and where architectural innovations are often circumscribed by the pre-existing fabric of buildings
adapted for cult use.[13] Only later, after Constantine's conversion transformed the legal and institutional standing of Christianity, could the
Church call on public, state-sponsored patronage for its building programmes in such a way as to transform its physical environment.[14]
There is a significant echo of this analysis in the only extant narrative of urban change from late antiquity, Gregory of Tours' account
of the tale of the Seven Sleepers of Ephesus. They were Christians
who were walled up in a cave outside the city during the persecution of Decius (249–51), and who were awoken two centuries later
in the reign of Theodosius II (408–50). As one of them returns to
Ephesus he is astonished by its transformation:

Approaching the gate of the city, he saw the sign of the cross above the
gate and in astonishment, he marvelled [at it] . . . Entering the city he heard
men swear oaths in Christ's name and saw a church, a priest who was rush-
ing around the city, and new walls; and being greatly astonished he said to
himself, 'Do you think that you have entered another city?'[15]

Yet, while allowing for such general trends, we must be careful
not to assume a simple, linear picture of evolution.[16] Even after
Constantinian patronage introduced the basilican form of church
building, a wide diversity of types—according to criteria such as size,
plan, and location—continued to exist.[17] As will be seen, there was
no inevitable linear development towards the use of apsidal basilicas by the Christians of northern Italy.[18]

[13] White, *God's House, passim.*   [14] Ibid., 147–8.
[15] Gregory of Tours, *Passio sanctorum martyrum septem dormentium apud Ephesum*, 7.
[16] Much art-historical analysis of the development of ecclesiastical architecture has
sought to achieve greater respectability (and hence rebut accusations that its values
are utterly subjective) by sprinkling its narratives with scientific metaphors, derived
primarily from biological evolution (see Wharton, *Refiguring the Post Classical City*,
1–14, esp. 3–7, for a review of some important examples of this trend). What such
analyses reveal by their insistence on an inexorable progression from one form to
another, however, is a misunderstanding (albeit a popular one) of the evolutionary
processes, based on what Stephen Jay Gould eloquently describes as 'the conflict
between "bushes" and "ladders" as metaphors for evolutionary change' (*Ever Since
Darwin*, 56–62).
[17] White, *God's House, passim.* On size and its physical limitations, see the judicious remarks, also relevant to the dimensions of the giant ants in the film *Them!*,
in Gould, *Ever Since Darwin*, 171–8.
[18] The best recent studies, with ample bibliography, of north Italian churches are:
Cantino Wataghin, 'La cattedrale in Italia', and ead., 'Le "basiliche doppie" paleocristiane'.

Theodore, Fortunatianus, and the cathedral of Aquileia

The easiest way to appreciate these changes is to examine some church buildings in their urban context. Nowhere is the evidence better suited to this than at Aquileia, where the cathedral complex was rebuilt twice in the course of the fourth century. The earliest form of the Christian building on this site is irrevocably lost to us, buried beneath the remains of later structures. In the early fourth century, most probably shortly after Constantine's conversion in 312, the whole complex was rebuilt under the direction of bishop Theodore (see Figure 2).[19] This first custom-built church comprised two parallel halls connected by a transverse hall and a series of small rooms; somewhere between the parallel halls lay a baptistery. Although Theodore's church reused foundation courses from earlier buildings, and this did much to determine its shape and orientation,[20] it was possible to make adaptations to the needs of Christian liturgy.[21] Entrance to the building was from the road flanking the eastern wall of the complex; this led to a vestibule, but not the church halls themselves. Within the complex, it seems that the two parallel halls were used for distinct liturgical purposes. The southern hall, where the mosaics showing Eucharistic Victory and the story of Jonah advertised the benefits of eternal salvation offered by Christianity to fully fledged converts, seems to have been used primarily in the baptismal liturgy, perhaps leaving the northern hall as the church usually used by the congregation. Whatever the precise details of the ceremony, it is clear that the baptismal liturgy would have involved an elaborate procession through the rooms of the complex.

This initial stage of architectural elaboration reveals much about the developing profile of Christianity at Aquileia. In the first place, the congregation seems to have harboured a lingering desire for secrecy. From the outside, it was impossible to see into the central liturgical spaces of the building, indicating that the rituals performed there were physically separate from the rest of civic life in Aquileia. Such separation is reiterated in the elaborate nature of the

---

[19] Above pp. 74–6.

[20] White, *God's House*, 115, 136, 198 n. 114. Cf. above p. 78.

[21] The fundamental description is Corbett, 'Early Christian Buildings at Aquileia'. His description of the baptismal liturgy, and its attendant procession through the building, is out of date, however; see now Menis, 'La liturgia battesimale', esp. 72–4.

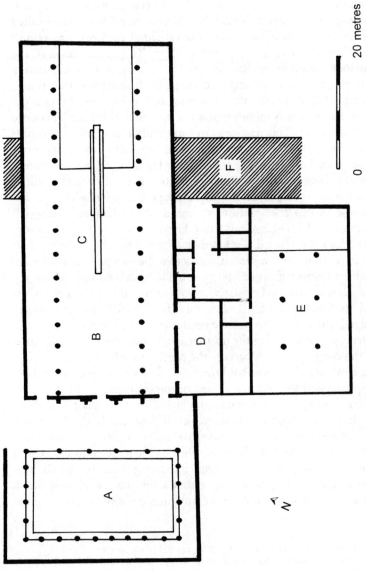

FIG. 4. Aquileia: the cathedral in the later fourth century
KEY A: portico B: new basilica C: *solea* D: baptistery E: Theodorean south hall F: street

0   20 metres

N

liturgy, particularly that associated with baptism. Being a Christian
involved moving from the street into the church and hence away
from public scrutiny. Undergoing baptism required further separation as the initiate moved through the various rooms and halls of
the complex. Thus, fulfilling the ritual requirements of Christian
life involved a real, physical dislocation between the Christian congregation and the wider urban community: the liturgical space of
Theodore's cathedral was not yet in the public domain. Such secrecy
is hardly surprising in the religious climate after the Diocletianic persecution. To be sure, Constantine had joined the side of the Church,
but there was no guarantee that his successors would do likewise:
a Christian triumph was not yet guaranteed.

Yet for all its clandestine character, this architectural metamorphosis reveals a self-conscious change in the status of the Christian
congregation in Aquileian society. In the mosaic pavements of both
halls are inscriptions acclaiming Theodore's construction of the
church, but that in the northern hall gives the clearest indication
of the interrelationship between the Theodorean building and its
immediate predecessor: it acclaims the bishop in the usual manner,
but rather than attributing the construction of the building to him,
it remarks simply that he increased it.[22] Taken together with investment necessary to pay for the elaborate mosaic decoration of the
building, this inscription demonstrates that the Christian community of Aquileia was aware that Theodore's reconstruction of their
liturgical building represented a new, monumental phase.

The northern hall of Theodore's church was subsequently rebuilt,
probably in the mid-340s during the episcopate of Fortunatianus.[23]
This new edifice (Figure 4), while not quite a true basilica (it lacks
an apse), shared many of the features of the basilican churches built
since Constantine's conversion. The main features of the building
were arranged along a central axis, with its entrance, preceded by a
porticoed court, now to the west. The door of the church was on

---

[22] 'Theodore felix hic *creuisti* hic felix': Kähler, *Die spätantiken Bauten*, 34; cf.
Chevallier, *Aquilée*, 106.
[23] It seems to be the basilica under construction mentioned in Athanasius'
account of his visit to Aquileia in 345 (*Apol. Const.* 15). Athanasius is describing regular congregations in undedicated buildings: in this context, the identification of the
church in question as the cathedral at Aquileia seems inescapable: Bertacchi, 'La basilica postteodoriana', 77–84; Jäggi, 174–7; Mirabella Roberti, 'Osservazioni sulla basilica postteodoriana', 863–75. The arguments of dalla Barba Brusin, 'Cronologia e
dedicazione', 2–3, in favour of a later date, between 387 and *c.* 407, are unconvincing.

the same axis as the nave, which was flanked by colonnades and aisles, and which culminated at the eastern end with a sanctuary and altar. In terms of ritual character, this church was more suited to the performance of grand processional—and ostentatiously public —liturgies, such as those celebrated in Rome, Jerusalem, and Constantinople,[24] and elsewhere in northern Italy at Milan (Paul. Med., *V. Ambr.* 52).[25]

This rebuilding of the northern hall marked a substantial increase in its dimensions, from 17.25 × 37.40 m of the Theodorean hall to 30.95 × 73.40 m.[26] Moreover, the building seems to have been more imposing as a whole: the architectural embellishments were more elaborate, with finely worked columns and a stone porch, while the overall platform of the church was raised by approximately 1 metre, which probably made it a more imposing structure than its predecessor.[27] Fortunatianus' basilica, like its Theodorean predecessor, marks a further stage in the increasing monumentality of the cathedral site. And just as the building itself was becoming a more visible feature in the urban landscape of Aquileia, so too the liturgy celebrated within was no longer shielded from the prying eyes of the urban community as a whole. With this new church, Aquileian Christianity became more integrated into the public life of the city; the clandestine mentality underlying the Theodorean building had evaporated to be replaced by greater self-confidence in the episcopate of Fortunatianus.

Indeed, in the course of the fourth century, Christianity came to occupy a more dominant position in the topography of Aquileia. At the beginning of the century, its presence may have been limited to nothing more than the pre-Theodorean building adopted, but not necessarily adapted, for liturgical use. By the end of the century, the site had been rebuilt twice with increasing monumentality. Some indication of the greater prominence of Christianity in Aquileian topography can be gleaned from the ground plan of Fortunatianus' new basilica. At some 73.40 m in length, it was approximately twice the length of its Theodorean predecessor, and this

---

[24] Baldovin, *Urban Character.*

[25] This quality was enhanced later by the insertion of a *solea*, a raised platform running down the middle of the nave, along which the bishop and clergy would have processed at the beginning and end of services: Bertacchi, 'La basilica postteodoriana', 62–71 and tavola II; cf. Mathews, 'Early Roman Chancel Arrangement', 73–95.

[26] Jäggi, 173–6.

[27] Mirabella Roberti, 'Osservazioni sulla basilica postteodoriana', 869.

extension of the building required the appropriation of property to the east of the original site. It is here that the rising power of the Church is most obvious: whereas the eastern limit of Theodore's church had been determined by the line of a road, Fortunatianus' basilica was built *over* this road.[28] This is significant. Everything suggests that the street grids of northern Italy were assiduously protected by municipal councils throughout late antiquity and the early middle ages.[29] For Fortunatianus' new basilica to break free from the constraints of the urban strait-jacket suggests, then, that Aquileian Christians enjoyed considerable social prominence and power.

The cathedral was not the only monumental Christian presence in the city, however: by the end of the fourth and the beginning of the fifth century a considerable area of the southern part of the city was given over to Christian oratories, all decorated with sumptuous mosaics.[30] This coincides with increased construction undertaken in the episcopate of Chromatius (388–407/8), whose energetic programme led his friend Rufinus to designate him the Bezalel of his day, after the skilled craftsman who had fashioned the tabernacle for Moses (Exod. 35).[31] Areas beyond the city walls were being colonized by the new faith, as the cemeteries saw the erection of various martyr shrines. Again, as is shown by the extensive remains of the cruciform church, measuring some 65 m in length, unearthed at the southern suburb of Beligna, the Aquileian congregation could afford to build on a magnificent scale.[32] The city also saw patronage by outsiders: in the early fifth century, eastern immigrants helped to build the church known today as the basilica di Monastero and housed in the Museo Paleocristiano;[33] while sometime around 400 the consular governor of *Venetia et Histria*, Parecorius Apollinaris,

---

[28] Jäggi, 175.

[29] The evidence is collected in Ward-Perkins, *CAMA*, 179–86.

[30] Chevallier, *Aquilée*, 104.

[31] Rufinus, *Prologus in omelias Origenis super Iesum Nave*, ed. W. A. Baehrens, *CCL* 20 (1961), 271, lines 16–23.

[32] Jäggi, 179–84; Chevallier, *Aquilée*, 108–9.

[33] Ruggini, 'Ebrei e orientali', 192–6, accepted the designation by the excavator, G. Brusin, that the building was originally a synagogue; this is now untenable: Bertacchi, 'Le basiliche suburbane di Aquileia', 225–7; and esp. Noy, *JIWE* i, p. xiv. The use of the apparently Judaizing formula of the dedication *d(omi)n(o) Sab(aoth)*, a crucial element in its identification as a synagogue, may be more ambiguous: it could well have entered Christian usage by the late fourth century, especially as most of the Christians who worshipped there were Syrians, and thus from an area where Jewish and Christian interpenetration was an everyday reality (cf. Drijvers, 'Syrian Christianity and Judaism', *passim*).

dedicated a *basilica apostolorum* in the city (*CIL* 5. 1582). Such examples show how the new religion could come to occupy a more prominent position in the life of a city. As the cathedral complex became larger and more lavish, it is safe to assume that this mirrors increments in the social profile of the Christian community. If Aquileia, like Ephesus, had its Seven Sleepers who returned after two hundred years, then they too would have marvelled at the utter transformation of the city they had left: between the mid-third and early fifth centuries, Aquileia, like the Ephesus of legend, had acquired a thoroughly Christian aspect.

Milan: emperors, bishops, and churches in an imperial capital

Milan is a popular subject for the study of the transformation of urban life in the late empire. Such analyses have tended to concentrate on the impact on the city of the episcopate of Ambrose, during which many new churches, primarily built to house the relics of martyrs and apostles, rose in the cemeteries outside Milan's walls.[34] First, however, I want to describe the sort of city Ambrose inherited from Auxentius in 374, and determine to what extent Christianity had changed Milan's appearance in the period since Constantine and Licinius proclaimed religious toleration in the city in 313. Any attempt to reconstruct the Christian topography of Milan during the fourth century is bound to be difficult in a city where even the imperial palace has not yet been found by archaeologists.

Our image of Milan's ecclesiastical topography at the time of Ambrose's election is lamentable. Literary sources give only occasional hints as to the presence of church buildings, such as the revelation that Ambrose's discovery of the relics of Gervasius and Protasius occurred in a basilica housing the relics of SS Felix and Nabor.[35] The existence of several churches, some of them quite large,

---

[34] Such interpretations owe much to Ambrose himself and his contemporaries: Calderini, 'La tradizione letteraria', 78–82.

[35] Paul. Med., *V. Ambr.* 14. 1: 'Per idem tempus sancti martyres Protasius et Gervasius se sacerdoti [*sc.* Ambrose] revelaverunt. Erant enim in basilica positi in qua sunt hodie corpora Naboris et Felicis martyrum: sed sancti martyres Nabor et Felix celeberrime frequentabantur, Protasii vero et Gervasii martyrum ut nomina, ita etiam sepulcra incognita sunt . . .' Cf. Ambrose's own account (*Ep.* 22. 2), on which Paulinus surely depends: 'Dominus gratiam dedit; formidantibus etiam clericis iussi eruderari terram eo loci qui est ante cancellos sanctorum Felicis atque Naboris.' For the origin of the cult of Nabor and Felix, perhaps in the time of bishop Maternus, see pp. 148–9 above.

before Ambrose's building programme is also commonly accepted. In 355, the Council of Milan met in a church which was perhaps the cathedral, although complete certainty on this point is impossible.[36] Milan, like Rome, had its *tituli*, churches which originated as private properties owned by members of the pre-Constantinian Christian community. Ambrose mentions a *basilica Faustae* near the shrine of SS. Nabor and Felix (*Ep.* 22. 2); the Portian basilica probably originated in this way too.[37] No less an authority than Ammianus Marcellinus attests the existence of a shrine *ad Innocentes* from the reign of Valentinian I (364–75).[38] Apart from their meagre existence as names in the literary tradition, some of these early churches can be located in the archaeological record. The area outside the western walls, a suburban park known as the Hortus Philippi,[39] saw the construction of many martyr shrines, some of which, including the *basilica Faustae* and SS Nabor and Felix, existed prior to Ambrose's election, and whose existence has been confirmed by excavation.[40]

Moving within the walls of Milan it is possible to posit a firm identification for the church described by Ambrose as the *basilica nova* (see Figure 5). Emergency excavations conducted in the Piazza del Duomo in 1943 (for the construction of air-raid shelters),

[36] Hilary of Poitiers is terribly imprecise, stating merely that the bishops met 'ad ecclesiam' (*Coll. ant. Par.* App. II. 3). McLynn, *Ambrose*, 29 and n. 101, rightly queries the assertion of Krautheimer, *Capitals*, 77, that 'the size of the synod of 355, attended by more than three hundred bishops, not counting their clerics, the emperor, his suite, and the congregation, suggestions that it met in the large new cathedral', that is the church of S. Tecla, under the Piazza del Duomo. This is based on the otherwise uncorroborated report of Socrates, *HE* 2. 36. But the only surviving list of bishops at the council suggests that it was a more select gathering: cf. pp. 49–50 above. Some support for the council assembling in the cathedral might be sought from Ambrose, who, in a letter to the people of Vercelli recalling the activities of their illustrious bishop Eusebius, remarks that Eusebius and Dionysius of Milan 'raperentur de ecclesia maiore' (*Ep.* 63. 68: text in *PL* 16. 1208). Yet Michaela Zelzer, in her new edition of the letter (*CSEL* 82/3 (1982): 271 app. crit.), suggests convincingly that the word *maiore* is a later interpolation. On the other hand, bearing in mind the importance of the synod, I cannot think of any reasons for doubting that the council *did* convene in the cathedral.

[37] Ambr. *Ep.* 20. 1: 'Portiana hoc est extramurana basilica'. Cf. Lewis, 'San Lorenzo Revisited', 203 and n. 23. For *tituli* at Milan, see Calderini, 'Milano archeologica', 591–2; and id., 'La tradizione letteraria', 76, 97–8.

[38] Amm. Marc. 27. 7. 5; cf. McLynn, *Ambrose*, 29–31.

[39] McLynn, *Ambrose*, 209–11. There were other gardens colonized by new churches, such as that where S. Nazaro was erected: Paul. Med., *V. Ambr.* 33.

[40] See now, above all: Sannazaro, 'Considerazioni sulla topografia'.

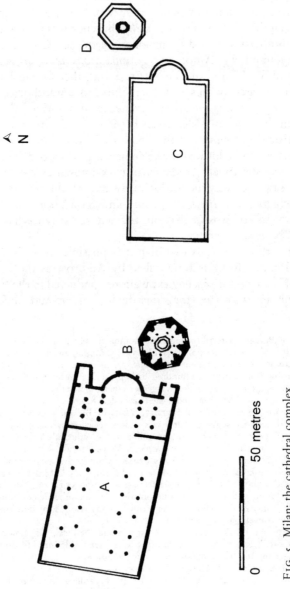

FIG. 5. Milan: the cathedral complex

KEY A: *basilica nova* B: baptistery of S. Giovanni alle Fonti C: site of *basilica vetus*
D: baptistery of S. Stefano alle Fonti

0   50 metres

and pursued further in 1960–2, revealed extensive remains of a colossal church, later known as S. Tecla, which can be safely identified as the *basilica nova*.[41] It was of basilican form, including an apse, and measured some 80 × 45 m, divided into a broad central nave flanked on either side by two colonnaded aisles. This was a truly enormous building by fourth-century standards. In Italy it was matched only by Constantine's Lateran basilica at Rome, while Fortunatianus' new northern hall at Aquileia was almost 1500 m² smaller.[42] Despite the conscious efforts of the architects to construct a basilican church, the whole edifice is slightly trapezoidal in plan: this was perhaps determined by the street plan in this part of Milan or by the buildings underlying the church.[43] Next to this lay the church which Ambrose described as the 'basilica of the baptistery' and as the 'old basilica' and the 'small basilica of the church'.[44] That baptistery is probably the small building excavated in the northern transept of the current cathedral, which was known in the middle ages as S. Stefano alle Fonti,[45] while the *baptisterii basilica* itself is probably the church known in the middle ages as Sta Maria Maggiore, and which was demolished in the fourteenth century to make way for the new cathedral.[46] In effect, then, Milan had

[41] For good descriptions: Apollonj Ghetti, 'Le cattedrali di Milano', 37–53 (including a review of earlier studies); Calderini, 'Milano archeologica', 595–8; Krautheimer, *Capitals*, 74–7.

[42] Krautheimer, *Capitals*, 76; cf. McLynn, *Ambrose*, 28 and n. 100.

[43] Krautheimer, *Capitals*, 76; cf. Calderini, 'Milano archeologica', 597, for a photograph of an inscription reused in S. Tecla's foundations.

[44] The source is Ambrose's letter (*Ep.* 20) to his sister Marcellina describing his conflict with the dowager empress Justina. He talks of the 'Portiana hoc est extramurana basilica' and the 'basilica nova hoc est intramurana quae maior est' at *Ep.* 20. 1; at 20. 4 he recalls how 'in baptisterii tradebam basilica'; while at 20. 10 he describes how 'ego in basilica veteri totum exegi diem'; while at 20. 24 he recounts how 'cum fratribus psalmos in ecclesiae basilica minore diximus'. Cf. Calderini, 'La tradizione letteraria', 70–7.

[45] Apollonj Ghetti, 'Le cattedrali di Milano', 28–32.

[46] The *baptisterii basilica* must have been the church in which Ambrose conducted the rest of the Easter Week liturgy: Ambr., *De Sacr.* 1. 3–10; cf. Lenox-Conygham, 'Topography of the Basilica Conflict', 361, and esp. Piva, 'L'ipotetica basilica doppia', 129–32. He describes to Marcellina how, later in the week, he taught in the *basilica vetus* (20. 10: *ego in basilica veteri totum exegi diem*). This church is distinguished from the *basilica nova* which, Ambrose tells us, filled up with his adherents while he was teaching (20. 13: *dum leguntur lectiones, intimitatur mihi plenam populi esse basilicam etiam novam*). Ambrose's description of the *basilica vetus* is qualified further when he recounts how *cum fratribus psalmos in ecclesiae basilica minore diximus* (20. 24). Thus it is clear that the *baptisterii basilica*, the *basilica vetus*, and the *ecclesiae basilica minor* were the same church.

acquired a double cathedral by the time of Ambrose's election in 374 (see Figure 5).[47]

A number of features of this complex are worth noting, because they reveal much about the social standing of the Milanese Christian community. First, the immense size of the *basilica nova* and its location, taken together, are instructive. It rose within the walls and its construction probably demanded the destruction of a considerable number of buildings already standing on the site.[48] Secondly, the materials used to build it were sumptuous and expensive: fine white marble plinths for columns hewn from African breccia.[49] The scale, richness, and location of this basilica point to a possible context for the construction of the building. The lavish decoration of the *basilica nova* may have been Hilary of Poitiers' target when he complained that the adherents of Auxentius of Milan should be satisfied that they can worship God in fine buildings.[50] The scale of the site puts the *basilica nova* in the same class as the imperial foundations at Rome, Trier, and Constantinople. As Milan was also an imperial capital, it is probable that it was built with imperial patronage. The basilican plan of the church, evocative of Constantine's foundations in Rome and Palestine, and a precocious feature among the churches of northern Italy, supports this contention. Beyond this, any assertion about the origins of S. Tecla can only be conjectural, but the suggestion that the church was built with the patronage of the emperor Constans during the 340s remains attractive.[51]

The splendour of the basilica was complemented, insofar as it can be deduced, by the episcopal house or palace. No archaeological remains of this building have ever been identified, but hints in Paulinus of Milan's account of it indicate that it may have been similar to the urban dwellings of aristocrats. Paulinus mentions various rooms: there was the bishop's bedroom (*cubiculum*), a portico, and an upper storey.[52] This is enough to suggest an imposing building with different rooms for distinct purposes, and it accords well with what is known about the use of domestic space by late antique

---

[47] Cf. Lusuardi Siena, 'Il complesso episcopale', 124–8, suggesting, however, that the *basilica vetus* is a different building entirely from the *baptisterii basilica* and the *ecclesiae basilica minor*.

[48] Krautheimer, *Capitals*, 76.   [49] Calderini, 'Milano archeologica', 596.

[50] Hil. Pict., *Contra Aux.* 12; connection drawn by McLynn, *Ambrose*, 27–8.

[51] Krautheimer, *Capitals*, 77; reiterated by McLynn, *Ambrose*, 29.

[52] Paul. Med., *V. Ambr.* 20 (*cubiculum*), 46 (*in extrema parte porticus*), 47 (*in superioribus domus*).

aristocrats to advertise their social power.[53] It represents the appropriation of the traditional symbols of social power by the Christian hierarchy in Milan, a phenomenon observable right across the
empire.[54]

The potency of such symbolic form was not lost on Ambrose,
who, as soon as he assumed the episcopate, embarked on a building campaign where the architectural form of his churches served
to stamp his prestige and power on his city.[55] Within the city, he
seems to have built a second baptistery. To the south-east of the
apse of the *basilica nova* (S. Tecla) there stood a sumptuous,
octagonal baptistery known in the middle ages as S. Giovanni alle
Fonti. A verse inscription, now preserved in a manuscript known
as the Lorsch sylloge, suggests that this baptistery was built by
Ambrose.[56] The bishop's most impressive constructions, however,
lay outside Milan's walls. One of his first new buildings was a mas-
sive basilica of imposing cruciform plan built on the porticoed
street on the road leaving Milan for Rome. This church, soon
known as the *basilica apostolorum* or *basilica in Romana*, but now
called S. Nazaro, was designed to house relics of the apostles Peter
and Paul, sent to Ambrose by Pope Damasus.[57] Perhaps the most
important new church, however, was that which rose outside the
city's western walls probably between 379 and 386.[58] The very
existence of this church soon became symbolic of the divine sanc-
tion of Ambrose's victory over his heterodox opponents, when it
became the resting place for the relics of the martyrs Gervasius and
Protasius.[59] Nevertheless, the church seems never to have lost its popular designation as the *basilica Ambrosiana*; indeed, its inseparable
identity with the bishop was reinforced when Ambrose was buried

[53] Ellis, 'Power, Architecture, and Decor'; for a north Italian example, cf.
Bertacchi, 'Edilizia civile', 349–53, and figs. 4–7.

[54] Brown, *Power and Persuasion*, esp. 146–52.

[55] Ambrose's architectural ambitions are mentioned in the *de excessu Satyri* 1.
20, dating to 378. On his programme as a whole: Krautheimer, *Capitals*, 72–81;
McLynn, *Ambrose*, 226–37.

[56] *CIL* 5, p. 617, no. 2. An Ambrosian date is argued by Mirabella Roberti, 'Il
battistero di Sant'Ambrogio', and Paredi, 'Dove fu battezzato Sant'Agostino'. Cf., however, McLynn, *Ambrose*, 235 n. 55, suggesting that the inscription served simply 'to
claim the baptistery for himself and thus to override its "Arian" connotations'. A
firm conclusion either way is probably impossible.

[57] Full discussion of the church in Lewis, 'Function and Symbolic Form'; ead.,
'Latin Iconography'. For the name, *basilica in Romana*, reflecting the church's location on the road to Rome: Ambr., *Ep.* 22. 1; cf. McLynn, *Ambrose*, 211, 231–2.

[58] Discussion in *Milano capitale*, 127–9.   [59] See above p. 122.

there in 397.[60] Although Ambrose's foundations were impressive, the bishop's architectural programme marks him out not so much as an innovator as the continuator of a development stretching back into the mid-fourth century. With its expansive cathedral complex, the church of Milan was already an ostentatious presence in the city; Ambrose's buildings served to emphasize this further.

At Milan, as at Aquileia, the fourth century saw the Church come to occupy a significant position in the topography of the city. Just as the area around Theodore's double cathedral took on the character of a Christian quarter, so too the *basilica nova, basilica vetus*, baptistery, and episcopal dwelling meant that the eastern sector of Milan was dominated by its ecclesiastical buildings. They made that area of the city an architectural focus of the Christian presence in the same way as the circus, Herculean baths, and imperial palace demonstrated the presence of the court in the western part of the city.[61] Yet the architectural development of Milanese Christianity differs from that at Aquileia in one significant way. Whereas the emperor's presence at Aquileia was both intermittent and transient, Milan was the permanent or semi-permanent home of several imperial courts between Maximian and Honorius. Thus the dialogue between the institutions of church and state was more intense at Milan than at Aquileia. The Milanese churches, as the disputes between the empress Justina and Ambrose show, were the focus not just for ecclesiatical ceremonial, but for that of the emperors also.

The creation of Christian environments in northern Italy

The study of specific examples like Aquileia and Milan is instructive in that it demonstrates how particularly rich sites can yield pictures of the way the monumental presence of the Church evolved during the fourth century. While they provide paradigms for the architectural development of Christianity in north Italian cities, it must be recognized that they cannot be taken as typical of the region as a whole. Both (and especially Milan) were major imperial cities, and this political importance was a significant factor in their overall development during late antiquity, including the monumental growth of

[60] The name is recorded by Ambrose himself: 'in basilicam quam appellant Ambrosianam' (*Ep.* 22. 2). Ambrose's burial: Paul. Med., *V. Ambr.* 48.

[61] Arslan, 'Urbanistica di Milano romana', 203, talks in terms of the bipolarity of late Roman Milan.

their churches. Even so, each city shows individual peculiarities, primarily the importance of imperial patronage for Milan. While they developed analogous structures, these could arise in starkly distinct circumstances. Thus, although both cities had double cathedrals by the end of the 370s, that at Milan had come into existence through a process of gradual architectural embellishment (the addition of the *basilica nova* to the *vetus*), whereas the one at Aquileia was the conscious creation of Theodore in the years after Constantine's conversion. Also, just as we ought not to generalize about Milan from Aquileia (or vice versa), so we ought not to assume that developments in either centre were typical of the region's cities as a whole. In every case it is necessary to consider the particular circumstances obtaining at individual cities. Nevertheless, it is possible to see certain features in the architectural evolution of Christianity across the region which have much in common with developments at Aquileia and Milan.

An important factor in determining the social prominence of Christian communities is the location of their church buildings. The religious space of a pagan city was, as has been noted, dominated by its temples. Any picture of a 'Christian triumph' would assume the erection of large churches within cities, signifying a transformation of their religious topography. The typical analysis of this change in northern Italy has been rather negative,[62] yet at Milan and Aquileia churches had risen within the walls by the middle of the fourth century. Even allowing for the undeniable power of the Christian communities in those cities, it is clear that intramural ecclesiastical (if not always episcopal) complexes were a broader phenomenon.[63] That at Aosta was built right on the side of the forum, close to the *capitolium* itself.[64] So too at Padua, the Christian building (perhaps not a church) which yielded the mosaic of Eutherius was close to the forum.[65] By the early fifth century a large and sumptuous church, on the site of the medieval cathedral of S. Giusto, had been built within the walls of Trieste, only metres away from the forum.[66]

---

[62] Bullough, 'Urban Change', writing of the church of SS Gervasius and Protasius at Pavia, states: 'Its extra-mural site is, in my view, fairly typical of early episcopal churches in north and central Italy' (90 n. 28).

[63] Cantino Wataghin, 'La cattedrale in Italia', 35–50.

[64] Bonnet and Perinetti, 'Les premiers édifices chrétiens', 480.

[65] Cf. n. 62 above.

[66] A column of the *capitolium* is visible behind a grille in the façade of the campanile of S. Giusto (personal observation on site). Cf. Cantino Wataghin, 'La cattedrale in Italia', 38.

Intramural churches were also present at Verona (under the present cathedral),[67] Grado (in the Piazza della Vittoria),[68] and Poreč (the primitive church beneath the Euphrasian basilica),[69] while the early fifth-century baptistery at Emona also represents a monumental Christian presence inside a city's walls.[70]

Even where intramural churches did exist, there could be considerable variety as to where precisely they were located. The early cathedrals of Trieste and Aosta, and the Christian building of Eutherius at Padua, were close to the traditional centres of secular and religious power: the forum and its temples. Not even the episcopal complexes of Milan and Aquileia enjoyed such prominence. The rather more peripheral nature of the Milanese and Aquileian cathedrals is mirrored at Verona in the early buildings erected on the northern periphery of the city, on the site of the medieval and modern cathedral. The Veronese case is instructive in other ways too. During the early middle ages, the centres of some towns (Milan, Aquileia, Brescia) literally shifted from the traditional focus of power (whether palace or forum) to the area around the cathedral, while at Trieste and Aosta the cathedrals rose beside the fora themselves: in both sets of examples the cathedral ultimately assumed a central position in urban topography. But at Verona the cathedral is still a peripheral building, while the forum remained the centre of town throughout the medieval period (as it is today), with only brief periods of interruption, and no church has ever been built near it.[71] Only local contexts can explain such differences. At Milan, the city's traditional political centre fell into disuse after the court withdrew to Ravenna; at Aquileia, the various disasters which befell the city in the fifth and sixth centuries granted the bishops considerable prominence and ensured a central location for the cathedral in the post-antique town; but at Verona, where the street plan was jealously preserved, the capacity of the church to encroach upon the old urban centre was considerably restricted.

A second significant factor was the interrelationship between Christian edifices and previous buildings on the same spot. There was a variety of responses. At Milan, the development of the *basilica nova* required the destruction of existing buildings from the outset,

[67] Zovatto, 'Arte paleocristiana a Verona', 562–74.
[68] Lizzi, *Vescovi*, 157; cf. Bognetti, 'Una campagna di scavi', 7–9.
[69] For full documentation, see pp. 86–9 above.
[70] See pp. 179–80 above.   [71] La Rocca, '"Dark Ages" a Verona', 53–70.

and their replacement by a radically different structure. This, however, seems an anomalous development, and even at Milan, it must be remembered, the trapezoidal alignment of the walls of the basilica probably reveals some influence on the shape of the Christian buildings by earlier structures. A more typical model seems to be one of gradual adaptation of existing buildings. This was clearly the case in the Theodorean complex at Aquileia and the pre-Euphrasian churches at Poreč, and a similar pattern exerted itself at Aosta, where the cathedral developed organically within confines imposed by a third- and early fourth-century *domus*.[72] Such developments are particularly clear in smaller Christian buildings: the oratories in Aquileia and Eutherius' building at Padua are good examples. So too is the early fifth-century baptistery and portico at Emona: not only did this develop within the strict confines of the existing insula, but it also exploited the presence of a bath building on the site as a ready-made source of water for the baptismal ablutions.[73] Of course, such adaptations did not always slavishly follow the ground-plans of existing buildings. Walls were knocked down and rooms enlarged to suit liturgical needs, and the laying of mosaic pavements—or *opus sectile* ones at Milan and Aosta—in many of these Christian buildings required considerable capital investment, which surely reflects the increasing social profile of Christianity. Later, as some church buildings were renovated, the investing of new wealth in more sumptuous buildings was accompanied by an increase in their size which led to the edifice breaking free of the confines of the urban street grid, as is most obvious in Fortunatianus' new northern hall at Aquileia.

The area where the growing monumentality of church buildings most altered the appearance of the cities of northern Italy was in their suburbs. At Milan much of this development belongs to the age of Ambrose,[74] but some of it precedes him: the basilica of SS Felix and Nabor, the *basilica Faustae*, the *basilica Portiana*, and the shrine *ad Innocentes*, whatever form it may have taken. Similar extramural developments are visible in the fourth century at Aquileia, Brescia, and Vicenza.[75] By the early fifth century, most cities in the region had several extramural churches.[76] These suburban transformations

---

[72] Bonnet and Perinetti, 'Les premiers édifices chrétiens', 480.
[73] Plesnicar-Gec, 'La città di Emona', 372.   [74] McLynn, *Ambrose*, 226–37.
[75] Aquileia: Bertacchi, 'Le basiliche suburbane di Aquileia', 224–33; Brescia and Vicenza: Cuscito, *Primo cristianesimo*, 38–43.
[76] Picard, *Souvenir*, 327–43.

were the most profound in terms of the changing image of north
Italian cities. The first indicator a visitor received of the wealth
and character of a city in antiquity came from its suburbs.[77] In the
late third century, the image projected by Milan was dominated by
its walls and the colonnaded street with its triumphal arch erected
by Maximian; everything emphasized that the city was an imperial
capital. By the later fourth century, however, the city's image—and
that of most other cities in northern Italy—had changed. Churches
were springing up outside their walls, and anyone who could have
returned to northern Italy two centuries after the persecutions, like
the Seven Sleepers had done at Ephesus, would have been im-
pressed by the outwardly Christian aspect of the region's cities.

For all that, it is impossible to draw a single, all-encompassing
blueprint for the transformation of the cities of northern Italy.
Types of church building varied enormously, from the vast imperial *basilica nova* at Milan, to Theodore's double church at Aquileia,
to small buildings such as that paid for by Eutherius at Padua, or
the baptistery and portico at Emona. Nor could every city boast
intramural churches. Some cities did not see an intramural Christian presence until very late indeed: at Pavia, for example, there was
no church built inside the walls until the Ostrogothic period;[78] the
first church underlying the Lombard cathedral at Brescia seems no
earlier than the sixth century;[79] and at Ravenna the appearance of
an intramural church, the Basilica of Ursus, most probably follows
the establishment of the imperial court there by Honorius in the early
fifth century.[80] Such variations from place to place reflect local differences in terms of the social prominence and influence of the
Christian community. The Church was a powerful organization in
Milan and Aquileia; it must also have exercised a certain amount of
clout in Aosta if the erection of a church building by the forum
at the end of the fourth century is any guide. Likewise, the absence
of intramural churches in many centres until a relatively late period
suggests that Christianity may not yet have been the dominant force

[77] Dyson, *Community and Society*, 149–53.
[78] Bullough, 'Urban Change', 91.   [79] Cuscito, *Primo cristianesimo*, 42.
[80] *Pace* Wharton, *Refiguring the Post Classical City*, 108–9, who dates it to the
late fourth. Such a dating is based, however, on a misinterpretation of Agnellus of
Ravenna's notice of bishop Ursus' death: cf. Picard, *Souvenir*, 488. The very form
of the basilica, a five-aisled, apsidal basilica measuring 60 × 35 m, suggests a conscious imitation of the *basilica nova* at Milan.

in local society. Indeed, there is other material which must be set beside the picture presented thus far, which shows that the more ostentatious Christian presence in the region occurred against a background of considerable religious diversity, and that not every soul in northern Italy had been seduced into accepting baptism.

Christians, pagans, and Jews

Christian expansion had not taken place in a religious vacuum: the new religion grew into a space already occupied by other beliefs. In the fourth century, however, the gradual emergence of Christianity as the faith of the imperial élite transformed the interrelationships between the various religions in northern Italy much as it did in the rest of the empire. As Christian toleration of other beliefs declined, so the religious dynamic of the region was transformed. The Church, intermittently supported by the state, directed its wrath against any rival group.[81] In many cases, these opponents would have been of a decidedly Christian hue themselves, such as heretics, variously defined, whose legacy of internal conflict continued to haunt the north Italian churches, and probably Manichaeans too.[82] These were rivals from within; in addition, Christian monopolization of the sacred forced new identities on other groups. The various pagan cults, never before a coherent system, were now lumped together and demonized.[83] Together with the Jews, they constituted threatening external 'others' in the religious landscape of northern Italy.[84]

Capitolium and church: Christianity and paganism

In the course of the fourth century, as we have just seen, church buildings came to dominate many, though by no means all, urban

---

[81] Cf. Beard, North, and Price, *Religions of Rome*, i. 369–75.

[82] Augustine's decision at Milan to 'leave the Manichaeans' because he could 'not remain in that sect' (*Conf.* 5. 14. 25) suggests that he may have been in contact with a group there. Cf. Lieu, *Manichaeism*, 137, for the importance of Manichaean cell networks in furthering Augustine's career. Although explicit evidence for a Milanese cell is lacking, their presence in western centres outside Rome (e.g. at Salona in Dalmatia: ibid., 86) and Ambrose's invective against them (*Hexameron* 1. 8. 30; 3. 7. 32), unless it is a *topos*, makes its existence probable.

[83] See esp. North, 'Development of Religious Pluralism'.

[84] On the process of demonizing religious 'others', see now Pagels, *The Origin of Satan*, esp. chs. 4–6.

landscapes in northern Italy, occupying a prominence previously reserved for the temples of the pagan gods. It would be rash to imagine that this transformation was swift. A more likely scenario is that of churches and temples standing side-by-side in the urban landscape, with both receiving worshippers. Our evidence for the continued vibrancy of paganism, however, is scanty—an inscription here, a sermon there—but there is just enough to show that even by the end of the century, northern Italy was still home to many pagans. In the last chapter, for example, we encountered vivid evidence of religious conflict between pagans and Christians in the Val di Non at the end of the fourth century. The narratives of these events show that in the Alto Adige temples still stood and pagan rituals and processions were still performed. Such material might lull us into accepting the traditional image of a paganism relegated to the countryside, but this is a thoroughly mistaken picture.[85] It is clear, rather, that the worship of the old gods may well have continued to take place within the walls of many north Italian cities for much of the fourth century.

The last period for which there is evidence of temple building on a large scale in the region is under the tetrarchy. The architectural embellishment of Milan, after its adoption as an imperial residence by Maximian, may have included sacred buildings. Ausonius' description of Milan (*Ordo urbium nobilium* 35–45) tells us of a number of buildings with sacred connotations. There were *templa* (ibid. 40), a reference which might mean Christian churches, but which could equally indicate pagan temples.[86] Ausonius also mentions Herculean baths in the city (ibid. 41), and these must surely be part of a tetrarchic building programme: as part of Diocletian's sacralization of the imperial office, Maximian took on the nature of Herculius, semi-divine lieutenant to the senior Augustus.[87] Apart from this, however, little is known of the pagan religious life of late Roman Milan.[88]

---

[85] For redress, see Roblin, 'Paganisme et rusticité'.

[86] Thus Green, *Ausonius*, 574.

[87] This is, however, conjecture, based on the location of the baths in the western part of the city which was redeveloped at the time of the tetrarchy: Arslan, 'Urbanistica di Milano romana', 196–8.

[88] Cf. Calderini, 'Milano archeologica', 563–9, demonstrates the inadequacy of our knowledge. Aur. Vict., *Caes.* 39. 45, yields a vague record of tetrarchic building programmes: 'Veterrimae religiones castissime curatae, ac mirum in modum adhuc nouis cultisque pulchre moenibus Romana culmina et ceterae urbes ornatae, maxime Carthago, Mediolanum, Nicomedia.'

There is little explicit evidence for the renovation or construction
of temples in other north Italian centres, but in one case the role of
direct imperial intervention is recorded. At Como, north of Milan,
a temple of Sol was erected by Axilius Iunior, a *curator* of T.
Flavius Postumius Titianus, *corrector Italiae*, by direct order of
Diocletian and Maximian themselves.[89] Apart from this our picture
is sketchy. Statues of the tetrarchs, replete with inscriptions recording their dedicants' devotion to the imperial *numen*, were set up at
Susa, Milan, Padua, and Miramare near Trieste.[90] These evoke comparison with the erection of similar images outside the Temple of
Hadrian at Ephesus at around the same time, but the northern Italian
instances lack such a precise context.[91]

Another city where paganism can be seen to have retained its vitality was Verona. Bishop Zeno's preaching gives the impression that
his Christian community did not yet dominate the city's population. He was scandalized about the knowledge of Christian mys-
teries among pagans (*Tract.* 2. 3. 10). Worse than that, he was
horrified by the potential for sacrilege when pagans and Christians
were actually married to one another. Advising widows not to
remarry, he paints a lurid picture of what might happen if a
Christian widow were to marry a new, pagan husband. Feast days
of the two religions might overlap and the pagan sacrificial food
become confused with that being offered as part of the Christian
sacrament. Apart from blasphemy this could lead to marital strife,
even violence, resulting in the woman being confined to the house
by her husband's orders, and so unable to come to church (*Tract.*
2. 7. 14–15). There is probably a deal of exaggeration here, but
there is an interesting aside in the course of Zeno's histrionics.
Establishing as his premise the coincidence of pagan and Christian
festivals, he remarks that this often happens (*Tract.* 2. 7. 14: 'ut saepe
contingit'). He uses the present tense, with the clear implication that
when Veronese Christians went to worship, they would have met
their pagan neighbours, en route to the temple, in the street.

[89] *AE* 1919: 52: 'Templum Dei Solis | iussu DD NN Diocletiani | et Maximiani
Augg. | T. Fl. Post. Titianus u. c. corr. | Ital. perfecit ac dedicauit | curante Axilio
Iuniore | u. c. curatore c[. . .]'; cf. *NSc* (1917), 272; *PLRE* 1. 919–20 'Titianus 9'.
[90] Susa: *CIL* 5. 7248–9; Milan: *CIL* 5. 5807/8; Padua: *CIL* 5. 2187–9 (erected by
different people); Miramare: *CIL* 5. 8205. Ward-Perkins, *CAMA*, 26, suggests that
CIL 5. 4327–8, recording the erection of unspecified items by a governor called
Gaudentius at Brescia, may also indicate imperial statues, although the date of
Gaudentius' tenure of office is unknown: cf. *PLRE* 1. 386 'Gaudentius 8.'
[91] Foss, *Ephesus After Antiquity*, 70–2.

To Zeno, then, paganism was a real threat to the integrity of the souls under his care. Yet his picture is strangely at odds with what else is known of Veronese paganism in the fourth century. The only independent evidence suggests that, by the early 380s, the traditional focus of pagan worship, the *capitolium*, was in a state of decay. At some time between 379 and 383, Valerius Palladius, consular governor of *Venetia et Histria*, ordered the erection in the forum at Verona of a statue that had previously been in the *capitolium*.[92] This was hardly looting: Palladius' dedicatory inscription announced that the statue had long lain ('diu iacentem') in the *capitolium*, toppled from its perch at some point. A *capitolium* strewn with fallen statues does not sound like a vibrant centre of pagan ritual.[93] Whatever ceremonies Zeno's pagan rivals were attending they are unlikely to have been in the *capitolium*: perhaps they were the rituals of privately funded cults, which continued to flourish thanks to the support of wealthy pagans even after the government had withdrawn the financial props of state cults.[94]

Verus Israel: Judaism and Christianity in northern Italy

Rather more evidence survives to show the uneasy relationship between Christians and Jews in the fourth century. Despite efforts by the state to retain a certain studied neutrality in Jewish–Christian relations,[95] confrontations at a local level could be both verbally and physically aggressive, as Christian mobs took matters into their own hands.[96] Even if this coincided with a general hardening of attitudes,[97] it remains true that the Jews had long been demonized by Christian authors: the continuance of Judaism after Christ's ministry meant that Christians were faced with awkward rival claimants to their Scriptural heritage, a factor not lost on pagan polemicists against Christianity.[98] Unsurprisingly, therefore,

[92] *CIL* 5. 3332: 'Hortante beatudine | temporum DDD NNN | Gratiani Valentiniani | et Theodosi [*sic*] Auggg. | statuam in capitolio | diu iacentem in | cereberrimo [*sic*] fori | loco constitui | iussit Val. Palladius | u. c. cons. Venet. et Hist.'

[93] Ward-Perkins, *CAMA*, 33, 89–90.

[94] Cf. Matthews, 'Symmachus and the Oriental Cults', 175–95.

[95] As Theodosius had tried to do at first over the burning of a synagogue at Callinicum on the Euphrates frontier in *c.* 389: McLynn, *Ambrose*, 298–315.

[96] Hunt, 'St. Stephen in Minorca', 114–19.

[97] Millar, 'Jews of the Graeco-Roman Diaspora', 116–19.

[98] Lieu, 'History and Theology', 82–7.

and despite all evidence to the contrary, the 'end' of Judaism had long been a rhetorical commonplace in Christian views of history.[99] North Italian Christians ventured into these debates. Just as Eusebius of Caesarea had argued for the priority of Christianity over paganism and Judaism by insisting that the Hebrew patriarchs were 'Christians in fact if not in name' (*HE* 1. 4. 6), so Zeno of Verona absolved Abraham of any taint of sin (*Tract.* 1. 3, 43): to be sure, Abraham had been circumcised—the typical mutilation of a Jew (*Tract.* 1. 3 *passim*)—but this had been a historical necessity, and it ought not to impugn the fundamental Christianity of his beliefs (*Tract.* 1. 3. 6–7). Thus Zeno was participating in the debate as to which particular claimants—the Jews or the Christians—on the heritage of Scripture constituted the *verus Israel*, the chosen people of God.[100] For Zeno there could be no doubt: commenting on the crossing of the Red Sea (Exodus 14) he announced:

Egypt is his world; Pharaoh and his people the Devil and every iniquitous spirit. Israel is the Christian people, which is ordered to set forth and strive for what is to come.   (*Tract.* 2. 26. 2)[101]

This passage of Exodus was but one *locus classicus* of the Jewish–Christian debate to which north Italians such as Zeno made their own contributions. Further pungent examples of Zeno's anti-Semitism come in his sermons on Isaiah, none more so than his exegesis of Isaiah 1: 2, 'Hear, O heavens, and give ear, O earth; for the Lord has spoken: "Sons have I begotten and exalted, but they have rebelled against me."' Zeno comments:

This is the voice of the Lord by which He was already reproaching the incredulous Jews through the prophets and warning them of what would be in the

---

[99] It is stated explicitly in Eusebius' historical agenda: *HE* 1. 1. 2.

[100] Cf. Rutgers, *The Jews in Late Ancient Rome*, 219–33, esp. 220–1 and 223, on the place of Zeno's use of the Pentateuch in the exegetical tradition.

[101] Zeno was capable of reading Exodus 13–14 in different ways depending on his needs. Throughout *Tract.* 2. 26 his interpretation proceeds by typological (e.g. 'Maria [i.e. Miriam in Exodus 15: 20] . . . typus ecclesiae fuit'). Elsewhere, however, his interpretation rejects such empty allegorizing: the Red Sea passage is seen as an inferior *imago* of the *veritas* offered by Christian baptism: Jeanes, *The Day*, 231–5. This is given added force by Zeno's assertion that the Jews were never immersed in water, contrary to the condition of Christians at baptism: cf. Hillier, *Arator on the Acts of the Apostles*, 162–3. Indeed, in *Tract.* 2. 16, he provides a unique interpretation of the parting of the waters: rather than represent God's favour it meant that the Jews had in fact been rejected (cf. *Tract.* 1. 18. 1), while the waters had reared up on either side to avoid contact with iniquitous Jewish feet.

future before it happened. For it is characteristic of God to comprehend
what has happened and to know what is to happen. He says: 'Sons have
I begotten and exalted.' The Jews, by their measureless infidelity, have
merited the hatred of our Lord; just as the grace of God's love is great, so
will be the future punishment of their offences. For it is certain that that
son, who has abandoned his father, will be punished severely . . . Thus
the Jews, who have spurned God their father, by whom they were reared,
who have forgotten their great honour and are ignorant of their great priv-
ilege, are wretched and miserable . . . Israel was exalted, when for three
days shadows and gloom enveloped all of Egypt; Israel was exalted, when
alone it feared or felt nothing of the many great torments of the Egyptians
. . . 'But they have rebelled against me': for they led Him to the cross.
(*Tract.* 1. 61. 5–8)

For Zeno, the Jews were a terrifying example to his congregation
of the dangers of turning away from God:

God is angry with the Jewish people and, lest they repent, shames them
with public reproofs . . . They are an example for us, my brothers: with
all your strength avoid doing likewise, and rejoice through the Lord Jesus
Christ that by the misfortune of others you learn the discipline of God.
(*Tract.* 1. 30)[102]

Isaiah inspired exegesis by Ambrose and Jerome too,[103] and the
prophet featured in the heresiological catalogue of Filastrius of
Brescia, again with reference to Judaism (e.g. *Div. heres. lib.* 155 on
Isaiah 6: 2). Indeed, Filastrius begins his work with an extensive list
of Jewish 'heresies' (*Div. heres. lib.* 1–28), marking the use in north
Italian circles of what became a familiar trope in anti-heretical
works: the association of Jews and heretics as a common enemy (cf.
Ambr., *De fide* 2. 15. 130).

It is uncertain to what extent such harping on the Jews and their
faults reflects actual conflict. For example, a familiar topic in Zeno's
sermons is how the wretchedness of the Jews in the present con-
trasts with their former enjoyment of God's favour:

The temple of Solomon, which they had taken for granted, has fallen . . .
Lamentation is imposed on their priests. Sacrifice is taken away. Anointing
has ceased. Circumcision is void. The Sabbath is a stigma. New moons and

---

[102] Cf. *Tract.* 1. 8; 1. 47; for commentary see Jeanes, *The Day,* 121–7.
[103] Evans, *To See and Not Perceive,* 157; Sawyer, *Fifth Gospel,* 54–61, 147 (and
100–25 *passim* for context).

feast days are held in odium. The Romans wield power over their kingdom. (*Tract.* 2. 17)[104]

In the absence of explicit evidence of actual conflict between Jews and Christians in fourth-century Verona, it is hard to see the use of the Jews here as anything other than a 'hermeneutical device [used] to define a premature closure of biblical discourse, short of the new realm of meaning it would enter in the light of the Incarnation'.[105] To put it another way, Zeno is emphasizing the damnation of the Jews purely to impress upon his congregation their special relationship with God.

Yet there may have been actual conditions of religious rivalry between the region's Jews and Christians. We saw that Jewish expansion in northern Italy, although of a different character, occurred at approximately the same time as that of Christianity.[106] During the fourth century, and later, the region was home to several flourishing Jewish communities, some of which have left traces in the material record.[107] Brescia, for example, had a synagogue, as is clear from an inscription recording a certain Coelia Paterna, *mater synagogae Brixianorum*;[108] indeed, the city's Jews were derided in several pungent sermons by bishop Gaudentius.[109] While such Jewish communities were the target of many anti-Semitic sermons,[110] evidence for actual violence against north Italian Jews is sparse. A tenth-century *Vita* narrates that St Innocentius of Tortona saw the conversion to Christianity of 'omnes Gentiles seu Judaei' (*sic*) as a primary aim of his episcopate.[111] Further, any Jews who did not submit to baptism were expelled from the city, while

---

[104] This formula is repeated in *Tract.* 1. 51: 'Salomonis templum hostili uastatione subuersum cum ruina sua iacet sepultum: ubi sacrificant? Sacerdotes iam non habent: qui eorum pro salute sacrificant?' The concept of Judaism's historical bankruptcy is common to all Zeno's anti-Jewish tirades: for example *Tract.* 2. 21: 'Iudaicum populum universum salutis suae amisisse praesidium diuini carminis textus ostendit.'

[105] Markus, *Signs and Meanings*, 24–5.   [106] See above pp. 99–101.

[107] Full details in Ruggini, 'Ebrei e orientali', 214–29.

[108] Noy, *JIWE* i. 5 (pp. 6–8) (= *CIL* 5. 4411; cf. *IG* 14. 2304), a fragment bearing the word *archisynagogos*.

[109] Lizzi, *Vescovi*, 124–7.

[110] Lizzi, *Vescovi*, 164–5 (Chromatius of Aquileia), 193 and n. 116 (Maximus of Turin).

[111] On this text: Savio, 'La légende de S. Innocent', 377–84; and esp. now. Picard, 'Le modèle épiscopal', 372–8, esp. 376 on the assimilation of pagans and Jews in the text. Cf. Ruggini, 'Ebrei e orientali', 221–3 n. 87.

the synagogue was destroyed and a church built in its place (*Vita S. Innocenti* 4–5). This account has been accepted as reliable, but such confidence seems misplaced.[112] The text is riddled with anachronisms. It narrates the fiction of Constantine's leprosy, conversion, and curative baptism at the hands of Sylvester of Rome (*Vita S. Innocenti* 4);[113] while the general tenor of the *Vita* is to present Innocentius as a model of episcopal sanctity.[114] It is also striking that in Ambrose's letters on the burning of the synagogue at Callinicum, not a single reference is made to Jewish–Christian tension in northern Italy: all the examples he cites are from the Levant or Egypt (*Ep.* 40. 15), while the only Italian evidence he produces of Christian attacks on synagogues comes from Rome in the late 380s (*Ep.* 40. 23).[115] Yet there was certainly some religious rivalry between Christians and Jews in northern Italy. At Grado this may have taken the form of active proselytism of Jews by Christians. In the early fifth century, a former Jew named Peter was buried in the church which now lies underneath the Byzantine basilica of S. Eufemia and set in its mosaic pavement an epitaph boasting of his conversion to Christianity.[116]

Construction, competition, and pluralism

The evidence presented in this chapter has been diffuse, and the picture it yields is one of considerable complexity. There is an undeniable increase in the scale and frequency of church building throughout the region, but against this must be set evidence for the continued vitality of paganism and Judaism. Traditional pictures of 'Christian triumph' are inadequate to explain such a nuanced picture of religious pluralism. Indeed, in the clandestine character of

[112] *Pace* Hunt, 'St. Stephen in Minorca', 116.

[113] Cf. Fowden, 'Last Days of Constantine', 153–5.

[114] Picard, 'Le modèle épiscopal', 371, 374–8, 383–4.

[115] On Ambrose's letter, cf. Millar, 'Jews of the Graeco-Roman Diaspora', 104–5. The view sometimes taken of Ambrose's claim that he wished he could have burned a synagogue himself (*Ep.* 40. 8) should not be taken as evidence of violence between Jews and Christians in northern Italy. Rather, it is part of the bishop's rhetorical strategy whereby he made the affair at Callinicum part of a personal struggle with Theodosius I: McLynn, *Ambrose*, 298–309.

[116] Brusin, 'L'epigrafe musiva di Petrus'; with Noy, *JIWE* i. 8 (pp. 13–16). This is, perhaps, a manifestation of the zeal commonly associated with converts: cf. Sawyer, *Fifth Gospel*, 100–1, 115–18, for energetic Christian proselytizing by former Jews.

Theodore's Aquileian church and the vitriol of Zeno of Verona's sermons, it is possible to glimpse Christian communities to whom the 'triumph' of their faith may not yet have been an obvious fact.

As ever, it is difficult and unwise to generalize for every north Italian city from a few specific examples, as the differing experience of each community was embedded in the particularities of local contexts. Magnificent, imperial Christian basilicas could be built at Milan, where the emperor and his court were resident for long periods of time. Likewise, any uneasiness between church and synagogue could only occur in cities that supported sizeable populations of both Christians and Jews. This variability of Christian experience from place to place across the Po valley mirrors the unevenness of the spread of the Church there. Some Christian communities were plainly large and influential forces in local urban society, as at Aquileia and Milan. Elsewhere, as is eloquently demonstrated in the grim protests of Zeno at Verona, Christians might have formed only a small religious minority. The implication is clear. Despite incontrovertible evidence for the expansion of the Church and its increasingly monumental presence in the cities, congregations still lived side by side with members of other religious groups. By the end of the fourth century, northern Italy was not yet a thoroughly Christian space.

EPILOGUE

The changing world of Chromatius of Aquileia

At various times in the first decade of the fifth century, the Gothic leader Alaric led an army through the passes of the Julian Alps into Venetia and the Po valley. The invasions provoked panic throughout northern Italy, to the extent that the emperor Honorius no longer felt safe at Milan and retreated to Ravenna, behind its protective ring of marshes. The response of the population of Aquileia, despairing of any effective imperial intervention, was to turn to its bishop, Chromatius, for reassurance. As part of his campaign to strengthen their spiritual resolve, he called on his old friend Turranius Rufinus, a fellow member of the Aquileian *chorus beatorum* under bishop Valerian, to prepare a Latin translation and continuation of Eusebius of Caesarea's *Ecclesiastical History*. In this narrative, the Christian people of Aquileia would find examples of how devotion to God had been rewarded by protection from adversity. In these uneasy days, this was what they needed to believe.[1]

Chromatius stands at the head of a list of Aquileian bishops who provided leadership for the city in the insecure period of barbarian invasions.[2] After the city was sacked by the Huns in 452, it rose again grouped around its cathedral complex, a symbol of the increasingly central role played by the Church in Aquileian society. Just over a century later, when Alboin and his Lombard armies flowed through the Julian Alps into the plains of Venetia, the people of Aquileia again looked to their bishop for reassurance. This time the reaction was more drastic. Bishop Paul decided that the exposed position of Aquileia was no longer tenable and, like many of his fellow bishops in north-eastern Italy, he led his people away from the plains to the comparative security of islands in the coastal lagoons (Paul. Diac., *HL* 2. 10).

---

[1] Invasions: Heather, *Goths and Romans*, 208–13. Reaction: Lizzi, *Vescovi*, 171–9. Chromatius and Rufinus: Thelamon, 'Une oeuvre destinée à la communauté chrétienne d'Aquilée'.

[2] For historical background, see Humphries, 'Italy 425–605'; these themes will be explored more fully by me in the sequel to this study.

With Paul and his contemporaries we enter a different phase in the dialogue between church and society from the one observed in the period covered by this study. In the 560s it was Christianity that was determining the shape of society, and religious concerns exercised a greater influence on how north Italians conceived of their identities. Religious, local, and political loyalties, for example, became inextricably intertwined. Thus, when in 610 a substantial part of the population of the bishopric of Aquileia living in exile at Grado opted to reject the side their bishop was taking in the Three Chapters controversy, they not only repudiated him, but also Grado itself in favour of a return to Aquileia, as well as allegiance to Constantinople for the Lombard dukes of Friuli. In the third and fourth centuries, the picture had been almost totally the reverse. When Zeno of Verona had addressed his congregations as the *aetheriae gentes*, they were not society itself, but an element within it.

This study has argued that the origins and development of Christian communities in northern Italy were in large measure determined by an established matrix of social networks. The medieval sources that have determined the shape of all previous studies of the topic do not reflect this situation; rather, they represent anachronistic projections of later ecclesiastical power struggles onto an earlier period. Even contemporary records, such as lists of conciliar subscriptions, are by themselves inadequate to explain the early development of north Italian Christianity (Chapter 2). But by fitting whatever meagre data such sources and the archaeological record yield into the framework of the human environment of northern Italy (Chapter 1), it is possible to explain why Christianity appeared in certain centres but not at others. In particular, it was in towns and cities, which for economic or administrative reasons had constantly changing populations, that there existed the environment of interpersonal contact crucial for the dissemination of the gospel (Chapter 3).

In the period between Constantine's conversion and Ambrose's death, the development of north Italian Christianity continued to manifest strong regional characteristics. Involvement in the Donatist schism and the Christological controversy had been fitful, and was dictated largely by periods of imperial presence in northern Italy itself. Constantius II's residence at Milan in 355 was the most fateful. North Italian bishops had hitherto been rather remote from the centre of the theological (as opposed to personal) debates of the controversy, but this ended with the emperor's determination to

impose a homoian settlement throughout his realm. Not only were
bishops required to submit to a credal formula that many found
repugnant, but during their periods of exile in the east they came
face to face with different shades of Christological opinion. With
the return of Eusebius of Vercelli to northern Italy in 362, the region's ecclesiastical politics changed character, from a situation where
orthodoxy was defined, in effect, by allegiance to champions such
as Athanasius of Alexandria, to one where credal minutiae assumed
greater importance. In these new circumstances it took Auxentius
of Milan all of his theological and political—not to mention linguistic
—acumen to retain his see. For all that, the broadening of north
Italian theological horizons occurred along idiosyncratic north
Italian lines. As Filastrius of Brescia's definition of Arius' beliefs
as homoianism shows, north Italian perceptions had been shaped
both by Constantius' visit in 355 and by the prevalence of homoian
bishops in the Balkans (Chapter 4).

Involvement in a wider arena of ecclesiastical politics influenced
more than the theological evolution of the north Italian episcopate.
The resulting struggles provided Ambrose of Milan with an impetus
to acquire for himself the regional supremacy necessary to secure a
pro-Nicene victory in the west. In many respects, however, Ambrose's
achievement was anomalous: ecclesiastical administration in northern Italy was generally embedded in the region's social networks.
Bishops' regional spheres of influence developed within an existing
framework of interconnections between neighbouring towns and
cities. At a more local level, a bishop's leadership of his congregation involved him in the patronage networks and power relationships of civic society (Chapter 5).

The fourth century also saw the continued expansion of the church
in northern Italy (Chapter 6). Despite the favour Christianity now
enjoyed with the state, the establishment of new congregations was
subject to much the same constraints as in the pre-Constantinian
period. The scatter of new communities continued to follow patterns
laid down by existing social networks, particularly along communications routes, even into seemingly remote areas such as the Alto
Adige. There was, of course, consolidation in some areas, most notably
in *Venetia et Histria*, but by 400 the dissemination of Christianity
across the region as a whole was still patchy.

Looking within the cities, we see a reflection in microcosm of
the unevenness of Christian growth (Chapter 7). To be sure, in

some centres the Christian population displayed increasing self-confidence as the century progressed. In centres such as Aquileia, as is clear from the growing monumentality of its cathedral complex already in the first half of the fourth century, the Christian presence would have been hard to ignore. Yet this was no universal phenomenon. In many other centres, large church buildings did not appear until much later, or they were relegated to peripheral parts of town. More importantly, Christianity did not yet hold a monopoly on the sacred. As the histrionics of bishops such as Zeno of Verona show, pagans and Jews continued to flourish in the cities of northern Italy. In short, north Italian Christianity continued to exist in an essentially pluralist environment even at the end of the fourth century.

The picture of early Christianity in northern Italy yielded by an approach sensitive to its social environment is very different from the traditional narrative based on medieval sources. Gone are the planned apostolic missions to centres such as Aquileia, Ravenna, and Milan, in favour of a more haphazard, anonymous dispersal of the Christian message. Similarly, some of the great ecclesiastical centres of the early medieval period make only a fleeting appearance in the fourth century. Apart from archaeological remains hinting at a Christian community at Classe and the participation of its bishop Severus at the Council of Serdica, the church of Ravenna has hardly been glimpsed in these pages. The Ravennate church only becomes important to the outside world in the fifth century, with the removal of the imperial court to the city and the occupation of the see by dynamic bishops like Peter Chrysologus. Also looking forward into the fifth century, it is clear how ephemeral was Ambrose's achievement of ecclesiastical hegemony for Milan. His successor Simplicianus managed to preserve the illusion enough for Vigilius of Trento to send him relics of the martyrs of the Val di Non. Yet, at a council held at Turin around this time, the Milanese church had to insist on its rights; interestingly, it could provide no more compelling justification for this position than the vanished glory of Ambrose.[3]

In essence, the picture I have painted is rather more sketchy than that which earlier generations would have drawn. In addition, it defies

---

[3] Munier, *Conc. Gall.*, 57–8; for comm. see Lizzi, *Vescovi*, 209–10 and nn. 192–5. On the vexed problem of the Council of Turin, see most recently: Kulikowski, 'Two Councils of Turin'.

efforts at generalization, as Christian presence and practice varied markedly across northern Italy. Northern Italy is also very different from other parts of the Mediterranean world, even those in the west. To be sure, northern Italy was beginning to acquire its rural parishes by 400, but their distribution was uneven and the general picture differs drastically from the image of a Christian countryside offered by many parts of north Africa. Such regional peculiarities have important ramifications for the study of early Christianity not just in northern Italy, but in the Roman empire as a whole. If a realistic picture of the processes of evangelization, dissemination, and consolidation is to be achieved, it must be sensitive to the special dynamics of local society: this was the framework that guided all aspects of ancient life, and no study of the early Church should ignore it.

In the early fifth century, Chromatius of Aquileia found himself working within these constraints. He might well be offering guidance to the people of Aquileia, but that guidance was directed particularly at the city's Christian population. On the night of the Paschal Vigil in one of those uncertain years during the Gothic invasions, Chromatius preached to the faithful in an effort to calm their fears (*Sermo* 16. 4):

Since this is the night on which, once, the firstborn of the Egyptians were struck down and the sons of Israel set free, so we pray to the Lord with all our hearts, with all our faith, that He might free us from the attacks of all our foes, and from our fear of all our enemies. . . . For as He says through the prophet: *Invoke me on the day of tribulation, and I will deliver you, and you shall glorify me.* (Ps. 49 [50]: 15)

Chromatius spoke as a Christian who lived within a society where non-Christians were present, and he saw his congregation much as Zeno had done, as *aetheriae gentes* living among pagans and Jews. In the gathering gloom induced by Alaric's invasion he could not vouch for the safety of the pagans and Jews who lived in Aquileia; as for devout Christians immersed in prayer, he could be more certain: 'uincuntur tenebrae noctis lumine deuotionis', 'the shadows of night are vanquished by the light of devotion' (*Sermo* 16. 3).

APPENDIX

The martyrs of northern Italy

This appendix will list the data available for martyrs in northern Italy, supplementing the information on earliest north Italian Christianity presented in Chapters 2 and 3. Material will be arranged by city. In the catalogue, references will be given to the *Bibliotheca Hagiographica Latina* (*BHL*), and to any relevant commentary in the *Bibliotheca Sanctorum* (*BS*); an asterisk indicates that the martyr or group of martyrs is listed in the *Martyrologium Hieronymianum* (*Mart. Hier.*). The dates given for each martyrdom are approximate, based on the details given in the *passiones*. Each catalogue will be followed by a brief commentary; a general conclusion will analyse the utility of these texts for a reconstruction of Christian experience, particularly persecution, in northern Italy before Constantine.[1]

Catalogue

Aquileia

* Cantius, Cantianus, Cantianella: *BHL* 1543–9; *BS* 3. 758–60; tetrarchic (284–305).
(*) Chrysogonus: *BHL* 1795–7; *BS* 4. 306–8; tetrarchic (284–305).
* Felix and Fortunatus: *BHL* 2860; *BS* 5. 588–91; tetrarchic (284–305).
* Hilarus (or Hilarius): *BHL* 3881; *BS* 7. 728–30; under Numerian (283/4).
* Protus: cf. under Cantius, Cantianus, Cantianella, with whom he was martyred.

Aquileia quickly developed a cult of martyrs,[2] around which there arose a complex hagiographical tradition.[3] The Aquileian martyrs are universally attributed to the late third or early fourth centuries, mainly under the tetrarchy. That the imperial government should be so interested in Aquileia at this time is reasonable, bearing in mind the city's considerable strategic importance. Thus many of the *passiones* may reflect a certain reality, especially the interesting detail of Hilarus' execution under Numerian as he is an obscure

---

[1] The only treatment of the subject is Delehaye, *Origines du culte*, 322–40; however, Picard, *Souvenir*, is a useful supplement especially on episcopal martyrs.
[2] Niero, 'I martiri aquileiesi'.   [3] See Ch. 2 above.

emperor. It is worth noting some difficulties. The Chrysogonus listed in the *Mart. Hier.* appears to have no connection with the Aquileian saint: cults associated with martyrs of that name are known in Milan, Zara, Ravenna, Carthage, and Rome, leaving ample scope for confusion. The *passio* of Chrysogonus, however, links him to a certain Anastasia from Sirmium, a city with which Aquileia had many contacts.

The earliest recorded cult is that of Felix and Fortunatus. Chromatius of Aquileia (388–407/8) mentions them as one of the glories of the sacred heritage of Aquileia (*Sermo* 7), but by the time of the *Mart. Hier.* they—and Fortunatus in particular—had also become associated with Vicenza, where a church was erected in their honour. The reason for this connection is impossible to ascertain. All that can be said is that Vicenza, an important city in north-eastern Italy, was well placed for its early Christian community to have had contact with Aquileia. For all that, however, there is no direct evidence of cooperation between them, even when the bishops of several Venetic churches were active in support of Athanasius' efforts to gain an audience with Constans in the 340s.

Brescia

* Faustinus and Iovitta: *BHL* 2836–40; *BS* 5. 483–5.

Their *passio* (*BHL* 2836) relates that they suffered under Hadrian. This, however, is probably a spurious detail: the texts associated with their cult have evidently undergone a long and complex process of shaping and reshaping.[4] Their entry in the *Mart. Hier.* is also problematic, listing them as having been venerated 'in Britannis'. This is very probably a corruption of 'in Brixia'.[5]

Imola (Forum Cornelii)

* Cassian: *BHL* 1625–9; *BS* 3. 909–12.

Cassian's is among the earliest martyr cults to develop in northern Italy. Prudentius describes visiting his tomb (*Peristephanon*, 9), above which was a painted representation ('colorum picta imago martyris') of his martyrdom (by being stabbed with the nibs of his students' pens), but mentions no date for the event. Cassian's cult was widely disseminated: it is mentioned by Gregory of Tours (*Gloria Martyrum* 42); and Pope Symmachus (498–514) dedicated an altar to him at Rome. This popularity is probably due the patronage of the cult by the bishops of Ravenna: Peter Chrysologus was buried

---

[4] See Savio, 'SS. Faustin et Jovite'.   [5] *Comm. Mart. Hier.* 99–100.

at Imola so as to be near him;[6] and he appears in the procession of martyrs in S. Apollinare Nuovo.[7]

Milan

* Gervasius and Protasius: *BHL* 3513–22; *inventio* in 386 described by Ambrose (*Ep.* 22), Augustine (*Conf.* 9. 7. 16), and Paulinus (*V. Ambr.* 14).
* Nabor and Felix: *BHL* 6028–9; *BS* 9. 689–93; tetrarchic (after 296).
* Victor: *BHL* 8580–3; *BS* 12. 1274–5; tetrarchic (after 296).
* Valeria: *BHL* 8699–704; usually associated with Felix, Nabor, and Victor.

All materials purporting to recount the earliest history of the church of Milan must be treated with caution because of the manner in which traditions were manipulated in the middle ages.[8] For example, although Ambrose, Augustine, and Paulinus are unanimous that Gervasius and Protasius were unknown prior to their miraculous *inventio*, there exists a tendentious medieval *passio* (*BHL* 3514) that narrates their deaths. The text reports the events from the perspective of a certain 'servus Christi Philippus' who claims to have recovered the martyrs' bodies:[9] this is clearly a fabrication based on the location of their *inventio* and subsequent burial in churches in the Hortus Philippi.

Likewise, the texts of the *passiones* of Nabor and Felix and of Victor bear the hallmarks of early medieval fabrication. The narratives are almost identical verbally; compare, for example, their opening sentences:

Regnante impio Maximiano Imperatore cum in civitate Mediolanensi esset persecutio ingens Christianorum, erant ibi quidam milites Nabor et Felix notissimi Imperatori.   (*BHL* 6028)

Regnante impio Maximiano Imperatore, in civitate Mediolanensi erat persecutio ingens Christianorum. Erat autem ibi quidam miles, nomine Victor, notissimus Imperatori.   (*BHL* 8580)

These verbal and narrative similarities—which reflect the close association between their cults—persist for much of both *passiones*, although the climax of each account is different (Nabor and Felix are executed at Lodì, Victor outside Milan).

Of particular interest is the note in the *Passio SS. Naboris et Felicis* (*BHL* 6028) that their relics were translated to Milan from Lodì by bishop

---

[6] Picard, *Souvenir*, 146–9.
[7] Deichmann, *Frühchristliche Bauten*, pls. 105, 121; id., *Ravenna. Kommentar*, i. 149.
[8] See Ch. 2 above.
[9] A similar narrative pattern is found in the Roman *gesta martyrum*. See Cooper, 'The Martyr, the *Matrona*, and the Bishop'.

Maternus in the first half of the fourth century. This association is eloquently reflected in the fifth-century mosaics in the vault of the chapel of S. Vittore in Ciel d'Oro.[10] Nabor and Felix are shown flanking Maternus opposite the depiction of Ambrose standing between Gervasius and Protasius, implying that Milanese tradition already credited Maternus with the *inventio* of these martyrs. This tradition might well reflect reality. The cult of Nabor and Felix was well established at Milan by 386, when the bodies of Gervasius and Protasius were found 'ante cancellos sanctorum Felicis atque Naboris' (Ambr., *Ep.* 22. 2). But, when describing that discovery, Ambrose remarks that the church of Milan had been 'sterile of martyrs' (*Ep.* 22. 7: 'sterilem martyribus ecclesiam Mediolanensem') and hitherto had merely taken other cities' martyrs (*Ep.* 22. 12: 'Perdiderat civitas [*sc.* Mediolanum] suos martyres quae rapuit alienos'). This means, therefore, that Felix and Nabor must have been imported to the city. Whether this actually happened under Maternus is impossible to ascertain.

Padua

Justina: *BHL* 4571–8; tetrarchic (after 286).

Justina is not attested until the sixth century. Once again there is need for a vigilant awareness of medieval fabrication, especially bearing in mind her association with the protobishop of Padua, Prosdocimus (cf. *BHL* 6960–1). Prosdocimus is of uncertain antiquity: no record of him exists prior to the dedication of a chapel to him and Justina by Venatius Opilio in the early sixth century. The surviving *Vita* (*BHL* 6960–1) portrays him as dying early in the reign of Antoninus Pius (138–61), but makes Justina, his protégée, live until the tetrarchic persecutions, a century and a half later! Such documents, and indeed the whole fostering of his cult, seem designed to grant the Paduan church a certain apostolic prestige.[11]

Poreč

Maurus: *II* 10/2. 64; (?) tetrarchic.

Like Ravenna (see below), Poreč attracted the cults of various saints and martyrs from elsewhere, as is eloquently demonstrated by the sixth-century mosaics in the Euphrasian basilica. Only one martyrdom can be associated with the city itself, that of Maurus. His death is recorded in an inscription from the primitive church underlying the Euphrasian basilica. This document is of no assistance in dating Maurus' death, although, on the basis of the most likely date for persecutions in other north Italian cities

---

[10] Picard, *Souvenir*, 39.   [11] See in full: Picard, *Souvenir*, 641–4.

(see below), it may be conjectured that he suffered under the tetrarchy. A surviving *passio* of Maurus (*BHL* 5786–91) is of no use: it discusses an African Christian, martyred at Rome under Numerian, who somehow came to be identified with the martyr of Poreč.[12]

Ravenna

* Apollinaris: *BHL* 623–32; (?) Flavian (69–79).

As with Milan and Aquileia, the hagiographical traditions of Ravenna are dauntingly complex; in particular, the city's bishops were active in appropriating and promoting the cults of saints from other centres (cf. above on Cassian of Imola). An additional layer of confusion is provided by the move of the court to Ravenna from Milan under Honorius: Delehaye suggests that this was responsible for the profusion of Milanese saints in the city.[13] Such imperial patronage was certainly important, as is demonstrated by the number of foundations made by Galla Placidia.[14]

The earliest developments at Ravenna itself of an indigenous martyr cult are associated with Apollinaris at Classe, whose veneration seems to begin in the fourth century if not before. Beyond that, however, details of Apollinaris are substantially irrecoverable. His cult, like so many, has been manipulated for political reasons in order to grant the Ravennate church apostolic status. Thus reports of his martyrdom under Vespasian ought to be treated with caution.

Trieste

Justus: *BHL* 4604; tetrarchic (after 286).

The city's patron saint, Justus, was martyred—so the *Martyrologium Romanum* and an early medieval *passio* maintain—during the Diocletianic persecution. As with many traditions, it is impossible to verify this one. The *Martyrologium* states that Justus was executed 'sub Manatio praeside', but no imperial official of this name is otherwise attested.[15] Any effort to pin down the date more closely soon runs into difficulty. The *passio* begins 'Temporibus Diocletiani et Maximiani imperatorum, consulatus eorum

---

[12] Full discussion in Delehaye, 'Saints d'Istrie et de Dalmatie'.

[13] Delehaye, *Origines du culte*, 322–8.

[14] Oost, *Galla Placidia Augusta*, 273–8.

[15] *Mart. Rom.* 4 id. Nov.: cf. the unlocated Justus mentioned in the *Mart. Hier.* on 2, 3 and 16 Nov. The *passio* has 'Mannacius', which is at least closer to Umbronius Mannachius, the one form of the name known from fourth-century Italy, albeit from Aeclanum in Apulia: *PLRE* i. 542. But the *passio* is otherwise untrustworthy (see below).

quarto anno, imperii ipsorum nono, facta est persecutio',[16] which seems precise enough. But the accuracy is illusory, and the dating criteria do not agree with each other: the fourth shared consulship of Diocletian and Maximian was in 299; the ninth year of their joint rule was 295; and the Great Persecution did not begin until February 303.[17] The attestation of another martyr at Trieste, a certain Apollinaris (*BHL* 633), is also tendentious: this saint is evidently the protomartyr and protobishop of Ravenna, albeit in a heavily disguised form (*BS* 2. 249).

Vercelli

Theonestus: not known to *BHL* or *BS*.

The *Vita Antiqua* of Eusebius of Vercelli (*BHL* 2748) records that he built a church in honour of a martyr Theonestus. This is impossible to verify, but the story does not inspire confidence: the *Vita Antiqua* is a tendentious and unreliable document, which makes Eusebius himself a martyr.

Vicenza

Felix and Fortunatus: see under Aquileia.

Persecutions in northern Italy

There is always the danger when dealing with martyr texts that too much is put down to the rehearsal of tropes, and not enough account is taken of the sources and motives of the hagiographer.[18] Taking a positivist line, it might seem that a great deal can be recovered from these texts about the various mechanisms by which persecution was implemented by the government. Many details seem in keeping with what is known about the persecutions from contemporary sources like Eusebius and Lactantius. For example, the Milanese martyrs Victor, Nabor, and Felix were detected during a purge of Christians from the army, a circumstance known to have accompanied the outbreak of the tetrarchic persecution. Similarly, the insistence that the Christians should offer sacrifice, as Maximian puts it to Victor, *per salutem [imperatoris] et statum reipublicae* rings true.

Yet a blithe acceptance of what such *passiones* tell us would be misplaced. While the generalities seem fine, the narratives often fall apart on their specifics. Turning again to the martyrdoms of Victor, Nabor, and Felix, they

[16] *AASS, Nov.* 1. 428.
[17] Cf. Delehaye, *Origines du culte*, 330: 'Sa Passion n'a rien historique.'
[18] Geary, *Living with the Dead*, 9–29.

go seriously awry when they begin describing the persecutors. In both texts, the prosecuting official is the *consularis* Anullinus. There are two problems here. First, the title is anachronistic: no *consulares* governed in northern Italy until after Constantine's victory over Maxentius; under Maximian, such governors were called *correctores*. Second, no-one called Anullinus seems to have filled an administrative post in northern Italy under the tetrarchy.[19] Even the detailed descriptions of tetrarchic Milan cannot inspire confidence. A strong classical tradition endured at Milan, preserving the memory of its Roman past long after the demise of the empire, and it is possible that the author(s) of these *passiones* drew on it for details of Milanese topography.

We may be on safer ground with regard to the chronological information preserved in the north Italian *passiones*. With a few exceptions (such as Faustinus and Jovitta at Brescia), they confine their narratives to the late third or early fourth century. While earlier martyrdoms are not impossible, the surviving accounts attesting persecution in the first and second centuries are too tendentious to inspire confidence. The inescapable conclusion must be that harassment of north Italian Christians by the imperial authorities was insignificant prior to the tetrarchic period. It seems unlikely that the region's Christian communities would have been large enough to attract attention even in the Decian persecution. This supports the picture painted in Chapters 2 and 3 of the retarded growth of Christianity in the region.

[19] It is possible that these *passiones* have been contaminated by north African materials. Two Anullini are known from the period. There was the Anullinus who served as proconsul of Africa and was Constantine's chief intermediary with the Carthaginian church in the early stages of the Donatist schism (*PLRE* i. 78–9, 'Anullinus 2'). A more likely candidate, however, might be C. Annius Anullinus, the *impius iudex* who presided over the trials of many Christians in a series of north African *passiones* (*PLRE* i. 79, 'Anullinus 3'). For detailed analysis: Humphries, 'Anullinus, Africa, and Aquileia'.

BIBLIOGRAPHY

Primary sources

This lists the major sources used for this study; full details of more minor works, such as the episcopal lists discussed in Chapter 2, will be found in the relevant footnotes. Classical authors are referred to in standard editions (Teubner, Budé, etc.).

Altercatio Hercaliani laici cum Germinio episcopo Sirmiensi, in *PLS* 1. 345–50.
Ambrose of Milan, *Contra Auxentium*, in *CSEL* 82/3. 82–107.
—— *De Fide*, in *CSEL* 78.
—— *De obitu Theodosii*, in *CSEL* 73. 369–401.
—— *De Sacramentis*, in *CSEL* 73. 13–85.
—— *De Spiritu Sancto*, in *CSEL* 79. 15–222.
—— *Epistolae*, in *PL* 16. 875–1286, and *CSEL* 82/1–3 (numbering follows *PL*).
Ammianus Marcellinus, ed. and trans. J. C. Rolfe (London, 1935–40).
Antonini Placentini Itinerarium, in *CCL* 175. 127–74.
Arnulf of Milan, *Liber gestorum recientorum*, in *MGH, SS* 8. 6–31.
Athanasius of Alexandria, *Apologia ad Constantium*, ed. J. Szymusiak (Paris, 1987).
—— *De Synodis*, in *Athanasius Werke* II, ed. H. G. Opitz (Berlin and Leipzig, 1935–41), i. 231–78.
—— *Epistola ad Afros*, in *PG* 26. 1029–48.
—— *Historia Arianorum*, in *Athanasius Werke II*, ed. H. G. Opitz (Berlin and Leipzig, 1935–41), i. 183–231.
Augustine of Hippo, *ad Donatistas post collationem*, in *CSEL* 53. 95–162.
—— *Breviarium Collationis cum Donatistis*, in *CCL* 149. 259–306.
—— *Confessions*, ed. J. J. O'Donnell (Oxford, 1992).
—— *Contra Cresconium*, in *CSEL* 52. 323–582.
—— *Epistolae*, in *CSEL* 34, 44, 57–8, 88.
Basil of Caesarea, *Epistolae*, ed. R. J. Deferrari (London, 1950–61).
Chromatius of Aquileia, *Sermons*, ed. J. Lemarié (Paris, 1969–71).
Church Councils:
    Acts of the Council of Aquileia, in *CSEL* 82/3. 325–68.
    Acts of the Council of Chalcedon, in N. P. Tanner (ed.), *Decrees of the Ecumenical Councils*, i (London and Washington, 1990), 75–103.

Acts of the Council of Nicaea, ibid., 1–19.

Codex Calendar of AD 354, in *MGH, AA* 9. 13–148.

Damasus, *Epistola 'Confidimus quidem'*, in *PL* 13. 347–9.

Eusebius of Caesarea, *Historia Ecclesiastica*, ed. K. Lake and J. E. L. Oulton (London, 1926–32).

Eusebius of Vercelli, *Epistolae*, in *CCL* 9. 101–10.

Filastrius of Brescia, *Diversarum hereseon liber*, in *CCL* 9. 217–324.

Gaudentius of Brescia, *Tractatus*, in *CSEL* 68.

Gregory the Great, *Dialogues*, ed. A. de Vogüé (Paris, 1978–9).

Jerome, *Chronicon*, ed. R. Helm (Berlin, 1956).

—— *De Viris Illustribus*, ed. E. C. Richardson (Leipzig, 1896).

—— *Epistolae*, ed. J. Labourt (Paris, 1949–).

Hilary of Poitiers, *Contra Auxentium*, in *PL* 10. 609–18.

—— *Collectanea Antiariana Parisina*, in *CSEL* 65.

Lactantius, *De mortibus persecutorum*, ed. and trans. J. L. Creed (Oxford, 1984).

—— *Divinae Institutiones*, in *CSEL* 19. 1–672.

Landulf Senior, *Mediolanenis historiae libri IV*, in *MGH, SS* 8. 32–100.

Libellus de situ civitatis Mediolanensis, in *RIS* n.s. 1/2.

Liberius of Rome, *Epistolae ad Eusebium Vercellensem*, in *CCL* 9. 121–4.

Lucifer of Cagliari, *de Athanasio*, in *CCL* 8. 3–132.

Martyrologium Hieronymianum, ed. G. B. De Rossi and L. Duchesne, *AASS* Nov. 2/1 (1894), 1–195.

Notitia Dignitatum, ed. O. Seeck (Berlin, 1876).

Notitia Galliarum, ed. O. Seeck, *Notitia Dignitatum* (Berlin, 1876), 261–74.

Optatus of Milevis, *Libri Septem*, in *CSEL* 26.

Palladius of Ratiaria, *Apologia*, in Gryson, *Scolies ariennes*, 274–324.

Panegyrici Latini, ed. E. Galletier (Paris, 1955).

Paul the Deacon, *Historia Langobardorum*, ed. and trans. A. Zanella (Milan, 1991).

—— *Liber de episcopis mettensibus*, in *MGH, SS* 2. 260–330.

Paulinus of Milan, *Vita Sancti Ambrosii*, in *PL* 14. 27–46.

Peter Chrysologus, *Sermons*, in *CCL* 24.

Rufinus, *Historia Ecclesiastica*, ed. Th. Mommsen (Leipzig, 1908).

Sulpicius Severus, *Chronica*, in *CSEL* 1.

—— *Vita Sancti Martini*, ed. J. Fontaine (Paris, 1968–9).

Turranius Rufinus, *Apologia contra Hieronymum*, in *CCL* 79.

Venantius Fortunatus, *Carmina*, in *MGH, AA* 4/1. 1–270.

—— *Vita Sancti Martini*, in *MGH, AA* 4/1. 293–370.

Vigilius of Trento, *Epistolae*, in *PL* 13. 549–58.

Zeno of Verona, *Tractatus*, in *CCL* 22.

Secondary works

ABULAFIA, D., *The Two Italies: Economic Relations between the Norman Kingdom of Sicily and the Northern Communes* (Cambridge, 1977).

ALFÖLDY, G., *Noricum* (London, 1974).

ALFONSI, A., 'Vicenza. Antico sepocreto cristiano a grandi sarcofagi sopra terra, e titoli funebri di età classica scoperti presso la chiesa di s. Felice', *NSc* (1908), 337–40.

AMIDON, P. R., 'The Procedure of St. Cyprian's Synods', *VChr* 37 (1983), 328–39.

APOLLONJ GHETTI, B. M., 'Le cattedrali di Milano ed i relativi battisteri', *RAC* 68 (1987), 23–89.

ARSLAN, E. A., 'Urbanistica di Milano Romana', *ANRW* II. 12. 1 (1982), 179–210.

ASHBY, T., *The Roman Campagna in Classical Times*, 2nd edn. (London, 1970).

AUBERT, R., 'Gregoire de Montelongo', *DHGE* 22 (1988), 6–9.

AUDIN, A., 'Lugdunum: colonie romaine et capitale des Gaules', in A. Latreille (ed.), *L'histoire de Lyon et du Lyonnais* (Toulouse, 1975).

BAGATTI, B., 'Note sul contenuto dottrinale dei mosaici di Aquileia', *RAC* 34 (1958), 119–22.

BAGNALL, R. S., *Egypt in Late Antiquity* (Princeton, 1993).

BALDOVIN, J. F., *The Urban Character of Christian Worship* (Rome, 1987).

BALDWIN, B., 'Acclamations in the *Historia Augusta*', *Athenaeum* n.s. 59 (1981), 138–49.

BARFIELD, L., 'The Iceman Reviewed', *Antiquity* 68 (1994), 10–26.

BARNES, T. D., *Tertullian* (Oxford, 1971).

—— 'Lactantius and Constantine', *JRS* 63 (1973), 29–46.

—— *Constantine and Eusebius* (Cambridge, Mass., 1981).

—— *The New Empire of Diocletian and Constantine* (Cambridge, Mass., 1982).

—— 'Religion and Society in the Reign of Theodosius', in H. Meynell (ed.), *Grace, Politics and Desire* (Calgary, 1990), 157–75.

—— *Athanasius and Constantius: Theology and Politics in the Constantinian Empire* (Cambridge, Mass., 1993).

BARONIUS, C., *Annales Ecclesiastici*, ed. A. Theiner, vols. i (Bar le Duc and Paris, 1864) and iv (Bar le Duc and Paris, 1865).

BAUER, W., *Orthodoxy and Heresy in Earliest Christianity* (Philadelphia, 1971).

—— *A Greek–English Lexicon of the New Testament and other Early Christian Literature* (Chicago, 1979).

BEARD, M., NORTH, J., and PRICE, S. R. F., *Religions of Rome*, 2 vols. (Cambridge, 1998).

BELLINATI, C., 'Luoghi di culto a Padova fino al sec. XII', in id. and L. Puppi (eds.), *Padova. Basiliche e chiese*, i (Vicenza, 1975), 1–19.

BERTACCHI, L., 'La basilica postteodoriana di Aquileia', *AqN* 43 (1972), 61–88.

—— 'Le basiliche suburbane di Aquileia', *Arh. Vest.* 23 (1972), 224–33.

—— 'Edilizia civile nel IV secolo ad Aquileia', *AAAd* 22 (1982), 337–57.

BESCHI, L., 'Verona romana. I monumenti', in *Verona* i. 369–552.

BILLANOVICH, M. P., 'Appunti di agiografia aquileiese', *RSCI* 30 (1976), 5–24.

—— 'San Siro. Falsificazioni, mito, storia', *IMU* 29 (1986), 1–54.

BINTLIFF, J., 'The Contribution of an *Annaliste*/Structural History approach to Archaeology', in id. (ed.), *The* Annales *School and Archaeology* (1991), 1–33.

BISCHOFF, B., *Manuscripts and Libraries in the Age of Charlemagne* (Cambridge, 1994).

BOBERTZ, C. A., 'The Development of Episcopal Order', in H. W. Attridge and G. Hata (eds.), *Eusebius, Christianity and Judaism* (Leiden, 1992), 183–211.

BOCCARDI, V., *'Quantum spiritualiter intellegi datur.* L'esegesi di Zenone di Verona', *Augustinianum* 23 (1983), 453–85.

BOGNETTI, G. P., 'Gli arcivescovi interpreti della realtà e il crescere dei minori ordini feudali nell'età ottoniana', in *Storia di Milano* 2 (Milan, 1954), 845–62.

—— 'Una campagna di scavi a Torcello per chiarire problemi inerenti alle origini di Venezia', *Bollettino dell'Istituto di Storia della Società e dello Stato veneziano* 3 (1961), 3–27.

BOLGAR, R. R., *The Classical Heritage and its Beneficiaries* (Cambridge, 1954).

BONNET, C., 'Les origines du groupe épiscopal de Genève', *CRAI* (1981), 414–33.

—— 'Developpement urbain et topographie chrétienne de Genève', *CRAI* (1985), 323–38.

BONNET, C., and PERINETTI, R., 'Les premiers édifices chrétiens d'*Augusta Praetoria*', *CRAI* (1986), 477–95.

BOWERSOCK, G. W., 'From Emperor to Bishop: The Self-Conscious Transformation of Political Power in the Fourth Century AD', *CPh* 81 (1986), 298–307.

BRADSHAW, P. F., *The Search for the Origins of Early Christian Worship* (London, 1992).

BRAUDEL, F., *The Mediterranean and the Mediterranean World in the Age of Philip II* (London, 1972).

—— *Civilization and Capitalism, 15th–18th century*, i: *The Structures of Everyday Life: The Limits of the Possible* (London, 1981).

BROWN, P., *Augustine of Hippo: A biography* (London, 1967).

—— *The Cult of the Saints: Its Rise and Function in Latin Christianity* (Chicago, 1981).

—— *Power and Persuasion in Late Antiquity* (Madison, 1992).

—— *Authority and the Sacred* (Cambridge, 1995).

Brown, T. S., 'The Church of Ravenna and the Imperial Administration in the Seventh Century', *EHR* 94 (1979), 1–28.

—— '*Romanitas* and *Campanilismo*: Agnellus of Ravenna's View of the Past', in C. Holdsworth and T. P. Wiseman (eds.), *The Inheritance of Historiography* (Exeter, 1986), 107–14.

Brown, T. S., Bryer, A., and Winfield, D., 'Cities of Heraclius', *Byzantine and Modern Greek Studies* 4 (1978), 15–38.

Brunt, P. A., *Italian Manpower 225 BC–AD 14* (Oxford, 1971).

Brusin, G., 'L'epigrafe musiva di Petrus', *NSc* (1947), 18–20.

—— *Aquileia e Grado*, 2nd edn. (Padua, 1952).

—— 'Il mosaico pavimentale della basilica di Aquileia e i suoi ritratti', *RAL* 22 (1967), 174–93.

Budischovsky, M.-C., 'La diffusion des cultes égyptiens d'Aquilée à travers les pays alpins', *AAAd* 9 (1976), 207–27.

—— *La diffusion des cultes isiaques autour de la mer Adriatique*, i (Leiden, 1977).

Bullough, D. A., 'Urban Change in Early Medieval Italy: The Example of Pavia', *PBSR* 34 (1966), 82–130.

—— 'Ethnic History and the Carolingians', in C. Holdsworth and T. P. Wiseman (eds.), *The Inheritance of Historiography* (Exeter, 1986), 85–105.

Buora, M., and Plesnicar-Gec, L., (eds.) *Aquileia-Emona* (Udine, 1989).

Burkert, W., *Ancient Mystery Cults* (Cambridge, Mass., and London, 1987).

Cagiano de Azevedo, M., 'Northern Italy', in M. W. Barley (ed.), *European Towns: Their Archaeology and Early History* (London, 1977), 475–85.

Caillet, J.-P., *L'évergétisme monumental chrétien en Italie et à ses marges* (Rome, 1993).

Calderini, A., *Aquileia romana* (Milan, 1930).

—— 'Indagini intorno alla Chiesa di S. Francesco Grande in Milano', *RIL* 73 (1939–40), 97–132.

—— 'La tradizione letteraria più antica sulle basiliche milanesi', *RIL* 75 (1941–2), 69–98.

—— 'Milano archeologica', *Storia di Milano*, i (Milan, 1953), 465–696.

Calderone, S., *Costantino e il cattolicesimo*, i (Florence, 1962).

Cameron, Averil, *Christianity and the Rhetoric of Empire*, (Berkeley, 1991).

Cantino Wataghin, G., 'La cattedrale in Italia: l'Italia settentrionale', *Actes du XI congrès international d'archeologie chrétienne*, i (Paris, 1989), 27–57.

—— 'Le "basiliche doppie" paleocristiane nell'Italia settentrionale: la documentazione archeologica', *An. Tard.* 4 (1996), 115–23.

CARVER, M. O. H., *Arguments in Stone* (Oxford, 1993).

CASADIO, P., 'Vitale da Bologna a Udine', in id. and C. Gnudi (eds.), *Itinerari di Vitale da Bologna. Affreschi a Udine e a Pomposa* (Bologna, 1990), 49–78.

CATTANEO, E., 'Appunti sui battisteri antichi di Milano', *RIL* 103 (1969), 849–64.

—— 'La tradizione e il rito ambrosiano nell'ambiente lombardo-medioevale', in G. Lazzati (ed.), *Ambrosius Episcopus* (Milan, 1976), 5–47.

—— 'Il governo ecclesiastico dell'Italia settentrionale nel IV secolo', *AAAd* 22 (1982), 175–87.

CERESA MORI, A., 'Gli horrea', *Milano capitale*, 102–3.

CESSI, R. (ed.), *Origo Civitatum Italiae seu Venetiarum* (Rome, 1933).

—— *Venezia Ducale*, i: *Duca e popolo* (Venice, 1963).

CHADWICK, H., 'Faith and Order at the Council of Nicaea: A Note on the Background of the Sixth Canon', *HThR* 53 (1960), 171–95.

—— 'The Origin of the Title "Oecumenical Council"', *JThS* n.s. 23 (1972), 132–5.

—— *Priscillian of Avila: The Occult and the Charismatic in the Early Church* (Oxford, 1976).

—— 'The Role of the Bishop in Ancient Society', *Protocol of the 35th Colluquy of the Centre for Hermeneutical Studies* (Berkeley, 1980), 1–14.

CHAFFIN, E., 'The Martyrs of the Val di Non', *Studia Patristica* 10 (1970), 184–203.

CHASTAGNOL, A., *Le Préfecture urbaine à Rome sous le Bas-Empire* (Paris, 1960).

—— 'L'Administration du diocèse italien au Bas-Empire', *Historia* 12 (1963), 348–79.

CHEVALLIER, R., *Le romanisation de la Celtique du Pô* (Rome, 1983).

—— *Roman Roads* (London, 1976).

—— *Aquilée et la romanisation de l'Europe* (Tours, 1990).

CHILVER, G. E. F., *Cisalpine Gaul* (Oxford, 1942).

CHOW, J. K., *Patronage and Power: A Study of Social Networks in Corinth* (Sheffield, 1992).

CHRISTIE, N., 'The Limes Bizantino Revisited: The Defence of Liguria, AD 568–643', *Rivista di Studi Liguri* 55 (1989), 5–38.

—— 'Byzantine Liguria: An Imperial Province against the Longobards, AD 568–643', *PBSR* 45 (1990), 229–71.

—— 'The Alps as a Frontier AD 168–774', *JRA* 4 (1991), 410–30.

CHRISTIE-MURRAY, D., *A History of Heresy* (Oxford, 1976).

CIPRIANO, M. T., 'Aquileia (Veneto). Le anfore del Museo', in Giardina, *Società* iii. 139–43.

CLARK, G., 'Cosmic Sympathies: Nature as the Expression of Divine Purpose', in G. Shipley and J. Salmon (eds.), *Human Landscapes in Classical Antiquity: Environment and Culture* (1996), 310–29.

—— 'Victricius of Rouen: Praising the Saints', (forthcoming).

CLARKE, J. R., *The Houses of Roman Italy, 100 BC–AD 250* (Berkeley, 1991).

COLAFEMMINA, C., *Apulia cristiana: Venosa, studi e scoperte* (Bari, 1973).

COOPER, K., 'The Martyr, the *Matrona*, and the Bishop: Networks of Allegiance in Early Sixth Century Rome', *JRA* (forthcoming).

CORBETT, G. U. S., 'A Note on the Arrangement of the Early Christian Buildings at Aquileia', *RAC* 32 (1956), 99–106.

COWDREY, H. E. J., 'Archbishop Aribert II of Milan', *History* 51 (1966), 1–15.

—— 'The Papacy, the Patarenes and the Church of Milan', *Transactions of the Royal Historical Society*, 5th. ser., 18 (1968), 25–48.

CRACCO RUGGINI, L., 'Storia totale di una piccola città: Vicenza romana', in ead. and A. Broglio (eds.), *Storia di Vicenza*, i: *Il territorio—la preistoria —l'età romana* (Vicenza, 1987), 205–303.

CRACCO RUGGINI, L., and CRACCO, G., 'L'eredità di Roma', in *Storia d'Italia*, v: *I documenti* 1 (Turin, 1973), 5–45.

See also: RUGGINI, L.

CRAMER, P., *Baptism and Change in the Early Middle Ages, c. 200–c. 1250* (Cambridge, 1993).

CREED, J. L., *see under* Lactantius *in primary sources.*

CUSCITO, G., 'Africani in Aquileia e nell'Italia settentrionale', *AAAd* 5 (1974), 143–63.

—— 'Testimonianze archeologico-monumentale sul più antico culto dei santi nella *Venetia et Histria*', *AqN* 45–46 (1974–5), 631–68.

—— 'La diffusione del cristianesimo nelle regioni alpine orientali', *AAAd* 9 (1976), 299–345.

—— *Il primo cristianesimo nella 'Venetia et Histria'* (Udine, 1986).

DAGRON, G., *Naissance d'une capitale* (Paris, 1974).

DALE, T. E. A., '*Inventing* a Sacred Past: Pictorial Narratives of St Mark in Aquileia and Venice, ca. 1000–1300', *DOP* 48 (1994), 53–104.

DALLA BARBA BRUSIN, D., 'Cronologia e dedicazione della basilica post-teodoriana settentrionale di Aquileia', *Arte Veneta* (1975), 1–3.

D'ARMS, J., *The Romans on the Bay of Naples* (Cambridge, Mass., 1970).

DATTRINO, L., 'S. Eusebio di Vercelli: vescovo "martire"? vescovo "monaco"?', *Augustinianum* 24 (1984), 167–87.

DAVIS, N. Z., *The Return of Martin Guerre* (Cambridge, Mass., 1983).

DAVIS, R., *The Book of Pontiffs* (Liverpool, 1989).

DE CLERQ, V. C., 'Fortunatien d'Aquilée', *DHGE* 17 (1971), 1182–5.

DEGRASSI, A., 'I culti romani della Venezia tridentina', *Archivio Veneto* 26 (1940), 95–112.

—— *Il confine nord-orientale d'Italia romana* (Berne, 1954).

DEICHMANN, F. W., *Frühchristliche Bauten und Mosaiken von Ravenna* (Wiesbaden, 1958).

—— *Ravenna. Haupstadte des spätantiken Abendlandes.* II *Kommentar,* 3 vols. (Wiesbaden, 1974–89).

DE LAET, J., *Portorium* (Bruges, 1949).

DELEHAYE, H., 'Saints d'Istrie et de Dalmatie', *AB* 18 (1899), 370–84.

—— *Commentarius perpetuus in Martyrologium Hieronymianum,* ed. H. Quentin, *AASS,* Nov. 2. ii (Brussels, 1931).

—— *Les origines du culte des martyrs,* 2nd edn. (Brussels, 1933).

DE ROSSI, G. B., *La Roma sotterranea cristiana* (Rome, 1864–77).

DE SALVO, L., *Economia privata e pubblici servizi nell'impero romano. I corpora naviculorum* (Messina, 1992).

DE VEER, A. C., 'Le séjour de Caecilianus à Brescia', *BA* 31 (1968), 822–4.

DIEHL, Ch., *Études sur l'administration byzantine dans l'exarchat de Ravenne* (Rome, 1888).

DITCHFIELD, S., *Liturgy, Sanctity, and History in Tridentine Italy* (Cambridge, 1995).

DORIGO, W., *Late Roman Painting* (London, 1971).

DOUGLAS, M., *How Institutions Think* (Syracuse, N. Y., 1986).

DRIJVERS, H., 'Syrian Christianity and Judaism', in J. Lieu et al. (eds.), *The Jews among Pagans and Christians in the Roman Empire* (London, 1992), 124–43.

DUBOIS, J., *Les martyrologes du moyen âge latin* (Turnhout, 1978).

DUCHESNE, L., *Fastes épiscopaux de l'ancienne Gaule* (Paris, 1907–15).

—— 'Libère et Fortunatien', *MEFRA* 28 (1908), 31–78.

DUNBABIN, K. M., *The Mosaics of Roman North Africa* (Oxford, 1978).

DUNBAR, D. G., 'The Delay of the Parousia in Hippolytus', *VChr* 37 (1983), 313–27.

DUNCAN-JONES, R., *The Roman Economy: Quantitative Studies* (Cambridge, 1974).

—— *Structure and Scale in the Roman Economy* (Cambridge, 1990).

DUVAL, Y. M., 'Les sources greques de l'exégèse de Jonas chez Zénon de Vérone', *VChr* 20 (1966), 98–115.

—— 'Vraix et faux problèmes concernant le retour d'exile d'Hilaire de Poitiers et son action en Italie en 360–363', *Athenaeum* n.s. 48 (1970), 251–75.

—— 'L'influence des écrivains africains du IIIe siècle sur les écrivains chrétiens de l'Italie du Nord dans la seconde moitié du IVe siècle', *AAAd* 5 (1974), 191–225.

—— 'Aquilée sur la route des invasions (350–452)', *AAAd* 9 (1976), 237–98.

—— 'Les rapports de la Gaule et de la Cisalpine dans l'histoire religieuse du IVe siècle', *AAAd* 19 (1981), 259–77.

—— 'Aquilée et Sirmium durant la crise arienne (325–400)', *AAAd* 26 (1985), 331–79.

DVORNIK, F., *The Slavs in European History and Civilisation* (New Brunswick, 1962).

—— *Byzantium and the Roman Primacy*, 2nd edn. (New York, 1979).

DYSON, S. L., *The Creation of the Roman Frontier* (Princeton, 1985).

—— *Community and Society in Roman Italy* (Baltimore, 1992).

EDWARDS, M., *Optatus: Against the Donatists* (Liverpool, 1997).

EHRHARDT, A., 'The First Two Years of the Emperor Theodosius I', *JEH* 15 (1964), 1–17.

ELLIS, S. P., 'Power, Architecture, and Decor: How a Late Roman Aristocrat Appeared to his guests', in E. K. Gazda (ed.), *Roman Art in the Private Sphere* (Ann Arbor, 1991), 117–34.

ELSNER, J., *Art and the Roman Viewer* (Cambridge, 1995).

ENO, R. B., 'The Significance of the Lists of Roman Bishops in the Anti-Donatist Polemic', *VChr* 47 (1993), 158–69.

ESLER, P. F., *Community and Gospel in Luke–Acts* (Cambridge, 1985).

—— (ed.), *Modelling Early Christianity: Social-Scientific Studies of the New Testament in its Context* (London, 1995).

EVANS, C. A., *To See and Not Perceive: Isaiah 6. 9–10 in Early Jewish and Christian Interpretation* (Sheffield, 1989).

FARMER, S., *Communities of Saint Martin: Legend and Ritual in Medieval Tours* (Ithaca, 1991).

FASANARI, R., *Il portale di San Zeno (marmi)* (Verona, 1964).

FASOLI, G., 'Rillegendo il "Liber Pontificalis" di Agnello Ravennate', *Sett.* 17 (1970), 457–96.

FEENEY, D., *Literature and Religion at Rome: Cultures, Contexts, and Beliefs* (Cambridge, 1998).

FELDMAN, L. H., *Jew and Gentile in the Ancient World: Attitudes and Interactions from Alexander to Justinian* (Princeton, 1993).

FERRUA, A., 'Due iscrizioni della Mauretania', *RAC* 53 (1977), 225–9.

FEVRIER, P. A., 'Permanence et heritages de l'antiquité dans la topographie des villes de l'Occident', *Sett.* 21 (1973), 41–138.

FINN, T. M., 'Social Mobility, Imperial Civil Service and the Spread of Christianity', *Studia Patristica* 17/1 (1982), 31–7.

FISHWICK, D., *The Imperial Cult in the Latin West* (Leiden, 1987).

FOSS, C., *Ephesus After Antiquity* (Cambridge, 1979).

FOWDEN, G., 'The Last Days of Constantine: Oppositional Versions and their Influence', *JRS* 84 (1994), 146–70.

FRAYN, J. M., *Sheep-Rearing and the Wool Trade in Italy during the Roman Period* (Liverpool, 1984).

—— *Markets and Fairs in Roman Italy* (Oxford, 1993).

FREDERIKSEN, M., *Campania*, ed. N. Purcell (London, 1984).

FREND, W. H. C., 'A Note on the Influence of Greek Immigrants on the Spread of Christianity in the West', in *Mullus. Festschrift für Theodor Klauser* (Munster, 1964), 125–9.

—— *The Donatist Church*, 2nd edn. (Oxford, 1971).

FROVA, A., 'Il circo di Milano e i circhi di età tetrarchica', in *Milano capitale*, 423–31.

FUMAGALLI, V., *Paesaggi della paura* (Bologna, 1994).

GABBA, E., *Italia romana* (Como, 1994).

GAMBLE, H. Y., *Books and Readers in the Early Church* (New Haven, 1995).

GARNSEY, P., 'Economy and Society of Mediolanum under the Principate', *PBSR* 44 (1976), 13–27.

GARNSEY, P., and SALLER, R., *The Roman Empire* (London, 1987).

GARNSEY, P., and WOOLF, G., 'Patronage of the Rural Poor in the Roman World', in A. Wallace-Hadrill (ed.), *Patronage in Ancient Society* (London, 1989), 153–70.

GAUDEMET, J., *Conciles gaulois du IVe siècle* (Paris, 1977).

—— 'Mutations politiques et géographie administrative: l'Empire romain de Dioclétien', in *La géographie administrative et politique d'Alexandre à Mahomet* (Leiden, 1981), 255–72.

GEARY, P. J., *Furta Sacra: Thefts of Relics in the Central Middle Ages* (Princeton, 1990).

—— *Living with the Dead in the Middle Ages* (Ithaca, 1994).

GELICHI, S., MALNATI, L., and ORTALLI, J., 'L'Emilia centro-occidentale tra la tarda età imperiale e l'alto Medioevo', in Giardina, *Società* iii. 543–645.

GENTILI, S., 'Politics and Christianity in Aquileia in the Fourth Century AD', *AC* 61 (1992), 192–208.

GEORGE, J. W., *Venantius Fortunatus.* (Oxford, 1992).

GEORGE, M., *The Roman Domestic Architecture of Northern Italy* (Oxford, 1997).

GEORGI, D., 'The Early Church: Internal Jewish Migration or New Religion?', *HThR* 88 (1995),

GILLIARD, F. D., 'The Apostolicity of the Gallic Churches', *HThR* 68 (1975), 17–33.

GINZBURG, C., *I benandanti* (Turin, 1966).

GLASS, D. F., *Studies on Cosmatesque Pavements* (Oxford, 1980).

GODMAN, P., *Poetry of the Carolingian Renaissance* (London, 1985).

GOODMAN, M., *Mission and Conversion: Proselytizing in the Religious History of the Roman Empire* (Oxford, 1994).

GOTTLIEB, G., 'Les évêques et les empereurs dans les affaires ecclésiastiques du 4e siècle', *MH* 33 (1976), 38–50.

GOULD, S. J., *Ever Since Darwin: Reflections in Natural History* (London, 1978).

GOULDER, M., *A Tale of Two Missions* (London, 1994).

GRANT, R. M., *Gods and the One God* (London, 1986).

GREEN, R. P. H., *The Works of Ausonius* (Oxford, 1991).

GREENHALGH, M., *The Survival of Roman Antiquities in the Middle Ages* (London, 1989).

GREGORY, T. E., *Vox Populi: Popular Opinion and Violence in the Religious Controversies of the Fifth Century AD* (Columbus, Ohio, 1979).

GRIBOMONT, J., 'Les plus anciennes traductions latines', in J. Fontaine and Ch. Pietri (eds.), *Le monde latin antique et la Bible* (Paris, 1985), 43–65.

GRIFFE, E., *La Gaule chrétienne à l'époque romaine* (Paris, 1964–6).

GRUEN, E. S., *Studies in Greek Culture and Roman Policy* (Leiden, 1990).

GRYSON, R., *Le prêtre selon Saint Ambroise* (Louvain, 1968).

—— 'Les élections ecclésiastiques au IIIe siècle', *RHE* 68 (1973), 353–404.

—— 'Les élections épiscopales en Orient au IVe siècle', *RHE* 74 (1979), 301–45.

—— 'Les élections épiscopales en Occident au IVe siècle', *RHE* 75 (1980), 257–83.

—— *Scolies ariennes sur le concile d'Aquilée* (SChr 267: Paris, 1980).

GUARNIERI, C., 'Nota sull'elezione episcopale in Apulia all'inizio del V secolo', in E. De Sanctis, *Puglia paleocristiana e altomedievale*, iv (Bari, 1984), 97–106.

GUILLOU, A., *Régionalisme et indépendance dans l'Empire byzantin au VIIe siècle* (Rome, 1969).

GUTKIND, C. A., *Urban Development in Southern Europe: Italy and Greece* (New York, 1969).

HAAS, C., 'The Arians of Alexandria', *VChr* 47 (1993), 234–45.

HAMMOND, C. P., 'A Product of a Fifth Century Scriptorium Preserving Conventions Used by Rufinus of Aquileia', *JThS* n.s. 29 (1978), 366–91.

HANSON, R. P. C., *Tradition in the Early Church* (London, 1962).

—— *The Search for the Christian Doctrine of God: The Arian Controversy, 318–381* (Edinburgh, 1981).

—— 'The Achievement of Orthodoxy in the Fourth Century', in R. Williams (ed.), *The Making of Orthodoxy* (Cambridge, 1989), 142–56.

HARNACK, A. VON, *The Expansion of Christianity in the First Three Centuries*, 2 vols. (London, 1908).

HARRIES, J. D., *Sidonius Apollinaris and the Fall of Rome* (Oxford, 1994).

HARVEY, A. E., 'Elders', *JThS* n.s. 25 (1974), 318–32

HAY, D., 'Scholars and Ecclesiastical History in the Early Modern Period: The Influence of Ferdinando Ughelli', in P. Mack and M. C. Jacob (eds.), *Politics and Culture in Early Modern Europe* (Cambridge, 1987), 215–29.

HEAD, T. F., *Hagiography and the Cult of Saints: The Diocese of Orléans, 800–1200* (Cambridge, 1990).

HEATHER, P. J., *Goths and Romans 332–489* (Oxford, 1991).

HEFELE, K. J., and LECLERQ, H., *Histoire des Conciles*, i (Paris, 1907).

HEGERMANN, H., 'The Diaspora in the Hellenistic Age', in W. D. Davies and L. Finkelstein (eds.), *The Cambridge History of Judaism*, ii: *The Hellenistic Age* (Cambridge, 1989), 115–66.

HENGEL, M., 'The Pre-Christian Paul', in J. Lieu et al. (eds.), *The Jews among Pagans and Christians in the Roman Empire* (London, 1992), 29–52.

HERRIN, J., *The Formation of Christendom* (Oxford, 1987).

HILLIER, R., *Arator on the Acts of the Apostles: A Baptismal Commentary* (Oxford, 1993).

HOBSBAWM, E. J., *Nations and Nationalism since 1780: Programme, Myth and Reality* (Cambridge, 1990).

HODGES, R., 'Spatial Models, Anthropology and Archaeology', in J. M. Wagstaff (ed.), *Landscape and Culture: Geographical and Archaeological Perspectives* (Oxford, 1987).

HOLDER, A., *Alt-celtischer Sprachschatz* (Leipzig, 1896–1913).

HOMES DUDDEN, F., *The Life and Times of St. Ambrose* (Oxford, 1935).

HUMPHREY, J. H., *Roman Circuses* (London, 1986).

HUMPHRIES, M., '*In Nomine Patris*: Constantine the Great and Constantius II in Christological Polemic', *Historia* 46 (1997), 448–64.

—— 'Zeno and Gallienus: Two Gentlemen of Verona', *Classics Ireland* 4 (1997), 67–78.

—— 'Savage Humour: Christian Anti-Panegyric in Hilary of Poitiers' *Against Constantius*', in Mary Whitby (ed.), *The Propaganda of Power: The Role of Panegyric in Late Antiquity* (Leiden, 1998), 201–23.

—— 'Trading Gods in Northern Italy', in H. Parkins and C. Smith (eds.), *Trade, Traders and the Ancient City* (London, 1998), 203–24.

—— 'Italy 425–605', in Averil Cameron, B. Ward-Perkins, and Michael Whitby (eds.), *The Cambridge Ancient History*, xiv: *Late Antiquity, 425–600* (Cambridge, forthcoming).

—— 'Anullinus, Africa, and Aquileia: The Formation of a Hagiographical Tradition', (forthcoming).

HUNT, E. D., 'The Traffic in Relics: Some Late Roman Evidence', in S. Hackel (ed.), *The Byzantine Saint* (London, 1981), 171–80.

—— 'St. Stephen in Minorca: An Episode in Jewish–Christian Relations in the Early 5th Century AD', *JThS* n.s. 33 (1982), 106–23.

—— 'Did Constantius II Have "Court Bishops"?', *Studia Patristica* 19 (1981), 86–90.

—— 'Constantine and Jerusalem', *JEH* 48 (1997), 405–24.

HUSKINSON, J. M., *Concordia Apostolorum* (Oxford, 1982).

HYDE, J. K., 'Medieval Descriptions of Cities', *BJRL* 48 (1965–6), 308–40.

HYDE, W. W., *Roman Alpine Routes* (Philadelphia, 1935).

JÄGGI, C., 'Aspekte der städtebaulichen Entwicklung Aquileias in frühchristlicher Zeit', *JbAC* 33 (1990), 158–96.

JEANES, G. P., *The Day Has Come! Easter and Baptism in Zeno of Verona* (Collegeville, 1995).

JONES, A. H. M., 'The Cloth Industry of the Roman Empire', *EconHR* n.s. 13 (1960), 183–92.

—— *The Later Roman Empire 284–602* (Oxford, 1964).

KÄHLER, H., *Die spätantiken Bauten unter dem Dom von Aquileia und ihre Stellung innerhalb der geschichte des frühchristlichen Kirchenbaues* (Saarbrücken, 1957).

KELLY, C. M., 'Later Roman Bureaucracy: Going Through the Files', in A. K. Bowman and G. Woolf (eds.), *Literacy and Power in the Ancient World* (Cambridge, 1994), 161–76.

KELLY, J. N. D., *Jerome* (London, 1975).

—— *Early Christian Doctrines*, 5th edn. (London, 1977).

KINNEY, D., 'The Evidence for the Dating of S. Lorenzo in Milan', *JSAH* 31 (1972), 92–107.

KLEINBAUER, W., '*Aedita in turribus*: The Superstructure of the Early Christian Church of S. Lorenzo in Milan', *Gesta* 15 (1976), 1–9.

KRAUTHEIMER, R., *Early Christian and Byzantine Architecture*, 4th edn. (Harmondsworth, 1986).

—— *Three Christian Capitals* (Berkeley, 1983).

KULIKOWSKI, M. E., 'Two Councils of Turin', *JThS* n.s. 47 (1996), 159–68.

LABOURT, J., (ed.), *Saint Jérôme: Lettres* (Paris, 1969–70).

LAMPE, G. W. H. (ed.), *A Patristic Greek Lexicon* (Oxford, 1961).

LANE FOX, R., *Pagans and Christians* (Harmondsworth, 1986).

—— 'Literacy and Power in Early Christianity', in A. K. Bowman and G. Woolf (eds.), *Literacy and Power in the Ancient World* (Cambridge, 1994), 126–48.

LANZANI, V., 'Ticinum: le origini della città cristiana', *Storia di Pavia*, i: *L'età antica* (Pavia and Milan, 1984), 349–68.

LANZONI, F., *Le origini delle diocesi antiche d'Italia* (Studi e Testi 35: Rome, 1923).

LA ROCCA [HUDSON], C., ' "Dark Ages" a Verona. Edilizia privata, aree aperte e strutture pubbliche in una città dell'Italia settentrionale', *Archeologia Medievale* 13 (1986), 31–78.

—— 'Public Buildings and Urban Change in Northern Italy in the Early Medieval Period', in J. W. Rich (ed.), *The City in Late Antiquity* (London, 1992), 161–80.

LAURENCE, R., *Roman Pompeii: Space and Society* (London, 1994).

—— 'Land Transport in Roman Italy: Costs, Practice, and the Economy', in H. Parkins and C. Smith (eds.), *Trade, Traders, and the Ancient City* (London, 1998), 129–48.

LECLERQ, H., 'Pavement', *DACL* 13/2 (1938), 2734–54.

LEINHARD, J. T., 'Did Athanasius Reject Marcellus?', in M. R. Barnes and D. H. Williams (eds.), *Arianism after Arius* (Edinburgh, 1993), 65–80.

LEMERLE, P., 'L'archeologie paleochrétienne en Italie. Milan et Castelseprio, "Orient ou Rome" ', *B* 22 (1952), 169–84.

LENOX-CONYGHAM, A., 'The Topography of the Basilica Conflict of AD 385/6 in Milan', *Historia* 31 (1972), 353–63.

LEPELLEY, C., *Les Cités de l'Afrique romaine au Bas-Empire* (Paris, 1981).

LEMARIÉ, J., (ed.) *Chromace d'Aquilée: Sermons* (Paris, 1969–70).

LETTICH, G., 'Concordia e Aquileia', *AAAd* 22 (1982), 67–87.

LEWIS, S., 'Function and Symbolic Form in the *Basilica Apostolorum* at Milan', *JSAH* 28 (1969), 83–98.

—— 'The Latin Iconography of the Single-Naved Cruciform *Basilica Apostolorum*', *Art Bulletin* 51 (1969), 205–19.

—— 'San Lorenzo Revisited: A Theodosian Palace Church at Milan', *JSAH* 32 (1973), 197–222.

LIEBESCHUETZ, J. H. W. G., *Continuity and Change in Roman Religion* (Oxford, 1979).

—— *Barbarians and Bishops: Army, Church, and Politics in the Age of Arcadius and Chrysostom* (Oxford, 1990).

—— 'The End of the Ancient City', in J. W. Rich (ed.), *The City in Late Antiquity* (London, 1992), 1–49.

LIEU, J., 'History and Theology in Christian Views of Judaism', in ead. et al. (eds.), *The Jews among Pagans and Christians in the Roman Empire* (London, 1992), 79–96.

—— ' "The Parting of the Ways": Theological Construct or Historical Reality?', *JSNT* 56 (1994), 101–19.

LIEU, J., RAJAK, T., and NORTH, J. (eds.), *The Jews among Pagans and Christians in the Roman Empire* (London, 1992).

LIEU, S. N. C., *Manichaeism in the Later Roman Empire and Medieval China* (Manchester, 1985).

LIZZI, R., '*Codicilli* imperiali e *insignia* episcopali: un'affinità significativa', *RIL* 122 (1988), 3–13.

—— *Vescovi e strutture ecclesiastiche nella città tardoantica (l'*Italia Annonaria *nel IV–V secolo d. C)* (Como, 1989).

—— 'Ambrose's Contemporaries and the Christianization of Northern Italy', *JRS* 80 (1990), 156–73.

LÖFSTEDT, B., and PACKARD, D. W., *A Concordance to the Sermons of Bishop Zeno of Verona* (New York, 1975).

LOPREATO, P., 'Il battistero cromaziano di Aquileia', *AAAd* 34 (1989), 209–18.

LUCCHESI, G., 'Ancora sull'antico calendario italico', *RSCI* 32 (1978), 140–52.

LUISELLI, B., and ZANELLA, A., *Paolo Diacono. Storia dei Langobardi* (Milan, 1991).

LUSUARDI SIENA, S., 'Il complesso episcopale di Milano: riconsiderazione della testimonia ambrosiana nella *Epistola ad sororem*', *An. Tard.* 4 (1996), 124–9.

McCLURE, J., 'Handbooks Against Heresy in the West', *JThS* n.s. 30 (1979), 186–97.

MACCORMACK, S., *Art and Ceremony in Late Antiquity* (Berkeley, 1981).

MACDONALD, W. L., *The Architecture of the Roman Empire*, ii: *An Urban Appraisal* (New Haven, 1986).

McLYNN, N. B., *Ambrose of Milan: Church and Court in a Christian Capital* (Berkeley, 1994).

MacMULLEN, R., *Paganism in the Roman Empire* (New Haven, 1981).

—— *Christianizing the Roman Empire, AD 100–400* (New Haven, 1984).

MAGIE, D., *Roman Rule in Asia Minor* (Princeton, 1950).

MAIER, J.-L., *Le Dossier du donatisme*, i (Berlin, 1987).

MAIOLI, M. G., 'Il complesso di via Dogana e altri mosaici tardoantichi in Faenza', in R. Ling (ed.), *Fifth International Colloquium on Ancient Mosaics*, ii (Ann Arbor, 1995), 189–206.

MALAISE, M., *Inventaire préliminaire des documents égyptiens découverts en Italie* (Leiden, 1972).

—— *Les conditions de pénétration et de diffusion des cultes égyptiens en Italie* (Leiden, 1972)

—— 'La diffusion des cultes égyptiens dans les provinces européennes de l'Empire romain', *ANRW* II. 17. 3 (1984), 1615–91.

MARKUS, R. A., *Christianity in the Roman World* (London, 1974).

—— 'Ravenna and Rome, 554–600', *B* 51 (1981), 556–78.

—— *The End of Ancient Christianity* (Cambridge, 1990).

—— *Signs and Meanings: World and Text in Ancient Christianity* (Liverpool, 1996).

—— *Gregory the Great and His World* (Cambridge, 1997).

MARTIN, L. H., *Hellenistic Religions* (New York, 1987).

MARUCCHI, O., 'Le recente scoperti nel Duomo di Parenzo', *Nuovo Bullettino di Archeologia Cristiana* 2 (1896), 14–26, 124–34.

—— 'Notizie', *Nuovo Bullettino di Archeologia Cristiana* 16 (1910), 165.

MARUSIC, B., 'Krscanstvo i poganstvo na tlu Istre u IV i V stoljecu', *Arh. Vest.* 29 (1978), 549–72.

MARUSIC, B., and SASEL, J., 'De la cella trichora au complexe monastique de St. André à Betika entre Pula et Rovinj', *Arh. Vest.* 37 (1986), 307–42.

MATHEWS, T. F., 'An Early Roman Chancel Arrangement and its Liturgical Function', *RAC* 38 (1962), 73–95.

—— *The Early Churches of Constantinople* (University Park and London, 1971).

MATTHEWS, J. F., 'Symmachus and the Oriental Cults', *JRS* 63 (1973), 175–95.

—— *Western Aristocracies and Imperial Court AD 364–425* (Oxford, 1975).

—— 'Hostages, Philosophers, Pilgrims, and the Diffusion of Ideas in the Late Roman Mediterranean and Near East', in F. M. Clover and R. S. Humphreys (eds.), *Tradition and Innovation in Late Antiquity* (Madison, 1989), 29–49.

—— *The Roman Empire of Ammianus* (London, 1989).

MEEKS, W. A., *The First Urban Christians* (New Haven, 1983).

—— 'Review of P. F. Esler, *The First Christians in their Social Worlds* (London, 1994)', *JRS* 85 (1995), 316–17.

MELLOR, R., 'The Local Character of Roman Imperial Religion', *Athenaeum* n.s. 80 (1992), 385–400.

MENANT, F., *Campagnes lombardes au Moyen Âge* (Rome, 1993).

MENIS, G. C., *I mosaici cristiani di Aquileia* (Udine, 1965).

—— 'Le giurisdizioni metropolitiche di Aquileia e di Milano nell'antichità', *AAAd* 4 (1973), 271–94.

—— 'La basilica paleocristiana nelle regioni delle Alpi orientali', *AAAd* 9 (1976), 375–420.

—— 'Rapporti ecclesiastici tra Aquileia e la Slovenia in età paleocristiana', *Arh. Vest.* 29 (1978), 368–76.

—— 'La cultura teologica del clero aquileiese all'inizio del IV secolo', *AAAd* 22 (1982), 463–527.

—— 'La liturgia battesimale ad Aquileia nel complesso episcopale del IV secolo', *An. Tard.* 4 (1996), 61–74.

MERCATI, G., 'Il più antico vescovo di Parma conosciuto', *Studi e documenti di storia e diritto* 23 (1902), 3–6.

MESLIN, M., *Les Ariens d'Occident 335–430* (Paris, 1967).

MEYENDORFF, J., *Imperial Unity and Christian Divisions* (Englewood Cliffs, 1989).

MILANESE, M., *Genova romana* (Rome, 1993).

MILANO, E., 'Eusebio di Vercelli, vescovo metropolita. Leggenda o realtà storica?', *IMU* 30 (1987), 313–22.

MILLAR, F., 'The Jews of the Graeco-Roman Diaspora between Paganism and Christianity, AD 312–438', in J. Lieu et al. (eds.), *The Jews among Pagans and Christians in the Roman Empire* (London, 1992), 97–123.

—— *The Roman Near East 31 BC–AD 337* (Cambridge, Mass., 1993).

MILLER, M. C., *The Formation of a Medieval Church: Ecclesiastical Change in Verona, 950–1150* (Ithaca, 1993).

MIRABELLA ROBERTI, M., 'La posizione dell'altare nelle più antiche basiliche di Aquileia e di Parenzo', *RAC* 26 (1950), 181–94.

—— 'Osservazioni sulla basilica postteodoriana settentrionale di Aquileia', in *Studi in onore di Aristide Calderini e Roberto Paribeni*, iii (1956), 863–75.

—— 'Il battistero di Sant'Ambrogio a Milano', *Rech. Aug.* 4 (1966), 3–10.

—— 'Iulium Carnicum centro romano alpino', *AAAd* 9 (1976), 91–101.

—— 'Partizioni dei pavimenti musivi delle basiliche cristiane dell'area aquileiese', *AAAd* 22 (1982), 413–28.

—— 'Architettura padana tardoantica', *RIL* 123 (1989), 3–16.

—— 'Milano e Como', in *La città nell'Italia settentrionale in età romana* (Rome, 1990), 479–98.

Misurare la terra: centuriazione e coloni nel mondo romano, il caso veneto (Modena, 1984).

MITCHELL, S., *Anatolia: Land, Men, and Gods in Asia Minor*, 2 vols. (Oxford, 1993).

Mócsy, A., *Pannonia and Upper Moesia* (London, 1974).

Mohrmann, C., *Liturgical Latin* (London, 1959).

—— *Études sur le Latin des Chrétiens*, iii: *Latin chrétien et liturgique* (Rome, 1965).

Mollat, G., 'Bertrand de Saint-Geniés', *DHGE* 8 (1935), 1075–8.

Monachino, V., 'Comminio e primato nella controversia ariana', in I. D'Ercole and A. M. Stickler (eds.), *Comunione interecclesiale: collegialità —primato—ecumenismo* (Rome, 1972), 319–402.

Monti, P., 'Faenza. Tracce di un edificio paleocristiano', *NSc* (1961), 18–21.

Moorhead, J., *Theoderic in Italy* (Oxford, 1992).

Moreau, J., 'Pont Milvius ou Saxa Rubra', *La Nouvelle Clio* 4 (1952), 369–73.

Morelli, G., 'Monumenta Ferdinandi Ughelli: Barb. lat. 3204–3249', *Miscellanea Bibliothecae Apostolicae Vaticanae* 4 (Studi e Testi 338: Vatican City, 1990), 243–80.

Morin, D. G., 'Deux petits discours d'un évêque Petronius, du Ve siècle', *RB* 14 (1897), 3–8.

Mumford, L., *The City in History* (London, 1961).

Niero, A., 'I martiri aquileiesi', *AAAd* 22 (1982), 151–74.

Noble, T. F. X., *The Republic of St Peter* (Philadelphia, 1984).

—— 'Literacy and Papal Government in Late Antiquity and the Early Middle Ages', in R. McKitterick (ed.), *The Uses of Literacy in Early Mediaeval Europe* (Cambridge, 1990), 82–108.

Nock, A. D., *Conversion* (Oxford, 1933).

North, J., 'Conservatism and Change in Roman Religion', *PBSR* 44 (1976), 1–12.

—— 'The Development of Religious Pluralism', in J. Lieu et al. (eds.), *The Jews Among Pagans and Christians in the Roman Empire* (London, 1992), 174–93.

—— 'Religion and Rusticity', in T. J. Cornell and K. Lomas (eds.), *Urban Society in Roman Italy* (London, 1995), 135–50.

Obolensky, D., *The Byzantine Commonwealth* (London, 1971).

Oost, S. I., *Galla Placidia Augusta* (Chicago, 1968).

Origone, S., *Bizanzio e Genova* (Genoa, 1992).

Osborne, R., *Classical Landscape with Figures* (London, 1987).

Otranto, G., *Italia meridionale e Puglia paleocristiane. Saggi storici* (Bari, 1991).

Padovese, L., *L'originalità cristiana. Il pensiero etico-sociale di alcuni vescovi norditaliani del IV secolo* (Rome, 1983).

Pagels, E., *The Gnostic Gospels* (New York, 1979).

—— *Adam, Eve, and the Serpent* (New York, 1988).

—— *The Origin of Satan* (London, 1996).

Pallottino, M., *A History of Earliest Italy* (London, 1991).

PANCIERA, S., *Vita economica di Aquileia in età romana* (Venice, 1957).

PANELLA, C., 'Le merci: produzione, itinerari e destinari', in Giardina, *Società* iii. 431–59.

PANTO, G., and MENNELLA, G., 'Topografia ed epigrafia nelle ultime indagini su Vercelli paleocristiana', *RAC* 70 (1994), 339–410.

PAREDI, A., 'Dove fu battezato Sant'Agostino', *Rech. Aug.* 4 (1966), 11–26.

—— ' "Barnabas, Apostel der Mailänder": nuovi studi su le origini e il rito della chiesa di Milano', *RIL* 125 (1991), 33–40.

PARK, C. C., *Sacred Worlds: An Introduction to Geography and Religion* (London, 1994).

PARKER, R., *Athenian Religion: A History* (Oxford, 1996).

PASCAL, C. B., *The Cults of Cisalpine Gaul* (Brussels, 1964).

PAVAN, M., 'La provincia romana della Pannonia Superior', *Memorie Lincei*, 8th series, 6 (1955), 373–574.

PELIKAN, J., *Christianity and Classical Culture* (New Haven, 1993).

PENCO, G., *Storia della chiesa in Italia*, i: *Dalle origini all Concilio di Trento* (Milan, 1977).

PICARD, J.-CH., *Le souvenir des évêques. Sépultures, listes épiscopales et culte des évêques en Italie du Nord des origines au Xe siècle* (Rome, 1988).

—— 'Le modèle épiscopal dans deux vies du Xe siècle: S. Innocentius de Tortona et S. Prosper de Reggio Emilia', in *Les fonctions des saints dans le monde occidental (IIIe–XIIIe siècle)* (Rome, 1991), 371–84.

PIETRI, CH., *Roma Christiana. Recherches sur l'église de Rome, son organisation, sa politique, son idéologie de Miltiade à Sixte III (311–440)* (Rome, 1976).

—— 'Appendice prosopographique à la *Roma Christiana* (311–440)', *MEFRA* 89 (1977).

—— 'Les origines de la mission lyonnaise: remarques critiques', in *Les Martyres de Lyon (177)* (Paris, 1978), 220–31.

—— 'Une aristocratie provinciale et la mission chrétienne: l'exemple de la *Venetia*', *AAAd* 22 (1982), 89–137.

—— 'Chiesa e comunità locali nell'occidente cristiano (IV–VI d. C): l'esempio della Gallia', in Giardina, *Società* iii. 761–95.

—— 'La politique de Constance II: un premier "césaropapisme" ou l'*imitatio Constantini*?' *EAC* 34 (1989), 113–72.

PIETRI, L., *La ville de Tours du IVe au VIe siècles: naissance d'une cité chrétienne* (Rome, 1983).

PIGHI, G. B., 'Scrittori latini di Verona Romana', in *Verona* i. 261–365.

PILSWORTH, C., *Sanctity in Early Medieval Northern Italy* (forthcoming).

PIVA, P., '*Domus episcopalis* e sala di udienza: dove si trova il *secretarium* teodoriano di Aquileia?', *An. Tard.* 4 (1996), 74–7.

—— 'L'ipotetica basilica doppia di Milano e la liturgia ambrosiana', *An. Tard.* 4 (1996), 129–32.

PLESNICAR-GEC, L., 'La città di Emona nel tardoantico e suoi ruderi paleocristiani', *Arh. Vest.* 23 (1972), 367–75.

—— 'Aquileia ed Emona', *AAAd* 9 (1976), 119–32.

—— 'Emona in età romana', in M. Buora and L. Plesnicar-Gec (eds.), *Aquileia-Emona* (Udine, 1989), 34–57.

PORTA, P., 'Mosaici paleocristiani di Padova', in R. Ling (ed.), *Fifth International Colloquium on Ancient Mosaics*, ii (Ann Arbor, 1995), 235–44.

PRICE, S. R. F., *Rituals and Power: The Roman Imperial Cult in Asia Minor* (Cambridge, 1984).

PROSS GABRIELI, C., *L'Oratorio e la Basilica Paleocristiana di Trieste. Via Madonna del Mare* (Rocca S. Casciano, 1969).

PURCELL, N., 'The Creation of Provincial Landscape', in T. Blagg and M. Millett (eds.) *The Early Roman Empire in the West* (Oxford, 1990), 7–29.

RAJAK, T., 'The Jewish Community and its Boundaries', in J. Lieu et al. (eds.), *The Jews among Pagans and Christians in the Roman Empire* (London, 1992), 9–28.

RANDO, D., *Una chiesa di frontiera. Le istituzioni ecclesiastiche veneziane nei secoli VI–XII* (Bologna, 1994).

REDDÉ, M., *Mare Nostrum* (Rome, 1986).

RICHARDS, J., *The Popes and the Papacy in the Early Middle Ages 476–752* (London, 1979).

—— *Consul of God: The Life and Times of Gregory the Great* (London, 1980).

RICHMOND, I. A., and HOLFORD, W. G., 'Roman Verona: The Archaeology of its Town-Plan', *PBSR* 13 (1935), 69–76.

RICKMAN, G., *Roman Granaries and Storage Buildings* (Cambridge, 1971).

—— *The Corn Supply of Ancient Rome* (Oxford, 1980).

RIVES, J. B., *Religion and Authority in Roman Carthage* (Oxford, 1995).

RIVET, A. L. F., *Gallia Narbonensis* (1988).

ROBERTS, C. H., 'Elders: A Note', *JThS* n.s. 26 (1975), 403–5.

ROBINSON, I. S., *Authority and Resistance in the Investiture Contest* (Manchester, 1978).

ROBLIN, M., 'Paganisme et rusticité. Un gros problème, une étude des mots', *Annales, ESC* 8 (1953), 173–83.

ROUECHÉ, C., 'Acclamations in the Later Roman Empire: New Evidence from Aphrodisias', *JRS* 74 (1984), 181–99.

ROUGÉ, J., 'Ports et escales dans l'empire tardif', *Sett.* 25 (1978), 67–124.

ROUSSEAU, P., *Basil of Caesarea* (Berkeley, 1994).

RUBIN, Z., 'The Church of the Holy Sepulchre and the Conflict between the Churches of Jerusalem and Caesarea', in L. I. Levine (ed.), *The Jerusalem Cathedra*, ii (Jerusalem and Detroit, 1982), 79–105.

RUGGINI, L., 'Ebrei e orientali nell'Italia settentrionale fra il IV e il VI secolo d.C.', *SDHI* 25 (1959), 186–308.

—— *Economia e società nell'* Italia Annonaria. *Rapporti fra agricoltura e commercio dal IV al VI secolo d. C.* (Milan, 1961).

RUTGERS, L. V., *The Jews in Late Ancient Rome* (Leiden, 1995).

SAID, E. W., *Culture and Imperialism* (London, 1993).

SANNAZARO, M., 'Considerazioni sulla topografia e le origini del cimitero milanese *Ad Martyres*', *Aevum* 70 (1996), 81–111.

SARTORI, F., 'Verona romana', in *Verona* i. 161–259

SASEL, J., 'Barbii', *Eirene* 5 (1966), 117–37.

—— 'Lineamenti dell'espansione romana nelle Alpi orientali e nei Balcani occidentali', *AAAd* 9 (1976), 71–90.

SAVIO, F., 'La légende des SS. Faustin et Jovite', *AB* 15 (1896), 5–72, 113–59.

—— 'La légende de S. Innocent, évêque de Tortone', *AB* 15 (1896), 377–84.

—— *Gli antichi vescovi d'Italia dalle origini al 1300 descritti per regioni. Il Piemonte* (Turin, 1898).

SAWYER, J. F. A., *The Fifth Gospel: Isaiah in the History of Christianity* (Cambridge, 1996).

SCAGLIARINI CORLIATA, D., 'La villa di Desenzano', in *Milano capitale*, 260–3.

SCHÜRER, E., *The History of the Jewish People in the Age of Jesus Christ (175 BC–AD 135)* 3/1 (Edinburgh, 1986).

SCOURFIELD, J. H. D., *Consoling Heliodorus: A Commentary on Jerome, Letter 60* (Oxford, 1993).

SEECK, O., *Regesten der Kaiser und Päpste für die Jahre 311 bis 476 n. Chr.* (Stuttgart, 1919).

SELEM, P., *Les religions orientales dans la Pannonie romaine* (Leiden, 1980).

SETTON, K. M., *Christian Attitude to the Emperor in the Fourth Century* (New York, 1941).

SILVAGNI, A., 'Studio critico sopra le due sillogi medievali di iscrizioni cristiane Milanesi', *RAC* 15 (1938), 107–22, 249–79.

SIMONETTI, M., 'Qualche osservazione sul *De Trinitate* attribuito a Eusebio di Vercelli', *Rivista di Cultura Classica e Medioevale* 5 (1963), 386–93.

—— *La crisi ariana nel IV secolo* (Rome, 1975).

SIVEC, I., 'Il periodo delle migrazioni dei popoli e l'alto Medioevo', in M. Buora and L. Plesnicar-Gec (eds.), *Aquileia-Emona* (Udine, 1989), 58–64.

SMITH, C. A., 'Analysing Regional Social Systems', in ead. (ed.), *Regional Analysis*, ii: *Social Systems* (New York, 1976), 3–20.

SMULDERS, P., *Hilary of Poitiers' Preface to his* Opus Historicum (Leiden, 1995).

SNYDER, G. F., *Ante Pacem: Archaeological Evidence of Church Life before Constantine* (Macon, Ga., 1985).

SONJE, A., 'Krstionice gradevnog ansambla Eufrazijeve bazilike u Poreču', *Arh. Vest.* 23 (1972), 289–322.

SOUTER, A., *A Glossary of Later Latin to 600 AD* (Oxford, 1949).

SPELLER, L. 'A Note on Eusebius of Vercelli and the Council of Milan', *JThS* n.s. 36 (1985), 157–65.

SPINELLI, G., 'Ascetismo, monachesimo e cenobitismo ad Aquileia nel IV secolo', *AAAd* 22 (1982), 273–300.

STANCLIFFE, C., *St Martin and his Hagiographer* (Oxford, 1983).

STARK, R., *The Rise of Christianity: A Sociologist Reconsiders History* (Princeton, 1996).

STARR, C. G., *The Roman Imperial Navy 31 BC–AD 324* (Ithaca, 1960).

STUCCHI, S., 'Le basiliche paleocristiane di Aquileia', *RAC* 23–4 (1947–8), 169–207.

SUSINI, G., 'Pavimento musivo con iscrizione di un edificio paleocristiano faentino', *NSc* (1961), 21–3.

SUTHERLAND, C. H. V., *The Roman Imperial Coinage*, vi (London, 1967).

SZYMUSIAK, J. M., *Athanase d'Alexandrie. Deux apologies*, 2nd edn. (Paris, 1987).

TABACCO, G., *The Struggle for Power in Medieval Italy* (Cambridge, 1988).

TAVANO, S., 'Il recinto presbiteriale nelle aule teodoriane di Aquileia', *RAC* 36 (1960), 105–21.

—— 'Una pagina degli *scolia* ariani. La sede e il clima del concilio', *AAAd* 21 (1981), 145–65.

—— 'La crisi formale tardoantica e i mosaici Teodoriani', *AAAd* 22 (1982), 549–69.

TEITLER, H. C., *Notarii and Exceptores: An Enquiry into the Role and Significance of Shorthand Writers in the Imperial and Ecclesiastical Bureaucracy of the Roman Empire* (Amsterdam, 1985).

THELAMON, F., *Païens et chrétiens au IVe siècle. L'apport de l'*Histoire ecclésiatique *de Rufin d'Aquilée* (Paris, 1981).

—— 'Une oeuvre destinée à la communauté chrétienne d'Aquilée: l'*Histoire Ecclésiastique* de Rufin', *AAAd* 22 (1982), 255–71.

THOMSEN, R., *The Italic Regions* (Copenhagen, 1947).

TIBILETTI, G., *Storie locali dell'Italia romana* (Como, 1978).

TOZZI, P. L., 'Iscrizioni latine sull'arte lanaria bresciana e Virgilio, *Georgiche* IV, 277–8', *Athenaeum* n.s. 49 (1971), 152–7.

TRAMONTIN, S., 'Origini del cristianesimo nel Veneto', in G. Folena (ed.), *Storia della cultura veneta*, i: *Dalle origini al trecento* (Vicenza, 1976), 102–23.

TROMBLEY, F. R., *Hellenistic Religions and Christianization, c. 370–529* (Leiden, 1993).

TRUZZI, C., *Zeno, Gaudenzio, e Cromazio. Testi e contenuti della predicazione cristiana per le chiese di Verona, Brescia e Aquileia (350–410 ca.)* (Brescia, 1985).

—— 'L'ordinazione episcopale di Cromazio di Aquileia nel suo contesto storico-culturale', *AAAd* 34 (1989), 27–44.

TURNER, C. H., 'Adversaria critica: Notes on the Anti-Donatist Dossier and on Optatus, Books i, ii', *JThS* 27 (1926), 283–96.

TURRINI, G., *Millennium Scriptorii Veronensis dal IV al XV secolo* (Verona, 1967).

UGHELLI, F., *Italia Sacra*, ed. N. Coleti (Venice, 1717–22).

VAN ANDEL, T. H., and RUNNELS, C., *Beyond the Acropolis: A Rural Greek Past* (Stanford, 1987).

VAN DAM, R., *Leadership and Community in Late Antique Gaul* (Berkeley, 1985).

—— *Saints and their Miracles in Late Antique Gaul* (Princeton, 1993).

VECCHI, A., 'I luoghi comuni nell'agiografia. Saggio sulla leggenda veronese di S. Zenone', *Augustinianum* 24 (1984), 143–66.

VON REDEN, S., 'The Piraeus—A World Apart', *G&R* 42 (1995), 24–37.

VON SIMPSON, O. G., *Sacred Fortress* (Princeton, 1987).

WALLACE-HADRILL, A., 'Introduction', in id. and J. Rich (eds.), *City and Countryside in the Ancient World* (London, 1991), ix–xviii.

—— *Houses and Society in Pompeii and Herculaneum* (Princeton, 1994).

WARD-PERKINS, B., *From Classical Antiquity to the Middle Ages: Urban Public Building in Northern and Central Italy AD 300–850* (Oxford, 1984).

WEITZMANN, K., 'The Ivories of the So-called Grado Chair', *DOP* 26 (1972), 45–94.

WHARTON, A. J., *Refiguring the Post Classical City* (Cambridge, 1995).

WHITBY, MICHAEL, *The Emperor Maurice and his Historian* (Oxford, 1988).

WHITE, L. M., *Building God's House in the Roman World: Architectural Adaptation among Pagans, Jews, and Christians* (Baltimore, 1990).

WHITTAKER, C. R., 'Late Roman Trade and Traders', in P. Garnsey et al. (eds.), *Trade in the Ancient Economy* (Cambridge, 1983), 163–80.

—— *Frontiers of the Roman Empire* (Baltimore, 1994).

WICKHAM, C., *Early Medieval Italy: Central Authority and Local Power 400–1000* (London, 1981).

WIEDEMANN, T. J., *Emperors and Gladiators* (London, 1992).

WILD, R. A., 'The Known Isis-Sarapis Sanctuaries of the Roman Period', *ANRW* II. 17. 4 (1984), 1739–1851.

WILKEN, R. L., 'The Christians as the Romans (and Greeks) Saw Them', in E. P. Sanders (ed.), *Jewish and Christian Self-Definition*, i (London, 1980), 100–25.

—— *John Chrysostom and the Jews: Rhetoric and Reality in the 4th Century* (Berkeley, 1983).

WILKES, J. J., *Dalmatia* (London, 1969).

WILKINSON, J., *Egeria's Travels in the Holy Land* (Warminster, 1981).

WILLIAMS, D. H., 'The Anti-Arian Campaigns of Hilary of Poitiers and the "Liber Contra Auxentium"', *Church History* 61 (1992), 7–22.

—— 'Ambrose, Emperors and Homoians in Milan: The First Conflict over a Basilica', in id. and M. R. Barnes (eds.), *Arianism after Arius* (Edinburgh, 1993), 127–46.

—— *Ambrose of Milan and the End of the Arian–Nicene Conflicts* (Oxford, 1995).

WILLIAMS, R., 'Does it Make Sense to Speak of Pre-Nicene Orthodoxy?', in id. (ed.), *The Making of Orthodoxy* (Cambridge, 1989), 1–23.

WILMART, A., 'Deux expositions d'un évêque Fortunat sur l'Évangile', *RB* 32 (1920), 160–74.

WILSON, R. J. A., 'Roman Mosaics in Sicily: The African Connection', *AJA* 86 (1982), 413–18.

—— *Piazza Armerina* (London, 1983).

WISEMAN, T. P., '*Conspicui postes tectaque digna deo*: The Public Image of Aristocratic and Imperial Houses in the Late Republic and Early Empire', in *L'Urbs. Espace urbain et histoire (Ier siècle avant J.-C.–IIIe siècle après J.-C.)* (Rome, 1987), 393–413.

YARNOLD, E. J., 'The Ceremonies of Initiation in the *De Sacrimentis* and *De Mysteriis* of S. Ambrose', *Studia Patristica* 10 (1970), 453–63.

—— *The Awe-Inspiring Rites of Initiation*, 2nd edn. (Edinburgh, 1994).

ZANKER, P., *The Power of Images in the Age of Augustus* (Ann Arbor, 1988).

ZEILLER, J., *Les origines chrétiennes dans la province romaine de Dalmatie* (Paris, 1906).

—— *Les origines chrétiennes dans les provinces danubiennes de l'Empire romain* (Paris, 1918).

—— 'L'Organisation ecclésiastique', in A. Fliche and V. Martin (eds.), *Histoire de l'église*, ii (Paris, 1946), 387–402.

ZOVATTO, P. L., 'Il significato della basilica doppia. L'esempio di Aquileia', *RSCI* 18 (1964), 357–98.

—— 'Il "defensor ecclesiae" e le iscrizione musive di Trieste', *RSCI* 20 (1966), 1–8.

—— 'Arte paleocristiana a Verona', in *Verona* i. 553–613.

—— 'Paolo da Concordia', *AAAd* 5 (1974), 165–80.

INDEX

Abundantius, bishop of Trento 173, 181
acclamations 164, 165–6
Adriatic Sea 31
Aelianus, C. Marius, decurion at Genoa, Tortona, and Vercelli 34
Aesontius, local god at Aquileia 37
Africa 15
  Christian expansion in 10, 98–9
  links with northern Italy 77, 78
Agnellus of Ravenna, historian 60–1
Agricola and Vitalis, Bolognese martyrs venerated at Milan 55, 148–9
Alps 23
  as barrier 25–6
  as frontier in late empire 40–2
  centre and periphery 28
  religious dynamics 36–7, 175–6
  Christianity in 176, 177–83
  see also Val di Non
Altino 30, 144, 173, 175
Alto Adige, see Alps, Val di Non, Trento
Ambrose, bishop of Milan 17–18, 57, 62, 66, 187, 214
  and Arianism 120–2, 134
  at the Council of Aquileia 120, 150
  building projects 165, 201–2, 205
  character 121, 126–7, 150, 160
  and cult of saints 54–6, 122, 148–9, 151, 157
  early career 149–50
  election 119
  episcopal leadership 121, 123, 125, 149–53, 179, 185
  and Gratian 119–21, 143
  opposition to 132, 168–9
  and papacy 151, 157–8, 201
  and Theodosius I 123–6, 169
  and Valentinian II and Justina 121–3, 125, 169
  writings:
    De Fide 119–20, 212
    De obitu Valentiniani 125
    De obitu Theodosii 125–6
    De Sacramentis 123, 124–5
    Hexameron 207 n. 82

Ammianus Marcellinus, historian 197
Anatelon, legendary bishop of Milan 58, 61, 62–3
Anemius, bishop of Sirmium 132, 143
Antenor, Trojan hero commemorated at Padua 36
Antioch in Pisidia 8
Antoninus, martyr of Piacenza 55–6
ants, giant 190 n. 17
Anullinus, alleged persecutor in northern Italy 227 and n. 119
Anullinus, Constantinian proconsul of Africa 111
Aosta 28
  Christianity at 178–9, 203, 204
Apennines 23–5
Apollinaris, 'apostle' of Ravenna 60–1, 91, 225, 226
Apollinaris, Parecorius, governor of *Venetia et Histria*, patron of church at Aquileia 195–6
apostolicity 60, 62–3, 64–5
Apulia, social dynamics of 29 n. 36
Aquae Gradatae, necropolis near Aquileia 73–4, 144–5, 159, 183–4
Aquileia 1, 14, 26, 204
  church buildings at 74–8, 158–9, 163–5, 167–70, 191–6
  church of 154–5
    administrative apparatus 158–60
    apostolic claims and status 1–2, 64–5, 73, 77
    baptismal liturgy 161–3, 191–3
    chorus beatorum at 142–4, 175, 184
    episcopal list 1–2, 63–5
    martyrs of 73–4, 221–2
    origins 73–9
    regional influence 132, 139, 140–5, 175, 183–4
  economy 31–2
  links with Balkans 31–2
  pagan religions at 36–7, 38–9
  social dynamics 32–3, 142, 194
  strategic importance 40
archives, ecclesiastical 68, 71, 158–60

Rome (378) 157
Seleucia (359) 50
Serdica (343) 48–9, 127–8
Sirmium (351) 116, 155
Turin (*c.* 400) 219 and n. 3
Venetian and Gallic (late-360s) 131–2
see also Nicaea, creed of
cities:
  physical fabric of 28–9, 188–207
  social dynamics of 5–6
Cividale 1 and n. 1
Classis, port of Ravenna 31
  Christians at 91
Claterna 92, 174
Claudius, Roman emperor 37
cloth trade 30
Coelia Paterna, Jewish patron at Brescia
  213
Como 28, 34 and n. 62, 38, 174
Concordia 41, 144
Conrad II, German emperor 58
Constans I, Roman emperor 115, 140,
  147–8, 169, 200, 222
Constans II, (east) Roman emperor 60
Constantine I, Roman emperor 45, 190,
  193, 196
  building projects 200
  convenes church councils 46–8, 51–2
  conversion 112, 214
  in northern Italy 82
  supports Church 111–15
Constantius, bishop of Faenza 47, 111
Constantius II, Roman emperor 16
  and Arianism 49–50, 154
  ecclesiastical policies in Italy 115–17,
  118–19, 120–1, 126, 147–8,
  155–6
Coronatus of Verona, author of the *Vita
  Zenonis* 67–9, 71
countryside, Christianity in 10, 98–9,
  181–4
Cremona 27, 31 40
  Christians at 92
Crispinus, bishop of Padua 49
customs network (*portorium*) 33

Dalmatia, Christian communities in
  102–4
Damasus I, bishop of Rome 153
  and cult of saints 54–5, 149, 201,
  and northern Italy 156–7, 168
Decius, Roman emperor 190
Desenzano di Garda, Roman villa 77

dioceses, diocesan administration 2–3,
  10–12, 137 n. 3, 137–53, 158–61
  fluidity 160–1
  relationship to secular administrative
  structures 139, 160
Diocletian, Roman emperor 208–9
Diogenes, bishop of Geneva 174
Dionysius, bishop of Milan 49–50, 57,
  116–19, 147–8, 197 n. 36
Donatist schism, northern Italian
  involvement in 46–48, 82, 109,
  111

Easter 11, 114, 169, 220
Egeria, Gallic pilgrim to Jerusalem 10
Emona 33, 40
  Christians at 142, 174, 179–80, 204–5
Ephesus in Asia Minor 39, 208
  see also Seven Sleepers of Ephesus
Epiphanius, bishop of Salamis, *Panarion*
  of 133
episcopal lists 1–4, 56–7
  Aquileian 1–2, 57, 63–5
  Brescian 58
  Genevan 177 n. 19
  manipulation of 57
  Milanese 57, 61–3
  Paduan 58–9
  Ravennate 60–1
  Trento 57, 181 n. 42
  see also apostolicity and *Liber
  Pontificalis* (Roman)
Eusebius, bishop of Bologna 152, 173
Eusebius, bishop of Caesarea in
  Palestine 56, 211, 216
Eusebius, bishop of Vercelli 52, 66,
  145–6, 179
  at council of Milan (355) 49–50,
  116–17, 118–19, 148, 197 n. 36
  character 160
  De Trinitate attributed to 130,
  161 n. 90
  eastern exile 93, 129
  legend of 66
  returns to the west 117, 129–30, 143
  Sardinian origins and early career at
  Rome 94, 154
Eustasius, bishop of Aosta 178
Eutherius, Christian patron at Padua
  83–4, 165, 205
evangelization, processes of 52–3, 95–9,
  103–5, 172–5, 182–6, 220
Eventius, bishop of Pavia 173